Love Theory in Later Ḥanbalite Islam

STUDIES IN ISLAMIC PHILOSOPHY AND SCIENCE

Published under the auspices of
the Society for the Study of Islamic Philosophy and Science

Love Theory
in Later Ḥanbalite Islam

Joseph Norment Bell

State University of New York Press · Albany 1979

Published by
State University of New York Press
Albany, New York 12246

Printed in the United States of America

Library of Congress Cataloging in Publication Data

Bell, Joseph Norment.
Love theory in later Ḥanbalite Islam.

Bibliography: p.
1. Love (Islam) 2. Ḥanbalites. I. Title.
BP188.16.L68B44 297'.5 78-5904
ISBN 0-87395-244-8

To my father Walter Herman Bell, Sr.

Contents

Tables

Acknowledgments

SINCE THE RESEARCH which has resulted in the present publication was first undertaken the list of those to whom I am indebted for advice and assistance has grown quite long. I should like to take this opportunity to extend my thanks to them all. In particular I wish to mention Professor Rudolf Mach, who first suggested that I investigate some aspect of the idea of love in Arabic literature, Professors Muhsin Mahdi and Jaroslav Stetkevych, whose counsel and encouragement over several years was invaluable, and Professor Lois Giffen, who kindly offered a number of suggestions for the improvement of the final version of the manuscript.

I should also like to express my gratitude to the Foreign Area Fellowship Program and the Center for Middle Eastern Studies of the University of Chicago for their support of this study.

1. Introduction

Over a period of centuries and particularly in the early 1400s followers of the Ḥanbalite school of jurisprudence[1] made significant contributions to the literature in Arabic dealing with sacred and profane love. Owing to a widely accepted stereotype of Ḥanbalism, this fact appears as something of an anomaly to many modern Middle Easterners and Orientalists alike. In some Arab countries today to dub a person a Ḥanbalite is to charge him, at the very least, with a certain rigidity of thought and conduct. It is often asked jokingly how it is that the Ḥanbalites should have been interested in love. This popular image is undoubtedly somewhat unfair, but it did not develop in a vacuum. From the beginning the mainstream of Ḥanbalism has resolutely and at times courageously defended a strict-constructionist interpretation of Islamic orthodoxy. The forefather and prime authority of the school, Aḥmad b. Ḥanbal (164/780–241/855), suffered imprisonment and corporal punishment because he refused to sanction the Muʿtazilite doctrine of the created Koran imposed by the humanist caliph al-Maʾmūn. In subsequent times Ḥanbalism continued to oppose, on occasion with violence, Shīʿism, speculative theology, Platonizing mysticism, and other movements or ideas which it perceived as threats to primitive Islam.

Yet Ḥanbalism has never been a monolith. Many Sufis, for instance, some of them conspicuous figures in the history of Islamic mysticism, have found their place within its ranks. As a rule, despite some celebrated examples to the contrary, the school does not seem to have circumscribed unduly the intellectual pursuits of its adherents. Ḥanbalites, from the outset, have distinguished themselves in nearly every field of scholarly endeavor and the school has given Islam some of its greatest religious thinkers. Although as a system of law Ḥanbalism no longer possesses a widespread following—it is in fact the most restricted of the Sunni rites, in matters of faith and morals it has had a considerable influence on Islamic modernism and, according to one view, has given encouragement to a more liberal and independent approach to the traditional sources of dogma.[2] The most notable manifestation of the school in recent times is the conservative Wahhābī reformist movement, which in the eighteenth century played a decisive role in the formation of the modern kingdom of Saudi Arabia and has since continued to inspire much of Saudi religious policy.

Very likely as a consequence of its self-appointed role as defender of the true faith, Ḥanbalism, to a greater extent than any of the other three major legal schools of Sunni Islam, has come to be associated with a particular theological point of view. For the most part, Ḥanbalite writings on love reflect typical dogmatic and ethical concerns of the school. This study investigates, in most cases for the first time in depth, the treatment of love found in the works of four representative Ḥanbalite authors: Abū 'l-Faraj Ibn al-Jawzī (d. 597/1200); Aḥmad Ibn Taymīya (d. 728/1328); his student Ibn Qayyim al-Jawzīya (d. 751/1350); and Marʿī b. Yūsuf al-Karmī (d. 1033/1624).[3] Their work constitutes a small but exceptionally important part of the Muslim literature on love—a literature to which Western scholars have increasingly turned their attention.

Up to the present time much of the interest in the medieval Arabic conception of love has been generated by the controversy over the origins of the courtly love theme.[4] Studies on this question are numerous. The theory of an Arabic origin, defended by A. R. Nykl, Lawrence Ecker, and others, has been strongly opposed by Romanists like A. Jeanroy and D. Scheludko.[5] Criticisms of the Arabic theory have generally focused on the fact that its advocates have failed to demonstrate an indisputable case of direct filiation in poetry, although they have managed to compile long lists of parallel motifs (Ecker gives thirty-two) in addition to pointing out historical circumstances favorable to cultural contact, for instance, the campaigns in Syria and Spain of William IX (1071–1127), the poet-duke of Aquitaine and grandfather of Eleanor. Opponents of the theory have succeeded in finding all the motifs common to Arabic and Provençal poetry in other literatures, though not all of them in any single literature, and they have shown that the rhyme and strophic form adopted in Provençal may have had other sources than the Arabic, medieval Latin poetry being considered the most likely alternative.[6]

The Ḥanbalite writers considered in the present inquiry did not deal strictly with imaginative literature. Determined by the varying needs of sectarian polemic, the scope of their concerns is much broader, comprehending aspects of medieval psychology, religious ethics, speculative theology, and mysticism, as well as problems in prophetic tradition and the more properly gratuitous disciplines of anecdotal literature and poetry. The possibility of their writings having influenced any contemporary European authors, moreover, is to be discounted from the outset. Nevertheless the cultures of the Arab world and Western Europe in the Middle Ages had an obvious underlying unity, and the close kinship of much in their respective literatures remains undeniable, however scant examples of direct influence may be.

This point was made some years ago by G. E. von Grunebaum. His observations, no less valid now than when they were first expressed, suggest for the comparatist an approach which should prove more profitable than the traditional stress on filiation, whether the object of study be expository works, imaginative literature, or some combination of the two. In an article addressed to Father A. Denomy's thesis that the Western theme of courtly love stemmed not from the poetry and narrative of the Arabs but from their philosophy, specifically from the mystical philosophy of Avicenna,[7] Professor von Grunebaum showed that Latin sources which might account for the origin of the courtly theme were available to the troubadours at a time when Avicenna's *Treatise on love* was unknown in the West and copies of his *De anima* (translated between 1135 and 1153, or after the death of William of Aquitaine) must have been rare.[8] His concluding remarks bear quotation here:

> In postulating Eastern influences to account for a phenomenon of Western culture in the period under consideration, it is frequently not sufficiently thought out what it means that, to a very large extent, medieval Orient and medieval Occident arose from the same roots. . . . The interaction between East and West in the Middle Ages will never be correctly assessed or appraised unless their fundamental cultural unity is realized and taken into consideration. It is that essential kinship of East and West that will account both for Europe's receptiveness to Arabic thought and to the growth in the Occident of ideas and attitudes that on first sight appear too closely akin to their oriental counterparts not to be attributed to mere borrowing.[9]

There is certainly no lack of evidence to support Professor von Grunebaum's view with regard to the West, and much the same may be said for the Muslim East. In particular, the debt of the expository literature on love in Arabic to antiquity is clear and undeniable. This holds not only for works in philosophical and scientific disciplines but also for that semitechnical *adab* literature, which synthesizes the various aspects of medieval Muslim education. (The occurrence in Arabic verse and narrative prose of motifs common in books of the *adab* genre should likewise come as no surprise.) Material of Jewish origin had long been available to the Arabs, both through Koranic restatements and in a large body of inherited Jewish tradition. Greek thought, which for years had been filtering into the Islamic intellectual milieu, became immediately accessible with the great Abbasid translation movement of the ninth and tenth centuries. Since most writers on love were not professional philosophers, however, Greek influence reached them rather indirectly, often after considerable distortion of the original ideas. Direct quotations from translated texts are rare in their works, and the numerous acknowledged citations of Greek sages, not always properly ascribed, consist generally of neat aphorisms taken from a common stock of such sayings. Plato, Aristotle, Hippocrates, Galen, and Empedocles are among the authorities most often cited on matters pertaining to love.

Taking into consideration only the most obvious sources, it may be observed that a significant proportion of the fundamental motifs recurring in Arabic treatises on love, including many typical of imaginative literature, are to be found in the works of Plato and Aristotle or in the Hebrew Bible. Thus, for example, the following, all of which will be seen again in the course of this study:

from Plato and Aristotle—

the definition of *eros* (*ʿishq* among the Arabs) as excessive love or an excess of feeling (Plato *Phaedrus* 237–38; *Laws* viii. 837);

the exclusive character of such excessive love (Aristotle *Ethics* ix. 10. 1171a);

the description of love as a divine madness, neither fair nor foul (Plato *Phaedrus* 265; *Symposium* 202);

the ennobling power of love (Plato *Symposium* 178);

love as a consequence of similarity or complementarity (Plato *Symposium* 189–93; *Lysis* 214; *Laws* viii. 837);

the necessary reciprocity of friendship resulting from a congeniality of natures—a principle applied to *love* in the Arab context (Plato *Lysis* 221–22);

the distinction between friendship (love in Arab theories) caused by similarity, which is permanent, and that proceeding from utility or pleasure, which ceases when no further advantage is to be obtained from the beloved (Aristotle *Ethics* viii. 3–4. 1156b–1157a);

the thesis that nothing which is possessed can be the object of desire or love, only the continued possession of it in the future or its continued existence being considered lovable, that is, something which is still a nonexistent with respect to the lover (Plato *Symposium* 199–200);

love as the progressive apprehension of the stages of beauty (Plato *Symposium* 209–212);

the contemplation of beautiful faces, especially those of beardless youths (Plato *Phaedrus* 251–53; *Symposium* 179; *Laws* viii. 837);

the concept of ordinate love, each object except the last being loved for the sake of another higher than itself (Plato *Lysis* 219–20);

the question whether the happy and self-sufficient man needs friends—in the Muslim context, whether God as self-sufficient can be described as loving (Aristotle *Ethics* ix. 9. 1169b);

the denial of love between God and man (Aristotle *Ethics* viii. 7. 1159a);

the contrary assertion, that love is the means of all intercourse between God and man (Plato *Symposium* 203);

from the Old Testament—

love conceived as obedience to the divine law (Deut. 4:37–40; 6:5, 13–15);

the close association of the love and fear of God (Deut. 10:12);

the love-sacrifice of Abraham, the "friend" of God (Gen. 22:1–19; Isa. 41:8; cf. James 2:20–23;

Joseph in Egypt as the paragon of chastity (Gen. 39:7–20).

As with similar theories in the Latin West, it was in a society permeated with these and other Greek or Jewish ideas that Muslim theories of love began to take shape. Together with a number of Koranic passages, certain sayings of the Prophet, a considerable store of ascetic and mystical maxims, and a vast quantity of romantic anecdotes and verse, both Bedouin and urban in flavor, these ideas inherited from antiquity became an integral part of the raw material on which Muslim thinkers were to draw in their discussions of love. It was the same complex of themes that formed the intellectual background for much of later Arabic poetry and narrative.

At this stage a broad comparative study reflecting the approach suggested by Professor von Grunebaum would no doubt be premature. The prerequisite for such a study, a comprehensive assessment of medieval Arab attitudes towards love, is lacking at present and is unlikely to be available in the near future. Even if it were possible to exclude from one's sources the immense corpus of imaginative literature—romances, anecdotes, and verse, which contains by far the greater share of the treatment of love, the subject remains a crucial issue in disciplines as diverse as philosophy, theology, mysticism, ethics, medicine, and astrology. In Arabic alone, not to mention Persian, in which much relevant information has been preserved, there is a proliferation of works covering these fields, many of them still in manuscript. Almost any of these works may contain an important section on love. A survey of this literature would be a project requiring more than one lifetime, and, unfortunately, reliable secondary sources are conspicuous by their absence.[10] The task now facing the historian of the idea of love in Islam, therefore, is to prepare the monographs on which more generalized studies must rely. Much the same may be said with regard to other questions in the history of Islamic thought.

Once the groundwork has been laid for a proper understanding of literate Muslim culture, however, the comparatist will be free to investigate how similar or identical motifs, whether or not themselves genetically related, were treated in two fundamentally kindred civilizations which shared the same Neoplatonic heritage and faced the common problem of reconciling the discursive thought of Greece with the concrete givens of Semitic religion. Research which takes as a point of departure the essential unity of medieval Europe and the Islamic East, I believe, promises to reveal more about the kinship between the two, and about the distinctive characteristics of each, than the attempts to uncover isolated, and late, examples of filiation or mutual dependence to which so much effort has been devoted.

Assuming this basic approach, what can be said regarding methodology? It is a tempting thing to envisage a technique or a set of concepts appropriate for later syntheses which would also facilitate the painstaking chore of collecting information now before us and thus hasten the transition to the more pleasant task of analysis. To a certain extent, undoubtedly, the desired conceptual apparatus is already available. In his controversial book *Agape and Eros*, the Swedish bishop Anders Nygren attempted to trace the history of the Christian doctrine of love from its sources in the New Testament and the dialogues of Plato to its rarefied expression in the writings of Martin Luther. Faced with problems similar to but less insurmountable than those encountered by the Arabist, Nygren adopted a method of *motif research* which he described as "concerned less with the historical connections and origins of motifs than with their characteristic content and manifestations."[11] He distinguished as fundamental and conflicting motifs the two kinds of love named in the title of his book—primitive Christian *agape*, a wholly selfless and disinterested love impossible among men but for the grace of God, and the heavenly *eros* of Plato, representing the individual's quest for his own highest spiritual good. Under the term *nomos* he isolated a third motif, the Old Testament conception of love as arising within the framework of divine law and expressed through submission to that law. By reducing to one of these fundamental motifs, or to a combination of them, the doctrine of love held by each author he studied, Nygren was able to impose a considerable degree of order, perhaps to the point of oversimplification, on an otherwise very confused body of information.

Agape and eros, it should be remarked, is a book with a frankly polemic aim. The author asserts the purity of the primitive Christian, and subsequently Lutheran, *agape* motif over against the synthesis of *agape* and *eros* in the Catholic theology of Augustine and Thomas Aquinas—the *caritas* doctrine. The inevitable reaction ensued. To date, in fine Western tradition, Protestant, Catholic, and Jew have all been represented in the controversy.[12] Whatever one may think of Nygren's reasons for writing *Agape and Eros*, however, or of the passions his work aroused, there is no doubt that the technique of motif research he employed has proved stimulating and useful. The thought of composing a Muslim analogue to Nygren's book, entitled perhaps *Nomos and Eros*, is an enticing one.

There are, of course, various models from which to choose. But it must be reiterated that neither Nygren nor the other writers who have dealt systematically with the Western idea of love were faced with the severe textual problems still regularly met by the student of medieval Islam. Nor were they plagued by a lack of secondary sources. Moreover, at least one strongly analytical work on theories of love in the West,

Robert G. Hazo's *The idea of love*, has been the product of extensive collective research.[13] Taking into consideration the state of our knowledge of Islamic intellectual history, I have concluded that the dangers involved in relying on the kind of conceptual apparatus developed by authors like Nygren and Hazo outweigh the obvious advantages to be gained. A consistent reduction of Ḥanbalite attitudes towards love to a limited set of motifs or critical notions would run the double risk of personal error in interpretation and suppression of aspects of the school's teaching which may appear to be loose ends but could prove relevant to future studies. On the assumption that a first study of this kind will be useful in the preparation of a broader synthesis, I have decided to follow the texts where they lead. Without neglecting entirely the lessons of Western historians, particularly those of Nygren, I have attempted to treat each of the four Ḥanbalite writers surveyed here in the way which best reveals the total character of his work on love. Accordingly, nothing which these men call by the name love or its major synonyms has been completely overlooked. Where either a genetic or a motif approach has seemed especially appropriate, it has been adopted. As far as possible, however, it is the texts themselves which have dictated the method and scope of this research and the form of its presentation.

So much for matters of approach and method. At last we may inquire about the nature of the beast with which we are dealing. Into what literary tradition, it may be asked, does the Ḥanbalite treatment of love fall, and what is its place within that tradition? There are in fact a number of answers to this question, just as there are a number of contexts in which problems involving the idea of love can arise. For now, it will be convenient to reply only with regard to those Ḥanbalite works devoted exclusively to love and immediately related issues. This will mean temporarily passing over the important contributions of Ibn Taymīya, the subject of almost a fourth of this study, as well as the most mature statements of his student Ibn Qayyim al-Jawzīya.

The Arabic treatise on love underwent an interesting evolution, developing eventually into a distinct literary genre. In the course of the third and fourth centuries after the Hijra (ninth and tenth A.D.) discussions of love appeared in a variety of contexts: theological works; belletristic compositions with an ethical and sociological bent such as the *Qiyān* of al-Jāḥiẓ (d. 255/868) on slave-girls, or his *Treatise on love and women*[14]; early ascetic and mystical texts like al-Muḥāsibī's (d. 243/837) "Chapter on love"[15]; and an assortment of literary anthologies. With regard to form and, to some extent, theoretical content, it was a particular type of anthology which was to have the greatest influence on future works dealing with love. Many anthologies of love literature appear to have been completely lacking in organization, resembling in this respect the *Maṣāriʿ al-ʿushshāq* of the Ḥanbalite Jaʿfar b. Aḥmad al-Sarrāj (d. 500/1106).[16] Others, in the manner of biographical dictionaries, were divided into sections devoted to individual poets celebrated for their romantic verse. This seems to have been the format employed by Muḥammad b. ʿImrān al-Marzubānī (d. 384/994) in his work known as *al-Riyāḍ fī akhbār al-mutayyamīn min al-shuʿarāʾ*.[17] There were still other compilations, however, characterized by a thematic arrangement. It was these which set the pattern for Arabic treatises on love. Specifically, two such anthologies, the *Kitāb al-zahra* of Muḥammad b. Dāwūd al-Iṣfahānī al-Ẓāhirī (d. 297/909)[18] and the *Iʿtilāl al-qulūb* of Abū Bakr Muḥammad b. Jaʿfar al-Kharāʾiṭī (d. 327/938),[19] are to be singled out for having had a formative influence on later works in the genre.

It is true that Ibn Dāwūd's book is short on analysis, while al-Kharāʾiṭī's *Iʿtilāl* lacks it almost totally, but many of the chapter headings these two scholars established were to evolve into major topics of love theory. To cite an example particularly relevant to this study, Lois Giffen has shown that the *Iʿtilāl*, from the point of view of overall structure, is the ancestor of the somewhat more analytical *Dhamm al-hawā* by the Ḥanbalite Ibn al-Jawzī.[20] In turn, the most sophisticated of the extant Ḥanbalite treatises on love, Ibn Qayyim al-Jawzīya's *Rawḍat al-muḥibbīn*, is heavily dependent on *Dhamm al-hawā*. The much later *Munyat al-muḥibbīn* of Marʿī b. Yūsuf is constantly indebted to both the *Dhamm* and the *Rawḍa*. In all of these later texts particular stories and poems may at times be traced to the *Iʿtilāl*, but the influence of the early work is to be seen primarily in the classification and arrangement of subject matter.

In another way, al-Sarrāj's haphazardly compiled *Maṣāriʿ al-ʿushshāq* also left its mark on the genre. Later writers drew incessantly on the material related in his book.[21] Among those who did so extensively were Ibn al-Jawzī and, through him, Ibn Qayyim al-Jawzīya. This fact is significant, for it shows that the *Maṣāriʿ* constituted an essential element in the literary background of the Ḥanbalite doctrine of love. Al-Sarrāj's primary devotion, however, seems to have been to belles-lettres, and the greater share of his material bears little relation to the moral teaching of his successors in the school of Aḥmad.[22]

On the basis of the preceding remarks it is possible to give a limited reply to the first of our original questions. With the exception of al-

Sarrāj's *Maṣāriʿ*, the Ḥanbalite treatises on love are in their structure and to a considerable degree in their content typical examples of the thematically arranged anthology. In answer to the second question, a few preliminary impressions regarding the distinctive position of these treatises in their genre must suffice for the moment. *Dhamm al-hawā* and *Rawḍat al-muḥibbīn*, it should be mentioned, represent by any standard major achievements in the development of Arabic expository literature on profane love. Marʿī b. Yūsuf's *Munya* is a production of secondary importance. The first two works, moreover, differ notably from the usual anthologies of their kind in that literary concerns are subordinated to religious ones. A strong moralizing tone, often accompanied by anti-Sufi polemic, constantly pervades the text, and in the *Rawḍa* issues which are specifically theological arise. Both books should be understood primarily as apologies for legalistic Islam presented in a form which would appeal to a wide variety of readers. They attack libertine secularism on the one hand and what Nygren would describe as *eros* religion on the other. Interestingly, some radical departures from this approach are to be found in *Munyat al-muḥibbīn.*

2. Selection and Organization of Literary Material: Ibn al-Jawzī's *Dhamm al-hawā*

THE *Dhamm al-hawā* or *Censure of passion* of Abū 'l-Faraj ʿAbd al-Raḥmān b. ʿAlī al-Baghdādī, known as Ibn al-Jawzī (d. 597/1200),[1] represents at once the definitive selection of traditional material to support the Ḥanbalite doctrine of profane love and the first major analytical treatment of the subject produced by a Ḥanbalite jurist. The book exercised considerable influence on later works, including, as we know, Ibn Qayyim al-Jawzīya's *Rawḍat al-muḥibbin*. The lengthy article on love compiled by the Egyptian encyclopedist al-Nuwayrī (d. 733/1332) for his *Nihāyat al-arab* was borrowed in its entirety from Ibn al-Jawzī's work.[2]

The author of *Dhamm al-hawā* was one of the most prolific writers in the history of medieval Muslim scholarship. A glance at the list of titles Ibn Rajab attributes to him or the protracted catalogue established recently by ʿAbd al-Ḥamīd al-ʿAlwajī suffices to reveal the extraordinary volume of his work. According to Brockelmann his productivity was surpassed only by that of al-Suyūṭī.[3]

Ibn al-Jawzī's bent for what was of necessity hasty composition did not leave him without critics in his own *madhhab.* Ibn Rajab notes that he often wrote on subjects in which he was not well versed, merely organizing passages selected from the works of others. More seriously, he was said to rely too heavily on personal interpretations (*ta'wīl*) of certain points, and his knowledge of prophetic tradition, like that of the earlier Ḥanbalite Ibn ʿAqīl (d. 513/1119), by whom he was influenced, was held to be inadequate. Muwaffaq al-Dīn Ibn Qudāma repudiated his works on Sunna and the method he followed in them. Interestingly, Ibn Taymīya seems to have been more favorable towards him.[4]

Despite his failure to satisfy certain more conservative followers of the rite, Ibn al-Jawzī is reported to have maintained a staunch devotion to Ḥanbalism.[5] His preoccupation with love and the passions was a reflection of the typical concerns of the school. Very likely, had his allegiance been other, he would still have dealt with the subject. His unbounded curiosity seems to have required that he devote a work to every topic which occurred to him.[6] But the *Dhamm* is clearly the product of a characteristically Ḥanbalite concern with the literature of asceticism and piety, in which love was an inescapable issue. Much of the material related in the work was heard by the author directly from Ḥanbalite teachers like Muḥammad b. Nāṣir (d. 550/1155).[7]

The compilation of the *ḥadīth*, anecdotes, and verse contained in *Dhamm al-hawā* was greatly facilitated for Ibn al-Jawzī by his acquaintance with al-Sarrāj's *Maṣāriʿ*, which he knew through the woman traditionist Shuhda bint Aḥmad.[8] "Our masters taught us traditions from him [al-Sarrāj]," he writes, "and the last person who related to us from him was Shuhda bint al-ʿIbarī. It was under her that I read his book called *Maṣāriʿ al-ʿushshāq* as she had heard it from him."[9] To a considerable degree Ibn al-Jawzī's selection bears al-Sarrāj's imprint. But *Dhamm al-hawā* differs none the less most significantly from the *Maṣāriʿ*. Whereas it is impossible to consider the latter a representative Ḥanbalite work, Ibn al-Jawzī's book is in form and content the recognizable prototype of the most important extant treatise on love by a member of the Ḥanbalite school, Ibn al-Qayyim's *Rawḍa*. Moreover, although *Dhamm al-hawā* is heavily dependent on borrowings from the *Maṣāriʿ*, Ibn al-Jawzī demonstrates greater selectivity than al-Sarrāj and attempts a systematic classification of the material he uses. One finds foreshadowed in a number of chapters in the *Dhamm*, though with far less balance, the plan *ʿaql-naql-shiʿr* (rational argumentation, tradition, poetry), which Ibn al-Qayyim utilized in most of the chapters of *Rawḍat al-muḥibbīn*. The adoption of this structure may be considered a cardinal factor in the development of the Ḥanbalite doctrine of love. Ibn al-Jawzī's personal contribution in this area should not be exaggerated, however. While in much of the *Rawḍa* tradition receives only slightly more space than the arguments of reason, in *Dhamm al-hawā* its preponderance is still overwhelming. For example, chapter three, "*Fī dhikr mujāhadat al-nafs . . .*," has only four and one-half lines of introductory argumentation, and many others have none at all. Furthermore, Ibn al-Jawzī's concern with *isnāds* is fastidious, whereas Ibn al-Qayyim usually omits the traditional documentation of his material, often replacing it with introductory remarks of an interpretive nature.

Dhamm al-hawā is divided into fifty chapters of greatly varying length. But because series of chapters frequently deal with virtually the same subject, the outline of the work can be reduced to the following main headings:

I. The moral make-up of man
  1. Reason (*ʿaql*), chapter one
  2. Passion (*hawā*), chapter two
  3. Striving against the soul (*jihād al-nafs*), chapter three
  4. Patience (*ṣabr*), chapter four
  5. The heart (*qalb*), chapters five through ten

II. Vices and virtues
  A. The sins of passion
    1. Glances and gazing (*naẓar*), chapters eleven through twenty
    2. Seclusion with women; the temptations afforded by women, chapters twenty-one and twenty-two
    3. Sins in general and their consequences, chapters twenty-three and twenty-four
    4. Fornication and adultery (*zinā*), chapter twenty-five
    5. Homosexuality (*liwāṭa*), chapters twenty-six through twenty-eight
    6. Warning against punishment and exhortation to repentance, chapters twenty-nine and thirty
  B. Virtues
    1. Chastity or temperance (*ʿafāf*), chapters thirty-one and thirty-two
    2. Marriage and licit intercourse, chapters thirty-three and thirty-four

III. Passionate love (*ʿishq*)
  1. The nature of love, chapter thirty-five
  2. The causes of love, chapter thirty-six
  3. The censure of passionate love, chapter thirty-seven
  4. The reward of the lover who conceals his passion and remains chaste, chapter thirty-eight
  5. The evil consequences of passionate love, chapters thirty-nine through forty-eight
  6. *Remedia amoris* and various counsels, chapters forty-nine and fifty.

As is apparent from this outline, the two subjects to which Ibn al-Jawzī devotes the greatest number of chapters in *Dhamm al-hawā* are *ʿishq*-love and the wandering of the eye. A similar emphasis will be found in Ibn al-Qayyim's writings on profane love.

In view of the extensive influence Ibn al-Jawzī's book had on later treatises, both in structure and choice of material, it will be of some use to provide a fairly detailed summary of the work. The following is an analytical description of *Dhamm al-hawā* based on the outline given above.

I. The moral make-up of man

Reason (I,1)

In a manner characteristic of works on ethics, Ibn al-Jawzī opens his treatise with a discussion of the two opposing elements in man's moral constitution: reason and passion.[10] For the faculty of reason the scholar mentions several definitions current at the time. Reason is called an intuition (*gharīza*) by which knowledge is obtained, a simple substance (*jawhar basīṭ*), a transparent body (*jism shaffāf*), or simply light. Attempting a more precise definition, Ibn al-Jawzī describes reason as "an intuition, as it were, a light cast into the heart, which is in readiness to apprehend things, knowing the possible from the impossible and grasping the consequences of things. This light may be strong or weak. If it is strong, it overcomes temporal passions through the realization of their consequences." That the seat of reason is the heart, he adds, is the opinion of most scholars, including al-Shāfiʿī. Substantiation of this view is found in Koran 22:46, "So that they should have hearts with which to understand (*yaʿqilūna bi-hā*)."[11] Among the opponents of this opinion are the followers of Abū Ḥanīfa, who hold that the seat of reason is the brain.[12]

After this brief introduction, Ibn al-Jawzī sets out to demonstrate the nobility of reason by relating a number of traditions from the Prophet as well as sayings from various other authorities. Symptomatically, and given the subject somewhat ironically, the evidence of *naql* is given decided priority over that of *ʿaql* in his argument. The brief deductive proof with which he follows up the relation of tradition can be reduced to a single sentence: the nobility of things is to be discerned by their fruit, and the fruit of reason is known to all.[13]

To object that in hesitating to defend reason on the basis of its own arguments Ibn al-Jawzī may have been seeking to avoid circularity is to credit him with greater philosophical sophistication than appears to have been his. The relative weight given to tradition and deduction in this context is typical of his treatment of many other subjects. Despite this disinclination to rely on rational argumentation, in a tradition he relates from Ibn ʿUmar, Ibn al-Jawzī ranks reason above the very pillars of Islam: "Truly a man may be among the people of fasting, prayer, pilgrimage, and holy war, but on the Day of Resurrection he will be rewarded only in proportion to his reason (*bi-qadri ʿaqlihi*)."[14] Here, however, he is thinking of reason in a moral context as the harness of the passions, not as the source of dialectic. His definition of reason quoted above reveals a similar moral emphasis.

Ibn al-Jawzī's reluctance to resort to rational proofs, illustrated in his discussion of *ʿaql*, seems to reflect the fact that in this period, as one century earlier when Ibn ʿAqīl was forced to retract his opinions sympathetic to speculative theology, the Ḥanbalite school had not yet recovered from its phobia of Muʿtazilism and its misgivings with regard to *kalām*. This attitude towards dialectic would have to be modified before Ḥanbalism could develop a more systematic conception of love and the passions.

Passion (I,2)

Hawā (roughly passion) is mentioned in Ibn al-Jawzī's *Ṣayd al-khāṭir* in surprisingly scholastic terms. Its purpose is described as the attraction of the beneficial (*maṣāliḥ*), while its complement, *ghaḍab* or anger, serves to repel the harmful.[15] Thus, although the range of meaning of *hawā* is rather broad in Arabic, it is clear that what Ibn al-Jawzī basically means by the term is the concupiscible appetite, with *ghaḍab* thus corresponding to the irascible appetite.

Accordingly, despite the title and major emphasis of his *Dhamm al-hawā*, he begins the second chapter of the work with the recognition that *hawā* plays a necessary role in life.

> Know that the concupiscible appetite (*hawā*) is the inclination of a nature (*ṭabʿ*) towards that which is suited to it, and that this inclination has been created in man as necessary to his survival (*li-ḍarūrati baqāʾihi*). For if he had no penchant for eating, he would not eat; if none for drinking, he would not drink; and if none for mating, he would not marry. This is the case with all things which he desires, for the concupiscible appetite attracts to him what is beneficial, just as the irascible appetite (*ghaḍab*) repels that which is harmful. Consequently, it is not right to censure *hawā* absolute-

> ly, but only when it is exaggerated, that is, when it goes beyond merely attracting the beneficial and repelling the harmful.

But, his argument continues, since it is usual for no one to stop at the limit of the beneficial, *hawā* is generally considered blameworthy. As Ibn ʿAbbās is reported to have said: "Nowhere did God mention *hawā* in his Book without blaming it."[16] On these grounds, although *Dhamm al-hawā* is specifically directed against sensual passion, the author includes the censure of *hawā* in general as well.[17]

Hawā, the reader is warned, invites man to pursue temporal pleasures without thought for the outcome of his acts. The best defense against it is reason, which distinguishes man from the other animals. The reasonable man should resist *hawā* by considering the consequences of what he does. For example, he should realize that addiction to his desires leads eventually to the cessation of pleasure in them without, however, allowing him to give them up. They become as essential for him as bread itself. Thus the man who is addicted to wine or physical union has not one-tenth of the pleasure experienced by one who is not so addicted. For the man who has already fallen into the snares of *hawā* a firm resolve to give up that which is harming him and, simultaneously, the gradual abandonment of those things which he even suspects may be harmful is prescribed. Ibn al-Jawzī suggests seven thoughts for the reader's contemplation which should facilitate this effort. Most of these are variations on the theme of considering the consequences of one's acts.[18]

Turning to the arguments of *naql*, Ibn al-Jawzī cites a number of Koranic verses and *ḥadīth* as well as nonprophetic traditions on themes which were to become elements of Ibn al-Qayyim's teaching on love. One of these is Koran 18:28, "And he follows his low desires and his case exceeds due bounds (*wa-kāna amruhu furuṭan*),"[19] which provides authority for the doctrine of the Golden Mean that the Ḥanbalites cherished and simultaneously, by associating *hawā* with the idea of excess, parallels the definition of *ʿishq* as excessive love which Muslim theoreticians took over from al-Jāḥiẓ.[20]

Other citations liken the unrestrained following of *hawā* to idolatry. Al-Ḥasan b. ʿAlī al-Muṭawwiʿī said: "The idol of every man is his *hawā*. . . ." From the Prophet is related a tradition in the same vein: "There is no god under heaven more odious to Allah than a man's passion when he has yielded to it (*hawā muttabaʿ*)." From the Koran (45:23): "Hast thou considered him who takes his lusts (*hawā*) for his god? . . ." Quotations such as these anticipate a later Ḥanbalite equation of love for objects other than God with *shirk* (idolatry or polytheism). It is not surprising to find the *ḥadīth* on *hawā muttaba*ʿ among the traditions which the author of the *Rawḍa* borrows from this section of *Dhamm al-hawā*.[21]

Finally, and rather inconsistently in view of his opinions on Sufism, Ibn al-Jawzī cites a number of Sufi traditions, not from the Prophet, which tell how certain holy men having renounced all their passions spent the rest of their lives floating in the air.[22] Ibn al-Qayyim usually omits material of this nature when borrowing from *Dhamm al-hawā*.

In the verses of poetry Ibn al-Jawzī cites to reinforce his argument against passion, a predominant motif is the paronomasia *hawā* = *hawān*, emphasizing that passion brings its victim to disgrace. Al-Aṣmaʿī once heard it said:

> Inna *'l-hawāna* huwa *'l-hawā* quliba 'smuhū:
> fa-idhā *hawīta*, fa-qad laqīta *hawānā*.
>
> (Truly disgrace is passion with its name altered:
> when you yield to passion, you meet disgrace.)[23]

A number of verses utilizing the same play on words are taken up again in *Rawḍat al-muḥibbīn*.

In summary, *hawā* for Ibn al-Jawzī is already a technical term, corresponding approximately to the concupiscible appetite of scholasticism. Although it has a necessary function in human survival, few people limit it to its proper role. Accordingly, *hawā* is condemned by the Koran, religious tradition, and the arguments of reason together.

Striving against the soul (I,3)

Since the seat of the passions is considered to be the soul, the effort to resist them is called "striving against the soul" (*jihād al-nafs*). Ibn al-Jawzī, at the beginning of his chapter entitled "*Mujāhadat al-nafs wa-muḥāsabatuhā wa-tawbīkhuhā* (Striving against the soul, holding it accountable, and reprimanding it)," states that the soul must be resisted since it is "innately disposed to love *hawā*." Employing a common pun on the word *jihād* (striving, holy war), he repeats and explains the traditional aphorism that *jihād al-nafs* is greater than holy war against the enemy (*jihād al-aʿdā'*): "Know that striving against the soul is greater than holy war for one reason: the soul is beloved and that to which it invites man is beloved, for the soul only attracts man to that which it desires. Now since it is desirable to conform to the wish of one's beloved even in something disliked, how much more is it desirable to acquiesce when the beloved invites man to something which is itself loved."[24]

Patience (I,4)

According to Ibn al-Jawzī the only means of resisting soul and passion is patient endurance (*ṣabr*), which, one learns, is mentioned about seventy times in the Koran and repeatedly in the *ḥadīth*. Al-Ḥārith al-Muḥāsibī is cited as saying: "Everything has an essence; and, whereas the essence of man is reason, the essence of reason is patience." There are two aspects of patience: patience is enduring the undesirable (*ṣabr ʿalā 'l-makrūh*) and patience in the privation of what one loves (*ṣabr ʿani 'l-maḥbūb*).[25] Though *Dhamm al-hawā* has basically little more to say on the subject, this must not obscure the fact that patience was a major element in Ḥanbalite ethics and became the object of several treatises by followers of the *madhhab*.[26]

The heart (I,5)

The heart, theater of the conflict between reason and passion, is held to be originally free from all evil, but the five senses deliver to it harmful information together with the useful. Consequently, it is necessary to block the paths by which the heart receives sensations likely to distract it from worship of the Maker, the purpose for which it was created.[27] Ibn al-Jawzī demonstrates the dangers of the heart's being engrossed in worldly preoccupations by the sheer amassing of traditions.

Among the themes recurring in these traditions is one which J.-C. Vadet has pointed to in discussing al-Kharā'iṭī's *Iʿtilāl al-qulūb*: the rusting of the heart (*ṣada' al-qalb*) and how to cure it.[28] The corrective measures suggested in *Dhamm al-hawā* are summed up in a saying of Ibrāhīm al-Khawwāṣ: "The remedy of the heart is fivefold: reciting the Koran with reflection, an empty belly, vigil by night, humble entreaties at dawn, and keeping company with the righteous."[29] While Ibn al-Jawzī devotes two chapters to the rusting of the heart, the author of *Rawḍat al-muḥibbīn* does not emphasize the subject and borrows only one tradition on it from the *Dhamm*.[30] Ibn al-Qayyim's lack of concern for this traditional theme may be explained by the fact that its metaphorical character rendered it of little use in the reasoned argument which he was attempting to construct.

In the tenth chapter of *Dhamm al-hawā* are collected traditions which command that man free his heart from all preoccupations save love for God. Among the reasons given for having an "empty heart" (*qalb fārigh*) devoted to God is the divine jealousy, a subject dealt with at length by Ibn al-Qayyim. On this latter question Ibn al-Qayyim owes a number of traditions to Ibn al-Jawzī.[31]

II. *Vices and virtues*

A. THE SINS OF PASSION

Glances and gazing (naẓar) (II,A,1)

Ibn al-Jawzī opens his treatment of the various sins of passion with the subject of the amorous regard or *naẓar*. The faculty of vision, we are told, is one of the means of delivering information to the heart, and indulging it causes *hawā* to occur there. Accordingly, the Law has prescribed that this faculty be restrained, as in Koran 24:30, "Say to the Believers that they cast down their eyes. . . ." (trans. Bell). The reason for this command, the author explains, is to be found in the second half of the verse: ". . . and guard their private parts (*wa-yaḥfaẓū furūjahum*)."[32]

In orthodox Islam the consensus with regard to *naẓar* could only follow the Koranic injunction. But by the time of Ibn al-Jawzī the Ḥanbalites, in reaction to certain Sufi practices as well as to the views of the Ẓāhirites Ibn Dāwūd and Ibn Ḥazm, felt obliged to come to the defense of the traditional teaching. Accordingly, about a tenth of the *Dhamm* is devoted to *naẓar*. Later, Ibn al-Qayyim gives over a similar portion of his *Rawḍa* to the same topic. It must not be overlooked, however, that the Ḥanbalite school from its inception had attached great importance to restraining the gaze. A saying ascribed to Aḥmad b. Ḥanbal implies that repentance is not valid unless *naẓar* is abandoned. Abū Bakr al-Marwazī reported:

> I said to Abū ʿAbd Allāh Aḥmad b. Ḥanbal, "A man repented and said, 'Though my back be scourged, I will never again disobey God,' but he did not give up *naẓar*." "What kind of repentence is this?" Aḥmad replied.[33]

The treatment of *naẓar* in *Dhamm al-hawā*, consists essentially of relating *ḥadīth*. In the traditions cited are adumbrated many of the points Ibn Qayyim al-Jawzīya raised later. One example is the interdiction of the second glance towards a woman—the first, if accidental, being allowed. This principle is found in a number of traditions spoken by the Prophet to ʿAlī b. Abī Ṭālib. The Prophet is reported to have said to ʿAlī, for example: "Do not follow up the first glance with another, for the first is permitted to you, but not the second."[34] Again, exploiting the common poetic comparison of the glance to an arrow, he said: "ʿAlī, beware of the second glance, for it is a poisoned arrow which stirs up desire in the heart."[35] One wonders why these admonitions are addressed to ʿAlī. The colporteurs of tradition may well have had in mind the fact that the majority of Sufis traced their spiritual lineage back to the fourth caliph. But the question merits more study.

Some of the traditions quoted by Ibn al-Jawzī connect the glance specifically with *ʿishq*-love: "A certain *ḥakīm* [presumably a pre-Islamic sage and most likely a Greek] said, 'The beginning of *ʿishq* is *naẓar*, as the beginning of fire is sparks (*sharar*).' " Another tradition, this one explicitly ascribed to a pre-Islamic source, tells of a group of philosophers who met one day with Alexander and discussed how love is born of the glance. "The glance," remarked one of them, "brings first sorrow (*asaf*) and then death (*talaf*)."[36] The *sajʿ* or rhymed prose of these two aphorisms, to be sure, strongly suggests an Arabic and probably Islamic origin. Their ascription however to pre-Islamic sources reveals that the Muslim intellectual world was aware of a certain indebtedness to antiquity for the association *glance-love-sorrow-death.*

After relating a great many traditions, Ibn al-Jawzī finally gives a comparison which he claims as his own. The subject is the first point mentioned above, the repeated glance. It is more feasible, he observes, exploiting an analogy in fact already used by al-Ghazālī, to cure *naẓar* by stopping it immediately after the first glance, just as, when a horse enters a narrow place, it is easier to extricate him before he has gone far in.[37]

But why, it had been objected, should one refrain from the second glance? A first glance can lead to love based on a hurried and inaccurate impression. If this occurs, a second look may bring consolation by revealing the beloved's faults. Ibn al-Jawzī meets this argument with a fourfold refutation. The second glance is not permitted (by Islamic law). The person seen, moreover, is probably even more attractive than was thought at first. Also, when a man makes up his mind to cast a second glance, Satan is there to embellish what is not beautiful. Finally, even if a man by means of a second glance ascertains that the person seen is not worthy of his love, it will be because the person does not suit his purposes that he is led to renounce him, not for the sake of God.[38] These same proofs are among those adopted by Ibn Qayyim al-Jawzīya, who treats this objection in greater detail.[39]

Within the discussion of *naẓar* Ibn al-Jawzī devotes a special chapter to the matter of gazing at beardless youths and keeping company with them. Religious men and scholars, he remarks, who may consistently refrain from glancing at women legally forbidden to them (*nisā' ajānib*) thanks to their infrequent contacts with members of the opposite sex, must also beware of looking at the youths in their company; for "there are few who have approached this enticement without falling into it." The extent of this danger as Ibn al-Jawzī conceived it, appears in the traditions he cites. For example, according to Anas, the Prophet said: "Keep not company with the sons of kings, for verily souls desire them in a way they do not desire freed slave-girls. Again, it was reported that al-Ḥasan b. Dhakwān said: "Do not sit with the sons of the rich, for they have faces (*ṣuwar*) like those of women and are a greater temptation than virgins."[40]

Ibn al-Jawzī was particularly concerned with the practice of gazing at boys when it was carried on in the guise of religion. This fact is stressed by a number of traditions and sayings related in the *Dhamm.* Abū al-ʿAbbās b. Aḥmad al-Mu'addib said to Abū ʿAlī al-Rūdhbārī: "Abū ʿAlī, whence did the Sufis of our time acquire this intimacy with youths?" Abū Saʿīd is reported to have said: "Few are the Sufis who are untainted in this regard [intimacy with youths]." In this same connection Abū Sahl, emphasizing more specifically *naẓar* and its affinity with a less restrained form of indulgence, said: "There will be in this community a people called sodomites (*al-lūṭīyūn*). They will be of three kinds: those who gaze, those who touch, and those who commit that act."[41] Although this last saying does not mention the Sufis by name, it may be assumed that Ibn al-Jawzī had them in mind in quoting it, since the majority of the traditions related in the same context are directed against them. Cited also are many anecdotes which recount how various mystics, even leaders among them, were smitten with lovesickness from looking at boys.

The extent of Ibn al-Jawzī's scorn for the Sufi custom of gazing at beardless youths is more apparent in his heresiographical work *Talbīs Iblīs* (*Satan's deceit*) than in *Dhamm al-hawā. Naẓar* is not simply immoral, it is linked with one of the most heinous of Sufi heresies, the belief in indwelling or incarnation (*ḥulūl*).[42] In matters such as this, which have doctrinal associations, Ibn al-Jawzī's mordant polemic is at its best. Combining keen observation with what often appears as a grain of sarcasm, he divides those mystics who engage in the practice of *naẓar* into seven classes, none of them flattering.[43]

The first and for Ibn al-Jawzī the most execrable class is composed of those Sufis who actually maintain the doctrine of *ḥulūl*, claiming that

God indwells in certain bodies in this world, often in human forms and especially in the beautiful. Cited earlier in the *Talbīs* is a story about Abū Ḥamza which exploits the common motif of a Sufī's misunderstanding a banal phrase or giving a spiritual interpretation to some everyday sound. One day when Abū Ḥamza was speaking in the mosque of Ṭarsūs, a crow cawed on the roof. The mystic cried out in reply, "Here am I, here am I." For this, it is said, he was justly accused of *ḥulūl* and *zandaqa* (Manichaeism).[44]

The practice of gazing at young boys or beautiful objects was a natural corollary of the doctrine of *ḥulūl*. Ibn al-Jawzī remarks that while some Sufis held God to be visible in this world to the heart only, others believed the beatific vision to be accessible to the faculty of sight. Others still maintained that they kept company with God and could touch him. It was not uncommon for a man to claim that he had witnessed God while gazing at a comely slave-boy.[45]

Not surprisingly, al-Ḥallāj is cited for *ḥulūl*, the following verses from the martyr's *dīwān* being given as evidence:

Subḥāna man aẓhara nāsūtuhū
  sirra sanā lāhūtihi 'l-thāqibī
Thumma badā fī khalqihī ẓāhiran
  fī ṣūrati 'l-ākili wa-l-shāribī
Ḥattā laqad ʿāyanahū khalquhū
  ka-laḥẓati 'l-ḥājibi bi-l-ḥajibī

(Praise to Him whose Humanity has manifested [to the Angels]
  the mystery of the glory of His radiant Divinity!
And Who, since then, has shown Himself to his [human] creature openly
  in the form of one "who eats and drinks,"
So that His creature could contemplate Him with his eyes,
  as if face to face)[46]

The explanatory additions in brackets, inserted by Massignon in his French translation, from which this English version is adapted, do not mitigate the clear allusion of these verses to the doctrine of indwelling as well as, in the last two lines, to the beatific vision in the flesh. Whether or not the verses are actually by al-Ḥallāj,[47] their attribution to him can only have increased the repugnance with which he was viewed in orthodox Muslim circles.

In the second class of mystics who practice *naẓar* are grouped those persons who dress as Sufis in order to pursue debauchery.

The third is composed of those who permit gazing at beautiful objects, although they do not teach *ḥulūl.* Abū ʿAbd al-Raḥmān al-Sulamī, towards the end of his *Sunan al-Ṣūfīya*, devoted a chapter to the licenses (*rukhaṣ*) of the Sufis in which he mentioned dancing, singing, and gazing at beautiful faces. In support of the last of these he cited the sayings of the Prophet: "Seek good from those who have beautiful faces," and "Three things clarify the vision: looking at greenery, looking at water, and looking at beautiful faces." Ibn al-Jawzī rejects these two traditions on the weakness of their *isnād*s, adding that al-Sulamī should have restricted the gazing of which he spoke to the face of one's wife or slave-girl only.[48] In this same category is placed Ibn Ṭāhir al-Maqdisī, who wrote a treatise defending the practice of gazing at beardless youths.

The fourth class is made up of those who maintain that their gaze is not one of desire (*shahwa*) but of admiration (*iʿtibār*) and consequently is harmless. Ibn al-Jawzī holds this claim to be untenable on the grounds that looking at beautiful faces is known to arouse desire in all sound men.

In this group falls Aḥmad al-Ghazālī, brother of Abū Ḥāmid and himself the author of a treatise on love. Aḥmid was once seen sitting alone with a young boy, a rose being placed between them. In this posture he would gaze alternately at the rose and the boy. When he was asked by the persons who discovered him whether they were intruding, he replied, "You are, by God!"[49]

In the fifth class are grouped those Sufis who associate with youths but refrain from immorality, thinking that their abstinence in the face of such temptation constitutes *jihād al-nafs* or the great "holy war" against the soul. They fail to realize, according to Ibn al-Jawzī, that merely to look at a young boy with desire is sinful and that their preoccupation with youths distracts them from thinking of God.[50]

The sixth class comprises those mystics who do not intentionally frequent young boys but who are joined by youthful disciples. Satan induces Sufis of this category to cast repeated unintentional glances at their juvenile *murīd*s until he obtains from them whatever he can manage.

In the last group are classified those Sufis who know that keeping company with youths and gazing at them is not permitted but who cannot control themselves. For Ibn al-Jawzī it was a platitude that young boys constitute a greater source of temptation than girls.[51]

This unflattering classification of the mystical practitioners of *naẓar* reveals that Ibn al-Jawzī's discussion of the subject was prompted no less by his attitude towards Sufism than by his concern for the everyday morality of the community. Reflecting Ḥanbalism's stand against the doctrine and practice of antinomian mysticism, he stresses a second dimension of the traditional *naẓar* theme of ascetic literature. Treatment of a given issue on several planes in this manner is typical of Ḥanbalite writings on love. The question of music (*samāʿ*), for example, is subjected to a similar development in *Talbīs Iblīs.*

Ibn al-Jawzī's initial objection to music is that it is morally perilous. On the profane level it distracts the listener's heart from meditating on the greatness of God and from serving him, while, at the same time, it makes him incline towards temporal passions and pleasures, especially towards carnality. The Ḥanbalite scholar, in fact, sees a clear correspondence between fornication and song: physical immorality is the pleasure of the soul (*nafs*), while song is that of the spirit (*rūḥ*). Now since taking pleasure in one thing invites man to do likewise in another, especially when some correspondence exists between the two, Satan can use song to lead men to graver transgressions.[52] True, Ibn al-Jawzī admits, listening to song, like the analogous practices of looking at youths or kissing girls of three, is only forbidden when there is danger of stirring up desire,[53] but since human nature is alike in all sound men and since singing is known to arouse romantic passion (*ʿishq*) and the love of this world, he who claims that song does not excite desire in him is either lying or ill.[54]

Yet the Sufis claim that song is edifying, that the mystic grasps it in intimations of something higher. This, Ibn al-Jawzī replies, is like the claim of one who looks at a beautiful woman and alleges that he does so only to contemplate God's creation. Such a defense is inadmissible, for human nature will have already run its course before any subtle intimations can be seized.

Let it be supposed, however, that human nature were not an obstacle to grasping the alleged intimations in song. Could one then find anything there? Practically nothing, maintains Ibn al-Jawzī, now thinking of the words, not the music: there is hardly anything in song which alludes to the Creator, for God is too great for it to be said of him that he is loved with *ʿishq.* This term which the Sufis dare to use with reference to God, the reader is told, is applicable only to that with which one can copulate.[55]

It should be remarked also that Ibn al-Jawzī in attacking song on the basis of the words misunderstands the Sufi conception of music, which is basically that of Neoplatonism as generally reflected in Islamic thought. This view of music is explained in *al-ʿIqd al-farīd*:

> The philosophers maintained that music (*naghm*) is an excess (*faḍl*) of speech (*manṭiq*) which the tongue cannot express, and so nature expresses it by means of melodies. . . . When it appears, the soul falls in love with it (*ʿashiqahu*) and the spirit yearns for it. This is what led Plato to say: "The parts of the soul must not be prevented from loving (*muʿāshaqa*) each other." [i.e. it was through music that he learned of the love of the soul.] . . .
>
> Sometimes one may proceed by means of musical airs to the good of this world and the next, for they incite man to high morals, and the heart, being softened by them, remembers the pleasantness of the Heavenly Existence (*al-Malakūt*) and envisions it in its inner consciousness (*ḍamīr*).[56]

One discerns here not only the Sufi concept of the ennobling power of music, as distinct from speech, but also, in the first paragraph, a parallel to the relationship held by the mystics to exist between music and the love of the soul. This relationship, as has been seen above, Ibn al-Jawzī could conceive of only between music and vulgar *eros*. Thus in his argument against the intimations of the divine which the Sufis claim to experience in *samāʿ*, although he establishes that music arouses worldly passions in all sound men, he fails to deal effectively with the eventuality of its simultaneously exciting desires of a higher and more compelling nature. Rather, he undertakes to demonstrate the impropriety of the words sung to music, on the assumption that it is only through speech that one may claim to receive such intimations.

This misunderstanding serves to place in relief Ibn al-Jawzī's preoccupation with the Sufi application of the term *ʿishq* to love between God and man. Whether under the influence of Ashʿarism or as a consequence of his own legalistic view of religion, the Ḥanbalite, like the Christian Father Tertullian,[57] condemns outright the Neoplatonic concept of longing *eros*-*ʿishq*: "God has no quality towards which human nature can incline or souls yearn. Rather, the complete dissimilarity between the Divinity and his creatures produces in men's souls awe (*hayba*) and timidity (*ḥishma*). What the Sufi 'lovers' (*ʿushshāq*) maintain concerning love (*maḥabba*) to God is pure delusion."[58] The very basis of *eros*-*ʿishq* is rejected here, for, as will be seen, a kind of similarity between subject and object is considered to be among the preconditions for this egocentric type of love.[59]

The importance of the sacred dimension in Ibn al-Jawzī's discussion of such questions as *naẓar* and *samāʿ* should be apparent. This is not to say, of course, that these questions never arise in a more secular context. Most of the treatment of *naẓar* in *Dhamm-al-hawā* dwells on profane lovers who were reported to have indulged in the vices of glancing and gazing. The primary accused is the Ẓāhirite jurist Muḥammad b. Dāwūd al-Iṣfahānī. If Ibn al-Jawzī does not hesitate to cite Ibn Dāwūd against al-Ḥallāj, he none the less criticizes the Ẓāhirite's courtly relationship with Muḥammad b. Jāmiʿ al-Ṣaydalānī, for whom he wrote his *Kitāb al-zahra.*[60] Once, records Ibn al-Jawzī,

> Muḥammad b. Jāmiʿ entered the bath and made up his face. Picking up a mirror, he examined his visage and veiled it. Then he rode to Muḥammad b. Dāwūd. [Ibn Dāwūd], seeing the youth's face covered, feared that some harm had befallen him and inquired what was the matter. "I saw my face just now in the mirror," the boy answered, "and I covered it, because I wanted no one to see it before you." On hearing this reply, Ibn Dāwūd fell into a swoon.

It is not difficult to imagine the contempt—and perhaps also the curiosity—which stories like this one regarding the personal life of the Ẓāhirite must have aroused in Ibn al-Jawzī.

Another anecdote concerning Ibn Dāwūd related in *Dhamm al-hawā* represents him advancing the permissibility of visual contemplation of the beloved. The jurist, on his death bed, actually attributes his affliction to *naẓar* but does not recant. "The love of whom you know has brought about what you see," he complained. Being asked what kept him from possessing the person when it was in his power to do so, he replied, "It is the legitimate glance which has incurred what you see, but as for the forbidden pleasure, I was deterred from it by what my father reported to me: . . . from Ibn ʿAbbās that the Prophet said, 'He who falls in love (*ʿashiqa*), conceals [his passion], is chaste, and patiently abstains (*ṣabara*), is forgiven by God and received into Paradise.' "

Unlike Ibn al-Qayyim, Ibn al-Jawzī raises no ideological objections to this tradition on chaste love cited by the Ẓāhirite. On the contrary, he uses it as the theme of one of the chapters of *Dhamm al-hawā* (chapter thirty-eight, "On the reward of him who loves, remains chaste, and conceals"). He takes odds with Ibn Dāwūd only concerning *naẓar*, and his argument sums up his views on the ethical aspects of the question:

> Looking at a youth is only permissible in the absence of desire. But even if desire is lacking, it may be aroused by the act of looking at him. Our companions [the Ḥanbalites] offer two considerations on

> this point: 1. If the constitution (*ṭabʿ*) is sound, desire is present, and it is still necessary to forbid *naẓar*. 2. He who claims that he experiences no desire is a liar, and if we could believe him, he would be an animal, not a human being. It is clear however, from the words of Ibn Dāwūd, that he did not hold *naẓar* to be forbidden. In this he was mistaken, and the error led first to his disgrace before the people, and, finally, to his death. . . . If only this man had restrained his glance the first time, he would have been spared, but he understood only fornication to be forbidden.

From ancient times it had been something of a commonplace that when a youth grew a beard he began to appeal to girls and ceased to exert a strong attraction on men. This is the idea implicit in a description Horace gives of the youth Lycidas, who, although not for much longer, is still beardless. The poet, relating to the boy's older lover, Lucius Sestius, some of the sorrows he will experience in Pluto's realm, tells him:

> Nec tenerum Lycidan mirabere, quo calet iuventus
> Nunc ommis et mox virgines tepebunt.
>
> (Nor will you gaze on tender Lycidas, for whom all youths are now ablaze with love and virgins will soon be warm.)
>
> *Odes* i.4.19–20

Ibn al-Jawzī did not share the ancient assumption. Not even when the beard begins to grow is it permissible to look at a youth. It is forbidden to look at anyone if pleasure results, and Arabic poetry reveals that many are seduced by the first signs of a beard. An example is found in these verses related by Nifṭawayh from Ibn Dāwūd, who is said to have composed them on his death bed:

> Mā la-hum ankarū sawādan bi-khaddayhī
> wa-lā yunkirūna warda 'l-ghuṣūnī?
> In yakun ʿaybu khaddihī budada 'l-shaʿrī,
> fa-ʿaybu 'l-ʿuyūni shaʿru 'l-jufūnī.
>
> (Why do they blame the blackness in his cheeks,
> when they do not blame the blossoms on their boughs?
> If the flaw of his cheeks is the down of his beard,
> then the flaw of his eyes is the fringe of his lashes.)

On hearing these lines Nifṭawayh exclaimed to the jurist, "You reject analogy in jurisprudence [a Ẓāhirite tenet] but affirm it in poetry?!"

"Because of overpowering passion and the natural disposition of the human soul," he replied. Ibn Dāwūd died, according to Nifṭawayh, that same night or the following day.[61]

After thus categorically rejecting *naẓar* towards women not one's own, boys, and even older youths, Ibn al-Jawzī devotes several chapters to practical aspects of the problem: God's punishment for *naẓar*; self-inflicted punishments; stories of men who asked that their sight be taken away out of fear of temptation; the reward of those who restrain their glances; how to cure the concern and anxiety arising from *naẓar*; and what to do when pleased by a woman one has seen.

Seclusion with women (II,A,2)

Closely allied with the question of *naẓar* is the forbiddance of seclusion with a woman other than one's own (*ajnabīya*). According to a number of *ḥadīth*s cited in this connection, when a man and a woman are alone together, the third present is Satan. When the Prophet was asked, "What if they are good people?" he replied, "Even if they were the Virgin Mary and John the Baptist!"[62]

In general, Ibn al-Jawzī views women not as objects of respect but rather as sources of temptation. This observation is borne out by a number of the traditions and stories he quotes. The Prophet is reported to have said, for example, "I have left after me no temptation for men more pernicious than women."[63] The story of the fallen angels Hārūt and Mārūt is in the same misogynous vein. Ibn al-Jawzī recounts several versions of this *ḥadīth*. The one translated here has the merit of having Aḥmad b. Ḥanbal in the *isnād* (. . . from Ibn ʿUmar that the Prophet said):

> When God placed Adam on the earth, the angels exclaimed, "Our Lord, shouldst thou put on the earth one who will corrupt it and shed blood, whereas we praise thee and glorify thee?" "Verily, I know things of which you are ignorant," he replied.[64] "But, our Lord," they objected, "we are more obedient to thee than men." Then God Most High said to the angels, "Bring forth two angels so that we may send them to the earth and observe how they act." "Take Hārūt and Mārūt, O Lord," they replied.
>
> These two being sent down to the earth, there appeared to them al-Zuhara [name of the planet Venus], one of the most beautiful of women. [When they saw her], they asked her to give herself to them. "No, by God," she answered, "not until you speak idolatry!" "By God, we shall never set up an equal to God," they retorted.

> Then she went away from them and returned carrying a child. When they asked her again, she said, "No, by God, not until you kill this child!" They swore that they would never kill him. So she withdrew and returned later with a cup of wine. On their asking her a third time, she cried, "No, by God, not until you drink this wine!" So they drank until they were drunk; then they possessed her and killed the child. When they were sober again, the woman derided them: "By God, not one of the things you refused me did you leave undone when you were drunk."
>
> Then they were made to choose between the punishment of this world and that of the next. It was the punishment of this world which they chose.[65]

Ibn al-Jawzī also relates a sweeping condemnation which Ibn ʿAbbās made of the temptations of women: "The unbelief of those who have departed was caused by women alone, and the unbelief of those who remain is also from women." Similarly, Sufyān al-Thawrī's word of caution is recorded: "Entrust me with a house full of riches, but do not entrust me with a black girl who is not permitted to me."[66]

These examples suffice to demonstrate that Ibn al-Jawzī in his moral teaching was concerned with women chiefly as a grave source of temptation for men. In *Dhamm al-hawā* at least, he places no emphasis on respect for women as a reason for abstaining from sexual immorality.[67] It is merely a question of obeying a command and avoiding punishment.

Sins (maʿāṣī) in general and their consequences (II,A,3)

The succeeding section of *Dhamm al-hawā* is devoted to the relation of traditions against sin in general. Among the more interesting motifs which appear are the jealousy of God when a Muslim sins,[68] the effect of sins and good deeds on facial beauty,[69] and the importance of conscience. Regarding the last of these al-Faḍl is reported to have said: "The smaller a sin seems to you, the greater it is in the eyes of God; and the greater it is to you, the smaller it is to God."[70] More indicative of Ibn al-Jawzī's attitude towards sin, however, is a saying ascribed to a certain sage (*ḥakīm*): "If you are able to avoid harming the one you love, then do so." When the sage was asked, "How does a man harm the one he loves?" he replied, "If you disobey God, you harm your own soul (*nafsaka* = yourself), and she is your greatest beloved."[71] Here is expressed unequivocally what is more or less understood in the rest of

Ibn al-Jawzī's preaching: the basic reason for refraining from sin is self-love. It is this principle which underlies his repeated exhortations to consider the consequences of acts before undertaking them. The Koran and Sunna provide the sanctions; self-love does the rest. Thus the Ḥanbalite approach to morality, as found in Ibn al-Jawzī, is both legalistic and egocentric. It has, except in rare cases,[72] very little to do with a sentiment of altruism. We shall see later to what extent this outlook characterizes the movement's treatment of love.[73]

Fornication and homosexuality
(II,A,4,5,)
The two sins singled out for particular censure in the *Dhamm* are *zinā* (fornication or adultery) and sodomy. Concerning *zinā* Aḥmad b. Ḥanbal said, "There is nothing more heinous after murder than adultery."[74] Through adultery, the Prophet had held, a man ceases to be a believer, unless he repents.[75] According to a rather colorful tradition, the Prophet in a vision found adulterers to be the most foul-smelling of people.[76] Another time he beheld them gathered in a house like an oven with a fire beneath.[77] According to a tradition from al-Ḥaytham b. Mālik al-Ṭā'ī, he ranked illicit relations with women as the second most deadly sin: "There is no offense after *shirk* [idolatry] more heinous to God than a man's placing his seed in a womb which is forbidden to him."[78]

The reason for abstaining from adultery implicit in the last tradition quoted from the Prophet is a practical one—the danger of injustice in succession. This objection along with others is stated explicitly in *Ṣayd al-khāṭir*, where Ibn al-Jawzī gives a list summing up the consequences of adultery. These are: the end of one's good name; the uncovering of one's private parts; the betrayal of one's Muslim brother; the disgracing of the woman, who ought to be treated as a sister or a daughter; confusion and injustice in inheritance; and the wrath of God.[79] If two of these objections to adultery, the betrayal of a fellow Muslim and especially the disgracing of the woman, reveal an altruism rarely expressed in the works of Ibn al-Jawzī, the remaining four rest typically upon practical considerations—the need for order in society or simply self-interest.

Against sodomy, which he observed to be widespread, especially among Sufis, Ibn al-Jawzī is equally vehement. Briefly, his argument runs thus: If God, in the Koran, dwelt more upon the homosexuality of Lot's people than upon their unbelief (*kufr*), although unbelief is the greater of the two sins, it was to warn men away from such acts. As is known, their punishment was stoning. Moreover, the Prophet said that both active and passive homosexuals should be stoned, while Abū Bakr and the Companions had a *lūṭī* burnt. According to Ibn ʿAbbās, the sodomite should be thrown upside down from the highest building in the town and then stoned.[80] In the hereafter the punishment for sodomy will be even more terrible. On Resurrection Day, unless they repent, the guilty partners will find themselves stuck together![81]

Lesbianism comes off no lighter. "Two women together," Ibn al-Jawzī writes, "are like two men together." Cited in this connection is the saying of the Prophet (from Wā'ila b. al-Asqaʿ): "The tribady (*siḥāq*) of women is fornication between them."[82] Later, Ibn Qayyim al-Jawzīya, as usual more sophisticated, would make a legal distinction between male homosexuality and Lesbianism.[83]

Following the section on fornication and sodomy, two chapters of *Dhamm al-hawā* are devoted to cautioning the reader against the punishments incurred for sins of passion and to exhorting him to repentance (II,A,6).

B. VIRTUES

Chastity or temperance (ʿafāf) *(II,B,1)*

Turning to the praise of chastity, Ibn al-Jawzī attempts to make his point merely by recounting traditions and anecdotes on the subject. Many of these fail to convince the modern reader, and some may even occasion a smile. An example is the story of ʿUrwa b. al-Zubayr, whose leg was attacked by gangrene. Being informed that it would be necessary to amputate, he refused a soporific and watched the operation. When he saw the severed member in the hands of the physicians, he seized it from them and addressed it, crying, "Praise be to God! He who made you carry me knows that I never walked on you to any forbidden thing."[84] A more convincing example, illustrating the Islamic principle that acts are judged by intentions, tells the story of a hermitess who was forcibly raped. During the act she held her hand in burning coals. When the ravisher inquired why she had done this, she replied that it was to avoid sharing in the pleasure and consequently in the sin. Hearing this answer, the man repented.[85]

The paragon of chastity for Ibn al-Jawzī, as for Islam in general, is Joseph. This rank he earned by declining the advances of Potiphar's wife (the wife of al-ʿAzīz in the Koranic version) despite her power to bring harm to him. A tradition relates that ʿAṭāʾ b. Yasār after successfully resisting the wiles of a Bedouin woman saw Joseph in a dream and was told that he was similar to the Hebrew prophet. In another less orthodox version of the story, told of Sulaymān b. Yasār, the hero, after fleeing from a temptress, is told by Joseph in a dream, "I am Joseph, who was troubled [by desire]; you are Sulaymān, who were not." As the editor of *Dhamm al-hawā* indicates in a footnote, the second version of the story gives precedence to an ascetic over a prophet—a view not typical of Ḥanbalism.[86]

Among the verses cited to grace the chapter on chastity, one compares illicit sexual relations to idolatry, thus touching on a point treated in detail by Ibn al-Qayyim. This verse, if we grant that it represents Ibn al-Jawzī's thought, suggests that the word temperance—in our ordinary usage—may more accurately apply to his conception of the virtue:

> Lastu mim-man yabghī ʾl-wiṣāla ḥarāman:
> inna fiʿla ʾl-ḥarāmi ka-l-ishrākī.

> (I am not one who covets union illicitly:
> to perform [such] an illicit act is like idolatry.)[87]

Here and throughout *Dhamm al-hawā* Ibn al-Jawzī's arguments are directed only against forbidden physical relations. Nowhere is complete abstinence recommended for its own sake. On the contrary, this Ḥanbalite not only preached but also practiced a reasonable indulgence in the pleasures of venery.[88]

Marriage and licit intercourse (II,B,2)

In accordance with his conception of temperence, Ibn al-Jawzī encourages marriage (*nikāḥ*) and licit sexual relations with slave-girls as well. The following is the purport of the traditions cited in this connection. Marriage is recommended for those who can afford it. For those who cannot, fasting, which effects a kind of castration, is suggested. Marriage would appear to be the best defense against the Tempter, since women are Satan's most effective weapon against men—except those who are married. Hence the man who has a son ready for matrimony and can afford to give him a bride should do so. Otherwise, if the son fornicates, the father shares the responsibility for the act. The example of the Prophet also encourages marriage, for he married fourteen women and left nine after him when he died. Finally, Aḥmad b. Ḥanbal recommended marriage, a number of sayings being related from him to this effect.[89]

Ibn al-Jawzī's views on the function of marriage are found not in *Dhamm al-hawā* but in *Ṣayd al-khāṭir.* The utility of marriage (*mankaḥ*), he maintains, is twofold: primarily to insure the survival of the race and secondarily to expel the harmful congested excess from the body. If it were not for man's desire (*hawā*) for intercourse, procreation would cease and the congested excess would cause physical damage. It is for these purposes that sexual intercourse has been created, not for the sake of mere pleasure. Pleasure is simply a device to attract man to the beneficial. For, were the object of sexual activity pleasure in itself, then the animals would not have been given a greater share of this activity than human beings.[90]

Also in *Ṣayd al-khāṭir* is found most of the advice Ibn al-Jawzī gives regarding marriage and sexual relations. But one counsel from the *Dhamm* commands attention because it pertains to the question of *naẓar*. It is advisable, the reader is told, for the man who is about to contract an alliance to view his prospective bride, since one of the two grounds on which she should be chosen is beauty (the other being piety). One stricken with passion should try to wed the object of his affection. If he is unable to do so, then he ought to choose someone who he believes will console him, that is, someone who is pleasing to his sight.[91] We discover here that *naẓar* for Ibn al-Jawzī, when it is intended as a step towards a legitimate union, is not only permitted but even recommended. The pleasures of sight are not to be condemned, then, as long as they can in no way be construed as enticements to the illicit.

Among other advice Ibn al-Jawzī tenders is a suggestion that concubines are to be preferred to wives, since most free women are of disagreeable temperament. One should especially avoid marrying a free woman if he knows she will not tolerate his marrying again or taking a concubine.[92]

An old man should not marry a young girl for the obvious reason that it is impossible to obtain complete pleasure when she is too young, whereas, when she matures, her desire is so great that the man, being advanced in years, cannot satisfy her. If he attempts to do so, a speedy death awaits him.[93]

The youth is advised to avoid overindulgence in physical relations in order to ensure the survival of his "essence" (*jawhar*) until old age. He should realize, furthermore, that the true pleasure of love comes from proximity to the beloved, embraces, and kisses, all of which strengthen love. It does not come from cohabitation, which actually decreases love and destroys the pleasure it yields. Thus the Bedouins loved passionately but spurned physical union, believing that it destroys love. As for the pleasure resulting from union, it is the affair of animals, not of man.[94]

In this same context Ibn al-Jawzī offers a rather Platonic interpretation of sexual intercourse, apparently an abridgment of a passage in the *Rasā'il Ikhwān al-Ṣafā'*. In his concluding remarks he minimizes the importance of physical pleasure. Lovemaking is not merely a physical act in his view; it has a spiritual meaning. This spiritual meaning is that the soul (*nafs*), which seeks ever greater proximity to the soul of the beloved, first by embraces, next by kisses, and then by sucking the tongue—as the Prophet, according to tradition, used to hug ʿĀ'isha, and kiss her, and suck her tongue—finally desires to come even closer to the soul of the beloved and resorts to physical union. Such, Ibn al-Jawzī assures his reader, is the spiritual—and, he implies, the true—meaning of intercourse. Sensual pleasure is but a byproduct.[95]

Ibn Qayyim al-Jawzīya later, sensing the incompatibility of such Platonism with his anti-Sufi position, consistently rejects signs of it wherever he recognizes them. Consequently, while he shares Ibn al-Jawzī's view of the advantages of marriage, we may assume that he would not have accepted his spiritual interpretation of sexual intercourse. We know that he specifically rejected the view that intercourse is harmful to love.[96]

Following the chapter in *Dhamm al-hawā* on marriage is another listing traditions and anecdotes which condemn the corrupting of other men's wives. The succeeding section of the work, more than half of it, is devoted to the subject of *ʿishq*.

III. *Passionate love (ʿishq)*

Although the greater part of Ibn al-Jawzī's treatment of *ʿishq* is made up not of his own arguments but of stories and *ḥadīth* culled from the oral tradition or borrowed from al-Sarrāj's *Maṣāriʿ*, still the considerable length of this section is an indication of how concerned he was with the subject. First, then, we ought to recall why he was so preoccupied with the question of romantic love. One possible explanation, that his interest, together with that of Ḥanbalism in general, is an outgrowth of lexicographical discussions of the term *ʿishq*, appears somewhat unlikely, since the classical dictionaries consecrate only very minor articles to the root *ʿ-SH-Q*. A second hypothesis, that Ibn al-Jawzī's work on *ʿishq* is a development of the treatment of the subject in works on ethics, would seem to be more plausible. But the primary cause of his concern, at least in so far as we have been able to discover it in his writings themselves, is his reaction to the views on *ʿishq* propounded by groups loosely describable as Islamic Platonists, that is, the Sufis and, to some extent, the Ẓāhirites, who were represented for him by Muḥammad b. Dāwūd. Bearing this in mind, it is interesting to observe how often he is inconsistent in his attitude towards the influences of Platonism.

The nature and causes of love (III,1,2)

On the essence (*māhīya*) of *ʿishq*-love, Ibn al-Jawzī informs the reader, opinions vary: most people call it simply by the names of its causes or of its consequences. There was however, he continues, fairly general agreement among the ancients on several points: *ʿishq* is the operation of an empty or unpreoccupied heart (*qalb fārigh*); it is madness (a saying to this effect is attributed to Socrates); and it leads to anguish or death. Some claim that it is a mentally caused disease (*maraḍ waswāsī*) similar to melancholy (*mālīkhūliyā*).[97] According to the Muʿtazilite Thumāma b. Ashras (d. 213/828), poets understand *ʿishq* better than do jurists.

Dissatisfied with the comments of his predecessors on the subject, Ibn al-Jawzī attempts to formulate the true definition of *ʿishq*. *ʿIshq*, he writes, is "the acute inclination of the soul (*nafs*) towards a form (*ṣūra*) which conforms to its nature (*ṭabʿ*). If the soul thinks intensely on this form, it imagines the possibility of obtaining it and begins to hope that it may. From this intense thought is born the malady [of love]."[98]

Al-Jāḥiẓ's definition of *ʿishq* as excessive love is mentioned by Ibn al-Jawzī but not dwelt upon.[99] The closest he comes to this definition in his own words is when he speaks of the "intense thought" which ends in malady.

ʿIshq, of course, is not the only word for love. Ibn al-Jawzī is concerned with the various names for love and the stages of the emotion they represent, perhaps in response to the Sufi stratification of love terminology.[100] Here again, however, he relies uncritically on tradition. Thus in the lists he cites in which the two words occur *ʿishq* is consistently ranked above *khulla*. For the more careful Ibn Qayyim al-Jawzīya, on the other hand, it is *khulla*, taken to signify the true devotion of love exclusively to one object, which represents the supreme stage of affection—one realized in this world only in the love of Abraham and Muḥammad for God.[101] The highest degree of love in the first of the lists given by Ibn al-Jawzī is *walah* or loss of discernment. In two others it is *tatayyum*, which is the same as *ta'abbud* (enslavement or worship). Mentioned in substantiation of the equation of the latter two terms are the expressions *Taym Allāh* (a name: Slave or Servant of God) and *rajul mutayyam* (a man enslaved by love).[102]

The term *maḥabba*, Ibn al-Jawzī says following al-Jāḥiẓ, is generic, while *'ishq* is considered a species of love. For instance, a man may love his father and his son, but this kind of love does not lead to death as does *'ishq*. When one loves his family, this is the love of reason (*maḥabbat al-'aql*), while *'ishq* is the love of the spirit (*maḥabbat al-rūḥ*).[103]

Turning to the causes of love, the scholar expands on a similar distinction in terms which again recall a passage of the *Rasā'il Ikhwān al-Ṣafā'*. According to the ancients, he writes, there are three kinds of souls: "the rational soul (*nafs nāṭiqa*), whose love is devoted to knowledge and the acquisition of virtues; the animal, irascible soul (*nafs ḥayawānīya ghaḍabīya*), whose love is devoted to power, victory, and leadership; and the appetitive soul (*nafs shahwānīya*), whose love is directed towards food, drink, and sexual relations." He makes it clear, in this context, that his purpose is to discuss only the causes of the love of the appetitive soul, which he calls *'ishq*.[104]

The primary cause of passionate love is *naẓar*. For love, as is evident from Ibn al-Jawzī's definition, occurs when the soul meets an object which conforms to its nature. Obviously it is the faculty of vision which is most often responsible for bringing about this meeting. It is persistent gazing, he adds, and not a lone glance, which results in love.

Another cause of *'ishq* is listening to amatory verse and song (*samā'*). This activity engraves images on the heart which the faculty of vision then proceeds to find beautiful. That *samā'* was one of the major factors in determining Ibn al-Jawzī's concern for love appears, as we have already seen, in his treatment of Sufi *samā'* in *Talbīs Iblīs*. The singling out of the two causes *naẓar* and *samā'*, however, is not original with the author of *Dhamm al-hawā*. We find them, for example, in the tradition mentioned above which ranks *'ishq* above *khulla*.[105]

The essential precondition of love, as it appears in Ibn al-Jawzī's definition of *'ishq*, is a kind of conformity between the subject and the object of the emotion. In advancing the necessity of such a relationship between lovers, the Ḥanbalite agrees with the view commonly accepted by medieval Muslim theoreticians of love. Interestingly, in his brief discussion of the question he records uncritically a saying which implies that men's souls exist prior to their bodies.[106] Ibn Qayyim al-Jawzīya was to become celebrated for his rejection of this Platonic doctrine.[107]

The censure of passionate love (III,3)

Is the kind of love known as *ʿishq* praiseworthy or reprehensible? Some authorities, Ibn al-Jawzī informs the reader, answer that *ʿishq* is praiseworthy, because it can proceed only from a delicate nature and because, so long as it is not excessive, it clarifies the reason and the mind. Others blame *ʿishq* because it imprisons the lover and makes a slave of him. In Ibn al-Jawzī's view, *maḥabba*-love and affection (*wadd*), together with an inclination towards the beautiful and suitable, are not to be blamed, since they are natural in mankind. "But *ʿishq*, which exceeds the limit of mere inclination and [normal] love and by possessing the reason causes its victim to act unwisely, is blameworthy and ought to be avoided by the prudent."[108] In this same connection Ibn ʿAqīl is cited to the effect that the wise man does not suffer from *ʿishq*.[109]

Perhaps after the example of Ibn ʿAqīl, who was heavily under the influence of the speculative theologians, Ibn al-Jawzī goes into a rather scholastic discussion of the relationship between love and pleasure. Pleasure is not sought for its own sake, but in order to avoid pain. Consequently, the pleasures of lovers are not real, for they lead to boredom and pain many times greater than that which the two partners have hoped to escape. Lovers are indeed far worse than beasts in their lack of self-control and their obedience to their passions. Unlike animals, which cohabit only to avoid pain, they seek satisfaction from a particular person and exploit their minds in contriving how to attain their lewd desires.[110]

Is it really Ibn al-Jawzī writing here? Perhaps. But, as the editor of *Dhamm al-hawā* points out, the same judgment is given by al-Ghazālī.[111] Since, furthermore, the argument follows on a long quotation from Ibn ʿAqīl, it is tempting to conclude that Ibn al-Jawzī in this attempt at formal argumentation is dependent on one of these two writers.

The conclusion of his argument on the relationship between love and pleasure is that *ʿishq* always leads to pain, since (1) even when satisfied, it must eventually end in separation, and, (2) even when the fear of God causes the lover to abstain from immorality, this abstinence in itself constitutes a kind of punishment.[112] (In *Ṣayd al-khāṭir*

Ibn al-Jawzī is constrained to admit that of the physical pleasures sexual intercourse is the greatest.)[113]

Most of the chapters of *Dhamm al-hawā* which follow the introductory discussion of *ʿishq* are mere compilations of stories illustrating the disasters which attend those who give themselves over to romantic love (III,4,5). The first of these, however, chapter thirty-eight, is revealed as an exception by its title: "Concerning the reward of those who fall in love (*ʿashiqa*), but are chaste and conceal [their passion]." The title is particularly interesting, of course, because it implies Ibn al-Jawzī's acceptance of the tradition which promises to the lover who remains chaste and dies the reward of a martyr. In fact, although he is reported to have considered it a fabrication, Ibn al-Jawzī is later cited as an authority for as well as against this tradition.[114] As we shall see, by the time of Ibn Qayyim al-Jawzīya the Ḥanbalite doctrine of love has developed to such an extent that the *ḥadīth* must be unequivocally excluded from the canon of prophetic sayings.

Remedia amoris (III,6)

Like Ovid in Latin antiquity and Andreas Capellanus in the Christian Middle Ages, Ibn al-Jawzī sees fit to close his treatise with a discussion of the remedies of love. It is true that unlike these two he has maintained throughout his work a constant stand against passion and romantic love; but in treating the consequences of passion he has more than once delved into the scandalous,[115] and the reader should not be left on such a note.

An ounce of prevention being worth a pound of cure, the first counsel Ibn al-Jawzī offers is to avoid the causes of romantic love altogether. These are mainly, as they are outlined in *Dhamm al-hawā*, glancing at another man's wife, or any *ajnabīya*, talking to her, or being in seclusion with her. The early Arabs, he notes, used to practice these things, believing that they could resist the temptations to fornicate. But it was this custom, opposed to law and prudence as well, which led to the tragedies of Majnūn Laylā and others like him. Their example should serve to warn men away from such practices.

Since it is not always possible to arrest *ʿishq* before it occurs, a number of remedies are suggested by Ibn al-Jawzī, but with the caution that when madness sets in cure becomes impossible.[116] How then is *ʿishq* to be treated? The suggestion that a second glance may cure love conceived at first sight is rejected once again. Repeated glances cause the form of the beloved to be engraved on the heart of the lover, thus strengthening *ʿishq* and awakening desire which may lead to fornication. If the glance has been repeated, the only cure is a firm resolve to keep away from the beloved; for absence from him slowly, imperceptibly, effaces his image from the heart.[117]

A number of considerations gathered from the *ḥadīth* are listed in the hope that they will aid in the treatment of *ʿishq.* A man should remember, for instance, that his very steps in the direction of the beloved are held against him. In addition, he is responsible for what he says to his beloved. Thus, in view of the dangers of intimate conversations, these should be avoided. Two other suggestions are particularly designed to take the spice out of a Muslim's life. When enjoying pleasures, the lover should meditate upon the bitterness of death. Also, when he is exposed to the temptations of passion, he should consider how ashamed he will be in God's presence if he yields.[118]

If a man follows this advice and removes himself far from his beloved but still finds himself overcome with anxiety, the solution to his problem lies in legitimate intercourse, which is known to arrest *ʿishq.* This may be accomplished either through marriage or by the purchase of a slave-girl.[119]

When the beloved is legitimate, but for some reason appears impossible to obtain, the answer is recourse to God in supplication, for God may well bestow on the lover the object of his desire. In this connection Ibn al-Jawzī relates a series of stories about men who succeeded in marrying the one they loved.[120]

In the case of an illicit passion, on the other hand, as when the object is a married woman or a young male, the only general cure to be recommended is self-restraint based on firm resolution and prayer to God.[121] A number of specific cures can also be applied. These are either of a physical or a spiritual nature (*ʿilāj al-ẓāhir* and *ʿilāj al-bāṭin*).

The first of the physical treatments is directed against the emaciation and fevers from which lovers are known to suffer. The patient should exploit various means of increasing the humidity of the body, such as smelling violets and nenufars, taking short baths, sleeping long hours, eating moist foods, and gazing at clear water in verdant gardens. Also, he should make a point of telling humorous anecdotes.[122]

If most of the foregoing suggestions seem to promise little consolation to the suffering lover, others are more realistic. Travelling is recommended in order to ensure the removal of oneself from the presence of the beloved. Also, in accordance with the precept "*ʿishq* is the operation of an unpreoccupied heart," application to one's work or some other activity is suggested as a means of consolation. Another possibility mentioned is to meet women in view of marriage or slave-girls for concubinage. Frequency of sexual relations is always a good remedy. Yet another means of treatment suggested is to visit the sick and to walk in funeral processions. Pleasant walks and songs, on the other hand, although commonly said to afford relief, are viewed as more likely to increase *ʿishq*.[123]

As for the spiritual cures, these are dependent upon a basic attitude of resignation (*ya's*) and a firm resolve to overcome passion. If there is any hesitation, the treatment will fail. The necessary resolve should be sustained by pride and disdain (*himma abīya*) of humbling oneself. He who does not have this pride can hardly hope to rid himself of the affliction of love. A proud man, on the contrary, will cease to love when he is ill-treated and humiliated by his beloved. His self-esteem will not permit him to love one whose nature is perfidy (*ghadr*), the dominant characteristic of women.[124]

Ibn al-Jawzī mentions in addition certain matters for consideration which, when borne in mind, should assuage love. For example, he recommends contemplation of the fact that a man's beloved wife will turn to another and quickly forget him when he dies, there being no fidelity in women. This opinion the author substantiates by relating a number of stories about widows who remarried.[125] Another such consideration is that the beloved is never quite what one imagines. If a man prefers an *ajnabīya* to his own wife, it will be simply because the new woman's faults have not yet appeared to him. Thus he should make an effort to concentrate on her shortcomings. For instance, he should consider the ugliness hidden under her clothes (a dubious suggestion!). As Ibn Masʿūd said: "If one of you is pleased by a woman, let him recall her foul-smelling parts."[126]

Yet another remedy is to imagine the loss of one's beloved, either through death or through some unforeseen separation.[127] Or the lover may imagine someone else in his own situation and then represent to himself the consequences of love for that person.[128]

The remaining cures Ibn al-Jawzī prescribes are for the most part of the same genre as those already mentioned. One suggestion, however, which approximates if only by its rhetoric the concept of sublimation, merits further attention. "One of the spiritual cures," he states, "is for a man to think on those virtues which may liberate him from his preoccupation with the beloved; for the *ʿishq* of the wakeful man is directed towards the virtues of knowledge and temperence."[129] This consideration receives a clearly Platonic development in the author's later work *Ṣayd al-khāṭir*. There *ʿishq* on the human level is contrasted with *maḥabba*-love for God, there being of course no question of

ʿishq for God. "There has occurred to me since [since the composition of *Dhamm al-hawā*]," he writes, "an interesting point which I shall explain here. It is that *ʿishq* is possible only in a motionless and ossified man." As for men of soaring zeal, the argument continues, whenever they witness or imagine the consequences of love, they perceive its drawbacks. Being thus consoled, they attach their desire to other objects. *ʿIshq* blinds one to the faults in the object of love; but those who disdain shortcomings persevere in their ascent to things higher. And though they may be touched by love, still they do not reach the stage of *ʿishq*, even when the inclination is strong. In cases where there exists a certain conformity between the two persons a kind of love may result, but not *ʿishq*. Indeed, the very nature of man seeks after a kind of perfection not to be found in human beings. Perceiving the faults of men, it turns away from them. If at this point a man's heart becomes attached to the love of the Creator, it can no longer pause on any inferior level. As for those men who possess gnosis (*maʿrifa*), they are engrossed in rapture (*walhān*), love for God having distracted them from all other loves. Their natures become "drowned in the intense gnosis and love (*maḥabba*)."[130]

Although this thought occurred to Ibn al-Jawzī after the composition of *Dhamm al-hawā*, it does not represent a change in his attitude towards *ʿishq* itself, which is still rejected as before. Yet it does reveal something new and apparently contradictory in his conception of the nature of man's love for God. In *Talbīs Iblīs*, as we have seen, he condemns the idea that *ʿishq*-love can be devoted to God: "God has no quality towards which human nature can incline or souls yearn."[131] Here, on the other hand, he seems to found man's love for the Creator on a longing for perfection inherent in his nature. This inconsistency, if indeed it is one, should not come as a surprise, for Ibn al-Jawzī's merit lies chiefly in his productivity, not in his ability to establish a logically coherent system. In fact, his position here calls to mind his tolerance of Platonic elements elsewhere. It is enough to remark that while still consistent in his rejection of the word *ʿishq* itself, he was no longer so rigorous in his attitude towards the concept of a longing, upward-tending love, which, for the Sufis at least, stood behind the term.

One final point to note in this thought from *Ṣayd al-khāṭir* is the emphasis placed on the exclusive character of man's love for God. This love prevents the heart from attaching itself to any lesser object and thus bars the possibility of its succumbing to an engrossing temporal passion such as *ʿishq*. Later Ibn Qayyim al-Jawzīya will make the idea of exclusive love for God the key to his more systematic teaching on the passions.

The preceding description of *Dhamm al-hawā*, I hope, has revealed the purport and something of the tone of Ibn al-Jawzī's major arguments regarding love and sexual ethics. Many of the questions raised by the scholar and discussed here will receive no further mention in the course of this study, but I should like to stress now that virtually all of the positions taken by Ibn al-Jawzī on matters of morality are reiterated in the works of Ibn al-Qayyim. One further word of caution: only a denuded sketch of *Dhamm al-hawā* has been offered here, and it must not be forgotten that the book is in form and to a great extent in content a literary anthology. This said, however, it remains undeniable that the distinctive slant of the *Dhamm* reflects primarily Ibn al-Jawzī's role as polemicist and preacher. Accordingly, the reader finds him reacting against the courtly views of the Ẓāhirite Ibn Dāwūd and the idealization of Bedouin love on the one hand and a variety of licentious customs on the other. Of the latter, in addition to adultery and homosexuality, the usual abhorrences, we know that he was particularly disturbed by the use of sexual stimulants and the libertine practices of certain religious groups.[132] In the matter of using religion as a cover for immorality the worst offenders in Ibn al-Jawzī's view were the Sufi's, and concerning his attitude towards this group something further should be said.

There is some evidence that the scholar may have had private motives for opposing Sufism.[133] But personal considerations could have served only to exacerbate his stand against the movement as he knew it. The hostility of Ḥanbalism towards certain manifestations of Islamic mysticism dates back to the Imām Aḥmad, who reportedly cautioned his followers: "Beware of al-Ḥārith [al-Muḥāsibī], for he is the source of affliction."[134] If Ibn al-Jawzī is more adamant against Sufism than Aḥmad, this is mainly a result of the development of Sufism itself. It may be of use to consider his view of that development in order to grasp the context of his objections both to the practices of the Sufis and to their notions about love.

His best known censure of Sufism is contained in *Talbīs Iblīs*. Christianity, Judaism, other religions, philosophy, and a number of Islamic factions also come under attack in the work, but more than half of the text is directed against the Sufis. Sufism, the reader is told, began as a movement to train the soul through spiritual exercise to avoid vice and to persevere in patience, sincerity, truth, and other virtues. But as each century passed, Satan beguiled the Sufis more. Eventually he convinced them that acts are more important than knowledge, and from that time on they were able to do no more than grope about in the darkness. The Sufis of his own time, according to Ibn al-Jawzī, had been completely deluded by Satan. They held the religious law to be merely an exoteric science intended for the common people, while they reserved esoteric knowledge to themselves. Among their heresies were their belief in God's indwelling in certain bodies and the doctrine of union with him. In the matter of sacred love, some claimed that they loved God with passionate *ʿishq*, as though he were a person of beautiful form.

Since there was no basis for any of this in the Koran or Prophetic tradition, Ibn al-Jawzī adds, the mystics proceeded to forge traditions of their own. In this connection the scholar brands as heretics many of the major writers on Sufism. Abū Nuʿaym, the author of *Ḥilyat al-awliyāʾ*, he remarks, went so far as to mention among the Sufis Abū Bakr, ʿUmar, ʿUthmān, ʿAlī, the Companions of the Prophet, and, indeed, Aḥmad b. Ḥanbal! In his *Qūt al-qulūb*, Abū Ṭālib al-Makkī, among other false traditions, related from a certain Sufi that God manifests himself to his saints in this world. Even al-Ghazālī's *Iḥyāʾ* is replete with fabricated traditions which the author did not realize to be spurious.[135]

Despite these express criticisms, Ibn al-Jawzī had high regard for certain aspects of the life of asceticism and mysticism. "No life in this world," he wrote, "is sweeter than that of the one who knows God. . . . His heart does not find its tranquility in wife or child, nor does it cling to the hem of love for any person. Rather, he lives among men with his body, while his spirit is with its Master."[136] Again he is found exclaiming, "How beautiful is the drunkenness of those who have lost themselves in God!"[137] Important for our knowledge of the continuity of Ḥanbalite thought is the fact that, on this point, he was merely repeating Ibn ʿAqīl, for whom nothing was more beautiful than the ardor of the mystic.[138] Ibn al-Jawzī, then, did not hold mysticism and asceticism to be wrong in themselves. Rather he believed them to be no longer properly understood by the Sufis of his day.

The Sufis' conception of asceticism or *zuhd* is crucial here, since it lies in Ibn al-Jawzī's view at the source of a number of their deviations from the Law. Although he is not explicit on the point, *zuhd* for him would seem to be not abstinence, as the Sufis see it, but simply perseverence in moderation and avoidance of attachment to the things of this world.[139] Certainly it is clear that he did not consider complete abstinence from permitted things to be implied by *zuhd*. This appears in his argument against Sufi asceticism in sexual matters. Abstinence from marriage he states to be clearly wrong, since it is opposed to the example of the Prophet and his Companions, who had many wives and concubines. Marriage for the purpose of procreation is in fact the highest form of worship, and there is nothing reprehensible in the attendant sexual pleasure. He quotes Ibn ʿAbbās as maintaining a similar view: "The best man in this community is he who has the most women." Concluding this argument from authority, he remarks that it has never been related of the Prophet that he abstained from the permissible (*mubāḥ*).[140]

Not content to refute the Sufi view of asceticism on the basis of tradition alone, Ibn al-Jawzī avails himself of rational proofs as well. His reasoning is not without interest. Although striving against the soul is considered to be the greatest form of holy war, those ascetics who abstain from something merely because the soul desires it are denying the soul its due. Since a man's soul is entrusted to his care, it is wrong to deprive it of those things it needs, and these, naturally are among the things it desires. Moreover, when one abstains from the permissible, the praise of men is substituted for the thing denied to the soul. There results a subtle temptation for the ascetic to consider himself better than those who do not abstain.[141]

The dichotomy implied here between the soul and the person to whom it is entrusted may strike the modern reader as naive or as smacking more of Neoplatonism than Ibn al-Jawzī intended. But the argument that human praise is substituted for renounced pleasures reveals, in comparison to most of his work, a refreshing degree of introspection. In the same vein of psychological analysis is the scholar's remark that, for the ascetic, abstinence itself may become an object of desire.[142] In this event, clearly, it cannot be attended by any merit.

For Ibn al-Jawzī, then, the Sufis' excessive mortification of the flesh and their denial of the legitimate desires of the appetitive soul led them to offenses no less grave than those they hoped to avoid. It was enough that their position on marriage was contrary to the known practice of the Prophet and his Companions. But the Ḥanbalite scholar was even more concerned, as has been seen, by those Sufi practices which he considered to be the sequel of abstinence from sexual relations with women, in particular the spiritual concert (*samāʿ*), usually accompanied by expressions of passionate *ʿishq* to God, and *naẓar*, the spellbound gazing at comely youths, with its overtones of perversion. The mystic who engaged in these activities faced the same temptations as the man given to their secular counterparts, but he ran the additional risk of falling into blasphemy and sodomy. Starting from a position of asceticism, the Muslim mystic had come by a circular route to a plight which was the same as or worse than that of the profane debauchee. With some variations therefore, the traditional moral preaching was appropriate to his case. This is how Ibn al-Jawzī, in his age, saw the situation of the adherents of the movement he calls Sufism, and as a reflection of this fact the concern with ascetic and moralizing literature in his work is complemented by a strong element of anti-Sufi polemic.

3. The Reaction to Ash'arism: Ibn Taymīya

A THIRD STRAND in the development of the Ḥanbalite teaching on love appears in the theological writings of Ibn Taymīya. The setting is primarily scholastic, the basic problems being the reality of love as an attribute of God and the nature of the love-relationship between God and man. He deals secondarily with aspects of mystical love. Only in comparatively rare instances is earthly love as such considered.[1] The question of profane *'ishq*, insofar as I can judge from the texts I have examined at least, has only a shadow of its importance for Ibn al-Jawzī or for Ibn al-Qayyim later.[2]

Ibn Taymīya was born in 661/1262 into a long line of Ḥanbalite jurists practicing in Ḥarrān in Upper Mesopotamia.[3] At an early age he came with his father to Damascus, which was then the seat of a thriving Ḥanbalite community under the hegemony of the Banū Qudāma. The most celebrated representative of this family had been the jurist Muwaffaq al-Dīn (d. 620/1223), mentioned above in connection with the rivalry between 'Abd al-Qādir al-Jīlī and Ibn al-Jawzī.[4] The figure of Muwaffaq al-Dīn may have offered something of a challenge to the young Ibn Taymīya, whose work Henri Laoust sees as a reaction to the earlier jurist's codification of Ḥanbalism.[5]

Ibn Taymīya's intellectual horizons were broader than was customary for the members of his school. He was familiar with speculative theology, philosophy, mysticism, and heresiography, in addition to the science of jurisprudence—the usual baggage of a Ḥanbalite scholar.[6] Towards a moderate mysticism he was not entirely unsympathetic,[7] but he was strongly opposed to the existential monism of Ibn al-'Arabī and his followers.

In practical life he was plagued by a series of intrigues.[8] Inquisition and imprisonment alternated with periods of good fortune. Among his most brilliant achievements in the political field, at least as related by his biographers, were his success in persuading the converted Īl-Khān

Ghāzān not to sack Damascus and his later role in securing the military support of the Mamlūks, who eventually defeated Ghāzān at Marj al-Ṣuffār.[9]

In 705, apparently in an effort to stifle his anti-Sufi polemic, he was taken to Egypt, where he was imprisoned successively in Cairo and Alexandria on charges of anthropomorphism.[10] Freed in 709, he continued to reside in Egypt until 712, when he returned to Damascus.[11] Two new imprisonments followed. The second of these was to be his last. He died in the citadel of Damascus in 728/1328, a month after having been deprived of books, paper, inkwell, and pen.[12]

The considerations which led Ibn Taymīya to treat the question of love reflect his polemic spirit. On the one hand, there was the question of the divine attributes. The later Ash'arites, in developing al-Ash'arī's refutations of Mu'tazilite positions, had strayed dangerously away from the intentions of their predecessor, who had attempted, with little success, to placate the Ḥanbalites. While the Ash'arites claimed to accept the terms with which the Koran and the Sunna of the Prophet describe God, their speculations on the divine attributes were in fact a violation of Aḥmad b. Ḥanbal's principle that the traditional descriptions of God should be received *bi-lā kayf*, that is without trying to understand them. In particular, the Ash'arite equation of God's love with his will was tantamount, for Ibn Taymīya, to a denial of the attribute of love, while related arguments led to the equally abhorrent position that man could not truly love God.[13] The Sufis of the day, on the other hand, under the influence of a monistic world view, seemed to have so perverted their original doctrine of love as to no longer affirm any real distinction between good and evil.[14] The contagion had spread to Ḥanbalism itself. Both the *qāḍī* Abū Ya'lā (d. 458/1066), author of *al-Aḥkām al-sulṭānīya*,[15] and his controversial student Ibn 'Aqīl[16] had favored the Ash'arite view of love,[17] while the authority of the great Ḥanbalite mystic Khwāja 'Abd Allāh al-Anṣārī al-Harawī (d. 481/1088) was being cited to support the Sufi denial of the distinction between good and evil.[18]

Ibn Taymīya's reaction is reflected in passages scattered throughout his dogmatic works. In these texts he outlines the final statement of the theological side of the Ḥanbalite teaching on love, centering his attention on love as a divine attribute and the mutual relationship of love between God and man. Love is far from an isolated or minor topic in the system of Ibn Taymīya. Related to the question of love, as we shall see, are such major tenets of the orthodox Muslim creed as the doctrine of predestination, the assertion of a wise plan (*ḥikma*) in

God's providence,[19] and the proper profession of monotheism, as well as the belief in a real distinction between good and evil and the rejection of the metaphorical exegesis of the Koran and Sunna.

The question of the Islamic conception of love having been a topic of secondary interest to date for all but students of poetry and mysticism, it was perhaps inevitable that the Ḥanbalite view on the subject be misunderstood. On the authority of an argument Ibn Taymīya recorded it has been thought that the jurist denied the possibility of man's loving God in himself, since love requires an affinity or identity between lover and beloved. Man could love only the divine law, not an unknowable God.[20] But the passage on which this conclusion is founded presents, in fact, an Ashʿarite argument cited by Ibn Taymīya merely for the sake of refuting it. The proposition that love for God means only love for worshipping and obeying him, or love for the divine law, he expressly rejects.[21] The mistaken interpretation to which I have referred began as a peripheral error in an otherwise excellent study, but it has engendered a certain following. In 1961 Anawati and Gardet, citing the work in question, wrote that according to Ibn Taymīya man could not love God himself but only his command.[22] As late as 1967 Gardet repeated this view and gave the following summary of the Ḥanbalite doctrine: "One can, then, and one should, love the law, the commandment, the kindness of God, not God Himself and in Himself."[23] Ibn Taymīya's own words are these: "God must be loved for himself (*li-dhātihi*). . . . If anyone says that he does not find in his heart that he loves God more than all else, either he is truthful, in which case he is an infidel . . . or he is mistaken. . . ."[24]

The same tradition is perhaps responsible for the misrepresentation of the primitive Ḥanbalite opinion on love. Michel Allard wrote in 1965 concerning the attitude of the early Ḥanbalites towards al-Muḥāsibī: "More precisely, we know that Ibn Ḥanbal, like his disciples, did not grant that one could speak of a love of God for men, or of men for God. A text from the *ʿAqīda* of Ibn Baṭṭa [d.387/997] is directed certainly, without naming them, at al-Muḥāsibī and his disciples: 'They claim to reach desire (*šawq*) and love (*maḥabba*) for God by killing in themselves all fear (*hawf*) and all hope (*rağā'*). This is pure innovation.' "[25]

Statements like this one from Ibn Baṭṭa, however, are nearly always made in reply to some opposing doctrines and thus connot be considered *in vacuo.*[26] A similar example from the *Kitāb al-Sunna* of the early fourth-/tenth-century Ḥanbalite leader Abū Muḥammad al-Ḥasan b. ʿAlī al-Barbahārī (d. 329/941), a teacher of Ibn Baṭṭa,[27] demonstrates this point: "Know that God is worshipped with nothing like fear of him. . . . Take care not to sit with those who preach longing (*shawq*) and love (*maḥabba*) and seclude themselves with women. . . ."[28] Like Ibn Baṭṭa in the preceding passage, al-Barbahārī is unquestionably stressing fear as a basis of worship, but it would be incompatible with the fundamental principles of Ḥanbalism that he should do so to the extent of rejecting the Koranic texts which affirm love between God and man.

Now the *Kitāb al-Sunna* of al-Barbahārī was in part intended to furnish the unsophisticated majority among the followers of Ibn Ḥanbal with rules of thumb for identifying heretics. Thus the author writes: "If you see a man attacking traditions [of the Prophet], he is a follower of passion,"[29] and again, "If a man on hearing a tradition says, 'We glorify God,' he is a Jahmite."[30] Undoubtedly al-Barbahārī himself did not refrain from criticizing traditions of suspicious purport, and it is patently absurd to suppose that he would have disapproved of glorifying God. The expression "we glorify God," which is to be understood in full as "we glorify God too much to grant that this anthropomorphic tradition truly describes him," is merely cited as a quick means of identifying those who deny the anthropomorphic attributes of God.[31] Likewise, al-Barbahārī's description of some heretics as "those who preach longing and love" is not meant to be an out-and-out denial of love between God and man but only a convenient sign by which to recognize those who, like al-Muḥāsibī perhaps, overemphasized love in their teaching to the exclusion of fear and awe. Similarly, Ibn Baṭṭa's statement does not show that he rejected love but merely that he placed greater stress on fear, probably in reaction to the mystical teachings current in his times.[32]

The view that love was denied a place in the history of Ḥanbalite doctrine must be set aside. Nevertheless, a basic change in the school's attitude towards dialectic had to be effected before treatments of the subject like those of Ibn Taymīya and Ibn Qayyim al-Jawzīya could be elaborated and preserved. The early Ḥanbalites did not possess and would not adopt the intellectual tools necessary for engaging in polemics on the question of love against their Ash'arite and Sufi adversaries. To realize how far Ḥanbalism had come in this respect by the time of Ibn Taymīya, or perhaps one should say how great was the leap the school had taken with him, it will be useful to consider some early examples of the Ḥanbalite attitude towards speculative theology (*kalām*).

In the context of affirming that God can be described only with the terms used in the Koran or with the words given as explanations of these by the Prophet and his Companions, a view shared ostensibly by the Ashʿarites, al-Barbahārī calls *kalām* innovation and perdition.[33] For al-Ashʿarī, however, *kalām* properly applied did not constitute innovation and did not lead to it. It was merely an effective means of responding to heresy and defending traditional Islam.[34] Shortly after his conversion from Muʿtazilism (ca. 300/912–13), al-Ashʿarī attempted to convince al-Barbahārī of this point, recalling how he had refuted the arguments of the Muʿtazilites al-Jubbāʾī (d. 303/916) and Abu Hāshim b. al-Jubbāʾī, his son, as well as the doctrines of the Jews, the Christians, and the Magians. Al-Barbahārī's answer reveals to what extent his mind was closed to the use of the methods of *kalām* in discussing theological questions: "Of all that you have said we know neither little nor much. We know nothing other than what ʿAbd Allāh Aḥmad b. Ḥanbal has said." It was to placate a Ḥanbalism of this nature, according to Ibn Abī Yaʿlā, that al-Ashʿarī composed his *Ibāna* and attached to it a creed of Ḥanbalite type. But even the *Ibāna* failed to satisfy al-Barbahārī.[35]

Ibn Baṭṭa, it is true, in the list of heretics he gives in *al-Sharḥ wa-l-ibāna*, omits mention of the Ashʿarites, as he likewise overlooks the Sufis.[36] But since Ibn Baṭṭa was writing during a period of Shīʿite ascendancy, as Allard has remarked, his omissions should perhaps be attributed to a certain solidarity among Sunnite forces in the face of a common enemy, not to any tolerance on his part for *kalām*.[37] Ibn Baṭṭa's true attitude towards the discipline is almost certainly represented by a maxim he relates from al-Barbahārī: "Sitting in assembly to pursue [religious] controversy (*al-mujālasa li-l-munāẓara*) closes the door of utility."[38]

The rift between Ashʿarism and Ḥanbalism, unintended by al-Ashʿarī himself, was destined to widen. In the circles of the *mutakallimūn*, this meant an ever greater reliance on reason at the expense of traditional knowledge. The Ashʿarite ʿAbd al-Qāhir al-Baghdādī (d. 429/1037–38) makes it clear which authority is to be given priority. "It is *permitted* (*yajūz*)," he writes, "to bring a Koranic proof to confirm what reason has already demonstrated."[39] An expression of the contrary view, on the popular level, was the destruction by fanatic Ḥanbalites of the edifice built over al-Ashʿarī's tomb.[40]

But the Ḥanbalite school could maintain a monolithic stance against *kalām* only with difficulty. Al-Ashʿarī, although he had been unable to win over the leading Ḥanbalites of his time, had succeeded in his *Risāla fī istiḥsān al-khawḍ fī ʿilm al-kalām* in demonstrating the inconsistency of their condemnation of speculative theology.[41] Asking the traditionalists opposed to *kalām* how they could claim that the Koran is uncreated when no explicit text can be found in the Koran or prophetic tradition to authorize this opinion, he obliged them to admit that they held their view only on the authority of Aḥmad b. Ḥanbal and his predecessors. Al-Ash'arī, whose intention was to establish that *kalām* was no innovation, since it was already present in the Koran and Sunna in the form of rational arguments, took advantage of his opponents' avowal to deliver an extremely well-placed blow: the early *'ulamā'*, including Aḥmad b. Ḥanbal, by affirming the doctrine of the uncreated Koran without clear support in the Koran or Sunna, were themselves engaging in *kalām*.[42]

Perhaps as a result of the disadvantages in controversy which the school's attitude towards dialectic imposed upon its followers, a situation strikingly summed up by the argument just cited, the fifth/eleventh century witnessed a current of defection within Ḥanbalism in the direction of Shāfi'ite Ash'arism and Mu'tazilism. The movement is represented chiefly by the *qāḍī* Abu Ya'la and al-Khaṭīb al-Baghdādī, their disciple Ibn 'Aqīl, and one of Ibn 'Aqīl's students, Abū 'l-Fatḥ b. Barhān.

While Abu Ya'lā, unlike al-Khaṭīb, did not abandon the Ḥanbalite school entirely, there is fairly convincing evidence to suggest that his attitude towards šhāfi'ism and Ash'arism was one of sympathy and compromise. His acceptance, after a preliminary refusal, of the post of *qāḍī* in the section of the caliphal palace in Baghdad,[43] indicates a readiness to accommodate when his interests were at stake. That some of his accommodations were in the direction of šhāfi'ism—and thus, perhaps, of *kalām*—has been suggested by George Makdisi: "At the beginning of his career, Abū Ya'lā was considered by the šāfi'ite Abū 'l-Ḥusain b. al-Maḥāmilī (d. 407/1016–17) as the Ḥanbalite most favored with good sense among all the Ḥanbalites of his acquaintance. Ibn Taimīya was later to hold against him his šāfi'ite tendencies which were to influence certain of his students."[44] A more direct indication of Abū Ya'lā's sympathies for Ash'arism is to be found in the fact that Ibn Taymīya links him together with Ibn 'Aqīl as a partisan of the view that God cannot be loved. On this issue, the later jurist claims, the two followed the Jahmites and the Ash'arite al-Bāqillānī.[45]

The biography of Abū Ya'lā written by his son, the author of *Ṭabaqāt al-Ḥanābila*, confirms that all was not well between the *qāḍī* and his fellow Ḥanbalites. The son goes to considerable lengths to show that the doctrines of his father were orthodox. Relating a saying of the Prophet according to which believers will see God face to face (*ʿiyānan*), he feels it necessary to record that his father held this *ḥadīth*, widely accepted in traditionist circles, to be *ṣaḥīḥ* or authentic.[46] Again, listing Abū Yaʿlā's works, he perhaps purposely begins by mentioning treatises on the Koran and faith and refutations of the Ashʿarites, the Karrāmīya, and the Bāṭinites.[47] Further on in the biography, Ibn Abī Yaʿlā particularly stresses his father's orthodoxy on the sensitive question of the divine attributes and his acceptance of all the terms with which God describes himself in the Koran.[48]

That this defense of the *qāḍī* was not gratuitous is evident from Ibn Abī Yaʿlā's apology for going on at length in praise of his father, a course which, he acknowledges, amounts implicitly to praise of himself. "We were only moved to this," he writes, "by the considerable talk of the opponents [of our father] and the lies and slander which they spread among their disciples. . . ."[49] It is not unlikely that the very points regarding which Ibn Abī Yaʿlā insists most on his father's orthodoxy were in fact those on which the *qāḍī* was the most distant from conservative Ḥanbalite opinion. These include, as has been seen, the problems of the beatific vision and the divine attributes—both intimately connected with the question of love between God and man, on which Abū Yaʿlā's views were criticized by Ibn Taymīya.

The case of Ibn ʿAqīl is better documented than that of Abū Yaʿlā. Thanks to the studies of George Makdisi on Ibn ʿAqīl and his age, to which the reader is referred,[50] only those points which are of immediate relevance to this study need to be mentioned here. During his period of flirtation with speculative theology, Ibn ʿAqīl is thought to have preferred Muʿtazilism over Ashʿarism. He was particularly reproached by his fellow Ḥanbalites for frequenting the Muʿtazilite scholars Abū ʿAlī b. al-Walīd (d. 478/1088)[51] and Abū 'l-Qāsim b. al-Tabbān.[52] Moreover, he expressly mentions the doctrines of the Muʿtazilites in his retraction of 465/1072.[53]

It is not unlikely, however, that his interest in *kalām* was first aroused by teachers of Ashʿarite allegiance, among whom the *qāḍī* Abū Yaʿlā should perhaps be numbered. Most of his teachers in the discipline of controversy (*munāẓara*) were Shāfiʿites[54] and may well have had Ashʿarite sympathies. One of Ibn ʿAqīl's most celebrated masters, al-Khaṭīb al-Baghdādī, himself once a follower of the school of Aḥmad b. Ḥanbal, was not only a Shāfiʿite but an Ashʿarite as well, although of the line which rejected the metaphorical interpretation of the divine attributes.[55] Ibn ʿAqīl's association with al-Khaṭīb, it might be added, was apparently one cause of the criticism he received from Ḥanbalite quarters. Immediately after naming the famous biographer-traditionist among his professors, he notes that the members of his *madhhab* objected to a number of his teachers.[56]

Whatever the nature and extent of Ibn 'Aqīl's sympathies for Mu'tazilism and Ash'arism respectively, the doctrines for which Ibn Taymīya criticized him, those which concern us here at least, represent the views of the later Ash'arites. Before his retraction, according to Ibn Taymīya, Ibn 'Aqīl held, unlike the Mu'tazilites, that God might well be seen in the next life; but he denied that the believer could experience any pleasure in this vision, thereby agreeing with the Ash'arite theologian Abū 'l-Ma'ālī al-Juwaynī (d. 478/1085).[57] The question whether pleasure is or is not experienced in the beatific vision is closely related to the possibility of the believer's truly loving God in himself, also denied by both Ibn 'Aqīl and al-Juwaynī.[58] Ibn 'Aqīl's later polemic against al-Juwaynī and his defense of the Ḥanbalites against the charge of anthropomorphism suggest that he may have ceased to profess these two doctrines after his retraction.[59] It is reported that he spared no effort in refuting the teachings of al-Juwaynī when the latter came to Baghdad.[60] None the less, from the point of view of the stricter Ḥanbalites, Ibn 'Aqīl always displayed traces of the speculation and allegorizing which had marked his earlier doctrine.[61]

The underlying reasons for the defection to Shāfi'ism of Ibn 'Aqīl's student Abū 'l-Fatḥ b. Barhān (d. 518/1124) are not known, but the immediate cause was an attack against him by his fellow Ḥanbalites.[62] The possibility of Ash'arite sympathies on his part is not to be excluded, since after leaving the Ḥanbalite school he proceeded to study jurisprudence under Abū Ḥāmid al-Ghazālī, who was an Ash'arite in theology. Later he received a chair in the Niẓāmīya, which seems to have provided an atmosphere favorable to *kalām*.[63]

All of the Ḥanbalite scholars mentioned here were subject to pressures from within their school. As a result of these pressures, Abū Ya'lā's divergences had to be suppressed by his son; al-Khaṭīb and Ibn Barhān chose to defect to Shāfi'ism; and Ibn 'Aqīl, the object of a personally motivated inquisition as well,[64] was obliged to recant. Two major factors seem to have been involved in bringing on the difficulties these men experienced: the reluctance of their school to adopt the methods and terminology of *kalām* in any form and their own failure to avoid the pitfalls of dialectic and to remain firmly attached to the dogma of traditional Islam.

In the succeeding generation, Ibn al-Jāwzī, at times cited by Ibn Taymīya along with Ibn 'Aqīl for Mu'tazilite tendencies,[65] was sympathetic towards the problems of Ibn ʿAqīl and his disciple Ibn Barhān but did not fail to stigmatize al-Ashʿarī as a source of dissension.[66] Generally he refrained from engaging in *kalām*, preferring the role of compiler and traditionist. Thus he was able to find his career within the ranks of Ḥanbalism.

Muwaffaq al-Dīn b. Qudāma, despite his eclecticism in law, was to reassert the closed point of view of al-Barbahārī on *kalām*. In his refutation of Ibn ʿAqīl's theology he left no doubt concerning his position:

> As for the details of his false arguments in speculative theology, we shall not plunge into them with him; but we know them to be false by virtue of their very source. We have already clearly shown, by what has preceded, the evilness of the science of speculative theology by virtue of its very source, the censure of it by our Imāms, the universal agreement of the learned men that its advocates are partisans of heretical innovations and error, that they are not considered to belong to the ranks of learned men, that whoever occupies himself with it becomes a *zindīq* and will not prosper.[67]

A more explicit condemnation of *kalām*, demonstrating complete disregard for its potential usefulness to the Ḥanbalites themselves, could not be asked for.

The events of the period following the death of Ibn Qudāma in 620/1223 called for a more flexible approach to dialectic. The spread of monistic Sufism through the works of Ibn al-ʿArabī (d. 638/1240), the unrest caused by the Mongol invasions, which seems to have favored the spread of popular mysticism, and the movement of Ashʿarism in the direction of philosophy, already evident in the theology of al-Shahrastānī (d. 548/1153), required that the Ḥanbalites defend their doctrinal positions in a language and style which could command the respect of their opponents and their hesitant sympathizers. For Ibn Taymīya there was clearly no alternative; the basic position of al-Ashʿarī had to be accepted. Dialectic, he states, is found in the Koran[68] and therefore constitutes a legitimate means of defending orthodox Islam. To be sure, the fundamental principles of religion (*uṣūl al-dīn*) are fixed, having been established on the authority of Koran and Sunna. Neither the methods of *kalām* nor its technical vocabulary may be exploited to deny any of these principles or to assert new ones. "But there is nothing reprehensible," he argues, "in addressing a group in its own technical terminology or its own language, if this becomes necessary."[69] By way of example, and anticipating a modern problem, Ibn

Taymīya adds that the Koran and prophetic tradition may be translated in order to explain them to those who do not understand the Arabic language. His approach to the language of theology is analogous. The use of terms like *jawhar* (atom), *'araḍ* (accident), and *jism* (substance), the fundamental vocabulary of Ash'arite atomism,[70] was condemned by the imams, he holds, only because of the false concepts attached to these words or because recourse to them was still unnecessary in their time. But Ibn Taymīya was living in another age. If true doctrine is first properly understood, he maintains, there is in fact great advantage to be gained from using the technical language of one's adversaries.[71]

Ibn Taymīya's attitude towards *kalām* is further reflected in his balanced assessment of al-Ash'arī, whose intention, he recognizes, was to stay within the scope of orthodox Islam. Al-Ash'arī's doctrine should be blamed only insofar as it opposes orthodoxy, but it is to be praised to the extent that it agrees with it.[72] His method itself is completely acceptable. Ibn Taymīya makes extensive use of it and frequently borrows from the theologian's *Maqālāt.*[73]

A good example of how Ibn Taymīya uses the language of *kalām* is found in his treatise on the will of God entitled *al-Irāda wa-l-amr.*[74] The work begins with a long and sophisticated exposition of the opinions of various groups in their own terminology. After thus demonstrating his technical virtuosity, perhaps in order to avoid the charge that he has not understood his opponents' doctrines, Ibn Taymīya proceeds to refute their positions. In doing this he uses arguments expressed in their own style, in addition to less technical proofs based on Koran and Sunna.

Although Ibn Taymīya clearly adopted the methods of *kalām*, he did so, as we have noted, only with a major reservation. The Koran and after it the Sunna of the Prophet remained for him the prime and infallible authorities in matters of dogma. The text of the Koran was not to be opposed by reason (*'aql*), personal opinion (*ra'y*), or analogical arguments (*qiyās*), nor might it be corrected by the experiential knowledge of the Sufis (*dhawq, wajd, mukāshafa*). A verse of the Koran could be opposed only by another which abrogates or interprets it, or by a saying of the Prophet in which it is explained.[75] Ibn Taymīya's rigorous adherence to this principle, his ability to combine the methods of speculative theology with an uncompromising respect for the traditional sources of dogma explains why his works were so widely received, not only by his contemporaries but also by modernists of the school of Muḥammad Rashīd Riḍā.

Two things have been established thus far: first, that the Ḥanbalite *madhhab* held a relation of love to exist between God and his creatures; and, second, that by Ibn Taymīya's time the school had acquired the sophistication in dialectic necessary for the defense and elaboration of this view. Before examining Ibn Taymīya's treatment of love more closely, however, it will be useful to look briefly at the opinions of his Ashʿarite adversaries. The most objectionable aspect of the Ashʿarite teaching on love for Ibn Taymīya was the equation of God's love with his will. This doctrine, in his view, was doubly disadvantageous, for it denied one of the attributes of God and weakened the argument for a real distinction between good and evil. By thus sapping the foundations of ethical behavior, Ashʿarite dogma was playing into the hands of antinomian Sufism.

The complete equation of love with will does not seem to have received unreserved sanction in Ashʿarism until the time of al-Juwaynī, although the available evidence shows that it had been one of several opinions tolerated by the school before his day.[76] The view is not found in the extant works of al-Ashʿarī himself, although it is foreshadowed in the theologian's affirmation of the divine will's all-encompassing character, a position he held in response to a variety of Muʿtazilite arguments which tended to exclude evil from the jurisdiction of God's will.[77]

A major step towards the equation of God's love with his will is found in two works of the theologian al-Bāqillānī (d. 403/1013), the *Inṣāf* and the *Tamhīd*. After acknowledging that God is to be described as living, knowing, omnipotent, hearing, seeing, and speaking,[78] al-Bāqillānī allows himself to be asked whether he also holds that God is angry, is pleased, loves, hates, befriends, and shows enmity, and whether these are among his attributes. He replies in the affirmative but adds that the meaning of these attributes is "God's *will* to reward those with whom he is satisfied, whom he loves and befriends, and to punish those with whom he is angered, whom he hates, and to whom he shows enmity. Nothing else!" Al-Bāqillānī's proof of this position is as follows. Either God's "anger, good pleasure, and the like must mean his will to do good or to do harm alone, or they must mean an aversion and a change arising in his nature when he is angered and a tenderness, inclination, and tranquility (*sukūn*) in his nature when he is pleased." But the nature of God cannot be subject to such sympathies and change, he argues, these being the characteristics of creatures. Thus the first opinion—the equation of God's good pleasure, anger, and love with his will—holds.

To the objection that one might by the same token qualify God with appetite (*shahwa*) as well, al-Bāqillānī is willing to admit that this is true, if by *shahwa* is meant his will to perform his acts. If, however, *shahwa* is taken to mean a desire of the soul or an inclination of the nature, then the term may not be applied to God. In any case, the theologian concludes, to so describe God is contrary to the Koran, the prophetic tradition, and the consensus of the Muslim community.[79]

Clearly stressed in al-Bāqillānī's argument is the immutability of God. God's good pleasure, his anger, and likewise his love are unchanging. What is decisive in the application of these attributes is the end-state of the man who is their object: God does not cease to be pleased with the man who he knows will die a believer even when he is in a state of disobedience, nor does he cease to be angered at one who he knows will die an unbeliever, even when he is obedient.[80]

According to the view of al-Bāqillānī, it will be remarked, God's love and hatred are one insofar as they are both equivalent to his will, but they are clearly different with respect to their objects. This distinction appears more explicitly in another argument. Asserting that nothing can happen in God's kingdom which he has not willed, al-Bāqillānī is forced to meet an objection which accepts with him for the sake of argument that love and will are one. What is meant, his opponent asks, by God's words "and God does not love iniquity"?[81] The objection assumes—the equivalence of love and will being given—that evil, since it is willed by God, must also be loved by him. This contradicts the Koranic text cited. Al-Bāqillānī offers two answers, the first his own and the second attributed by him to certain other Ash'arites (*"ba'ḍ aṣḥābinā"*).

For al-Bāqillānī himself the meaning of the Koranic verse is that God "does not reward, praise, or command iniquity. For the term love (*maḥabba*) can be applied only to that which is rewarded or brings praise to the doer. One who wills cannot be said to love all that he wills, just as a man who bribes an oppressive ruler is not said to love to do so, nor is a man who takes a bitter remedy. . . ." This answer shows plainly that for al-Bāqillānī God's love represents only a part of his will.[82] The theologian expresses the same idea in another way, explaining that God does not love iniquity as a religious law (*dīnan*).[83] The implication is that God may indeed love iniquity just as he wills it, but he does not love its existence as a standard of ethical or ritual behavior. From an Ash'arite perspective this is simply to say that God does not reward iniquity. Expressed in this fashion the distinction was to become important in the doctrine of Ibn Taymīya.

The second reply, belonging to certain unidentified Ash'arites, accepts the objection's assumption of the complete identity between love and will. The Koranic statement "and God does not love iniquity" means that he does not love it on the part of the good and obedient. This case is held to be analogous to that of Koran 39:7, "He is not pleased with unbelief in his servants," where "his servants" is interpreted to mean his believing servants, rather than mankind in general, the usual sense of the Arabic *ʿibād.*[84] The full ramifications of this interpretation are perhaps not apparent here, but the restriction of "servants" or "men" exclusively to believers in this context implies that there must be at least some men in whom God does love, and is satisfied with, iniquity and unbelief, just as he wills them.

With al-Juwaynī the Ashʿarite distaste for anthropomorphisms pervades every aspect of theology. Where al-Bāqillānī hesitated, al-Juwayni no longer does so. The Ashʿarites, he complains, are united, although not always openly, in affirming the all-inclusive jurisdiction of the divine will, but they differ with respect to the universal application of God's love and his good pleasure (*riḍā*, satisfaction). Their differences appear in their replies to the question: "Does God love the unbelief of the infidel and is he pleased with it?" Some Ashʿarite teachers, according to al-Juwaynī, would not admit the applicability of the word "love" in this case. They are divided into two factions. First there are those who hold that the attributes love and good pleasure denote God's acts of kindness (*inʿām*) and generosity (*ifḍāl*) and consequently number them among his attributes of act. They, like other Ashʿarites, deny that God's love can mean a longing (*taḥannun*) or inclination (*mayl*). Man's love for God, they add, is to be understood merely as obedience to him. (The premise on which this argument rests is typically Ashʿarite: God is above experiencing an inclination of the soul or even being the object of such an emotion.) Other authorities, al-Juwaynī continues, citing now the opinion held by al-Bāqillānī,[85] take love and good pleasure to mean will, but they add that will is called love and good pleasure when it has as its object a kindness to man, whereas, if its object is a punishment, it is called displeasure (*sukhṭ*).

For al-Juwaynī, however, the most reliable of the Ashʿarite doctors are unintimidated by Muʿtazilite objections and grant without hesitation that God's love means his will, as does his good pleasure. They assert that God loves impiety and is pleased with a punished unbelief.[86] In line with this view, al-Juwaynī states his preference for the interpretation of "servants" in the Koranic verse mentioned above (39:7) in the restrictive sense of the elect. The answer of al-Bāqillānī he describes as that of the theologians who distinguish between love and will.[87]

A controversial conclusion is deduced by al-Juwaynī from the equation of love and will. This is that God cannot truly be the object of love. The proof runs as follows. Love and will are one; and will can apply only to a thing occurring in time (*mutajaddid*), whereas God is preeternal, having no beginning. "For a willer may only will that something exist which does not already exist and which can exist or that something not cease to exist which can cease to exist. But that which is established as preeternal and insusceptible to nonexistence cannot be the object of will." Hence it cannot be the object of love. To make the preeternal and the abiding objects of will involves, in the view of al-Juwaynī, the absurdity of willing that a situation which is necessarily as it is be as it is. To cite his examples, one who wills cannot will the impossibility of the coexistence of two contraries, for this is impossible in itself. Nor can one who believes that black is necessarily black will that black be black, since he believes that this is the case necessarily and will continue to be so.[88] Al-Juwaynī concludes from this argument that man's love for God must be understood merely as his obedience to God, or, if it is permissible to add some precision to the theologian's formulation, as his will to obey and his love for obedience.[89] This is the very view which we have seen Ibn Taymīya refute.[90]

If God can be the object neither of will nor of amorous inclination as al-Juwaynī would have it, then it must also be improper to assert that a believer can experience pleasure, the product of love satisfied, in beholding God. Such is the conclusion drawn by the Ash'arite. Attempting to account for the pleasure held to accompany the beatific vision, he explains that God joins to the vision a separate joy or bliss (*rawḥ*). This pleasure is not considered to be a *result* of the vision, with which a punishment could as well have been linked, but an independent state occurring simultaneously with it.[91] The bearing of al-Juwaynī's interpretation of the vision on the question of love was not to escape the Neo-Ḥanbalite theologians.

Such are the major aspects of the Ash'arite teaching on love as it developed through al-Juwaynī and reached Ibn Taymīya. It is true that the Ḥanbalite doctor ascribes many of these views to such groups as the Jahmites or the Qadarites, but long before his time these names had become little more than terms of abuse for those who denied the attributes of God or for those who advanced the doctrine of human free will respectively. The two terms were both commonly applied to the Mu'tazilites.[92] The name "Jahmī" in particular was often applied to those who denied the attribute of love, the teacher of al-Jahm b. Ṣafwān (executed in 128/745–46), al-Ja'd b. Dirham (executed in 105/723–24), having been considered the first Muslim to deny that God loves.[93] To the extent that the Ash'arites' doctrine of love was felt to negate this attribute in God, the term Jahmī was applied to them as well. The later Ash'arites are frequently mentioned by Ibn Taymīya in connection with teachings ascribed to the Jahmites.[94] Admittedly it appears that Ibn Taymīya's *bête-noire*, the equation "love equals will," was held in common by the true Jahmites, thorough-going predestinarians; by the Mu'tazilites, free-willers; and probably by the original Qadarites as well.[95] But it is clear that the doctrine reached Ibn Taymīya primarily through Ash'arite channels and with Ash'arite corollaries.

4. Divine Will and Love in the Theology of Ibn Taymīya

Ibn Taymīya, with the Ashʿarites, granted the comprehensive jurisdiction of the divine will.[1] But he rejected the equation of God's love with his will which they had inherited from Muʿtazilism. The section on God's will in his creed entitled *al-ʿAqīda al-Wāsiṭīya* is preceded by a list of Koranic citations affirming the attribute of love.[2] Admittedly, the equation of the two attributes love and will did not represent the unanimous opinion of the Ashʿarite school, but it had remained a tolerated view and with al-Juwaynī had become predominant. The issue, as al-Juwaynī pointed out,[3] centers on the now familiar question whether God loves and is pleased with iniquity and unbelief. For Ibn Taymīya, the orthodox view is that God creates these and other evil or unpleasant things, despite his hatred of them, as means to a wise purpose (*ḥikma*)[4] which he loves. He wills them, but he does not love them.[5]

The two most objectionable formulations of the Ashʿarite view, that it is only in the pious that God does not love evil and that he does not love evil as a religious law (*dīnan*), had won adherents not only among the later *mutakallimūn* but also among certain Ḥanbalites. Ibn al-Jawzī, according to Ibn Taymīya, did not reject the latter of the two views, although he held it to be less probable than the orthodox position. Abū Yaʿlā, however, is clearly stated by the jurist to have subscribed to the Ashʿarite view.[6] This assertion is consistent with what has been said above with regard to the *qāḍī*'s opinions.[7]

A brief summary of the development of the theological controversy over God's love is provided by Ibn Taymīya in his treatise known as *al-Iḥtijāj bi-l-qadar.*[8] His representation of the conflicting views affords some insight into his own concerns in working out a doctrine of love.

The Qadarites (understand the Muʿtazilites), he explains, pointing to the consensus of Koran, *ḥadīth*, and the early community to the effect that God hates impiety, argued that, will and love being the same, God could not be said to will evil, just as he could not be said to love or command it. They were accordingly obliged to interpret metaphorically or to apply *ta'wīl* to those passages of the Koran which describe God as willing all that occurs.[9] The remark that this opinion required *ta'wīl* in order to be maintained was sufficient condemnation from Ibn Taymīya's standpoint.

The Jahmites, for their part, and some of the Ashʿarites, finding in the Koran, Sunna, and consensus that God is creator of all things and that he creates only what he wills, concluded, again on the assumption that love and will are one, that God must love all that occurs just as he wills it. If it were objected by Qadarites, Muʿtazilites, or others, that God describes himself as not loving iniquity and as being displeased with unbelief, the Ashʿarites would reply in the familiar fashion—the meaning of the Koranic texts is that God does not *will* iniquity and unbelief in *believers.* The Ashʿarites, in Ibn Taymīya's summary, are then, like the Muʿtazilites, obliged to recur to *ta'wīl*, in this case *ta'wīl* of the passages on love and satisfaction. Ibn Taymīya cites two Ashʿarite justifications for this position.

Given first is a form of the argument al-Juwaynī preferred. The Koranic statements that God does not love and is not pleased with iniquity and unbelief apply only in the case of those men in whom such evils do not occur, there being no doubt, the summary adds, that God does not love (or will) that which does not occur among the possible acts of men.[10] The complement of this view is that God loves all that exists or takes place.

While the fundamental error in the Qadarite position, for Ibn Taymīya, was the association of God's will and his love alike with only some occurrences—the good, the error in the first argument of the Ashʿarites is the association of both attributes with all that occurs and not with that which does not occur. The argument implies that God does not love faith on the part of infidels; he loves the sin and unbelief which exist but does not love the obedience and faith which do not exist.[11]

The second argument which Ibn Taymīya attributes to the Jahmites and the Ashʿarites is an expansion of al-Bāqillānī's opinion that God does not love evil as a religious law, as a standard of ritual and ethical behavior (*dīnan*). While for the Ashʿarites this second argument represents a different point of view from that of al-Juwaynī, Ibn Taymīya is able to classify the two together because, as will be seen,[12] his refutation of the second proof tends to reduce it to the first. The second argument, in his opinion, supports the interpretation which restricts the word servants (*ʿibād*) in Koran 39:7 to the elect. To say that God does not "love" evil as a religious law, according to an explanation Ibn Taymīya offers, is equivalent to saying that he does not "will" it as a religious law.[13] Al-Bāqillānī himself approximates this interpretation when he says that God "decrees" (*qaḍā*) the occurrence of sins in accordance with his will and intention (*qaṣd*), although he does not decree them as religion or holy law or as objects of reward.[14] Given the congruence of God's decree with his will,[15] it seems unlikely that al-Bāqillānī would have objected to saying that God "wills" sins but does not "will" them as a religion or holy law. What Ibn Taymīya seems to be implying by his observation is that, if the same distinction which applies to love in this context applies also to will, then al-Bāqillānī has failed in his attempt to preserve the separate identity of the two attributes.[16]

Ibn Taymīya also associates this second argument with Ashʿarite atomism, a system of which al-Bāqillānī was the most celebrated exponent.[17] According to this doctrine, causality is a mere illusion inferred from God's habit of willing certain things together or in a given sequence. Thus he wills blessedness together with faith and punishment together with unbelief in just the same way, for example, as he wills satiety together with eating. On such an assumption, according to Ibn Taymīya, the true meaning of the statement that God does not love or will iniquity and unbelief as a religious law is simply that it is not his habit to love or will their occurrence in conjunction with faith and salvation in the same individual. This, it will be recalled, is the purport of the first Ashʿarite argument. Both Ashʿarite arguments, then, would seem to be designed to allow the statement "God indeed loves evil, just as he wills it."[18] It is true that this opinion is qualified by the Ashʿarites with the observation that God does not love iniquity and unbelief in believers, but then iniquity and unbelief, according to the two Ashʿarite arguments, do not occur in believers. Ibn Taymīya does not raise the obvious objection that such is not the case. Perhaps he knew that this rebuttal in particular would go unheeded, since for the Ashʿarites the single atom of time in which a man is truly and finally a believer or an infidel is the moment before his death.[19]

Although Ibn Taymīya's view of causality and concomitance is opposed to the atomism of the Ashʿarites,[20] his arguments stress primarily the moral inferences of their doctrine of love, not the underlying ontological assumption. It was enough that neither their atomic philosophy nor their careful treatment of love and will had saved the Ashʿarites from recourse to *ta'wīl*. But more important for Ibn Taymīya, their assertion that God wills and loves without cause (*sabab*) and without a wise purpose (*ḥikma*), implying that he loves and wills both good and evil indifferently, amounted to a denial of any ultimate moral meaning in creation.

Ibn Taymīya lists a number of absurdities which follow from the equation of God's love with his will. Among these is the claim attributed to certain Sufi predestinarians that the *ahl al-ṣuffa*,[21] the Meccan emigrés who were obliged to seek lodging in the porch of the Medina mosque, fought with the Prophet in some battles and against him in others. They were justified in so doing, according to this view, because they always fought on the winning side, that is, the side God loved and had chosen to win. Other mystics, Ibn Taymīya reports, permitted not only fighting against prophets but even putting them to death. One shaykh is said to have held that he would not be sinning even if he were to kill seventy prophets, since God loves, just as he wills, all that occurs.[22]

Neglecting the atomic hypothesis and the practice of *ta'wīl*, Ibn Taymīya has preferred a *reductio ad absurdum* on the ethical plane. In this fashion he seeks to invalidate the entire Ashʿarite argument. Only the theologian who affirms in God love for certain things and hatred for others, satisfaction with some and wrath towards others, he states, can escape this moral pitfall.[23]

The argument from ethics demonstrates to Ibn Taymīya's satisfaction that the field of application of God's love cannot be completely congruent with that of his will, which includes all things and all occurrences. But the problem of the nature of the divine will itself and its relation to the attribute of love remains unsolved. Approaching this problem in another context, the jurist underlines the impropriety of postulating even of God's will, as distinct from his love, that it does not differentiate between things willed. Such a will, he argues, cannot be among the attributes of perfection. To be numbered among the attributes of perfection, will must discriminate between good and evil according to the dictates of knowledge (*ʿilm*) and wisdom.[24] Admittedly Ibn Taymīya may be objecting here primarily to the Ashʿarite view that God wills or chooses one of two similar potentials without cause or determining motive; but a secondary consideration is also hinted at: why must the Koranic affirmations of God's love and hatred be subjected to *ta'wīl*, whereas the expressions concerning his will are not? This question is dealt with explicitly in his *Risālat al-iklīl.*

Arguing against the position of the abstractionist theologians, Ibn Taymīya asks why they reject some attributes and not others. They do so obviously either for textual reasons, as when one passage of the

Koran is clearer than another, or for rational considerations, as when one meaning is suitable and another not. Neither procedure justifies the reduction of love to congruency with will. Textually, Ibn Taymīya argues, there is no difference between the Koranic affirmations of such attributes as mercy (*raḥma*), love (*maḥabba*), and exaltedness (*ʿulū*) on the one hand and volition (*mashī'a*) and will (*irāda*) on the other. Why, then, is it mercy and love which are denied and subordinated to will rather than the reverse? The rational approach, moreover, would not seem to support either procedure. "For," his argument continues, "if it is said that what is meant by mercy in the human context is a tenderness (*riqqa*) not ascribable to God, it may be answered that what is meant by will in the human context is an inclination (*mayl*) likewise unbefitting God. If it is objected that his [God's] will is not of the same kind as that of his creatures, it may be answered that his mercy is not of the same kind as that of his creatures, and the same may be said of his love."[25] Again, to paraphrase the rest of the argument, if it is objected that attributes like will, omnipotence, and knowledge are affirmed primarily by reason, not by traditional authority (*samʿ*), it may be rejoined that just as his determining (*takhṣīṣ*) a given potential demonstrates his will, so his beneficence demonstrates his mercy, and his providence his love. Thus, in the view of Ibn Taymīya, any argument which would deny love for the sake of subordinating it to will applies equally to will and is consequently invalid.[26]

If God's love cannot be subsumed under his will, what then may be said of the relation between the two attributes? For Ibn Taymīya will is in fact subordinate to love: "Every will necessarily requires a love, for everything willed is willed only because it is loved or because it is a means to something loved. If love is assumed not to exist, then will is an impossibility."[27] In this statement Ibn Taymīya implies that there are at least two different reasons for which a thing may be willed, but he goes further. Perhaps recalling an argument advanced by the Muʿtazilite Abū 'l-Qāsim al-Kaʿbī (d. 319/931–32),[28] he suggests that the distinction al-Bāqillānī made with regard to love applies, on the contrary, to will. Aware, however, that dialectic had failed the Ashʿarites in this context, Ibn Taymīya turns to revelation as the only reliable authority for his view.[29]

The forms of the word *irāda* (will) and the synonym *mashī'a* as they occur in the Koran and correct usage can clearly be understood in two different senses, corresponding roughly to the distinction between "willing" and "wishing" in English. Ibn Taymīya cites the following examples to demonstrate this distinction:

1. Fa-man yuridi 'llāhu an yahdiyahu yashraḥ ṣadrahu li-l-islām wa-man yurid an yuḍillahu yaj'al ṣadrahu ḍayyiqan ḥarajan (Koran 6:125).

   (Whomever God wills to guide, he opens his breast to submission, and whomever he wills to lead into error, he makes his breast strait and narrow.)[30]

   Mā shā'a 'llāhu kāna wa-mā lam yasha' lam yakun (a Muslim adage).

   (What God wills occurs, and what he does not will does not occur.)[31]

2. Yurīdu 'llāhu bi-kumu 'l-yusra wa-lā yurīdu bi-kumu 'l-'usra (Koran 2:185).

   (God wills ease for you, and he does not will for you hardship.)

   Wa-llāhu yurīdu an yatūba 'alaykum (Koran 4:27).

   (And God wills to turn to you in mercy.)

The first two examples represent, according to Ibn Taymīya, God's creative, existential will (*irada khalqīya kawnīya*), which applies to all that occurs but not to that which does not occur.[32] The second two express his religious, prescriptive will (*irāda dīnīya shar'īya*), which implies love for the thing willed and for those who may bring it about but which does not necessitate its existence.[33] An objection paralleling al-Juwaynī's remarks on love and satisfaction could have been raised here to the effect that the quotations Ibn Taymīya gives to represent the prescriptive will are addressed only to believers and imply in consequence the necessary occurrence of the good which is the object of that will. Although Ibn Taymīya does not consider this objection, he would have been able to answer it by citing Koran 3:108, "And God wills no injustice to the worlds," where the kind of will in question is clearly distinct from the will which includes both good and evil in its jurisdiction. The interrelation of the two aspects of God's will as conceived by Ibn Taymīya can be seen in the following diagram.

The object of the creative will, although willed by definition, is not necessarily loved. What then is the relation between God's love and the section "hated but occurring" of the sphere of the creative will? The object of the creative will, Ibn Taymīya answers, if it is not loved in itself, is willed solely because it leads to or is a necessary condition of something which God loves.[34] For example, God may have predes-

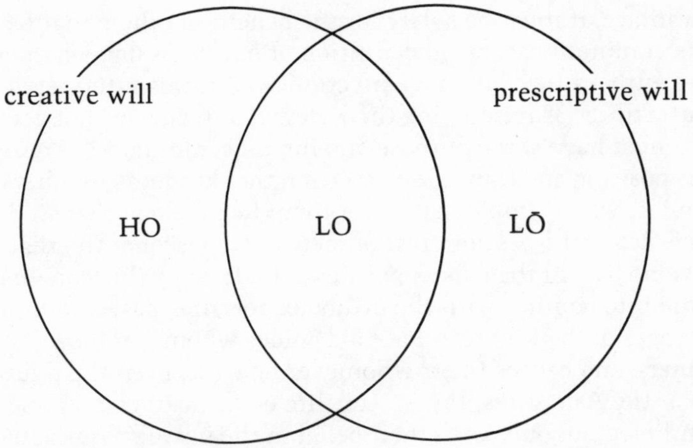

HO —comprehends events hated but occurring, willed creatively only

LO —comprehends events loved and occurring, willed creatively and prescriptively

LŌ —comprehends potential events loved but not occurring, willed prescriptively only

tined certain men to be sinners and unbelievers in order that others be saved. Creatively he has not willed obedience on the part of these sinners. But with his prescriptive will he has willed that they obey because he knows that it would be to their advantage to do so.[35]

Since it is out of the question to determine precisely what it is God loves which requires that some men be lost and that evil exist in the universe, the unknown factor must be represented by a general concept covering the various possibilities. Ibn Taymīya is able to fill the need for such a concept by recurring to the controversial term *ḥikma*,[36] designating God's wisdom or wise purpose.

The concept of *ḥikma*, often referred to by Ibn Taymīya as underlying God's decree,[37] is primarily utilized by the jurist to reestablish the moral significance of the universe in response to the Ashʿarite denial that God wills and creates for a motive or purpose.[38] The Muʿtazilites earlier had adulterated the concept of God's wisdom or *ḥikma* by associating it with the idea of motive or purpose (*gharaḍ*). They maintained that the Wise One (*al-Ḥakīm*, God) does nothing except for some *ḥikma* or some purpose, an act without purpose being patently foolish and absurd. That purpose might be to benefit himself or someone other than himself; but God being clearly above seeking his own advantage, it must be solely for the benefit of others that he acts.[39] The commonly accepted definition of *ḥakīm* as one who performs his acts with art (*iḥkām*) and perfection (*itqān*) was interpreted by the Muʿtazilites as reinforcing their view that God does not act at random but must have some purpose and intend some good.[40] Arguing from this position and from their assertion that kindness to others is good in itself, it was a simple matter for them to conclude that God must always act in the best interest of men and, consequently, that he can have no part in the existence of evil. In drawing this conclusion, they came into conflict with the orthodox doctrine, based on numerous passages of the Koran,[41] that God guides whomever he wills, including sinners, and causes to err whomever he wills, even the righteous.[42]

For the Ashʿarites, the Muʿtazilite doctrine of *gharaḍ* and *ḥikma* conflicted not only with their belief in the universal jurisdiction of the divine will, a fact remarked by Ibn Taymīya,[43] but also with their conception of the absolute transcendence and impassivity of God. Al-Shahrastānī, expressing his school's objection to the use of the term *gharaḍ*, purpose or aim, in the divine context, first remarks that the Muʿtazilites must be accepting the word with its usual implications of attracting the beneficial and repelling harm. According to all Muslims, his argument continues, God is clearly above this with respect to himself. But the Muʿtazilite claim that God's purpose implies only benefiting others is likewise unacceptable. For what could have been then, the theologian asks, the purpose in creating the universe in the beginning?[44] The purport of al-Shahrastānī's argument appears to be as follows. If God's purpose is to do good to others, then at a time when there were no others, that is, before creation, he could have had no purpose in bringing the universe into existence. If he had had a purpose, as the Muʿtazilites would have to concede, that purpose would have implied, in this one instance at least, a need or deficiency on his own part.

The Muʿtazilite reply, as related by al-Shahrastānī, suggests that God's purpose in creating the universe was to make it possible for his unity to be deduced from the signs (*dalāʾil*) pointing to him in creation. This reply, which is in fact still open to his prior objection, the theologian chooses to refute with a new argument. If God, who is described as the Wise One, has a purpose, then that purpose must necessarily be realized universally and without delay; otherwise it must be concluded that he is subject to ignorance and weakness, which is inadmissible. But God's purpose as defined by the Muʿtazilites has clearly never been realized. Therefore, he can never have had such a purpose.[45]

These arguments that al-Shahrastānī advances are not unlike those of other members of his school. It may be said that the major representatives of later Ash'arism rejected outright the idea of purpose in connection with the will and acts of God.[46] The concept of *ḥikma*, on the other hand, was not altogether discarded. It was opposed, rather, only insofar as it had been understood by the Mu'tazilites to be coextensive with or to include the idea of purpose. This assimilation of the two concepts is touched on by al-Shahrastānī in his refutation of another Mu'tazilite suggestion concerning the nature of the divine purpose. He dismisses the additional suggestion as unworthy of the effort devoted by the Mu'tazilites to the question of God's "*ḥikma*."[47] Al-Shahrastānī's argument suggests, I believe, that the Ash'arites were consciously attempting to free the word *ḥikma* from the connotation of purpose. To the extent that they retained the term, it was held to imply little more than the idea of perfection (*iḥkām*, *itqān*) in the acts of God.[48]

Ibn Taymīya accepts with the Ash'arites what he calls the orthodox objection to *gharaḍ* or purpose on the grounds that it implies a need or even an injustice on the part of God.[49] But he rehabilitates the somewhat more neutral term *ḥikma* by in fact substituting it for *gharaḍ*. For this he claims the authority of most Muslims as well as the followers of other religions.[50] God performs his acts, according to Ibn Taymīya, *li-ḥikma*, "for a wisdom." Although in view of the exigencies of the English language this expression is rendered here as "for a wise purpose" or "for a wise design," it must be understood that the term *ḥikma* was used by Ibn Taymīya specifically to avoid the idea of purpose. The suggestion that Ibn Taymīya's usage of *li-ḥikma* may be rendered merely by "out of wisdom" rather than by "for [the sake of] a wisdom" must be rejected, however, since the noun *ḥikma* in this expression is at times qualified by such modifiers as *maṭlūba* (sought after) and *maḥbūba* (loved).[51] Whatever rendering of the phrase *li-ḥikma* one may prefer, it must be borne in mind that in the thought of Ibn Taymīya God is definitely not moved by a "purpose," but neither does he will or create without some cause, reason, or end known to him in his infinite wisdom.

For Ibn Taymīya, God's wise design cannot be merely to benefit man. One of the hypotheses on which this Mu'tazilite position was based, the opinion that kindness to others is known to be good and praiseworthy to the reason and is thus good in itself, is held by the jurist to be clearly false. Kindness to others is good and laudable, on the contrary, because of something which reverts to the doer, whether praise, reward, or merely pleasure in the act of altruism. "If it be supposed," he argues, "that the existence or nonexistence of an act of kindness were indifferent to the agent, then he would not know such an act on his part to be good. Rather such an act would be considered absurd in the minds of rational thinkers."[52] Thus in the assessment of Ibn Taymīya the Muʿtazilite view of *ḥikma* and purpose, although originally advanced to avoid any suggestion of absurdity in the acts of God, itself leads to the absurd.[53]

But if God's *ḥikma*, as this argument implies, must be directed primarily back to himself and touches man only in a secondary sense, how can Ibn Taymīya reconcile his position with the orthodox Muslim conception of God's self-sufficiency? The key to the jurist's solution lies in his assertion that God "loves" his wise purpose. The effect of this assertion is however merely to defer the question of self-sufficiency to another stage of his argument. Ibn Taymīya is saying implicitly that the problem of a deficient or anthropopathic God should not be treated in connection with *ḥikma* because it belongs properly to the discussion of the nature of God's love.

But the representation of *ḥikma* as an object of love is more than a means of setting temporarily aside a complicated issue. It plays in Ibn Taymīya's theodicy the important role to which I have already referred. The beloved *ḥikma* explains the application of God's creative will to the existence of evil. God does not will evil with his prescriptive will, nor does he love it. But he wills its existence with his creative will, despite his hatred of it, for the sake of a *ḥikma* or wise design which he loves.[54]

Ibn Taymīya's God is obliged to function in this manner because, although omnipotent, he is subject to the laws of logic. The occurrence of obedience on the part of a certain person, for example, may necessitate the nonoccurrence of something which God loves more than he loves the obedience of that person. Or again, the existence of a thing which God hates may lead to the existence of another thing, the existence of which he loves more than the nonexistence of the hated thing. In this fashion, Ibn Taymīya remarks, all things have their contraries, with which they cannot coexist, and their inseparable attributes and concomitants, without which they cannot exist. "God has power over each of any two contraries," he maintains, "and can create either, but on condition that the other not exist; for the coexistence of two [contraries] is impossible in itself. It does not follow from his having power over them both that the two may exist together." To the objector who asks why God does not create two contraries together or a thing without its inseparable attributes Ibn Taymīya replies that this is like asking why God did not create Zayd, that is, any given individual, before his father. Clearly it is impossible for Zayd to have been created before his father and yet to remain his father's son.[55]

This argument explains for Ibn Taymīya the necessity of the existence of evil for the attainment of God's *ḥikma*. Since this *ḥikma* is loved by God in the same manner as such goods as faith and obedience, it therefore forms the link which subordinates God's creative will to his love. While the prescriptive will seems to have been in Ibn Taymīya's view virtually congruent with, if not equal to, God's love, the creative will, without *ḥikma*, would have been random and indifferent in its application. The concept of a wise purpose which is loved and sought by God[56] and for the sake of which some evil, although abhored, must exist allows Ibn Taymīya to justify God's willing the existence of evil and also enables him to avoid contradicting or in Ashʿarite fashion restricting the meaning of the Koranic assertions that God is displeased with iniquity and unbelief.

Having asserted that the relationship between God and his *ḥikma* was one of love, Ibn Taymīya felt himself unobliged to deal with the problem of a need or lack on the part of God which the concept of *ḥikma* might otherwise have entailed. The question remains, of course, whether or not God's love itself implies some deficiency on his part. Here, fortunately, the religious tradition made it unnecessary for the Ḥanbalite scholar to seek a solution. God's love is, in the first instance, his self-love, a purely internal function of the godhead which affects creation only secondarily. "He longs for his own beauty," says the Persian poet Farīd al-Dīn ʿAṭṭār (d. early seventh/thirteenth century).[57] This concept of the divine self-love, Ritter has observed, is commonly associated with the doctrine of self-sufficiency.[58] It is advanced in order to explain God's freedom from need for his creation or for anything other than himself.

The concept of God's self-love is not Koranic. It owed its wide acceptance in medieval thought to the spread of Neoplatonism.[59] In Islam, although neglected by earlier Sufis, the idea found particular favor with the later exponents of mystical doctrine.[60] Abū 'l-Ḥasan ʿAlī b. Muḥammad al-Daylamī (fl. late fourth/tenth century), in a discussion of God's love as the source of all love and being, quotes a passage from al-Ḥallāj on *ʿishq* which suggests the egocentric nature of the divine love. Sensing that the opinion must have a foreign origin, al-Daylamī compares it with sayings attributed to the pre-Socratics Empedocles and Heraclitus of Ephesus which propose love and strife as the fundamental principles of being. He believes al-Ḥallāj to have been the first

Muslim mystic to advance such a view.[61] For his own part, al-Daylamī proclaims the self-love of God outright: "God has never ceased to be described with love (*maḥabba*), which is an attribute subsisting in him. In his preeternity he considered himself for himself and in himself (or "by himself": *bi-nafsihi*) and he was conscious of (*wājid*) himself for himself and in himself. Thus he loved himself for himself and in himself, and there were there lover, beloved, and love, one thing without division, for he is pure unity (*ʿayn al-aḥadīya*), and in unity two things cannot coexist." For al-Daylamī it is this same original love which appears indirectly in the world of contingency.[62] Abū Ḥāmid al-Ghazālī expresses a similar idea. In the perfect and self-sufficient there can exist no desire for that which is other than itself. God loves his creatures and their acts only in the sense that they represent his acts. One who loves only his own works loves only himself.[63] Ibn al-ʿArabī falls in the same tradition. For the Murcian too, divine love is the source of being: God, loving to be known, created men; he loved them first for himself and secondarily for their own sake.[64]

The concept of God's self-love, then, was readily available to Ibn Taymīya in the Islamic religious milieu. He had to provide only a minimum of evidence for the idea in order to incorporate it into his own theological system. The necessary support he found in the doctrine of God's self-praise, taught in certain sayings of the Prophet. Here are two such sayings cited by Ibn Taymīya:

> There is none to whom praise is more beloved than God, and for this reason he praised himself.
>
> I do not number my praise for thee [but praise thee] just as thou hast praised thyself.[65]

Nothing, the scholar's argument runs, is praised or worshipped except that which is loved—a point which Ibn Taymīya claims to have substantiated elsewhere. Thus it may be said that men love God just as they praise him. But—Ibn Taymīya's argument continues in the same vein as one advanced by Saint Thomas Aquinas[66]—it is therefore all the more appropriate to assert that God not only praises but also loves himself. God's love for himself is necessarily the greatest of all loves, and his love for certain men and their acts is subordinate to this first love. This is demonstrable by analogy with the love of believers. If the believer loves certain creatures for the sake of God, for example the Prophet and the righteous, then this love is subordinate to his love for God. The same must be true in the case of God: his love for his creatures must be subordinate to his love for himself.[67]

The concepts of God's self-love and his *ḥikma* are at times juxtaposed in the writings of Ibn Taymīya.[68] This is to be explained by the need to preserve intact God's freedom from deficiency or want. The fact that God rejoices at the repentance of a sinner and loves the pious, the jurist argues, cannot be held to imply that he has need for or seeks perfection through anything other than himself. Everything worthy of love in his creatures is God's own work; and to say that he is perfected through his own acts is in no way different from saying that he is perfected through his attributes and essence. Ibn Taymīya calls this the argument of those who posit in God a *ḥikma* which he loves and for the sake of which he acts.[69] The Neo-Ḥanbalite God, then, remains perfect and sufficient in himself. Creation cannot be considered a response to a need existing in him; it is rather a natural and logical working out of the implications of his attributes—and particularly the attributes of love—through the divine acts which follow from them.[70]

5. Ibn Taymīya on Love Between God and Man

IT HAS BEEN seen how Ibn Taymīya establishes the possibility and, in his view, the necessity of affirming that God loves and how, through the concept of *ḥikma*, he relates divine love to the world of existence and to the occurrence of both good and evil. But God's love, for Ibn Taymīya, is not merely an abstract preference restricted to a cosmic role; it is also one aspect of an individual relationship, of the fundamental bond between the believer and his creator. Ibn Taymīya insists on the mutual character of this relationship and repeatedly describes his opponents as those who deny that God loves and is loved.[1] His comments on the divine name *al-Wadūd*[2] present one example of his insistence on this point. Although, after Ibn al-Anbārī, he appears to accept the opinion that *wadūd* in this case is the *faʿūl* pattern with the sense of the active participle (*fāʿil*) and means accordingly "one who loves," he also lists other opinions to the effect that the form has here the sense of the passive participle (*mafʿūl*) and thus means "beloved." If he prefers the first opinion, he none the less attempts to resolve the conflicting views by stressing the mutual connotation of the verb from which the word is derived.[3] This emphasis on the reciprocal nature of the love-relationship between God and man complements the jurist's treatment of love as a divine attribute and establishes the framework of the remainder of his teachings on the subject.

Several fundamental arguments used to deny the possibility of love between God and man, all inherited from antiquity, are singled out by Ibn Taymīya. The first is the argument that love requires a conformity or similarity (*munāsaba*) between the two lovers, a relationship impossible between the eternal and the contingent, that is, between God and man. According to the second, love, like will, can have as its object only a nonexistent or something which may cease to exist, and thus it cannot be directed to God. A third proof denies that God can truly love men because this would entail some need on his part for his creatures.[4]

The assumption of the first argument, that love depends for its occurrence on some kind of original affinity, relationship, or similarity (*munāsaba, mushākala*) between lover and beloved, formed a part of the Neoplatonic heritage and was well entrenched in the Islamic intellectual milieu. Supported not only by the prestige of the Greek philosophers but also by the authority of Koran and Sunna,[5] the existence of such an affinity between lovers was a constant given in discussions of earthly love. The idea could be subjected to varying interpretations but never rejected outright. Ritter has assembled a variety of Arabic sources, beginning with al-Jāḥiẓ, which make use of this concept.[6] Ibn Dāwūd al-Ẓāhirī, among others, relates a version of Aristophanes' myth of the halving of the original spherical man, attributing it to an unidentified philosopher.[7] Ibn Ḥazm, in *Ṭawq al-ḥamāma*, cites Ibn Dāwūd on this question. Although he rejects the image of a spherical soul proposed in the earlier Ẓāhirite's text, he retains the basic idea, suggesting that love is to be explained by a conjunction in the higher world between souls which share some affinity.[8] Ibn Taymīya's student Ibn Qayyim al-Jawzīya takes up the question again, quoting extensively from the relevant passage of Ibn Ḥazm's *Ṭawq.* He rejects both the Platonic myth and Ibn Ḥazm's alternative speculations on the grounds that they are based on a false premise—the existence of the soul prior to the body. Significantly, however, he leaves intact the related formula that some affinity must exist between lover and beloved.[9]

This hypothesis of a basic affinity or homology between lovers, commonly accepted as the explanation of earthly love, was not admitted by the Ash'arites in the context of a similar relationship between God and man according to Ibn Taymīya.[10] The essential condition of love thus being absent, there could be no love in either direction.[11] Among many Sufis, on the other hand, the theory was in vogue. Ritter mentions the example of Ṣadr al-Dīn al-Qunawī (d. 672/1273 or 673/1274), a disciple of Ibn al-'Arabī. In his *Nafaḥāt* al-Qunawī writes:

> They turn to God with the attribute (*bi-ṣifat*) of pure absolute love and seek nothing other than him. They do not love him and seek him out of their knowledge of him or because someone has informed them of him. Indeed, they do not know why they love him,

> and they have so specific request (*maṭlūb*) of him. Rather their turning to him is caused by an original, essential affinity (*munāsaba aṣlīya dhātīya*). . . . And this is the essential affinity which I have mentioned on various occasions in my books.[12]

Neither the Ashʿarite doctrine, which Ibn Taymīya ascribes to Ibn ʿAqīl as well as to al-Juwaynī,[13] nor the view of al-Qunawī was admissible from the standpoint of Ḥanbalite theology. Consequently, the problem facing Ibn Taymīya was to refute the Ashʿarite position on affinity, which led to the total denial of love, without, for that, being obliged to agree with al-Qunawī.

The Arabic word *munāsaba*, the word most commonly used to denote the affinity existing between lovers, is described by Ibn Taymīya as an equivocal term (*lafẓ mujmal*). It may have, for example, such divergent meanings as resemblance or blood relationship.[14] Again, in a usage derived from the first of these two meanings, the word may denote a comparison, as when a *munāsaba* or *nisba* between two things is denied in order to assert that one of them is in some way far greater than the other. To use Ibn Taymīya's own examples, one may say, for instance, that there is no *nisba* or comparison between a grain of mustard seed and a mountain or between dust and the Lord of Lords.[15] Ibn Taymīya grants that no *munāsaba* in any of the senses suggested here can exist between the eternal and the contingent. But love, he claims, requires another kind of affinity. *Munāsaba* properly understood refers to the fact that there is in the beloved some attribute (*maʿnā*) for the sake of which the lover loves him. God, who is qualified with every lovable attribute, is clearly a proper and worthy object of love. But it may be less clear why man is loved by God according to this interpretation. To explain the *munāsaba* underlying God's love for the faithful the jurist resorts to a kind of pun. The *munāsaba* in this latter case is the believer's "accord" (*muwāfaqa*) in what God commands, through obedience, and in what he loves, by loving it.[16] A play on words is hardly a sound basis for effective argumentation, and we shall see that Ibn Qayyim al-Jawzīya is obliged to restate this point in his teacher's doctrine with greater precision.[17]

Ibn Taymīya does not overlook another prevalent approach to *munāsaba*, the philosophical principle of imitation (*tashabbuh*). To account for the love of souls, Avicenna had taught that everything loves the object through the imitation of which it attains its perfection, as an apprentice loves his master. The ultimate object of this imitation, and thus of the love (*ʿishq*) of souls at all levels of existence, is the

Absolute Good. This concept of *tashabbuh* is not precisely to be equated with *munāsaba*; it is rather an assimilation of virtues to which souls are moved by knowledge of the fundamental affinity between them and their first cause.[18] The suggestion of the philosophers that the purpose of the human soul, like that of the heavenly souls which cause the movement of the spheres, is to imitate God, is unacceptable to Ibn Taymīya. Imitation, he argues, can only occur between beings whose aims are the same, as in the case of the imam and those whom he leads in the performance of prayer. But God is loved for *himself*, and he knows, loves, and praises *himself*, while man must seek his salvation in knowing, loving, and praising God. The principle of imitation would require that man be loved for himself and that he love and praise himself, which is inadmissible.[19]

For the affinity of natures which Ashʿarites, mystics, and philosophers alike understood from *munāsaba*, whether or not they in fact accepted the idea in the context of sacred love, Ibn Taymīya substitutes, on the one hand, the believer's awareness that God in his perfection is deserving of love and, on the other, man's accord with God in what he loves. In this fashion he is able to strike a mean between the views of the *mutakallimūn* and the Muslim Neoplatonists without sacrificing the dogma of commonsensical Islam.

The second Ashʿarite argument, which we have seen partially expressed by al-Juwaynī[20] and which Asín has shown to be reflected, although incompletely, in the Sufism of Ibn al-ʿArabī as well,[21] held that will, and consequently love, can be directed only towards a nonexistent or towards the continued existence of something which can cease to exist—the continued existence of a thing being considered as nonexistent, or more exactly as not-yet-existent, at the time it is willed. According to this view, God, being unsusceptible to nonexistence, cannot truly be an object of will or love.[22] The Ashʿarite justification of this argument's premise is summarized by Ibn Taymīya. "If the existent and the eternal (*qadīm*) may be willed," he writes, "then the world may be eternal, despite its being an object of will (*murād*) and of power (*maqdūr*), as certain philosophers hold [and as the Ashʿarites refused to admit]. For, among those who maintain that he [God] is a necessitator through his essence (*mūjib bi-dhātihī*) and that the world is eternal, some, like Abū l-Barakāt [al-Baghdādī (d. after 560/1164–65)] and others, qualify him with will."[23]

Although the Ashʿarite premise ill suits his own doctrine of love, Ibn Taymīya appears not to reject it out of hand. The considerations which lie behind his reaction are of some interest. As the Ashʿarite argument suggests, the problem has to do with the opposing doctrines of the world's eternity and creation *ex nihilo.* For the *mutakallimūn*, creation out of nothingness meant simply that the world has had a beginning. The doctrine could be understood from the point of view of common sense to mean that the existence of God was temporally prior to creation, that is, that the world came into existence after a time during which it did not exist. Or again, it could be understood according to a scheme like that of al-Shahrastānī, in which God is existentially but not temporally prior to the world—time, the measure of movement, being inapplicable to an unmoved God.[24]

Against the first position the philosophers raised the following objection. If God has always been a complete cause without deficiency, then his effect must always have existed with him. Therefore, the world can have had no beginning but is coeternal with God. In reply, the partisans of creation after a period of nonexistence, obliged to justify the delay in the effect of a perfect cause which the world's having had a beginning implied, asserted that God did not create simply out of the necessity of his nature. Rather, he chose the moment of creation according to his will, as a man resolves on one day to do something on the next.[25] To the philosophers' objection that in preeternity all instants were alike and that the divine will would thus have no means of specifying any one of them as the moment of creation, the theologians answered that it is the function of the divine will to specify without cause a given thing rather than its like.[26]

This last assertion was unacceptable to philosophers and Muslim fundamentalists alike.[27] Moreover, recourse to al-Shahrastānī's argument that God is outside of time was of no avail, at least against Abū 'l-Barakāt; for this most original philosopher had rejected the Aristotelean definition of time as the measure of movement for a new definition which made time the measure of being.[28] Abū 'l-Barakāt, however, in attempting to explain the occurrence of temporal phenomena, which clearly do have a beginning, seems to accept in theistic fashion that God wills their occurrence: "Among them [the proponents of the eternity of the world]," he writes, "are those who say that he created eternal things with perpetual being through his perpetual generosity and temporal events one after another. He willed and then created [these temporal events], and he created and then willed. Thus his creating necessitated [an act of] will and his willing, another [act of] creation."[29]

To this position the *mutakallimūn* believed they had an answer in the argument which we have seen summarized above by Ibn Taymīya.

The mere observation that will can have as its object only a nonexistent sufficed to demonstrate that anything willed by God must have been preceded by nonexistence. Therefore, the world could not be coeternal with God. It should be noticed that the Ashʿarite proof does not apply to the eternal things which Abū 'l-Barakāt describes as resulting from God's perpetual generosity. The argument as summarized by Ibn Taymīya is probably incomplete and may have been expanded by the theologians to include somehow the products of the divine generosity as well.[30]

On the eternity of the world Ibn Taymīya accepts in fact neither the position of the Ashʿarites nor that of the philosophers.[31] But in his treatise entitled *al-Irāda wa-l-amr* he specifies that it is a question which must be approached gradually. The first step, in his view, is to defend all Muslim positions against the arguments of those who hold the eternity of the world.[32] It is this attitude which explains why, despite the fact that it did not fit into his own theological system, he preferred to leave intact the Ashʿarite premise that will can have as its object only a nonexistent. The problem remained, then, for the sake of a united front against philosophy, to accommodate insofar as possible the Ashʿarite principle to the Ḥanbalite teaching on love. This Ibn Taymīya achieved by recurring to a parallel of the distinction discussed above between the prescriptive will and love on the one hand and the creative will on the other.

Two things are involved in the Ashʿarite premise, the jurist argues: the will that something be done or that it come into existence and the love of the very essence (*dhāt*) of a thing, a love which in no way affects the thing's essence in the matter of existence. Here the two aspects of will are considered as will of the means to a thing and will or love of its essence. The former, as the Ashʿarites claim, cannot be concerned with the existent, the abiding (*bāqī*), and the preeternal; but the latter clearly does concern them. Thus, if a man wills to build a house, he does so because he wills (or wants) the house itself for a dwelling. The process of building is but a means. The example demonstrates that the will to the essence or to the end is logically prior to the will to the means. Unless the end is willed, the will to build, to act, or to create is absurd. The example also shows to the satisfaction of Ibn Taymīya that the will for the essence continues after its object has come into existence, for a man would hate to see his house destroyed after its completion.[33] Accordingly, man can indeed direct both will and love towards the preeternal God, although only in the sense of love for his essence.

Conversely, God may also love things in their essence and he may continue to will and love them in this sense even after he has brought them into existence. God's love for individual objects is represented by Ibn Taymīya as part of a more general love which, ultimately, is the cause of all existence. This general love, as has been seen, is none other than God's ecstatic self-love.[34] "The Lord loves himself (*nafsahū*)," writes the jurist in a tortured Arabic which demands an equally tortured translation, "and among the accompaniments (*lawāzim*) of his love for himself is that it [his self] loves and wills that which he wills to do. And what he wills to do, he wills for an end (*ghāya*) which he loves. Thus love (*ḥubb*) is the final cause for the sake of which all things have come into being."[35]

The third argument against love between God and men is based on the doctrine of God's self-sufficiency. It denies love on God's part on the grounds that it would entail some need in him for the object of his love. The essentials of Ibn Taymīya's refutation have already been discussed. He replies, it will be recalled, that any reasoning which serves to deny God's love must apply also to his will, an attribute which his Ashʿarite opponents accepted.[36] Some additional aspects of the jurist's argument should be mentioned, however, because they are relevant to his view of the nature of the love-relationship between God and man.

Dealing specifically with the argument of those who deny attributes like love, wisdom (*ḥikma*), and satisfaction (*riḍā*) because these require a pleasure (*ladhdha*), which can occur only in a being subject to pleasure and pain, Ibn Taymīya once again argues that if these attributes are said to require a pleasure, the same must be said of will.[37] But he goes further. Even the philosophers, he remarks, admit that God experiences pleasure and delight, that he is *mustalidhdh* and *mubtahij*.[38] Moreover, it cannot be said that the notion of God's experiencing pleasure in any way calls into question his freedom from need or his immunity to harm. The sense of Ibn Taymīya's reasoning I take to be the following. God's self-sufficiency on the one hand and those attributes which like love are said to require pleasure on the other are attested with equal authority by both Koran and Sunna. Accordingly, it is impossible to deny the reality of any one of these attributes or its implications for the nature of God simply by asserting that its existence is incompatible with that of another.[39]

Ibn Taymīya realized that there might be legitimate objections to the term *ladhdha* itself. The question became, then, to know what the Ashʿarites meant by denying that God experiences pleasure. If they understood by this, his argument runs, that God cannot do anything at which he is joyous (*yafraḥ, yusarr*) and that he cannot cause men to do anything in which he takes delight, there would seem to be no support for their view. The joy and delight of God should not be denied simply because the terms used to denote them are nearly synonymous with a word tainted with fleshly connotations.

The word *ladhdha*, like *munāsaba*, Ibn Taymīya explains, is an equivocal term carrying derogatory meanings and lacks textual authority for its use with reference to God. This is not to say that it is wholly inapplicable in the divine context but only that it is unnecessary, given the existence of a more appropriate term sanctioned by tradition: the term *faraḥ* or joy. The Prophet is reported to have said that God is joyous (*yafraḥ*) at the repentance of a sinner. Therefore, the argument that denies God's love on the grounds that it involves a pleasure or *ladhdha* occurring in him upon the obtainment of the beloved may be shown to be invalid merely by substituting for *ladhdha* the unobjectionable term *faraḥ*. This substitution Ibn Taymīya holds to be possible because *faraḥ*, as it is understood in the human context, is in fact a pleasure arising from the obtainment of a loved object.[40]

Furnishing an example of how the word *ladhdha* is to be taken, Ibn Taymīya enters into a digression in which he defines his attitude towards the controversial term for love "*ʿishq*." *ʿIshq*, he maintains, despite the fact that some admit its applicability to the relationship between God and man in the sense of complete love,[41] is, like *ladhdha*, liable to be understood as connoting earthly pleasure and passion. Thus earlier authorities objected to describing God himself as loving with *ʿishq* on the grounds that the term denotes excess in love, whereas there can be no excess in God's love. They likewise rejected the use of the term *ʿishq* for man's love to God. Such an excessive love can only occur in conjunction with a corrupt representation of the beloved (*fasād al-taṣawwur li-l-maʿshūq*), they reasoned, but it is forbidden to form a false conception of God. Ibn Taymīya, although he mentions these arguments, apparently believed that they went too far in rejecting *ʿishq*. He suggests in his *Nubūwāt* an approach to the problem more to his liking. This is simply that the word *ʿishq*, since it is not found in the sacred texts, and since, further, it is ambiguous, is not to be applied to love between God and man.[42] As in his analogous treatment of *ladhdha*, the jurist is not maintaining after the fashion of Ibn al-Jawzī that the word *ʿishq* is absolutely inapplicable to sacred love[43] but merely that its use is unnecessary and confusing in this context and should be avoided.

Such, essentially, are the proofs with which Ibn Taymīya refutes three major elements in the arguments of the *mutakallimūn* against the reality of love between God and man—the propositions that there can be no affinity between the eternal and the contingent, that love can have as its object only a nonexistent, and that love requires a deficiency on the part of the lover. Both dialectic and the authority of Koran and tradition have their place in his method. God's love and the possibility of a reciprocal relationship of love between God and man are thus established for the Ḥanbalite jurist. Having seen how he demonstrates this, it remains to examine what he has to say concerning the nature of man's response to the divine initiative.

The end for which man was created, according to Ibn Taymīya, is the proper worship of God,[44] the conditions of which are perfect love and perfect humility.[45] God, in turn, is singularly worthy of the love that man owes him.[46] If this were not the case, it would have been improper for the Prophet to call men to love God and his messenger above all else.[47] Moreover, as we have seen, God is to be loved for himself.[48] Indeed, God alone is worthy of being loved for his own sake.[49] Thus, in the view of Ibn Taymīya, love for God cannot mean merely love for worshipping him, as the Ash'arites had argued,[50] or, according to a similar thesis, love for approaching him. On the contrary, love for worshipping or approaching any object is clearly dependent on love for that object in itself. The act of worshipping one who is not lovable in himself can hardly be considered an object worthy of love.[51]

This argument, as Ibn Taymīya knows, is open to the objection that man may love to worship and obey God merely for the sake of some compensation or reward. But if this were the case, he reasons, the compensation would become the true beloved which is loved for its own sake.[52] One would be able to say of a man who worships in view of a reward that the reward is to him a greater beloved than are God and his Prophet.[53] With this reply Ibn Taymīya succeeds in placing the objection in a very unfavorable light, at least in the minds of orthodox readers. But from the point of view of his opponents the comparison he makes between love for God and his Prophet and love for a reward is clearly invalid, since it implies that man ought to love God. They held such a love to be altogether impossible and consequently could not admit it as a term of a true comparison.

Perhaps himself unconvinced of this proof's validity, Ibn Taymīya musters an additional, although even more subjective, argument in his *Minhāj*. "The sweetness of faith experienced in the heart," he writes, "cannot arise from love of a compensation which has not yet been received. On the contrary, the agent who works for wages alone finds in his work only weariness, toil, and pain. If there were no meaning to love for God and his Prophet other than love for the reward which is received [in the afterlife], then a man could experience no sweetness of faith in his heart while in this world."[54] Here again Ibn Taymīya's argument may have fallen on deaf Ashʿarite ears. The reasoning is of too intimate a nature and recalls the jurist's assertion, quoted above, that a believer cannot truly deny the love for God which he perceives in his heart.[55] Statements such as these, which at times interrupt the cold progression of Ibn Taymīya's polemic, reveal something about the man. Convincing or not as arguments, they offer invaluable evidence for assessing the nature of Ḥanbalite religious experience.

Ibn Taymīya's train of thought reaches something of a climax when he suggests that God's beneficence—his beneficence in this world is the implication—may not properly be deemed a cause for loving him. Admittedly, it is not unthinkable that God should be loved for his acts of kindness, but love for him will be more nearly perfect if he is considered in the first instance as one sublimely qualified with the attributes of perfection. To entertain thoughts concerning his benefits is in this optic a harmful distraction. God must be loved only, or at least primarily, for himself, and this despite the fact that his beneficence also requires that he be loved.[56] An alleged saying of the Prophet which would confirm God's beneficence as a reason to love him, "Love God for the blessings with which he sustains you . . . ," is rejected by Ibn Taymīya as having a weak chain of authority.[57]

Another argument Ibn Taymīya gives to uphold the view that God must be loved primarily for himself rather than for a reward or compensation is that if God were not the ultimate object of love, then beholding him would not be the most beloved of all human experiences. This argument rests on two assumptions acceptable to most orthodox Muslims: that the greatest joy must be the result of obtaining the highest object of love and that the greatest of all joys is that experienced in the beatific vision, which is the consummation of man's love for God.

While reasoning of this nature may have served to confirm the orthodox in their belief, it was ineffective against the arguments of such "Jahmites" as al-Juwaynī and Ibn ʿAqīl, who did not share the underlying assumptions. Affirming the beatific vision but denying that God could be an object of love, they concluded that no pleasure could occur as a result of the vision. Although this conclusion would likewise be inferred by the Ashʿarite denial of causal relationships, it will be useful to reconstruct the theologians' argument here purely on the basis of their doctrine of love. If God were an object of love, they might have argued, then the relation of the beatific vision to this love would be analogous to that of physical union to earthly love. Now the pleasure resulting from union in earthly love clearly depends upon that love for its occurrence. But God cannot be loved. Therefore, no pleasure can result from the beatific vision. The pleasure which does accompany the vision is consequently an independent pleasure linked to that experience in time but unrelated to it causally.[58]

Having demonstrated to his own satisfaction that God, contrary to the assumption of the Ashʿarites, is indeed a proper object of love, Ibn Taymīya found it unnecessary to devote particular attention to their doctrine of the beatific vision. However, in the course of describing the opinion of al-Juwaynī, he implies that the independent pleasure to which this Ashʿarite theologian referred must be a created pleasure and must presumably result from the obtainment of some created object.[59] From this point Ibn Taymīya would have been able to reason that the created object thus becomes the ultimate object of love. The Ashʿarite position would then be open to the same objections with which he countered the assertion that love for God means merely love for a reward or compensation. His description of the created pleasure as resulting from the obtainment of a created object—something al-Juwaynī does not in fact say[60]—suggests that he had in mind such an argument as this.

The principle that God must be loved for himself, or, more precisely, that God alone must be loved for himself, left its mark on the remainder of Neo-Ḥanbalite speculation concerning the proper ordering of man's love. According to Ibn Taymīya's reasoning, everything loved must be loved either as an end in itself or because it is ordered to an end, and, further, God alone may rightly be loved as an end in himself. All other objects of love, therefore, must be loved only for the sake of God. The man whose love is not thus ordered is guilty of an unforgivable sin comparable to idolatry or polytheism (*shirk*).[61] From the writings of Ibn Taymīya it appears that he admitted two senses in which it may be said that a thing is loved for the sake of God. First, a thing may be loved because it is loved by God for itself. For example, men should love obedience and worship because these are loved by God. This is a parallel to the jurist's interpretation of *munāsaba* as accord (*muwāfaqa*) in the objects of will and love.[62] Second, a thing may be loved for the sake of God because it is an aid to proper worship, which in Neo-Ḥanbalite doctrine, as has been seen, includes love for God.[63] Food, drink, and clothing, which provide the strength and protection required for the exercise of religious obligations, are obvious examples of objects of love for the sake of God considered from this point of view. The passions, it will be remarked, have thus the legitimate role of enabling man to obtain those things necessary to worship.[64] Things may not be considered as objects of love for the sake of God in this second sense, however, if they are in some way objectionable in themselves. The sin of one man, for example, even if it could be shown that this sin was a necessary condition of faith on the part of ten other men, would not be a legitimate object of love.[65]

The principle that God is love's ultimate object is central to Ibn Taymīya's view of human love to God. Moreover, it represents a major dividing line in what I believe to be the logical progression of his treatment of love. Up to now this study has dealt primarily with Ibn Taymīya's refutation of Ashʿarite teachings, stressing particularly his discussion of love as a divine attribute and his affirmation of the reality of the love-relationship between God and man. To be sure, the question of properly ordering man's love does not lie entirely outside the Ḥanbalite's polemic against the theologians, but it must be viewed in another context as well. The stress of Ibn Taymīya's argument as outlined here has shifted gradually from theology to morality, and as the issues change, so do the adversaries. When doctrinal issues recede into the background and ethical problems assume the greater importance, Ibn Taymīya is less concerned with the Ashʿarites and devotes most of his attention to the Sufis.

With regard to the question of the ordering of human love Ibn Taymīya had to deal with a notable controversy which had arisen in primitive Sufism. Starting from the principle that God is uniquely worthy of love, many mystics had inferred that such affections as love for parents, children, wife, and worldly goods, and even love for Paradise itself, constitute distractions from love to God. Such an attitude towards secondary loves was reportedly recommended in a dream to Sarī al-Saqaṭī (d. 253/867–68 or 257/870–71), a disciple of al-Muḥāsibī.[66] This shows that the idea was well established among the early Sufis of Baghdad, and an anecdote in which Rābiʿa al-ʿAdawīya (d. 185/801) blames the ascetic Rabāḥ (Riyāḥ) al-Qaysī for loving the children of his family suggests that it had been current for some time.[67] It is already considered and rejected by Abū Ṭālib al-Makkī in his mystical manual *Qūt al-qulūb*.[68]

Ibn al-ʿArabī, within the context of his monistic system, had resolved the problem through recourse to a distinction between the physical and the spiritual loves of men for God. Physical love, according to the doctrine of Ibn al-ʿArabī, is love for God as benefactor. Spiritual love aims at the spiritual beauty of God. Mixed with physical love, which is necessary for engendering the intense emotions of the mystical experience, spiritual love leads man to seize the spiritual beauty of God reflected in things and enables him to love God in all things and all things through God.[69]

The pantheistic implications of Ibn al-ʿArabī's formulation were unacceptable to Ibn Taymīya, but so was the earlier Sufi thesis that the only valid love was love exclusively for God in his essence.[70] The older Sufi opinion, if granted, would have rendered superfluous the jurist's discussion of "love for the sake of God" and it would have been inconsistent with his interpretation of the affinity underlying love from man to God as *muwāfaqa* or accord in the objects of will and love, since God would be the only proper object of man's love. The problem facing Ibn Taymīya was to justify those secondary loves rejected by the earlier mystics without falling into a position like that of Ibn al-ʿArabī. In stating his argument he singles out for special criticism the Sufi claim that love for Paradise constitutes a distraction from love to God.

The Sufi view is typically expressed by such exclamations as this one cited by Ibn Taymīya: "I have not worshipped you out of longing for your Paradise or out of fear of your Fire but so that I may behold you and glorify you."[71] As this statement suggests, the early mystics, unlike the *mutakallimūn*, generally accepted the traditional position on the beatific vision. They also admitted that pleasure resulted from the experience. Thus the vision became in fact the analogue of physical union in earthly love, the only true union with the one true beloved. But, as one may also understand from the statement, these mystics tended to isolate the pleasure of the vision and to place it outside of or beyond Paradise. Ibn Taymīya seizes on this as the fundamental error in their position. All the favors which God has prepared for his saints, he argues, including the beatific vision, are found in Paradise.[72] Love for Paradise, therefore, at least in the sense of a desiring love, is no less justifiable than the Sufis' expressed longing for the beatific vision.

For Ibn Taymīya this argument is sufficient to demonstrate that God, although the ultimate object of love, is not the sole legitimate object of the affection. He does not see the need, consequently, to develop a further proof justifying temporal loves but is satisfied merely to point out their importance to the religious experience. The direction of human love and will towards those actions and worldly objects which God loves, he argues, need not conflict with love for God. On the contrary, love *for the sake of* God or, with reference to love among men, love *in* God (*al-maḥabba fī 'llāh*) is the strongest bond of faith, as the sayings of the Prophet affirm.[73] Complete love for God demands this "love in God," which is defined as love for all that God loves with corresponding hatred for all that he hates. This accord in love is to be achieved not through some religious universal such as the emotional experiences of the mystics but in a specifically Islamic way through obedience to the Prophet, whose message, according to Ibn Taymīya, revealed to men all that God loves and only that which he loves.[74]

Clearly not all types of love fall into the category of love in God or for his sake. If human love is not properly ordered with God as its end, it is termed "love with God" (*al-maḥabba maʿa 'llāh*). This, according to Ibn Taymīya, is the love which is comparable to polytheism or idolatry and to which the Koran refers in the Sura of the Cow: "Yet of mankind are some [the polytheists] who take unto themselves (objects of worship which they set as) rivals [*andād*] to Allah, loving them just as they [the polytheists] love Allah."[75] Underlying the comparison of improperly ordered love or "love with God" to polytheism is the conviction that to love a thing for its own sake is to devote to it a kind of love which is due to God alone, which is, in some sense, to make that thing an equal to God. This conviction is fundamental to Ibn Taymīya's prescriptions for human love.

As inordinate love may be likened to idolatry or polytheism, so "love for the sake of God" is analogous to the proper confession of the unity of the godhead (*tawḥīd al-ilāhīya*), that is, the full realization of the Muslim *shahāda*, "There is no god but Allah and Muhammad is the Prophet of Allah." The first part of the *shahāda*, as Ibn Taymīya interprets it in this context, requires that the Muslim love and hate only for the sake of God, while the second part affirms that a man's love for God is to be judged according to his obedience to the Prophet. A Koranic verse cited by the jurist stresses this latter aspect of the *shahāda* and points to God's reciprocal love: "Say, (O Muhammad to mankind): If ye love Allah, follow me; Allah will love you. . . ."[76]

It appears from the above that Ibn Taymīya's criterion for judging the legitimacy of love for a given object is in part a subjective one, for it is based not only on the inherent moral worth of the thing or the teaching of the Prophet but also on the end envisaged by the lover. Taking as examples love for food and love for power, we may imagine, for instance, that two men may both love food equally, one because without it he would be too weak to perform his prayers, another simply out of gluttony. Or again, two men may both seek the imamate, one in order to restore the strength of Islam and another out of love for personal power. The proximate goal is the same for both men in each of the two cases—the obtainment of the beloved object; but their ultimate aims are quite different. The touchstone is intention. But the situation is complicated by another factor. Inordinate love is blind, and men may consequently believe that they are doing for the sake of God many things which they are doing merely out of love for leadership, wealth, or some other worldly good.[77] The Sufis, in their ignorance, are particularly subject to this failing according to Ibn Taymīya.[78] In such cases, where human judgment proves insufficient, the teaching of the Prophet provides the guideline.[79]

A fuller picture of Ibn Taymīya's criterion for human loves now emerges. In order to practice "love for the sake of God" and to avoid idolatrous love, the believer must not only have the right intention, he must also know why he loves. Required of him is a cognizant, deliberate subordination of his love for every loved object to his love for God, either directly or through an intermediate goal itself subordinated to that love. The stress of Ibn Taymīya's teaching is accordingly different from that of the Koranic passages which compare unbridled passion to a god and the traditions of similar purport collected by Ibn al-Jawzī.[80] Such statements are metaphorical and mean simply that human passions should not be allowed free rein. For Ibn Taymīya the metaphor is almost lost. The believer must fulfill the conditions of "love for the sake of God" or find himself dangerously near objective idolatry or polytheism. Here, in the view of the jurist, lies one of the greatest shortcomings of the mystics—their failure consciously to subordinate their acts and utterances to their expressed love for God. This explains why he cites them as the prime example of those who love "with God."

Much of the remainder of Ibn Taymīya's anti-Sufi polemic deals with those same practices which Ibn al-Jawzī decried, namely, the spiritual concert and gazing at objects of beauty, in particular at comely youths.[81] The mystics' use of the word *ʿishq*, as has been noted, he also rejects, although in less absolute terms than his predecessor. Clearly, however, the mysticism of Ibn Taymīya's day was no longer that which Ibn al-Jawzī had known, and the rise of existential monism had led to a new stress on another old question related to the problem of God's love. That question concerned the reality of the distinction between good and evil. It is the last aspect of Ibn Taymīya's doctrine of love which will be discussed here.

The problem of the distinction between good and evil had been a moot point in the divergent systems of the *mutakallimūn*, although the dispute over the isue had represented little more than an intellectual exercise. The Mu'tazilites had advanced that a natural moral distinction between good and evil was accessible to the human reason. The Ash'arites qualified this view. For them, "reason does not indicate with regard to anything that it is good or evil in the matter of religious obligation."[82] Good and evil in the religious sense are known solely through revelation, and the qualification of things as one or the other reflects God's uncaused and unmotivated choice. Reason, for the Ash'arites, can only determine what is good or bad with respect to the interests of the individual—what conforms to his interests or conflicts with them.[83] The Ash'arite approach to the distinction between good and evil did not, therefore, allow for the position Ibn Taymīya held—that acts and objects possess qualities which God loves or hates and that it is on the basis of these qualities that they are classified as good or evil.[84]

The Ash'arites had relegated their doctrine on this question to the sphere of speculation. Translated into the realm of mysticism, however, and especially in the monism of Ibn al-'Arabī and his followers, it became a means of justifying the antinomianism practiced by many Sufis. This was at least how Ibn Taymīya saw the problem. The great Ḥanbalite mystic 'Abd Allāh al-Anṣārī had taught that the man who contemplates the divine decree no longer deems good to be good or evil to be evil.[85] In this, according to Ibn Taymīya, he had adopted the Ash'arite position that all occurrences are not only willed by God but also loved by him.[86] The upshot of this view is that good and evil can mean no more than suitable or unsuitable with respect to a given individual; for God they are one and the same.[87]

The Sufi monists, and in particular 'Afīf al-Dīn al-Tilimsānī (d. 688/1289–90 or 690/1291), had given the interpretation of a thoroughgoing antinomianism to the teaching of al-Anṣārī. Since all existence is one, they reasoned, there can be no real distinction between good and evil. The most that they would grant, according to Ibn Taymīya's understanding of their view, was that some aspects of existence are nobler than others.[88] In this connection al-Tilimsānī, one of many commentators on al-Anṣārī's handbook of mysticism *Manāzil al-sā'irīn*,[89] is clearly Ibn Taymīya's principal foe. Al-Tilimsānī's view that all things like waves of the sea are merely parts of the godhead is singled out by the jurist,[90] who demonstrates the ethical implications of this opinion with a story related from a certain Kamāl al-Dīn al-Marāghī.

> I read something of their [the monists'] teachings under al-'Afīf al-Tilimsānī, and I found it contrary to the Book and Sunna. . . . So

> I said to him, "If all existence is one, what distinction is there according to you between [a man's] wife, a woman who belongs to another [*ajnabīya*], and his sister?" "There is no distinction between them in our view," he replied. "Rather, those whose vision has been veiled have believed [the latter two] to be illicit, and we say that they *are* illicit for them. But for us nothing is illicit."[91]

Ibn Taymīya could only conclude that both the earlier mysticism of al-Anṣārī and the later teaching of Ibn al-ʿArabī and al-Tilimsānī tended to undermine the bases of recognized morality. As has been seen, this conclusion in itself constituted a sufficient disproof in his judgment. But he did not fail to gather additional arguments against the Sufi position. Some aspects of these will be mentioned here because they pertain to his doctrine of love.

A thing is good or evil for Ibn Taymīya insofar as it is loved or hated by God; and it is loved or hated by God on the basis of its inherent qualities. A given evil may be willed by God's creative will because it is a necessary condition of something loved, but it remains an object of God's hatred. The Sufis erred, according to the jurist, in believing that evils necessary to the existence of something lovable in itself are not only *willed* but also *loved* for the sake of that thing.[92] Moreover, they erred in asserting that the distinction between good and evil ceases to be real for the man advanced in mystical knowledge. On this latter point Ibn Taymīya reveals his preference for a modified version of the Muʿtazilite view. Without hesitation he asserts that a man can know a thing to be an objective good and love it or recognize it as evil and hate it on the basis of its conformity to his own interests.[93] The Ashʿarites, and with them the Sufis, would have admitted this, but only with respect to such worldly goods as food, clothing, and shelter, which are indifferent from the religious point of view. For Ibn Taymīya, however, the whole of morality, from the human aspect, is a function of personal pleasure and pain. Naturally a man cannot always know perfectly where his own interests lie. The role of revelation, accordingly, is to explain to him more fully just what his interests are. Man is taught that certain earthly pains must be accepted and certain pleasures renounced for the obtainment of a greater pleasure in the afterlife. The Sufis, Ibn Taymīya argues, even if they deny in theory such an objective distinction between good and evil, accept it in practice, since it constitutes the fundamental assumption underlying their ascetic rule.[94] Asceticism, in the view of the Ḥanbalite scholar, takes as a given his position that there can be no conflict between objective morality and self-interest based on knowledge.

The link between Ibn Taymīya's refutation of Sufi opinions on the distinction between good and evil and his treatment of the Ashʿarite doctrine of love is evident. The arguments are similar in each case because the fundamental question is the same in each: does God love some objects to the exclusion of others? From the point of view of the jurist's systematic thought, his anti-Sufi polemic may appear less important and less convincing than his disputation against the Ashʿarites. But Ibn Taymīya's refutation of the mystics has not been dealt with here merely as an appendage to complete the picture of his treatment of love. It is essential to the nature and purpose of his argument, which never proceeds in complete disregard of the religious needs of the believer. For if on the dogmatic level it is primarily against the Ashʿarite equation of God's love with his creative will that the Ḥanbalite doctor directs his rebuttals, it was still essentially in the antinomian mystics, the *malāmīs* and the Qalandarīs, that he was able to observe the practical consequences of this Ashʿarite teaching.

6. Love in the Works of Ibn Qayyim al-Jawzīya

THE THEOLOGY AND religious ethics of Ibn Taymīya are expressed once again and elaborated, often with a new refinement, in the work of his most celebrated student and literary heir, Ibn Qayyim al-Jawzīya (691/1292–751/1350). The Ḥanbalite doctrine of love, in particular, received in the writings of this prolific but sensitive scholar its definitive and most eloquent, if not its most original, statement. Drawing not only on the theology of Ibn Taymīya but also on the tradition of moralizing literature culminating in the work of Ibn al-Jawzī, Ibn al-Qayyim gives a more comprehensive presentation of Ḥanbalite thinking on the subject of love, in both its sacred and profane aspects, than either of his two predecessors. One significant new element, a pervasive but still cautious and reserved concern with formal mysticism reflected in his later works, adds a third and complementary dimension to his discussion of love. There are no unusual consequences in the realm of dogma, however, and one should be wary of the almost commonplace assertion that Ibn al-Qayyim was himself a mystic. His books on Sufism were, in fact, half-disguised polemics against the contemplative monism of the *shuhūdī* mystics and the existential unity taught by the *ittiḥādīya* coupled with a statement of Neo-Ḥanbalite spirituality. Like Ibn Taymīya in his controversy with the Ashʿarites, Ibn al-Qayyim states expressly that he is obliged to borrow the terminology of his contemporaries.[1] If at all, he was only slightly closer to mysticism in the accepted sense than was his teacher to speculative theology. But this did not restrict the scope of his interests. Three major strands of the medieval Islamic debate on love—the literary and ascetic, the theological, and the mystical—converge in Ibn al-Qayyim's treatment of the subject and give it a character of its own.

Although born as it were into the intricacies of Ḥanbalite jurisprudence—his father was the superintendent (*qayyim*) of the Jawzīya *madrasa* in Damascus[2]—Ibn al-Qayyim is known to have flirted with less orthodox systems in his youth. By his own avowal, he remained in the snare of false doctrine until God in his grace allowed him to meet Ibn Taymīya,[3] an event set by the biographers in 712, upon the jurist's return from Egypt.[4] By this time, however, Ibn al-Qayyim seems already to have been at least tending towards the positions of his celebrated new teacher and must not have been entirely unprepared for the fateful meeting. His recently deceased instructor in mysticism, Abū 'l-ʿAbbās Aḥmad b. Ibrāhīm al-Wāsiṭī (d. 711/1311),[5] was an associate of Ibn Taymīya, and the two men are known to have held each other in the highest regard.

Al-Wāsiṭī, who had left his native Iraq as a pilgrim, settled eventually in Cairo. Frequenting the mystical circles there, in particular the Shādhilīs, he adopted their path and, according to Ibn Rajab's generous report, profited from the experience. Journeying later to Damascus, he met Ibn Taymīya. Although previously a Shāfiʿite in law and himself somewhat the elder, he became a student of the jurist.[6] At Ibn Taymīya's suggestion he tempered his mystical doctrine through the study of the life and traditions of the Prophet and then, in the name of a more orthodox spirituality, undertook a campaign of polemics against the *ittiḥādīya* and other "innovators."[7] Ibn Taymīya did not conceal his respect for al-Wāsiṭī, whom he called "the Junayd of his age,"[8] while the Sufi in turn took up the cause of his controversial teacher. Perhaps it was during Ibn Taymīya's long and troubled stay in Egypt that al-Wāsiṭī wrote a well-remembered letter to the shaykh's disciples admonishing them to respect and follow him.[9] Reportedly, he always spoke highly of Ibn Taymīya, expressing reservations only concerning his criticism of certain "imams and ascetics."[10]

Al-Wāsiṭī's instruction can undoubtedly be considered a forerunner of Ibn Taymīya's influence on Ibn al-Qayyim, but it is rather for another reason that the mystic deserves mention here. It is not unlikely that, in his role as teacher, he exerted on the young scholar still another kind of influence, which, as friend and student, he could not have had on Ibn Taymīya. Was it Ibn al-Qayyim's early sessions with al-Wāsiṭī which first instilled in him the concern with formal mysticism which was to assert itself so strongly in his later works? The hypothesis does not appear to be unfounded. In particular, al-Wāsiṭī's commentary on the *Manāzil al-sā'irīn* of al-Anṣārī, left unfinished,[11] may have inspired Ibn al-Qayyim to record his own interpretation of al-Anṣārī's treatise in the voluminous *Madārij al-sālikīn.*[12]

It is more the technical presentation of Ibn al-Qayyim's writings on

Sufism than their introspective character which should be attributed to al-Wāsiṭī's inspiration, however, since it is clearly the influence of Ibn Taymīya which dominates all others in nearly every passage of his works. His devotion to the views of the great Ḥanbalite, so evident in his books, showed itself likewise in his life. He alone among Ibn Taymīya's partisans shared his last imprisonment. Held separately, he was released only after the shaykh's death in 728.[13] He continued none the less to defend the doctrine of his teacher, including all of his isolated opinions (*mufradāt*) according to Ibn Ḥajar,[14] and he suffered harassment at least twice again for his loyalty to the jurist's views on racing and divorce.[15]

The profound effect of Ibn Taymīya's thought on Ibn al-Qayyim cannot have been restricted to the impersonal realm of jurisprudence and *kalām.* The older man's sympathy for a moderate mysticism and his tendency to fall back on such logical intangibles as the "sweetness of faith" in his argumentation have already been mentioned,[16] and Ibn al-Qayyim himself records certain of his teacher's utterances which did not fail to leave their mark on the student. He once heard Ibn Taymīya say, he recalls: "Truly there is a Paradise in this world, and he who does not enter it does not enter the Paradise of the next." Another time he heard him say, "What are my enemies able to do to me? My Paradise, my Garden, is in my heart. Wherever I go, it is with me and does not leave me. My imprisonment is a retreat (*khalwa*); my murder, the death of a martyr (*shahāda*); and my exile, a pilgrim's journey (*siyāḥa*)."[17]

Was it while imprisoned with Ibn Taymīya in the citadel of Damascus that Ibn al-Qayyim came to appreciate the meaning of these words? It is impossible to tell. But in any event it was during this confinement, according to the biographers, that he acquired certain habits of devotion which he was never to forsake, and it is to this period that Ibn Rajab traces the understanding of Sufism reflected in his writings.[18] Ibn Rajab's opinion tends to confirm, certainly, that the fundamental spirituality of Ibn al-Qayyim should be attributed to a later influence than that of al-Wāsiṭī. But one is still entitled to suspect that the scholar's interest in the formal aspects of Sufism, a phenomenon of his later years clearly distinguishable from the more casual introspection of Ibn Taymīya, represents, at least in part, a swing of the pendulum back to the concerns of his youth. Whatever the remote causes, perhaps very complex, of Ibn al-Qayyim's adoption of Sufi models in certain of his writings, his immediate reasons, reflecting the exigencies of religious debate in his age, are readily apparent from his own words. It was no longer possible to avoid writing in the style of one's adversaries.

The preliminary periodization of Ibn al-Qayyim's works which follows will make it possible to trace the evolution of his discussion of love through varying contexts and to assess the importance he ascribed to the question at different stages of his career. In particular, it will be possible to substantiate my assertion that the growth of his interest in formal mysticism, with its distinctive effects on his treatment of love, occurred during the latter part of his life, and it will be seen that he returned afterwards to a more typically Ḥanbalite approach. Since almost all of the works considered would seem to have been written after the death of Ibn Taymīya, the period of Ibn al-Qayyim's intellectual development dealt with here can be assumed to extend roughly from 728 to 751, covering thus the last twenty-three years of his life.[19]

The early works consist for the most part of books on jurisprudence and tradition, monographs on a variety of individual topics, and several preliminary essays in theology. Assignable to the early period are such compositions as the *Kitāb al-maʿālim* on *fiqh*, which may have been an unpolished draft of Ibn al-Qayyim's *Iʿlām al-muwaqqiʿīn* or is perhaps to be identified with that work;[20] the *Tahdhīb Sunan Abī Dāwūd* on *ḥadīth*;[21] *al-Tibyān fī aqsām al-Qur'ān*, on God's oaths in the Koran;[22] *al-Dā' wa-l-dawā'*, on religious ethics, arguing that God has provided a cure for every moral disease;[23] *Rawḍat al-muḥibbīn*, a major work on profane and sacred love;[24] a no longer extant *Kitāb maʿrifat al-rūḥ wa-l-nafs*, on the soul, to which his presently available *Kitāb al-rūḥ* refers and on which it was probably based;[25] and a long didactic poem on theology known as *al-Qaṣīda al-nūnīya*.[26] Theology is also represented in this period by two other works: *Ijtimāʿ al-juyūsh al-Islāmīya*, which is a collection of quotations on the divine attributes from various earlier authorities,[27] and the now lost *al-Futūḥāt al-Qudsīya* on moral theology.[28] Of these theological works neither *al-Qaṣīda al-nūnīya* nor the *Ijtimāʿ* bears comparison with Ibn al-Qayyim's more mature books in the discipline, while *al-Futūḥāt al-Qudsīya*, if it had some of the creative sophistication of his later writings, must have stood very much alone in the early period. Most likely, the book was no more than a first attempt by the scholar in the field of moral theology, soon to be superceded by his *Miftāḥ Dār al-Saʿāda*.

In general these earlier works are characterized by a style less highly developed than that found in Ibn al-Qayyim's later writings, a heavy reliance on traditions of the Prophet and sayings culled from other trustworthy sources, and a considerable emphasis on law and practical religious ethics.[29] Since no strong concern with formal mysticism is evident in the works belonging to the early period—which began, as has been seen, with the death of Ibn Taymīya in the citadel of Damascus—it is difficult to accept without at least some qualification Ibn Rajab's suggestion that Ibn al-Qayyim's understanding of Sufism was an outgrowth of his meditations while in prison.[30] For the time being, at least in his writings, Ibn al-Qayyim was still primarily jurist and preacher.

In theology Ibn al-Qayyim's first mature treatise seems to have been his just mentioned *Miftāḥ Dār al-Saʿāda wa-manshūr wilāyat al-ʿilm wa-l-irāda*, in which he began to work out a strong scholastic underpinning for Ḥanbalite spirituality.[31] This lengthy book, marking the beginning of a new period, treats the excellence of knowledge, man's need for the religious law, God's "wise purpose" (*ḥikma*) as it is reflected in creation, the reality of the distinction between good and evil, and the role of prophecy—all in the general context of man's search for beatitude. Included in passing are sections against astrology and divining by the flight of birds, with which the *Miftāḥ* comes to an abrupt end.[32] Two other sizable theological treatises followed—*Shifā' al-ʿalīl fī masā'il al-qaḍā' wa-l-qadar wa-l-ḥikma wa-l-taʿlīl* and *al-Ṣawāʿiq al-mursala ʿalā 'l-Jahmīya wa-l-muʿaṭṭila*,[33] which was probably written only a few years after the completion of the *Shifā'*.[34] The first book deals with the questions of predestination, providence, and free will, while the second is addressed to the problem of the analogical and metaphorical interpretation (*ta'wīl*) of the Koran in *kalām*. In each of these three works on theology—the *Miftāḥ*, the *Shifā'*, and the *Ṣawāʿiq*—sacred love and the issues raised by Ibn Taymīya with respect to love as a divine attribute form an important but not the major concern.

Sometime after the composition of *Miftāḥ Dār al-Saʿāda* and, I am inclined to believe, after finishing his works on predestination and *ta'wīl*, Ibn al-Qayyim began the treatment of formal mysticism which culminated in his masterful commentary on al-Anṣārī's *Manāzil al-sā'irīn*. To a certain extent the seeds of this new turn in his interests were present already in the *Miftāḥ*. As the second half of that work he had originally proposed to write a long section on love, which was to include more than a hundred proofs, dealing especially with the reality and necessity of the love-relationship between God and man.[35] This section would have fulfilled the promise of the title to deal with both *ʿilm* (knowledge) and *irāda* (will), but at some point during the course of writing Ibn al-Qayyim decided to bring the work to a close without realizing his plan.

Returning to the project, he later composed a large book on love, no longer extant, entitled *al-Mawrid al-ṣāfī wa-l-ẓill al-ḍāfī fī 'l-maḥabba wa-aqsāmihā wa-aḥkāmihā wa-bayān ta'alluqihā bi-l-ilāh al-ḥaqq dūna mā siwāhū*—on love, its kinds and conditions, and its devotion to God alone, as the title explains. Ibn al-Qayyim claimed to have supplied in the *Mawrid* more than a hundred arguments in support of his position,[36] a fact which seems to confirm that the work represented the fruition of the plans announced in the *Miftāḥ*. Presumably it was in this lost book, rather than in the earlier *Rawḍat al-muḥibbīn*, that he gave his most mature statement on love. Ibn al-Qayyim wrote in a similar vein another now lost work, which on the basis of rather tenuous evidence I think to have been slightly prior to *al-Mawrid al-ṣāfī*. This book, generally cited as *al-Tuḥfa al-Makkīya*, contained discussions of love, refutations of the mystical doctrines of incarnation (*ḥulūl*) and union with God (*ittiḥād*), and sections on how the afterlife is to be preferred to existence in this world.[37] Yet another text which appears to have been produced during the same period is the also no longer extant *Qurrat 'uyūn al-muḥibbīn wa-rawḍat qulūb al-'ārifīn.* The title seems a calque on that of *Rawḍat al-muḥibbīn* but suggests a stronger emphasis on mysticism. *Qurrat 'uyūn al-muḥibbīn*, perhaps to be identified with the work listed by Ibn Rajab as *al-Farq bayn al-khulla wa-l-maḥabba wa-munāẓarat al-Khalīl li-qawmihi*, included eighty arguments on *khulla* or intimate, exclusive love—the stage of sacred love attained only by Abraham and Muḥammad according to Islamic tradition.[38] *Al-Tuḥfa al-Makkīya* and *Qurrat 'uyūn al-muḥibbīn* may admittedly have been written much earlier in Ibn al-Qayyim's life than I have implied here, but it remains certain that at some time after completing his *Miftāḥ* the Neo-Ḥanbalite scholar became sufficiently concerned with the question of love to write *al-Mawrid al-ṣāfī*, which, as I have suggested, was evidently his greatest work on the subject. It was very possibly Ibn al-Qayyim's interest in this the most subtle and clearly most intimate relationship between man and God that led him to think increasingly of the problems of mysticism in general. The same concern may also have reminded him of his early lessons in formal Sufism with Abū 'l-'Abbās al-Wāsiṭī.

Soon afterwards, in any event, Ibn al-Qayyim wrote his first major mystical treatise, *Ṭarīq al-hijratayn wa-bāb al-sa'ādatayn*, which was essentially a commentary on the *Maḥāsin al-majālis* of the Andalusian *shuhūdī* mystic Abū 'l-ʿAbbās Aḥmad b. Muḥammad of Almería, known as Ibn al-ʿArīf or Ibn al-ʿIrrīf (d. 536/1141).[39] Ibn al-ʿArīf's work, in turn, was an expansion of a small tract by the Ḥanbalite ʿAbd Allāh al-Anṣārī on the deficiencies (*ʿilal*) of certain stations of the mystical path[40] and thus was not entirely irrelevant to the development of Sufism in the school of Aḥmad. There seems to be no reason to doubt that Ibn al-Qayyim knew of the connection between the two texts.[41]

The next step was to confront the master himself. Al-Anṣārī had composed his celebrated *Manāzil al-sā'irīn* in an elusive language designed apparently to avoid shocking readers unsympathetic to mysticism and had thus left the work open to widely varying interpretations.[42] The *ittiḥādī* scholar and poet ʿAfīf al-Dīn al-Tilimsānī, as we know, had subjected the *Manāzil* to a monistic exegesis.[43] Indeed it was partly in response to al-Tilimsānī's work that Ibn al-Qayyim drafted his own commentary on the treatise, the *Madārij al-sālikīn*—a book which the Egyptian modernist Muḥammad Rashīd Riḍā called the finest work he had known on Sufism and religious ethics.[44] Ibn al-Qayyim went far beyond a mere defense of al-Anṣārī, however. Recognizing that the authority of the great Ḥanbalite Sufi had given sanction to *shuhūdī* mysticism in orthodox circles, he repeatedly attacked the shaykh's stand on annihilation or *fanā'*—for al-Anṣārī the extinction of the individual consciousness rather than of separate existence—as the final goal of the mystic. In place of *shuhūdī fanā'* Ibn al-Qayyim offered as the ideal of Ḥanbalite mysticism a life of love to God reflected in the practical realm of worship and obedience. Thus, although the structure of *Madārij al-sālikīn* and consequently the questions it deals with are typical of conventional Sufi treatises, the content recalls for the most part the characteristic moral stress of Ḥanbalism.

Ibn al-Qayyim's interest in Sufism did not cease with the completion of his commentary on al-Anṣārī's *Manāzil.* In the *Madārij* he promised a large volume on the spiritual concert (*samāʿ*), in which he very likely intended to take up more secular aspects of music, song, and poetry as well; and it seems that he successfully realized this project.[45] The treatise on *samāʿ*, however, marks the end of a period. In what my evidence suggests is the latest work among those discussed here, *Ighāthat al-lahfān min maṣāyid al-Shayṭān*, Ibn al-Qayyim departed from his concern with specifically mystical questions to recapitulate certain Neo-Ḥanbalite arguments in jurisprudence, ethics, and the polemic against Christians and Jews.[46]

Among all the texts which have been mentioned here, *Rawḍat al-*

muḥibbīn must be singled out for special consideration. Despite the apparently early date of its composition, the *Rawḍa* remains the most comprehensive source now extant for Ibn al-Qayyim's teaching on sacred and profane love, and it is in this book that he comes closest to achieving a synthesis of Ḥanbalite thinking on the subject. The structure of the work and the focus on human love were in accordance with the requirements of tradition. But despite the conventional format adopted, it is clear that in the *Rawḍa* the author is no longer writing about love merely to exhaust one aspect of Muslim ethics as Ibn al-Jawzī had done or to clarify a fascinating but confused literary question in imitation of other writers on profane love. The traditional structure was taken over simply as a tactical expedient. Ibn al-Qayyim composed his treatise primarily to explicate a central element of Neo-Ḥanbalite doctrine. Love (*maḥabba*), he states unequivocally in the *khuṭba* or introduction to the *Rawḍa*, is the means and final cause of creation and the soul's way to beatitude.[47] The purpose of the work, then, in conformity with the teaching of Ibn Taymīya, was to aid believers in properly subordinating all secondary affections to the supreme love owed to God. To attain his end Ibn al-Qayyim was obliged to treat profane love, which had been to some extent neglected by his teacher, as well as more specifically religious topics. The secular, theological, and mystical facets of love theory clearly involve many of the same fundamental questions, however, and for Ibn al-Qayyim the three aspects are intimately bound up together. Each, therefore, finds its place in the *Rawḍa*, if in varying degrees. Seldom is a given issue in profane love treated without reference to its counterpart in the sacred sphere.

It is true that *Rawḍat al-muḥibbīn* resembles Ibn al-Jawzī's *Dhamm al-hawā* in many ways and depends heavily on that work for its raw material. Examples of direct borrowing could be listed ad infinitum. But the differences one would expect to find between a "garden for lovers" and a "censure of passion" are there. While Ibn al-Jawzī, expressing an emphatically negative attitude, dwells on restraining fleshly desires, Ibn al-Qayyim is interested primarily in mobilizing human emotions for the sake of a positive spiritual goal. Even the word *hawā* itself is treated with a different stress in the works of the two men. Like his predecessor, Ibn al-Qayyim is obliged to recognize that, although *hawā* often refers to the concupiscible appetite, which is not of itself blameworthy, the term is nevertheless usually applied to reprehensible desires.[48] When he deals with the "censure of passion," moreover, he quotes extensively from Ibn al-Jawzī's *Dhamm.*[49] But the Neo-Ḥanbalite scholar makes it clear from the outset that it is not the purpose of his book to provide yet another condemnation of passion. In the war between reason and *hawā*, he maintains, the latter is not to be denied its right. Accordingly, he describes his *Rawḍa* as a "treaty of peace" between reason and *hawā*, adding that once this peace is concluded, the believer's struggle with his lower desires will become an easy matter.[50]

Another important factor distinguishing *Rawḍat al-muḥibbīn* from *Dhamm al-hawā* is the extent and sophistication of the theoretical discussion found in the two works. Ibn al-Jawzī's analyses are generally short, while those of Ibn al-Qayyim, by comparison, are fairly long. In addition, the method of chapter organization *reason-tradition-poetry*, adumbrated in *Dhamm al-hawā*, is common and more fully exploited in the *Rawḍa*. In a typical chapter, the question at hand is presented in an analytic and semitechnical fashion and then are listed the arguments from tradition—the sayings of the Prophet and other authorities. Selections of verse, preferably short, are cited in conclusion, either to provide examples of popular wisdom in support of the author's opinion or in order to emphasize a point by means of ornamentation. As employed in the *Rawḍa*, this arrangement reflects, on the one hand, the influence of Ibn Taymīya's attempt to merge the methods of the traditionists and the speculative theologians and, on the other, Ibn al-Qayyim's keen sense of rhetoric. Inevitably the standards of the science of tradition are sacrificed. Paralleling the new stress on rational argumentation, there is revealed in the *Rawḍa* a striking lack of concern with *isnād*s, the chains of authority about which Ibn al-Jawzī was so fastidious. The virtual absence of *isnād*s in the work should not, I believe, be attributed primarily to the fact that the author was away from his library at the time of writing—one explanation which has been proposed.[51] He demonstrates a similar carelessness with regard to these chains of authority in other works.[52] In the *Rawḍa*, it would seem, the critical apparatus of *ḥadīth* science was neglected because it was irrelevant to the construction of a doctrine of love. Moreover, *isnād*s are tedious to the reader, and Ibn al-Qayyim was an accomplished homilist who expressly intended his book to be *dulce* as well as *utile.*[53] Thus he made use of *isnād*s only when they were necessary to confirm or deny the validity of a tradition central to his argument.[54]

The uniqueness of the *Rawḍa* is particularly apparent when the treatise is considered together with the *Manāzil al-aḥbāb* of another

Syrian-born Ḥanbalite, Shihāb al-Dīn Maḥmūd b. Sulaymān b. Fahd al-Ḥalabī (d. 725/1325).[55] Al-Ḥalabī's work, antedating the *Rawḍa* by perhaps no more than two or three decades but untouched by Ibn Taymīya's influence, is merely a collection of anecdotes, verse, and learned quotations on love arranged under a variety of headings. Virtually devoid of commentary on the part of the compiler, the *Manāzil* can hardly be seen as an improvement on *Dhamm al-hawā*. *Rawḍat al-muḥibbīn*, on the other hand, whatever its intellectual shortcomings in comparison to Ibn al-Qayyim's own later writings, has many of the attributes of a major theoretical treatment of love. On reading the *Rawḍa*, one can only regret the loss of the author's more mature statement on the subject given in *al-Mawrid al-ṣāfī*.

In summary, it should be pointed out once again that the various shifts in stress or disciplinary framework discernible in the writings of Ibn al-Qayyim correspond to several fairly distinct periods in his career. In the earlier phase, although by no means a young man, the scholar had just emerged from the tutelage of Ibn Taymīya. Perhaps uncertain of his skill in theology, he devoted most of his attention to jurisprudence, *ḥadīth*, and a number of easily handled monograph topics. His zeal as a compiler, revealing the influence of Ibn al-Jawzī,[56] still overshadowed the development of his personal style, and one catches only glimpses of the polished and sophisticated expression which is the hallmark of *Miftāḥ Dār al-Sa'āda* and the works which follow it. Love was already a question of great importance to him; he devoted to it the whole of *Rawḍat al-muḥibbīn* and considerable portions of *al-Dā' wa-l-dawā'*. But his treatment of the subject is generally typical of this early period. The *Rawḍa*, as has been seen, draws extensively on the corpus of imaginative literature and especially on the selection available in Ibn al-Jawzī's *Dhamm al-hawā*. In both the *Rawḍa* and the *Dā'* the primary stress is still on matters of practical morality.

With the writing of *Miftāḥ Dār al-Sa'āda* Ibn al-Qayyim moved into a new period with respect to style and method alike. This period, beginning with a more technical interest in moral theology, saw a development in two directions—towards an increasingly studied scholasticism on the one hand and a more pervasive introspection on the other. Probably rather late in this second stage, sacred love became the major issue, and the studies consecrated to the subject seem to have served as a bridge to a third period marked by an unusual preoccupation with formal mysticism. In Ibn al-Qayyim's mystical writings sacred love quite naturally retains its importance, but the point of view from which it is discussed is determined by the Sufi context and the

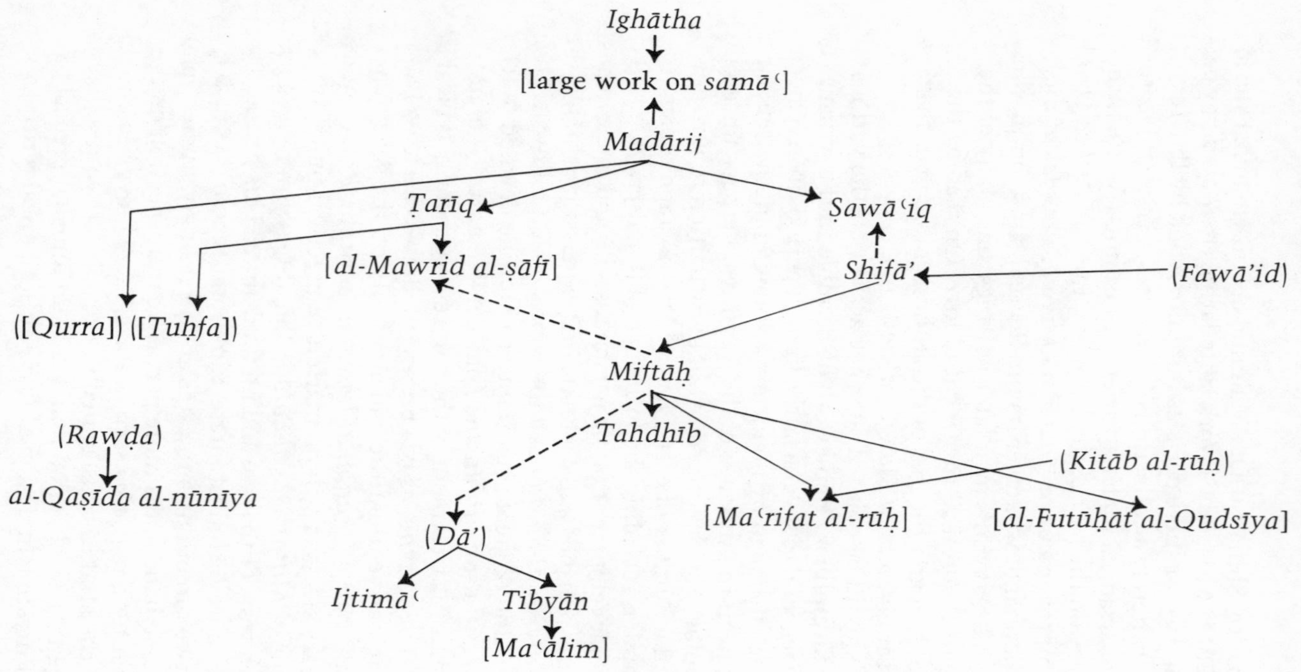

Fig.—Order of composition of some works of Ibn Qayyim al-Jawzīya from 728/1328 to 751/1350. Chronological order is from bottom to top. Arrows indicate that a work is cited or proposed in another. Broken arrows denote an uncertain identification of the work cited or proposed. Titles in brackets are not known to be extant or have not been definitely identified with extant works. Parentheses indicate that a title has been placed chronologically with others on grounds of style, subject, or an inconclusive reference in a later text.

attention devoted to it is limited by the necessity of treating each of the mystical stations dealt with by Ibn al-ʿArīf and al-Anṣārī—a task at times accomplished by the commentator in a rather forced manner.[57] Ibn al-Qayyim's *Ighāthat al-lahfān*, the only work which can be ascribed with relative certainty to the fourth and last period, demonstrates the persistence of the author's earlier concerns. It contains numerous observations on love and has, in particular, a section which returns to the subject of earthly *ʿishq*, the most important such passage I have found in the extant examples of his later writings.[58] The general tone of the treatment is more distinctly religious than in *Rawḍat al-muḥibbīn*, however.

Despite the variety of Ibn al-Qayyim's literary production and the changing emphasis of his works, it should be clear from the preceding discussion that the question of love remained crucial in his thought. It found a place in his early monographs which it was to retain throughout the period of his studies in theology and mysticism, although on the basis of the available evidence it seems that profane love in particular ceased for a time to enjoy its original importance. In the *Ighātha* both the secular and the religious facets of the subject were to appear again. None of the periods outlined here, however, can be said to have been devoted exclusively to a debate on love or any other single topic. The essential elements of Neo-Ḥanbalite dogma are never neglected, and the late composition of the *Ighātha* shows that even Ibn al-Qayyim's study of mysticism did not eclipse his interests of an earlier time. Throughout the evolution of the scholar's thought the fundamental theological positions remain the same, faithfully reflecting the doctrine of his teacher. It is, for the most part, only the style and the scope of his writings which set them apart from the compositions of Ibn Taymīya.

7. Affinity, Beneficence, and Beauty

In his *Madārij al-sālikīn* Ibn al-Qayyim asserts that love can be described only in terms of its causes, its signs and symptoms, its effects, and its precepts.[1] While taking care not to stray too far from the scholar's own approach, it will be convenient to restrict the discussion in this chapter and the next to his treatment of the causes of love, which involves directly or indirectly most of the basic issues to which he addresses himself. A corollary topic, the kinds of love as they are distinguished in the writings of Ibn al-Qayyim, will be reserved to a third chapter. It will not be necessary to devote special attention to the question of the precepts of love. Ibn al-Qayyim's observations on this subject resemble in their purely profane aspects the moral exhortations of Ibn al-Jawzī while in the realm of spirituality they mirror the teaching of Ibn Taymīya. To the scholar's study of the symptoms and effects of love there will be occasion to return briefly in a later chapter.[2]

Before examining Ibn al-Qayyim's treatment of the causes of love, one should no doubt attempt to ascertain his fundamental conception of the emotion in question. His remark concerning the ways in which love may be described, it will be noticed, reflects a certain hesitancy to offer a forthright definition of the term love itself. C. G. Jung, commenting on the wide range of experience covered by the word, expressed the difficulty faced by all writers who attempt to define it: "We find ourselves in the unprofitable situation of beginning a discussion about a matter and a concept of absolutely unlimited extent and indefiniteness."[3] Ibn al-Qayyim, together with a host of other Muslim writers, reveals the same perplexity, although it should be noted that the elusive nature of love seems to have become a major concern for him only when he began to write on mysticism. Commenting Ibn al-ʿArīf's rhymed declaration in the *Maḥāsin* to the effect that those who have tried to define love have done so according to their own experience (*dhawq*) and the extent of their own longing (*shawq*).[4] Ibn al-Qayyim agrees with the mystic and offers an elaboration of his own. Subjective, experiential states (*umūr wijdānīya dhawqīya*) like joy, affliction, and pain, he maintains, are known only through their symptoms and effects in the subject. Since these symptoms and effects vary from one person to another, the definitions given for the terms which denote the different subjective states likewise vary. This is the case with love. Its stages range from *ʿalāqa*, the attachment of the heart to the beloved, to *khulla* or intimate, exclusive love. Every lover perceives some of these stages and defines love accordingly, but the true definition always escapes him. No attempt to express the meaning of love in words, therefore, can reveal its real nature. The affection can be understood for what it is only through experience.[5] Its definition is its very existence.[6] In this reluctance to accept any verbal formula as a proper explanation of the meaning of love, Ibn al-Qayyim is echoing the conventional attitude of hesitation hinted at, when not expressly acknowledged, in one after another of the passages on the definition of love in Muslim writings. When the Neo-Ḥanbalite scholar sums up his discussion of the definitions of love (*maḥabba*) in *Ṭarīq al-hijratayn* with the remark that love has no better definition than the word *maḥabba* itself, he could well be recalling a similar statement made by the celebrated theoretician of mysticism al-Qushayrī in his *Risāla*.[7]

An early sign of this hesitation is found in the *Rawḍa*, where Ibn al-Qayyim refrains from offering any definitions of his own, choosing simply to enumerate the suggestions of others and remarking their proliferation.[8] In *Ṭarīq al-hijratayn* he rejects consistently as incomplete or as merely descriptive of love's consequences all the definitions Ibn al-ʿArīf assembled as well a number which he himself cites.[9] He repeats the process in the *Madārij*, but without mentioning Ibn al-ʿArīf.[10] The only formula which gains near acceptance, although not precisely as a definition, is a rather lyrical description of the self-effacement of the lover of God in worship and service attributed to the young Junayd.[11] The prevailing definition of love as an inclination (*mayl*) is rejected as too general on the grounds that a man may be inclined towards a thing and yet not love it because he knows it will bring harm to him. Love, for Ibn al-Qayyim, must be something more specific than inclination.[12] Another suggestion, that love is simply the lover's knowledge of the beloved's beauty, is likewise rejected—such knowledge being held by the scholar to constitute one of the causes of love rather than the affection itself.[13] Definitions which make love out as conformity of will, giving preference to the beloved, or sacrifice of self, although they parallel basic tenets of Neo-Ḥanbalite spirituality, are dismissed as referring merely to signs or effects of love.[14]

Despite Ibn al-Qayyim's almost totally negative attitude towards the various attempts by Muslim thinkers to express verbally the meaning of love, it is possible to draw certain conclusions regarding his fundamental conception of the sentiment. Love is not in his view a judgment, since judgment, like knowledge of the beloved's beauty, must be among its causes.[15] Nor is love constituted in an essential way by any of the acts typical of lovers, not even such subjective acts as conforming one's will to that of the beloved, for these are among its effects. Since love must therefore fall between the extremes of judgment and action, it would seem to lie in the area of tendency or inclination—Ibn al-Qayyim's aforementioned objection notwithstanding. But tendency as used in this sense is of the same nature as desire or longing;[16] and *shawq*, the Arabic term for desire or longing, defined as "the journey of the heart towards the beloved" by Muslim writers, denotes a kind of spiritual motion which is a consequence of love for the Neo-Ḥanbalite scholar, not its essence. One may say "I desired a person (or thing) because I loved him," but not the reverse, he remarks.[17] What remains after this process of elimination is a conception of love as *static tendency* which is as elusive as the author's original comments on the definition of love promised. It might be possible to express this understanding of love as an acquired, favorable disposition, but nowhere do the texts explicitly authorize such a formulation. Love, for Ibn al-Qayyim, like a point on a line, can be described only in terms of what lies on either side of it. Words are no substitute for personal experience as the source of true knowledge of the affection.

It would be obvious that Ibn al-Qayyim's refusal to define love involved certain dangerous implications for the Ḥanbalite position. Strictly adhered to, this approach would amount to handing the whole question over to the Sufi proponents of experience over knowledge, something the scholar could not allow. Accordingly, he felt the need to qualify a remark Ibn al-ʿArīf made to the effect that love has no form (*ṣīgha*) by which it can be expressed.[18] Every meaning (*maʿnā*), he states, has a form by which it is expressed, especially if it is a meaning known both to the elite and to the commonality. But a meaning may be clearly denoted by a word, as is the case with terms like drachma, bread, and water; or it may be above or beneath that to which the word refers, as is the case with the names of God, his book, and terms like love (*maḥabba*), desire, *eros* (*ʿishq*), death, and affection on the one hand and expressions like "atom" (*al-jawhar al-fard*) on the other. Thus, when Ibn al-ʿArīf writes that love has no form by which it is expressed, he intends to say only that the word love does not express the full meaning of the thing to which it refers.[19] The upshot of Ibn al-Qayyim's remarks is that love may be considered a proper object of analytical study. He makes this point clear further on in the same context. It is indeed necessary to distinguish between the man who merely knows *about* love and the one who has experienced it, he admits, and it must be affirmed that the latter is preferable to the former. But still more to be preferred is the one who both experiences love and also gives guidance concerning it to the community.[20] Reflecting the constant social and moral orientation of Ḥanbalite teaching, Ibn al-Qayyim's claim here is not only that love can be discussed but also that for the good of the Muslim community it ought to be.

With our author's basic conception of love thus circumscribed to the extent that the negative approach he adopted will allow, it is possible to return to the question at hand—the causes of love. As discussed by most writers, these can be grouped into three categories: causes residing or occurring solely in the subject; causes in the object; and causes common to both lovers. A fourth category, suggested by Nygren's *agape* doctrine, does not appear to be relevant to the Muslim views dealt with in this study.[21] The division I have just suggested, however, can be derived from Ibn al-Qayyim's own analysis. The causes and preconditions of love, as explained in *Rawḍat al-muḥibbīn*, are threefold: the qualities of the beloved; the lover's perception of them (*shuʿūruhu bi-hā*); and the affinity (*munāsaba*) existing between the natures of the lover and the beloved. Love depends upon these three factors, and its intensity is proportional to theirs.[22]

Affinity

The first of love's causes that Ibn al-Qayyim discusses in the *Rawḍa* is the affinity existing between lover and beloved, which falls into the category of causes affecting both subject and object. This is the *munāsaba* already touched on with reference to Ibn Taymīya's treatment of love between God and man.[23] Because the belief in such an affinity between lovers constituted one of the most fundamental and widely accepted elements in Muslim theories of love during the Middle Ages, some further general remarks on the subject may be appropriate.

Expressions of the ancient opinions which underlie both the Islamic idea of *munāsaba* or *mushākala* (resemblance) and the parallel concept of *similitudo* in medieval Western thought[24] are not uncommon in classical texts. They are found in the works of Plato and Aristotle, although in the case of Plato, typically, it is not always easy to determine just what position on the question he supports. Behind all of these opinions the reader senses the influence of popular wisdom couched in aphorisms of the "birds of a feather" variety.[25] This affinity with which writers on love have so long been concerned can be seen either as a relationship of similarity or as one of complementarity. The relationship of complementarity, in turn, can reflect either a desire for similarity, as in the student-teacher relationship discussed by Plato, or a desire for a mean between two extremes, as that of the dry to become moist rather than wet, to borrow an example given by Aristotle.[26] Hence much of the controversy turning on Aristophanes' rather ambiguous myth of the spherical man. Modern Western writers tend to interpret this image as expressing a desire for complementary union.[27] Muslim authors, most often, understood the myth and the term *munāsaba* itself to imply similarity.[28]

As it has been remarked earlier,[29] Islamic treatises on love did not as a rule represent the work of professional philosophers, and in most cases the idea of affinity, like other Greek elements in Muslim love theory, was not taken directly from the writings of Plato and Aristotle or their successors but from a common stock of sayings attributed to the major intellectual figures of antiquity. Among the authorities cited particularly often, the two physicians Hippocrates and Galen both touch on similarity. To Hippocrates is ascribed a definition of love as a mixing of two souls which is comparable to the mingling of two similar waters. Galen, paralleling the view of Aristotle and one of the arguments of Socrates in Plato's *Lysis*, is reported to have said that love arises between reasonable men because of their similarity in intelligence but cannot occur between two stupid men.[30]

Important in another way to the reception of the idea of affinity in Islamic theories of love were several controversial passages of the Koran[31] and certain traditions of the Prophet. Although Muslim arguments on the subject reflect more the influence of their Greek antecedents than that of indigenous sources, it was not without significance that the Koran and Sunna could be cited as sanctioning the hypothesis of a fundamental affinity between lovers. In the *ḥadīth* most often related in this connection the Prophet says: "Spirits are regimented battalions: those which know one another associate familiarly together, while those which do not know one another remain at variance."[32] Aḥmad b. Ḥanbal was among the transmitters of this tradition.[33]

By the late second/early ninth century at the latest, affinity or similarity (*munāsaba, mushākala, mujānasa, tashākul*, etc.), together with the corollary motif of the mingling of lovers' souls, seems to have become the most widely agreed upon element in Muslim definitions of love. Both the historian al-Masʿūdī, relating the opinions expressed in a fictitious or semihistorical symposium convened by the Barmakid vizier Yaḥyā b. Khālid (d. 190/805), and the mystic ʿAlī b. Muḥammad al-Daylamī (fl. late fourth/tenth century), apparently drawing on a different tradition concerning the same gathering, put definitions of *ʿishq*-love in the mouths of several leading Muʿtazilite and Shīʿite theologians of the period. Among the authorities quoted by the two writers are the Shīʿite Hishām b. al-Ḥakam al-Kūfī (d. 199/814) and the Muʿtazilites Abū 'l-Hudhayl al-ʿAllāf (d. 226/841), Ibrāhīm b. Sayyār al-Naẓẓām (d. 231/845), and Thumāma b. Ashras (d. 213/828). Many of al-Masʿūdī's personages and all of those mentioned by al-Daylamī name similarity as the basis of love, and al-Daylamī does not fail to point out similarity as the common element in the definitions the theologians offered.[34] From Ibn al-Qayyim one learns also that at least one of these men, Abū 'l-Hudhayl al-ʿAllāf, held like the Athenian in Plato's *Laws* that love must be reciprocal.[35] Presumably he was not alone in this opinion.

The celebrated writer of *adab* literature al-Jāḥiẓ, a Muʿtazilite and student of Ibrāhīm al-Naẓẓām, expresses the view of his school. He defines *ʿishq* as love (*ḥubb*) and desire—that is, the physical love of male and female for each other—accompanied by a similarity of nature (*mushākalat al-ṭabīʿa*). Al-Jāḥiẓ does not state that all loves proceeding from similarity must necessarily be reciprocal, but he does tell his readers that mutual loves are most often based on similarity. "It is rare," he writes, "to see *ʿishq*-love between two persons in which both share equally unless it be from some affinity of resemblance between them in looks, character, and refinement, or in their passions and natures."[36]

Al-Daylamī notes with apparent disapproval that the *mutakallimūn* did not go beyond similarity of nature, the mingling of spirits, and resemblance in constitution in their definitions of love.[37] Very likely he was alluding indirectly to their view that the affinity held to be necessary to the existence of love, although it may be found among humans, is lacking between God and man. In this connection, we may recall Ibn Taymīya's observation that certain theologians, among whom he cites al-Juwaynī and the Ḥanbalite Ibn ʿAqīl in particular, denied that men could love God or experience pleasure in the beatific vision on the grounds that there is no affinity between the eternal and the originated.[38]

As a consequence of the position taken by the theologians, Muslim mystics were divided on the question of affinity in sacred love. Al-Qushayrī (d. 465/1072) and Abū Ṭālib al-Makkī (d. 386/996) are silent on the issue in their chapters on love as we now have them, while a writer like al-Hujwīrī restricts the love of like for like to the realm of physical desire.[39] Others, however, gave unequivocal support to the idea. Abū Ḥāmid al-Ghazālī, feeling himself on certain ground in theology as well as in mysticism, did not hesitate to make a hidden affinity (*munāsaba khafīya*) between lovers the last and the greatest of his five causes of love—causes which, his argument runs, apply in reality strictly to love for God and only metaphorically to love for creatures.[40] It is to such an affinity that al-Ghazālī has recourse in attempting to explain the possibility of a disinterested love for a person in himself.[41] It is likewise, in his view, a secret affinity man has with the upper world that makes him desire God. Although man knows only the names and attributes of God, he may experience longing for him in the same way that a man who has never seen a woman would feel desire upon hearing one described.[42]

Al-Ghazālī does not overlook such observable affinities as, for example, the similarity of age and interest underlying friendship among children, but his major concern is the hidden relationship, which is of an inward nature and does not appear in a person's outward form. This secret affinity is of two kinds, he explains, that which may be discussed in writing, as the believer's resemblance to God through nearness in attributes, and that which it is forbidden to reveal. It is the latter which is alluded to in the Koranic statements, "Say: the spirit is (of) the affair [or 'command': *amr*] of my Lord" (17:85), and "So when I have formed him [Adam] harmoniously and breathed into him of my spirit, fall down prostrate before him. So the angels prostrated themselves before him all together . . ." (15:29–30). The first of these two passages, according to al-Ghazālī, shows that the human spirit is something divine (*amr rabbānī*) beyond man's comprehension, while the second, reiterating the same point, makes it known that this is why the angels were required to bow down to Adam. The *ḥadīth* which states that man was created in the image of God is to be interpreted in the same fashion.[43] Thus it is the presence of a divine element in man, the *rūḥ* or spirit, which constitutes the unrevealable affinity to which al-Ghazālī refers. The mystic-theologian did not permit himself to say more on the subject, but the few remarks pointed out here are sufficient to demonstrate that he affirmed, in the face of the objections of the *mutakallimūn*, an affinity which certainly borders on being a relationship of similarity as the basis of man's love to God. He did not recognize any grounds for love in the same sense on the part of God for man.[44]

Ibn al-ʿArabī, with only slight reservations, likewise endorses the idea of *munāsaba.* Noting that man enjoys only that with which he has an affinity (*al-munāsib*), he adds that the affinity between man and God, despite the fact that it is merely one of form or image (*ṣūra*), is nearer to perfection than that between a man and a youth or a woman. These human beloveds, he argues, cannot actually *be* an individual's hearing, sight, and other faculties as, according to a *ḥadīth*, God can. A boy or a woman can at most be the *object* of the lover's hearing or seeing.[45]

It has been seen that parallel views on affinity in the sphere of profane love are expressed by the Ẓāhirites Ibn Dāwūd (d. 297/909) and Ibn Ḥazm (d. 456/1064). Ibn Dāwūd's *Kitāb al-zahra* is primarily an anthology, and the youthful compiler had little of his own to say. But in the introduction he states that he intends to deal with the effects of similarity of natures.[46] Further on he relates the tradition of the Prophet describing souls as "regimented battalions," a corrupt version of Aristophanes' myth, Galen's saying to the effect that love can occur only between two men who are alike in being rational, and a number of other prose and verse citations on the same topic.[47] He also points out the reciprocity of love implied by similarity, observing that when *ʿishq* is fully requited, it must be the result of a resemblance of natures.[48] Ibn Ḥazm, a more sophisticated theoretician, discusses affinity at some length, stressing that it is a more fundamental cause of love than beauty or mere agreement in character. Like Ibn Dāwūd, he points to the reciprocity which typifies love based on a fusion of similar souls.[49] Following another position taken by his predecessor, he holds that true *ʿishq*, since it proceeds from an essential similarity, can end only with death.[50] As we know, however, he denies that the spirits of lovers are divided spheres, the apparent implication of Aristophanes' myth as related by Ibn Dāwūd, arguing that the relationship between souls springs rather from an affinity between their parts in the supernal world.[51] It is here that Ibn Ḥazm founds his argument on the controversial doctrine of the prior existence of souls, a teaching which had incurred considerable disapproval in the preceding century as al-Masʿūdī's unfavorable mention of it shows.[52] This is, of course, the issue over which Ibn Qayyim al-Jawzīya was later to reject the Ẓāhirite's views on affinity.

The teaching of the late-seventh-/thirteenth-century writer ʿAbd al-Raḥmān b. Muḥammad al-Anṣārī, known as (Ibn) al-Dabbāgh (d. 696/1296–97, or some five years after the birth of Ibn al-Qayyim) represents an interesting compromise in the direction of orthodoxy. After the fashion of al-Ghazālī, al-Dabbāgh makes affinity one of love's primary causes—he names beauty and beneficence as the other two and maintains that they influence sacred as well as profane love. Unlike al-Ghazālī, however, he uses expressions which imply that love between the eternal and the contingent is possible in both directions.[53] In one passage, more reminiscent of al-Daylamī, he calls God's love itself the true relation (*nisba*) between the divine and the created.[54] But his more usual conception of affinity involved a relationship which is recognizably one of similarity. This may be seen in his interpretation of Aristophanes' myth. The meaning of the myth is not that souls can be divided, he says, since they are not material substances, but rather that they may be alike in their receptivity to a particular thing, either innately or through training.[55]

In view of the emanationist character of much of al-Dabbāgh's work it might be assumed that he had more compelling reasons than the Ẓāhirite Ibn Ḥazm to stress the related idea that the human soul has known an earlier life. Yet as if in deference to the general censure of this notion by the traditionist party al-Dabbāgh declared that souls have had no existence whatsoever prior to the creation of their bodies.[56] The strong tone of his words would seem to exclude the possibility that he meant merely that there is no *individuation* of souls prior to the coming into being of their bodies—an interpretation which has been suggested with regard to certain similar remarks made by the *ishrāqī* martyr Suhrawardī Maqtūl (d. 587/1191).[57] But even if this were indeed the meaning of his statement, still, in a prior undifferentiated existence, there could be no basis for the specific similarities between particular souls which underlie earthly loves. Most probably, however, al-Dabbāgh's statement is to be taken at face value. In this case it can hardly be viewed as anything more than an attempt, sincere or otherwise, to appease the current of orthodox thinking which produced such lengthy condemnations of the doctrine of prior existence as that elaborated by Ibn al-Qayyim.[58]

The Ḥanbalites joined the majority of Muslim thinkers who dealt with love in making affinity the cause of the affection among men. Ibn al-Qayyim, although he treats the question primarily in his earlier works where his concern with earthly love is still great, is no exception. In the sphere of profane love he clearly adopts the usual interpretation that the affinity between lovers is one of similarity. Like tends towards like, he maintains, while contraries are at variance with one another. This, according to Ibn al-Qayyim, is the meaning of Koran 7:189, "He it is who created you from one soul (*nafs* [may also mean "person" as translated by Blachère]) and made from it its mate, so that he [Adam] might find repose in her." Man finds repose in woman, the Ḥanbalite's commentary runs, because she is of one genus and substance with him, because indeed she is from him. It is this essential affinity, not beauty of form or accord in intention, character, or righteousness, that is the fundamental cause of love, although these other things may also be among its causes.[59] Even when one person is beautiful and another perceives his beauty, if there is no affinity there can be no love or no strong love. In the words of one authority Ibn al-Qayyim cites, perhaps Muḥammad b. Dāwūd al-Ẓāhirī: "The essence of it [love] is that it is a mirror in which the lover (*al-muḥibb*) sees his character (*ṭibāʿ*) and his sensibility (*riqqa*) [reflected] in the image of his beloved. In reality he loves only himself, his character, and that which resembles him."[60]

The term *munāsaba*, according to Ibn al-Qayyim, can be extended to cover a temporary or accidental (*ʿāriḍa*) affinity resulting from proximity to a person or participation in a joint enterprise. But the love brought about by this kind of relationship is ephemeral, lasting only as long as the circumstances which produced it. Love proceeding from an "original" similarity on the other hand, like the attraction of iron to lodestone, depends for its continued existence on no other cause than this similarity itself.[61] So long as no insuperable obstacle is present, it will be both mutual and permanent.[62] Reciprocity and permanence thus constitute characteristic signs of love born of essential affinity. Apart from these two signs there are others, in particular the common occurrence of seeming coincidences between lovers, as when both fall ill with the same diseases or speak the same words while apart.[63]

With respect to these basic ideas about affinity Ibn al-Qayyim's view is not unlike that of most other Muslim writers. But the Neo-Ḥanbalite quickly joins issue with those authors who advance the corollary doctrine of the soul's prior existence. In *Rawḍat al-muḥibbīn*, as mentioned earlier, he quotes Ibn Ḥazm's passage in *Ṭawq al-ḥamāma* on the affinity between souls in their heavenly abode and then rejects the opinion expressed there on the grounds that it implies the existence of souls prior to their bodies. The human soul, Ibn al-Qayyim states in accordance with prophetic tradition, is created four months after conception. The allusion, of course, is to the time when the mother normally begins to feel the movement of the foetus.[64] Later on in the same work the scholar traces Ibn Ḥazm's position to the Peripatetics and remarks that Ibn Sīnā seems to have adopted it in the first hemistich of his *ʿAynīya* or "Ode on the soul":

> Habaṭat ilayka mina 'l-maḥalli 'l-arfaʿī
> ([A . . . dove] came down to you from the supernal abode.)

Ibn al-Qayyim had heard from Ibn Taymīya, however, that Jamāl al-Dīn al-Sharīshī, son of the commentator of al-Ḥarīrī's *Maqāmāt*, Abū 'l-ʿAbbās al-Sharīshī (d. 619/1223), had rejected the attribution of the *ʿAynīya* to Ibn Sīnā, noting (rightly if the poem is taken literally) that it conflicts with the view expressed by the philosopher in his technical works that the rational soul comes into existence with the body.[65]

In chapter eighteen of his extant *Kitāb al-rūḥ* (*Book on the spirit*) Ibn al-Qayyim discusses the question of the prior existence of souls at some length, with Ibn Ḥazm once again as a major adversary.[66] The idea as advanced by Muslim thinkers was usually associated with the *a-last* covenant, the circumstances of which are described in Koran 7:172: "And when thy Lord brought forth from the children of Adam, from their loins, their descendents, and made them bear witness about themselves: Am I not (*a-lastu*) your Lord? They said: Yes; we bear witness. Lest you should say on the day of Resurrection: We were unaware of this. . . ."[67] The Koranic passage, the reader is told, could be interpreted to refer to souls in a prior state of being or, as Ibn al-Qayyim preferred, to the *fiṭra*, man's innate disposition to turn to God. Ibn al-Jawzī, the author notes, was content to relate both interpretations—a remark which incidentally confirms my observation regarding the earlier Ḥanbalite's uncertainty on the issue.[68] On this and other pertinent scriptural texts Ibn al-Qayyim spares no effort in justifying his own exegesis.[69] Appealing to reason, he argues that spirits, had they had an existence prior to this earthly one, would necessarily recall it in some way, it being inconceivable that the soul should have once known its Lord and now no longer remember anything about him. The objection that the soul's attachment to the body renders such memories impossible is valid with respect to the recollection of details but not to the retention of generalities, especially since it is admitted that the soul can remember its first state in this life.[70] If there were any evidence in favor of the doctrine of the prior creation of souls, Ibn al-Qayyim adds, he would be the first to support it. But such is not the case. On the contrary, he concludes, as it is affirmed in a saying of the Prophet, God sends an angel to produce in man his spirit after a certain degree of foetal development. The angel is not said to bring with him a preexisting spirit which he "places" (*yudkhil*) in the body but rather to "breathe" (*yanfukh*) the spirit into it—an expression which the author somehow understands as implying no more and no less than the act of bringing into existence.[71]

There is little to be gained from further enumeration of Ibn al-Qayyim's arguments on this question or from comment on their validity. Of far greater relevance to this study are the motives which lay behind the scholar's refutation. His objections to the idea were not simply another manifestation of the Ḥanbalite tendency to adhere to the letter of Koran and Sunna. It seems certain that he experienced some difficulty in establishing his position on the basis of these sources. Rather, I am inclined to believe, Ibn al-Qayyim's objections expressed a tension between two fundamentally different religious systems, characterized by the *nomos* and *eros* motifs Nygren uses.[72] Both of these systems appealed ultimately to man's egocentric nature, but in very different ways. The Semitic, or *nomos*, tradition, with primarily a tribal or communal orientation, involved a legalism which reflected an attitude of this-worldly practicality. The cornerstone of this system was the moral responsibility of the individual before God and society. Accordingly, if a man conformed to the law, he would be rewarded; if not, he would be punished. When the belief in immortality began to prevail, the afterlife was viewed as a projection of earthly existence. As it was the whole man, body and soul, who obeyed or disobeyed, it was likewise the whole man who must be resurrected to salvation or damnation. This religious outlook eventually became crystallized in the doctrine of bodily resurrection, a teaching the function of which was to symbolize individual moral responsibility.

Hellenistic religious philosophy, the *eros* tradition, understood man's salvation differently. Its primary focus was on the highest good of each individual, and this good was held to be of a purely spiritual nature. The soul—alone able to attain the *summum bonum*—was an emanation of the divine in man—a prisoner in a material world which at best merely pointed the way to escape, as in the Neoplatonic view, and which at worst was totally evil and inimical, as the gnostics taught.[73] With the stress placed on the good of the individual immaterial soul, the community was inevitably neglected. *Eros* ethics, both in antiquity and under Islam, tended to be ascetic or antinomian. The various details of the *eros* scheme are, of course, extremely complicated, but its bare essentials can be summed up with relative accuracy under three characteristic doctrines: that the soul has had some kind of earlier and higher existence; that it differs in nature from the body; and that it is the soul alone which can reattain the lost beatitude. A partial deviation from these doctrines, for example al-Dabbāgh's statement that the soul is created with the body,[74] may generally be attributed to influences or pressures foreign to the basic system.

In reaction to the three theses of *eros* religion the *nomos* tradition was to assert the opposite of each: to maintain that the soul comes into being only *with* or *after* the creation of the body; to affirm its corporeality; and to stress the resurrection of the body. When one recalls that the last of these doctrines had prime importance in the *nomos* system, it is easy to see the logic in this reaction. If the soul has had a prior existence, then it is presumably not a body; and if the soul is not a body, then a purely immaterial resurrection is conceivable. This reaction occurred relatively early in Christian history, as Nygren points out. Its most fully typical representative was the late-second- and early-third-century theologian Tertullian (d. ca. 220). Consistent in his rejection of Christian gnosticism, Tertullian carefully opposed each of its major tenets—denying the idea of preexistence while affirming the corporeality of the soul and the resurrection of the whole man.[75]

Aspects of both the *eros* and the *nomos* traditions are interwoven in Neo-Ḥanbalism, but it is clearly the *nomos* view which predominates. Thus, like Tertullian, Ibn al-Qayyim not only disavows the doctrine of prior existence but also argues at length to prove the soul's corporeality.[76] In addition, he deals expressly with the necessity of the resurrection of the whole man.[77]

This predominance of the community-oriented, legalistic approach was not without its effects on the Ḥanbalite doctrine of love. In Neoplatonism and gnosticism, *eros* stood for the egocentric striving of the soul, the divine element in man, towards its own highest good, whereas the Ḥanbalite system conceived of love primarily, to use Nygren's formula, as "set within the scheme of law."[78] Accordingly, for Ḥanbalism as for traditionist Islam more generally, man's love finds its noblest expression in subordination of the will and in obedience to the divine command, while God's love, albeit exceeding human merit, is most often viewed as a reward for righteousness.[79] Ibn al-Qayyim scrupulously rejects all concepts incompatible with this fundamental outlook. Although he was willing, as I have shown in the preceding chapter, to adopt the vocabulary of the Muslim mystics and even the formal structure of their treatises, he would go no further towards reconciliation than the basic assumptions of the *nomos* tradition allowed. It should be clear that his refutation of the belief that souls exist prior to their bodies, with its implications of lost beatitude, was just one example of his consistent adherence to this tradition. It is very unlikely indeed, despite his claim to the contrary, that he would have been the first to advance the doctrine of an earlier existence of the soul had more cogent evidence in its favor been available.

The same concerns which motivated Ibn al-Qayyim's polemic against Ibn Ḥazm are reflected, as might be anticipated, in his treatment of mysticism. Thus, while not only Ibn al-ʿArabī and al-Qunawī but even al-Ghazālī can allude to some kind of original affinity between God and man when dealing with sacred love,[80] the Ḥanbalite, if he is to make use of anything resembling this concept, must come up with an interpretation of it which avoids the implication that there is something divine or incorporeal in man. He is unable to deny the relationship altogether. This would leave his position open to the "Jahmite" argument that there can be no love between God and man because there is no affinity between the eternal and the contingent. Perhaps to avoid being caught between the two extremes with no alternative but to opt for one or the other, Ibn al-Qayyim did not choose to discuss affinity in his writings on mysticism as extensively as he had dealt with it in connection with profane love. References to the question in his later works are extremely rare. Only from a passing remark, for example, does the reader of his *Madārij* learn that, with Ibn Taymīya, he rejected the philosophical doctrine of *tashabbuh* or imitation.[81]

It appears, in fact, that the Neo-Ḥanbalites did not thoroughly elaborate a standard approach to affinity in the context of sacred love. From a passage in *Ṭarīq al-hijratayn* it is clear that Ibn al-Qayyim could not have accepted in its entirety his teacher's rather awkward and forced explanation of the relationship as God's possession of lovable attributes on the one hand and man's being in accord (*muwāfaqa*) with the object of his prescriptive will on the other. Although he does not take issue with Ibn Taymīya by name, he states categorically that *muwā-*

faqa is an effect of love, not one of its causes.[82] In terminology at least, it should be added, this declaration represents a departure from a position he himself had taken earlier.[83]

Given the absence of an agreed definition of affinity, Ibn al-Qayyim might have preferred simply to omit all discussion of the idea in his mystical works. But in the course of interpreting al-Anṣārī's *Manāzil al-sā'irīn* he found himself obliged to deal with the problem. Al-Anṣārī, describing the station of love (*maḥabba*), calls it "the distinctive mark of the community [of Sufis], the sign at the beginning of the way, and the place where the relation is tied (*maʿqad al-nisba*)."[84] To explain this relation or *nisba* in sacred love Ibn al-Qayyim abandons the idea of similarity which he had used in the profane context and resorts to a concept of absolute complementarity or, it might be more accurate to say, of total dissimilarity. The only affinity existing between man and God, he advances, is the relationship of servanthood (*ʿubūdīya*) to divinity (*ulūhīya*): man (*al-ʿabd*) is servant (*ʿabd*) in every respect, while the Lord is God in every respect. This complementary relationship is inextricably tied up with love, the reader learns. When the bond of love is undone, so likewise is the bond of servitude.[85] (Ibn al-Qayyim's interpretation of affinity in this passage, although it differs in wording and emphasis, in fact parallels that offered by his teacher, since servanthood as understood by the two authors implies *muwāfaqa* or conformity of will, whereas the term "divinity," as opposed to "lordship" [*rubūbīya*], comprehends God's lovable attributes.)[86] Al-Anṣārī uses the term *nisba* again in his chapter on "submersion" (*gharaq*), and Ibn al-Qayyim, in even fewer words than before, repeats his former explanation.[87] In both cases the commentary is characterized by extreme brevity.

Drawing this sacred parallel to the master-slave relationship, a common motif in the literature on profane love,[88] Ibn al-Qayyim manages to arrive at an interpretation of affinity which excludes all trace of the divine from human nature. But he is able to do so only at the sacrifice of his more usual understanding of the concept as implying similarity. Significantly, moreover, although he does not deny that the relationship of complementarity or dissimilarity he proposes may be a cause of religious love, neither does he explicitly state that it is, as he does with similarity in the case of human affection. This apparent oversight, considered together with the brief and generally negative character of his statements and the fact that neither he nor Ibn Taymīya fully worked out a position on the question, suggests that the Neo-Ḥanbalite writers may have perceived the belief in an affinity between God and man, a basic tenet of the *eros* system, to be foreign to their own religious viewpoint. Ibn Taymīya's primary purpose in treating the subject, it will be recalled, was to counter the argument which denied love between God and man on the grounds that the necessary affinity is lacking.[89] It is difficult to escape the conclusion that the only reason Ibn al-Qayyim and his teacher did not reject outright the idea of affinity in the sacred context was to avoid playing into the hands of the theologians who advanced this argument.

Causes in the object: beneficence and beauty

In his *Fawā'id* Ibn al-Qayyim remarks that there are no separate causes with independent influence but only sets of causes.[90] The affinity of natures, therefore, although indisputedly the most potent of the causes of love, of earthly affections at least, normally requires the presence of ancillary factors in order to produce its effect. These secondary causes are at times no more than means of awakening one soul to an awareness of its affinity with another, but they may also act on their own to yield temporary loves. Al-Ghazālī, enumerating his five principles of love, points out, in addition to affinity, four such causes: self-interest or the desire for survival and perfection; beneficence of which the lover is the object; beneficence in general; and beauty, whether external or inward.[91] Taking into account al-Ghazālī's own arguments and restricting the discussion here to causes existing in the object of love, it is possible to reduce these four principles to the two on which most Muslim writers agree—beneficence and beauty, causes which correspond roughly to the loves of utility and pleasure.[92] Self-interest, although it underlies beneficence as a motive for love, has to do with the subject, while beneficence in general, of which the lover need not be a recipient, can be considered as an aspect of beauty of character.[93]

Like his predecessors, Ibn al-Qayyim names beneficence as one cause of love, although in strictly profane contexts he has little to say on love for benefactors as a separate category.[94] The disposition to love one's benefactor was generally considered by Muslim authors to be innate. This opinion was in accordance with a saying attributed to the Companion of the Prophet Ibn Masʿūd: "Hearts have been created with a natural disposition to love those who do good to them."[95] This natural love to benefactors was viewed as the gateway to man's love for

God by theorists committed to the reality of sacred love. For his part, Ibn al-Qayyim makes the point at some length in *Ṭarīq al-hijratayn.* After stating that divine beneficence has no cause outside of God himself and is therefore not earned by man, he asks: "How then should such a one [as God] not be loved, and how should man not blush to direct a particle of his love to an object other than him? Who is more worthy of praise and love than he?" This unmerited kindness of which man is the recipient, the argument continues, is visible to all, and it is the gate through which one must pass to enter into a relationship of love with God. But Ibn al-Qayyim makes it clear in the same context that to love God as benefactor is only a first step. From what he has known of the goodness of his Creator, the lover may infer that which he does not know. "God calls men to himself through this gate," the scholar writes, "so that, when they enter it, they are called through the other—the Gate of Names and Attributes, through which pass only the elite."[96]

Ibn al-Qayyim, then, like many theoreticians of religious love—Muslims, Jews, and Christians—considers love for God for his names and attributes or, as he says elsewhere, love for God as perfect and beautiful[97] a higher stage than love in response to his kindness.[98] It has been pointed out earlier in this connection how Ibn Taymīya at times voiced disapproval of loving God for his beneficence on the grounds that a love so motivated constitutes a distraction from the love owed to God as one qualified with the attributes of perfection.[99] Ibn al-Qayyim, however dependent upon his teacher in matters of dogma, had perhaps a more consistently realistic understanding of human nature. He recognized that love from beneficence alone is inherently inadequate since it comes to an end when the benefactor ceases to bestow his favor,[100] but he was also aware that as an emotion springing from man's essential nature it could not be separated from the total complex of human love to God. Only the vilest of hearts can resist love, he asserts, when the two causes of beneficence and perfection (or beauty) are united.[101] To the Sufis who disdained love and service to God for the sake of a reward he replies that it is best to long both for God himself and for his reward. It is humanly impossible to desire God and not to desire something from him.[102]

In an interesting corollary to this reasoning, Ibn al-Qayyim attempts, not too successfully, to present love for God as benefactor as an aspect of love for him as beautiful and perfect. Remarking in the *Fawā'id* that God's beauty is fourfold, comprehending his essence (*dhāt*), attributes, names, and acts, the scholar asserts that man must proceed step by step from an appreciation of the divine acts, or beneficence—the lowest of the stages of God's beauty, to love of the divine names and attributes and finally to love of God's essence. He concludes from this that God may rightly be loved for his kindness as well as for his essence, presumably on the grounds that the kinds of love involved in the two cases are alike in that they are both directed towards aspects of the divine beauty.[103] It hardly need be pointed out that Ibn al-Qayyim is confusing here self-interested love to one's own benefactor with love to benefactors in general for the beauty of their character. Had he recalled al-Ghazālī's distinction between these two kinds of love, he would have been obliged to give greater precision to his argument or to abandon it.[104]

What emerges from these details is that in the doctrine of Ibn al-Qayyim, although the scholar did not follow Ibn Taymīya in his near rejection of God's kindness as a cause of sacred love, beneficence is none the less subordinated to beauty. As we have seen, it is the love of beauty which sums up all the other aspects of man's love to God. In view of the importance Ibn al-Qayyim assigned to beauty, one might expect to find considerable analytical treatment of the concept in his works. But it seems that he never studied the subject carefully or with any degree of sophistication. Unlike many other writers on love, he apparently failed to take full advantage of the stock of classical notions about beauty which circulated in the Muslim intellectual environment. Among his predecessors, Abū Ḥāmid al-Ghazālī had improved on a suggestion discussed inconclusively by Socrates in *Hippias major*, carefully defining the beauty of any thing as the presence in it of "the perfection appropriate and possible to it." (Socrates does not specify that the necessary perfection must be possible as well as appropriate.)[105] Ibn al-Qayyim, likewise familiar with ideas inherited from the ancients, mentions specifically the definition of beauty as symmetry of constitution (*tanāsub al-khilqa wa-ʿtidāluhā wa-stiwāʾuhā*). Plotinus had cited this definition in fuller form as "the symmetry of parts towards each other and towards a whole . . ." and dismissed it on the grounds that it applies only to compounds.[106] The Neo-Ḥanbalite scholar rejects it because, as he observes with gross pragmatism, there are many things of symmetrical constitution which are not, for that, beautiful. In his view, the true nature of beauty, like that of love, escapes definition. It can be known only through description.[107] Accordingly, most of the chapter devoted to the subject in his *Rawḍa* consists simply of the enumeration of various well-known examples of beauty, including Joseph, the prophet Muḥammad, and the houris of Paradise, complemented by a few remarks on what qualities are considered beautiful in women.[108]

Despite Ibn al-Qayyim's unwillingness to deal with beauty in a discursive fashion, certain elements of his conception of the quality can be extracted from his works. He agrees with other Muslim writers in considering beauty to be something which men are naturally inclined to admire. It is for this reason, he explains, that God endowed all of his prophets with a comely appearance.[109] There is an inner as well as an outward beauty, according to Ibn al-Qayyim, and it is primarily the inner beauty—consisting of such attributes as knowledge, reason, generosity, temperance, and courage, as well as gratitude for divine benevolence—which God is said to love in men. As the tradition of the Prophet has it: "God is beautiful and loves beauty." Recognizing that this particular *ḥadīth* came in response to a question about beautiful clothing, Ibn al-Qayyim concludes that God also loves external beauty.[110] Inner beauty, he teaches in accordance with other *ḥadīth*s and the prevalent physiognomy of the age, embellishes one's external appearance. In proportion to his faith a certain beauty will appear in the face of the believer, however unattractive his natural features may be. True physical beauty, a gift with which only some are favored, likewise increases or wanes according as it is exploited for the sake of obedience or sin.[111]

Beyond this Ibn al-Qayyim had little to say on the nature of beauty, but he did not fail to reject theories relating to the concept which were incompatible with his fundamental point of view. The Platonic doctrine that men may progress through a hierarchy of stages to the apprehension of the ultimate beauty has been expressed variously by its Muslim proponents. One method of categorizing the different stages involved, found, for example, in the *Mashāriq anwār al-qulūb* of al-Dabbāgh, uses the terms "absolute beauty" (*jamāl muṭlaq*)—the necessarily existent beauty of God which is the source of all others—and "determinate beauty" (*jamāl muqayyad*). Determinate beauty is subdivided into universal and particular, and each of these in turn may be apparent (*ẓāhir*) or inward (*bāṭin*). According to al-Dabbāgh the lover proceeds from the apparent beauty to the inward and then from the particular to the universal. At this point, having apprehended the highest stage of determinate beauty, he readies himself to receive the light emanating from the absolute beauty.[112] Ibn al-Qayyim was not unfamiliar with this terminology, but he chose to apply it in a way of his own. In two of his earlier works he states that there are lovers (*'ushshāq*) of absolute beauty, who find the beauty they seek in every comely object, and lovers of determinate beauty, who perceive it only in a specific object. Those in the first group do not feel sexual desire (*ṭama'*) for their beloveds, while those in the second vary in this respect. In his comments on this distinction Ibn al-Qayyim casually brushes aside centuries of thought in the *eros* tradition in favor of a commonsense view of human nature. He inverts the Platonic ladder to argue that the most rational of lovers is the one who pursues determinate beauty and experiences carnal desire for his beloved, while even the lover of determinate beauty without desire is to be preferred to the lover of absolute beauty.[113] The particular case of love for a beautiful person as a locus of the manifestation of God he equates elsewhere with idolatry.[114] In another context, he summarily dismisses the related but more comprehensive doctrine that all existence is beautiful because it proceeds from God. The antinomian implications of this teaching he recognized as clearly irreconcilable with his own system.[115]

Ibn al-Qayyim does not go so far as to reject altogether the idea that a certain knowledge of the divine beauty may be inferred from the observation of its earthly counterpart. He holds every perfection in existence to be a sign or trace of God's own perfection.[116] But it is primarily, in his opinion, the revealed statements on the divine attributes found in the Koran or handed down in the prophetic tradition which enable men to know something of God's beauty. He argues further, beauty being the fundamental cause of religious love, that an individual's love for God is proportional to the knowledge which he acquires concerning the divine attributes. Thus the prophets, and particularly the two "friends of God" (*al-khalīlān*), Abraham and Muḥammad, are to be ranked among those who loved him best.[117] Conversely, those theologians who deny God's attributes cannot possibly love him.[118]

From the preceding remarks it should be clear that Ibn al-Qayyim's treatment of beneficence and beauty, however incomplete, conforms to his basic assumptions. In opposition to an opinion held by many Sufis and the similar view advanced on occasion by Ibn Taymīya, he considered love in response to God's beneficence to be legitimate. As elsewhere, he was following a pragmatic approach reflecting his realist's assessment of egocentric human nature. But it was necessary to establish a higher motive than mere beneficence for man's love to God. The doctrine of affinity, it has been seen, the scholar seems to have deliberately neglected in the sacred context. Aware of its implications, he offered beauty in its stead as the chief cause of love to God. Perhaps it was to assert the sufficiency of beauty as a cause that he stressed on a number of occasions the permanence of the love which it produces. Affinity, it will be recalled, was believed to constitute the sole grounds for permanence in earthly affections. Since the beauty of the divine attributes is limitless, Ibn al-Qayyim argued, there can be no end, even in Paradise, to man's longing to perceive it in all its aspects.[119] But the Platonic ladder is turned upside down. Beauty must be approached in a typically *nomos* fashion: the most complete knowledge of the divine beauty is to be obtained from Koran and Sunna. If, however, scripture and tradition are the prime sources of this knowledge, then it may be affirmed that the love of the mystics, in its highest stages a product of subjective experience, is imperfect. Likewise, it is possible to argue that the theologians who denied man's love to God did so because, in rejecting the revealed attributes, they had shut themselves off from knowledge of the beauty which is the cause of that love.

8. Glances, Gazing, and the Vision

IN A BRIEF passage in *Rawḍat al-muḥibbīn* Ibn al-Qayyim lists four causes of profane love occurring in the subject: glancing or gazing at the object (*naẓar*); finding it beautiful, or admiration (*istiḥsān*); contemplation of the object seen (*al-fikr fī 'l-manẓūr*); and desire to possess it (*ṭamaʿ*).[1] The first of these causes, the lover's gaze, is generally considered an act of the eye, but it may also be an act of the heart in response to the mere description of a beautiful person.[2] Accompanying the gaze there must be admiration, for unless the object is deemed beautiful or good no love can result. Equally necessary to the realization of love is the subject's contemplation of the object seen. This requires a heart unpreoccupied with more important things, otherwise no attachment will develop. For this reason, Ibn al-Qayyim observes, *ʿishq*-love is called the act or movement (*ḥaraka*) of an empty heart. Although these remarks from the *Rawḍa* apply only to profane love, the author also held the absence of distractions to be an essential precondition of sacred love. Writing in another context of the love man owes to God, he compares the preoccupied soul to a drunkard who has lost everything in a fire and remains unaware of the fact.[3] The necessity of the fourth cause, the desire to possess the beloved—physical lust, Ibn al-Qayyim recognizes as a disputed matter. His solution to the problem, pointed out above, is that this desire does not occur in lovers of "absolute" beauty and is not necessarily present in lovers of "determinate" beauty. But the strongest love in his opinion is that which is accompanied by a desire for physical union.[4]

There are other problems discussed by Ibn al-Qayyim which relate to the causes of love in the subject.[5] One of these deserves special mention before we turn to the topic of the amorous regard. It is the old question whether love is voluntary (*ikhtiyārī*) or involuntary (*iḍṭirārī*).[6] In one chapter of the *Rawḍa* the author poses this question and lists a number of opposing arguments. Love is said to be involuntary, since it is a kind of torture—which no one would choose of his own free will. By extension, in view of the fact that man has no control over love, to blame a lover is said to be like blaming a sick man for his illness. But other considerations suggest that love is voluntary. God has commanded men to shun passion, the reasoning runs. If love were not the result of a choice, the command would be unjust; for it is impossible to avoid something over which one has no control. Furthermore, God has reproved those entangled in illicit affections, and man is blamed or commended only on the basis of what he freely wills or chooses. Finally, God would not have threatened men with punishment for something against which they are impotent.[7] (The arguments for predetermined love, interestingly, are of a profane, light character, while those which claim that love is voluntary have a religious ring.) The correct view, according to Ibn al-Qayyim, is that the first stages of love—glances, exposing oneself to temptation, and contemplating the beloved—are voluntary actions, whereas the involvement which follows is involuntary and inescapable. Love is analogous to drunkenness: to drink is a voluntary action; to get drunk is the unavoidable consequence.[8] Excessive love (*ʿishq*) and drunkenness alike, though involuntary, are punishable, because the forbidden acts which lead to them are the result of a free choice. A corollary is that love, when it proceeds from a cause which has not been prohibited, such as an accidental glance, is not punishable, even if its object is illicit. In this case man is held responsible for the way he deals with his love, not for the emotion itself.[9]

There is a near parallel to this argument in the sphere of sacred love, where a distinction is made between longing for God which is involuntary and that which is voluntary and consequently more meritorious. According to Ibn al-Qayyim's view, man has an essential and uncaused need (*faqr*) for God, mirroring God's essential and uncaused self-sufficiency (*ghinā*). But there are two degrees of need for God. One comprises the universal need of all created beings for him as Lord and Creator (*faqr ilā rubūbīyatihi*) and is involuntary. The other is a need which springs from a man's knowledge of God and of himself—the need for God as sole object of worship (*faqr ilā ulūhīyatihi*). This second need, the prime factor in salvation, is voluntary.[10]

Glancing and gazing

Of all the causes of love occurring in the subject it was with the initial cause, the glance or gaze (*naẓar*), that Ibn al-Qayyim was most concerned.[11] Paralleling almost exactly the stress of Ibn al-Jawzī in *Dhamm al-hawā*, he devoted approximately one-tenth of his *Rawḍat al-muḥibbīn* to the subject. His treatment, in the *Rawḍa* and his other works as well, touches on a variety of topics. Generally these are related to one of three major issues, each of which has come up in earlier chapters of this study—the effect of the glance on sexual morality, Sufi *naẓar*, including the practice of gazing at beautiful youths, and the theological controversy over the beatific vision. If one considers the importance of these issues, in the context of which the amorous regard may be treated variously as the primary cause of love, one of its symptoms, or even its fruition (the case in chaste human love and man's love to God), the prominence of the subject in the works of Ibn al-Qayyim, and in the Muslim literature on love more generally, is easily understood. Associated with the debate on *naẓar* were the controversy over the propriety of listening to amatory verse and song, which like the glance may arouse love, and the issue of the permissibility of embraces, kisses, and other such acts between lovers to whom sexual union is forbidden.

In the circles which were destined to set the tone of Muslim orthodoxy it had been agreed at a fairly early date that the amorous glance and the loose practices associated with it were to be proscribed. The Muʿtazilites reacted,[12] and what was perhaps the most eloquent statement of their position has been preserved. In his *Qiyān*, al-Jāḥiẓ addresses himself to the opinion that the glance is forbidden, calling it the view of the "*ḥashwīya*" (roughly: anthropomorphists), among whom he almost certainly numbered the followers of Aḥmad b. Ḥanbal.[13] Citing numerous examples to confirm his own opinion, he argues that conversing with women and looking at them were respectable practices both in the Days of Ignorance and under Islam.[14] He likewise defends song and verse on the grounds that these two arts, like any form of speech, are to be judged solely by their content. They may indeed distract from worship as his opponents claimed, but many other pleasures have the same effect. Moreover, few men are able to spend their entire lives in devotions.[15] Al-Jāḥiẓ extends his argument to cover fondling and kissing as well. He maintains that in Koran 53:32, "Those who avoid the great sins and indecencies, except trivial acts (*lamam*)," God excluded from the category of offenses those actions covered by the term *lamam*, which some of the Companions of the Prophet interpreted to include kissing and touching or even intercourse without penetration of the vagina.[16]

Ibn Dāwūd and Ibn Ḥazm, the chosen antagonists of Ibn al-Qayyim on the issue of *naẓar*, are less consistent than al-Jāḥiẓ in recommending the practice. Ibn Dāwūd, for example, does not fail to point out in his *Kitāb al-zahra* that the glance, being the cause of love, becomes increasingly harmful once the affection has set in.[17] But his actions conveyed a different message to posterity. It was the stories of his relationship with Muḥammad b. Jāmiʿ, and particularly the anecdote which has him declare in his dying words that the glance is licit, which formed later writers' impressions of his teaching.[18] Ibn Hazm adopts in *Ṭawq al-ḥamāma* an attitude of sympathy towards love and the inclination of human nature to appreciate beauty, holding these feelings to be neither commanded nor forbidden.[19] None the less, he demonstrates considerable ambivalence towards the glance. In the earlier part of the *Ṭawq* he maintains that the eye has a "praiseworthy" (*maḥmūd*) role in conversations between lovers,[20] and he relates an argument he once had in which he advanced that it was wrong to deny one's soul the joy of meeting the beloved—a situation which presumably implies seeing him.[21] Towards the end of his book, however, Ibn Ḥazm recalls the rule that the first glance is permitted but the second forbidden and he describes the wicked man as one who allows his gaze to wander freely over beautiful faces. In the same context he also mentions the traditional injunction against a Muslim's listening to the singing of a woman who is not lawful for him (*ajnabīya*).[22] The emergence of such discrepancies in the final chapters of works on controversial topics is of course not unusual, since the authors often felt themselves obliged to conclude by appeasing readers whom they might have offended.[23] Given this fact, it would seem simple enough to select the statements expressed in the earlier portions of the *Ṭawq* as the more representative of Ibn Ḥazm's actual views. Certainly this is how Ibn al-Qayyim interpreted the book.[24] But for the sake of accuracy it should be remarked that this approach may not be fully justified, since in another of his works the Ẓāhirite again discredits *naẓar*, defining chastity as averting the glance and all organs of the body from that which is forbidden.[25]

In his own treatment of *naẓar* Ibn al-Qayyim stresses essentially the same evils pointed out earlier by Ibn al-Jawzī, but his discussion is somewhat broader in scope and his analysis typically more systematic.

In the strictly profane context, the fundamental arguments he cites in support of the practice can be conveniently grouped into four major categories, each of which is touched on but not always elaborated by his predecessor: 1) proofs based on Koran, Sunna, or opinions ascribed to men of unimpeachable authority; 2) arguments to the effect that such minor failings as glances and kisses should be tolerated as lesser evils than their likely alternative—the death of a Muslim stricken with love; 3) the view that a second glance may actually provide a cure for love conceived at first sight; and 4) the argument that chaste love is praiseworthy and the glance accordingly permissible within the limits of this ennobling relationship. At the risk of doing some violence to Ibn al-Qayyim's own organization, his refutation of each of these arguments will be discussed in the order given here before going on to the question of *naẓar* in the mystical and theological contexts.

1. Among the scriptural texts adduced in support of *naẓar* Ibn al-Qayyim singles out for comment Koran 7:185, "Do they not consider (*yanẓurū fī*) the kingdom of the heavens and the earth and what things Allāh has created, . . . ?"[26] His opponents held that the verse alluded to the visual contemplation of the whole of God's creation and that there could be no reason for excepting comely faces, these being among the most beautiful of his works.[27] This exegesis, Ibn al-Qayyim replies, resembles their justification of the "Satanic concert" (singing and, particularly, the spiritual concert of the Sufis) on the basis of Koran 39:17–18, "So give good news to My servants, Who listen to the Word [*al-qawl* = 'what is said'], then follow the best of it."[28] Contrary to their claims, he argues, what the two passages in question command is listening to the words of the Koranic revelation and gazing on those wonders of creation which increase faith and from which may be deduced the truth of what God has revealed through his prophets concerning his attributes and acts. The gaze which produces an attachment to forbidden forms can by no means be intended. It is prohibited elsewhere in the Koran, his argument concludes, and this despite the fact that the more recent danger of pederasty was not present among the Arabs at the time of the Prophet.[29]

Ibn al-Qayyim also discusses three well-known *ḥadīth*s cited by the advocates of *naẓar*: "Gazing at a comely face is an act of worship"; "Seek good from those with beautiful faces"; and the Prophet's recommendation to one of his contemporaries that he take a look at the woman he was thinking of marrying. The first two sayings were held to counsel the contemplation of beautiful faces in general, while the last was taken to show simply that *naẓar* is permissible, on the assumption that the Prophet would not otherwise have advised it.[30] Ibn al-Qayyim associates the first *ḥadīth* with mysticism and suggests that it must have been fabricated by a *zindīq* or some debauched lover. He tells the reader that his teacher Ibn Taymīya, when asked about the tradition, had declared it to be contrary to consensus and lacking even a weak (*ḍaʿīf*) *isnād*. The one who relates it, the jurist had stipulated, incurs the death penalty if he does not repent. The second *ḥadīth* is similarly dismissed as a fabrication, although Ibn al-Qayyim recognizes that it has a more convincing *isnād*. Sensing the need for caution in this case, the scholar remarks that the saying, even if it were authentic, could not be interpreted as sanctioning the pursuit of physical union (in his view the end actually desired by those who practice *naẓar*, whether or not they permit themselves to obtain it). What it teaches is rather that generosity and favors are to be sought from persons with beautiful faces. For Ibn al-Qayyim, this tradition is no more than a statement of the current physiognomic doctrine which held beauty of countenance to be an indication of nobility of character.[31] The third *ḥadīth*—interpreted as referring strictly to a man's viewing his prospective bride in order to forestall regrets which might occur after the conclusion of the marriage—is acceptable to the Neo-Ḥanbalite scholar. In such cases, where the advantages clearly outweigh the disadvantages, he recognized the legitimacy of the glance as Ibn al-Jawzī did earlier.[32] In like manner he declares in another context that gazing at a beautiful wife can be beneficial to a life of piety.[33]

The opinions from later authorities cited in favor of *naẓar* consist almost entirely of verse *responsa* ascribed to the founders of legal schools or to other figures held to be beyond reproach. Examples of such pieces are sufficiently numerous to suggest the existence of an autonomous poetic genre, the point of which was to amaze the reader by crediting the imams with an unexpected degree of tenderness towards lovers.[34] These metrical *fatwā*s give legal sanction variously to the amorous regard, embracing, and kissing. In the selections I have seen, a greater number are attributed to al-Shāfiʿī, known to have been a poet, than to any other imam; but none of the founders of the four principal schools of jurisprudence is overlooked.[35] Two lines purporting to quote a question addressed to Aḥmad b. Ḥanbal and the reply he gave are typical of the pieces:

Sa'altu imāma 'l-nāsi, najla 'bni Ḥanbalī,
ʿani 'l-ḍammi wa-l-taqbīli, hal fī-hi min bāsī?
Fa-qāla: idhā jalla 'l-ʿazā'u, fa-wājibun,
li-annaka qad aḥyayta ʿabdan mina 'l-nāsī.

(I asked the imam of men, the issue of the son of Ḥanbal,
about embracing and kissing, is there any wrong in them?
He said: if consolation is impossible, then they are obligatory,
for you will have given life to a man among men.)[36]

(The name of the jurist Ibn Ḥanbal in fuller form was Aḥmad b. Muḥammad b. Ḥanbal, which explains the expression "the issue (*najl*) of the son of Ḥanbal" in the first line.) Almost all of these *responsa* which Ibn al-Qayyim cites he rejects as slanderous falsifications. The few he suspects may be authentic he interprets to apply only to acts he considers licit.[37]

2. A similar but rather long *fatwā* in prose was ascribed to the Shaykh al-Islām Ibn Taymīya himself, most likely with the intention of needling his followers. Ibn al-Qayyim repudiates both the attribution and the substance of the *fatwā* and in the course of his argument has the occasion to discuss the view that glances and kisses constitute a lesser evil than the death of the lover. The text of the *fatwā*, quoted at some length in *Rawḍat al-muḥibbīn*, has Ibn Taymīya divide love into three stages—the last likened to madness. Lovers in the first stage, it states, should be satisfied with glances at the beloved, while those in the second may reveal their love to him. Among lovers having reached the final stage, some, who keep their secret, are said to perish as martyrs in accordance with the teaching of the *ḥadīth "Man ʿashiqa . . ."* on chastity. The rest, if in fear of death, are granted the right to kiss the beloved. (An opinion of certain unidentified authorities to the effect that the beloved is obliged to comply is also given in this connection.) Both the glance and the kiss are held to be justifiable on the grounds that they are preferable to the expiration of the lover. But fornication, in conformity with the rules of chaste love, is branded as inexcusable and said to be punishable by death.[38]

After reproducing the *fatwā* attributed to Ibn Taymīya, Ibn al-Qayyim takes note of a supplementary proof advanced by the partisans of *naẓar*. Certain jurists, they pointed out, had gone so far as to allow men to masturbate if they felt they were in danger of fornicating or to lie with their wives by day during fasts if they feared that their desire might otherwise cause damage to their reproductive organs.[39] Some had also allowed women to have recourse to artificial means of achieving satisfaction if they believed this necessary to avoid fornication. With such acts as these or indeed the death of the lover as alternatives, they asked, what evil is there in seeking cure through kissing and gazing.[40]

Beginning his rebuttal, Ibn al-Qayyim considers first the authenticity of the *fatwā* cited by his opponents. Remarking that it contradicts Ibn Taymīya's other writings and opinions on the same subject, he adds that he had seen the text long before copied in the hand of a man accused of being a liar.[41] He accepts, however, the ethical principle on which the argument of the *fatwā* is based, that a lesser evil may be resorted to for the sake of avoiding a greater one. But Ibn al-Qayyim stresses that gazing and kissing, contrary to the claims of the advocates of *naẓar*, lead to greater evils than does refraining from them. In support of his assertion he first points out the spiritual harm caused by these practices and then disputes the view that they offer the lover any real relief from his sufferings. Indulging in such acts, the argument runs, leads to the death of the heart and the corruption of faith, whereas abstinence, which is the preferred path, produces only emaciation or, at worst, a meritorious physical death. Moreover, the practices of gazing and kissing, far from preventing emaciation and death, actually increase the *ʿishq*-love which brings on these results. Reiterating this second point, the scholar dismisses the suggestion that the case at hand is analogous to the Muslim's obligation to eat pork or meat improperly slaughtered when necessary to avoid starvation. Desires, he reasons, are not to be compared to needs. Food is essential to life, but men can survive without engaging in sexual intercourse. Gazing, embracing, and kissing, therefore, are rather to be compared to certain fruits which might be harmful to a person suffering from a fever. No physician could recommend them to his patient.[42]

There remains the argument that other practices more heinous than these are tolerated in certain compelling circumstances. Ibn al-Qayyim does not address himself to this argument directly, choosing instead to discuss the permissibility of the seemingly graver sins. His reasoning can be read between the lines. Whereas he had affirmed that gazing, embracing, and kissing are responses to desires rather than to needs, his treatment of these other practices shows that he viewed them as conceivable expedients for averting real physical dangers. The man who fears that his daytime abstinence from sexual relations during Ramaḍān is about to cause his testicles to burst is allowed the following remedies in order of preference. If his seed will not release itself without coition, he may engage in a licit sexual union (with a wife or slave-girl), provided that he make up the day as he would if he were obliged by illness to eat food during the fast. If the only woman available is not allowable (*ajnabīya*) to him, he may in this case resort to onanism. Should this not result in an emission, then, according to a disputed opinion, he may make use of the hand of the *ajnabīya* to achieve his purpose (presumably without looking at her!). Hesitant to commit himself, Ibn al-Qayyim remarks that this last procedure, if indeed it is permissible, is analogous to a female physician's touching whatever parts of a man's body may be necessary to treat him or, again, to a male physician's doing the same with a woman.[43]

3. The third key argument for *naẓar*, a limited but fairly convincing application of the second, was probably utilized by its advocates as a means of inveigling the orthodox into taking a first step towards their position. They reasoned that in cases of love at first sight a second glance is permissible, since it provides the lover with an opportunity to detect the shortcomings of his beloved and thus to correct the initial impression which brought on his affection. Ibn al-Jawzī had dealt with this argument in *Dhamm al-hawā*. Ibn al-Qayyim, in his own reply, is content to relate an expanded version of one of the earlier Ḥanbalite's *fatwā*s cited in that work. The essential points of the rebuttal are familiar. The legitimacy of taking another look at the beloved is rejected on the grounds that the second glance is specifically prohibited by prophetic tradition—only the first, if accidental, being allowed—and that it is more likely to intensify than to diminish the lover's passion. Although it is admitted in Ibn al-Jawzī's *fatwā* that love at first sight may conceivably be cured by a second glance, such a cure itself is held to be improper. Its realization depends not on the lover's conforming to the divine command but simply on the fact that the beloved fails to suit his tastes.[44]

4. The last argument contended that *naẓar* was allowable in the context of a strictly chaste relationship. It was founded on the theses that love in itself is a natural emotion, neither praiseworthy nor blameful, and that chaste love is not only permissible but laudable, as taught by the *ḥadīth* "He who loves passionately, conceals it, is chaste, and dies is a martyr."[45] In this conception of love, it would seem, the risk of sin was held to be minimal in view of the excellence of the reward promised to the one who remained chaste. The practice of *naẓar* should lead to no greater harm than the wasting away and eventual demise of the lover—the very martyrdom to which he aspired. Ibn al-Qayyim interprets things differently. The partisans of this opinion, among whom he numbers Ibn Dāwūd and Ibn Ḥazm, advocated chastity because they believed that sexual union corrupts passionate love (*ʿishq*). It was primarily for this reason, in his judgment, whether or not they had religious motives as well, that they jealously guarded their affection from carnality.[46] In effect, he explains, they were following the pre-Islamic custom, likewise based on the belief that consummation

destroys love, which limited amorous relationships to conversations, glances, embraces, and kisses. This custom, according to some, had resulted in the lover's being allowed complete enjoyment of the upper half of a woman's body, while the part below the navel was reserved to her husband.[47] To illustrate the point of view of the early Arabs Ibn al-Qayyim cites a little conversation related by the philologist al-Aṣmaʿī (d. 213/828 or shortly thereafter). Exploiting a common motif, the dialogue aptly portrays the attitude in question and indicates its persistence under Islam as a characteristic distinguishing Bedouin from urban love.

> I [al-Aṣmaʿī] said to a Bedouin woman: "What do you consider love to be among you?" "Hugging, embracing, winks, and conversation," she replied. Then she asked: "How is it among you, city-dweller?" "He sits amidst her four limbs (*shuʿabihā*) and presses her to the limit," I answered. "Nephew," she cried, "this is no lover (*ʿāshiq*), but a man after a child!"[48]

There is little reason to doubt that Ibn al-Qayyim was right in ascribing to Ibn Dāwūd the opinion that intercourse puts an end to love. The Ẓāhirite, despite his perhaps unmindful repetition of the commonly held view that love from similarity ceases only with death, seems to say in the course of commenting the *ḥadīth "Man ʿashiqa . . ."* that the rule of chastity, even if it were not prescribed by divine law and public opinion, would still be an obligation on each of the two lovers for the sake of the preservation of their mutual affection.[49] In the same vein he also claims that a coquettish abandonment by the beloved yields more pleasure than repeated physical union.[50] Ibn Ḥazm, on the other hand, does not entirely accept his predecessor's position. Indeed, he goes so far as to reject even the view that union when prolonged and repeated is fatal to love. Only among the inconstant could he accept this as being the case. His own experience had taught him that the more often one has commerce with the beloved, the greater one's desire.[51] Nevertheless, he agrees with Ibn Dāwūd, on the second point, stating in virtually the same words that an abandonment out of coquetry can be more pleasant than a great deal of union and that the same is true of abandonment caused by the presence of a spy (*raqīb*).[52] Perhaps it was on the basis of remarks such as this, considered in conjunction with the general tenor of the stories related in the *Ṭawq*, that Ibn al-Qayyim equated Ibn Ḥazm's views on intercourse, wrongly it would seem, with those of Ibn Dāwūd and the early Bedouins.[53]

The passage in which Ibn al-Qayyim gives his explanation of the

Ẓāhirite position is not immediately concerned with the pleasures of the eye, but its bearing on the subject may easily be inferred. According to the author's understanding of the courtly ideal which he ascribed to Ibn Dāwūd and Ibn Ḥazm, the visual contemplation of the beloved, together with the associated practices of intimate conversation, embracing, and kissing, was justified as the highest degree of fulfillment compatible with the survival of love. As thus not only the cause but also the fruition of chaste relationships, the amorous regard was to him the hallmark of Arab Courtesy. To discredit the practice, it was necessary to undermine the conception of love which legitimized it. Accordingly, both the social customs which he believed fostered the idea of chaste love and the *ḥadīth* cited in support of it are dealt with by the Ḥanbalite scholar in his rebuttal. The ancient practices of innocent gazing and kissing he quickly rejects as contrary to divine law and good sense. They were declared illicit with the coming of the divine law, which restricted both the upper and lower halves of a woman to her husband alone; but they are also abhorrent to reason, since they constitute temptations to yet graver sins towards which men are already naturally inclined.[54]

Ibn al-Qayyim's precise attitude towards the tradition "*Man ʿashiqa . . .* ," which confers the rank of martyr on the chaste lover who dies concealing his passion, is somewhat difficult to define. Nevertheless, he explicitly denies that the saying can be understood as endorsing a courtly conception of love. Treatments of this tradition, ranging in emphasis from seemingly unmitigated repudiation to qualified approval, are found in several of his earlier works. The attribution of the saying to the Prophet he flatly dismisses, pointing out that a number of its narrators are unreliable, particularly the traditionist Suwayd b. Saʿīd on whom most of the *isnād*s converge.[55] In one work he observes that the word *ʿishq* does not occur in any authentic *ḥadīth*.[56] But the tradition "*Man ʿashiqa . . .*" is not simply foreign to the linguistic usage of the Prophet, it also conflicts with his teaching. The Prophet taught that only six classes of men are to be considered martyrs, and the lover is not among them.[57]. Following up this point in *al-Ṭibb al-nabawī*, Ibn al-Qayyim seems to reject the substance of the *ḥadīth* entirely. The reader is asked how martyrdom, being a most exalted rank, can be attained through *ʿishq*, which, since the passionate lover worships his beloved, is to be equated with idolatry in love.[58]

Elsewhere the scholar is more forbearing. In *Rawḍat al-muḥibbīn* he allows that the most that can be said for the tradition is that it comes from Ibn ʿAbbās, while in *al-Dāʾ wa-l-dawāʾ* he unhesitatingly ascribes it to this Companion, noting that it resembles certain of his other sayings.[59] But Ibn al-Qayyim will not admit that Ibn ʿAbbās in any way intended to declare *ʿishq* permissible or its perpetuation a meritorious aim. The one who dies of love, having endured his passion in chastity and concealment, is rewarded only if it was for the sake of God and in order to please him that he restrained himself. Such a lover, while not strictly speaking to be numbered among the martyrs, is certainly among those referred to in Koran 79:40–41, "And as for those who fear the time when they will stand before their Lord and restrain their souls from low desires, Paradise will be their retreat."[60]

As is generally the case in orthodox Muslim discussions of moral issues, it is the intention rather than the act which is crucial here. In a passage of the *Rawḍa* Ibn al-Qayyim recognizes a number of reasons why a lover may choose to remain chaste. Only three of these, in the context of his thought, can be taken as relevant to chastity for the sake of pleasing God. Ranked by the author in descending order of preference, the acceptable motives are reverence for God, desire for the houris of Paradise (no man being allowed both the pleasures of forbidden women or boys in this world and the delights of the houris in the next), and fear of divine retribution. None of these three motives, in the Ḥanbalite scheme, can be operative in those who in disobedience to God's will allow themselves the illicit pleasure of gazing at the beloved. Some or all of the remaining inducements to chastity, however, may well be involved in their case—the risk of shame, chaste conduct on the part of the beloved, shyness, fear for one's reputation, the wish to preserve one's standing in the eyes of the beloved as well as people in general, and, most especially, the desire to secure the love-relationship against the putatively ruinous effects of carnal union.[61] These are clearly motives to which no religious value can be attached, and one whose chastity springs from such considerations, in the view of Ibn al-Qayyim, has no right to expect a recompense from God.

The Ḥanbalite scholar's acceptance of the tradition "*Man ʿashiqa . . .*" in the particular sense described above is by no means to be understood as a concession to his opponents. It is quite inconceivable that he should have gone so far as to deny the rewards of Paradise to one who dies while waging what the Muslims called "the greater holy war"—the struggle against the temptations of the soul. But the fundamental position underlying his treatment of the *ḥadīth* remains the same throughout, whether or not fully expressed: that which bestows merit is not *ʿishq* itself but the effort to overcome it. The desire to perpetuate this idolatrous love, entailing recourse to the forbidden practice of gazing as a substitute for sexual relations, corrupts the intention of the man who would strive against his soul and thus robs him of his reward.

Ibn al-Qayyim's treatment of what he considered the basic hypothesis of courtly theory, the opinion that union destroys love, presents something of a problem. The argument in favor of this assumption, superficially at least, was fairly cogent, proceeding from the premise that coition is the end sought by love to the conclusion that love naturally ceases with the attainment of this end.[62] The scholar's assessment of this argument, although never entirely positive, appears to vary considerably according to the context in which he deals with it. In the passage of the *Rawḍa* where he ascribes the opinion that love ends with union to Ibn Dāwūd and Ibn Ḥazm his purpose is simply to demonstrate the moral inadequacy of the motive which inspired Ẓāhirite chastity. There is thus little to be gained from an unqualified denial of the validity of the view. Hence in this context, with an eye to the ethical implications of his statements, the author admits that illicit intercourse destroys love, adding that the fact is confirmed by observation; but he scorns the suggestion that the case is the same with licit union, which, he holds, produces an increased longing. Sexual appetite does indeed wane for a time after legitimate intercourse, but it soon returns. In a permissible relationship it is only overindulgence which, as with any desire, turns love into antipathy.[63]

The total subordination of this argument to considerations of religious morality is obvious. Prohibited union destroys love; licit union strengthens it—unless abused, in which case it too destroys love. Only a few pages earlier in the *Rawḍa*, writing in a more strictly theoretical vein, Ibn al-Qayyim advances a rather different opinion. In this life, only loves which do not proceed from an essential affinity cease with the attainment of the particular goal they seek.[64] It is otherwise with love directed towards an object conforming to the fundamental nature of the lover. Such love, according to my understanding of the author's reasoning, once it has been conceived, only increases with union. "It is well known," he claims, "that the love of one who has tasted that which suits him . . . is stronger than the love of one who has not." This conclusion is based on a *ḥadīth* in which God is reported to have asked the angels whether men had seen him. Men had not seen him, the angels replied, for if they had, they would give him greater praise.[65] Admittedly Ibn al-Qayyim may have been thinking primarily of licit love here as well, but, none the less, his position as stated in this context cannot be completely reconciled with that described above except on the clearly false assumption that he believed no illicit affections to be the result of affinity. We know that he held a conformity of natures, whether between members of the same or opposite sexes, to be the essential precondition of inordinate and idolatrous *ʿishq.*[66]

The existence of a contradiction in Ibn al-Qayyim's thought on this issue, I believe, must be recognized. In discussing the Ẓāhirites he saw no need to reject absolutely their assumption that love ends with union. His intent was merely to show that there was no merit in their abstaining from sexual gratification, since they hoped to preserve by this means a love which was itself illicit. But dealing with love based on affinity, widely held to be permanent, he yielded to the weight of tradition and repudiated the Ẓāhirite thesis. The contradiction was never resolved. Thus in the late work *Ighāthat al-lahfān* Ibn al-Qayyim may be found advancing the two opposing views on the very same page. First he states that one rarely recovers from the drunkenness of *ʿishq* in this life—an observation with which he explains why homosexuals persist in the intoxication of sodomy until the moment they are overtaken by divine punishment. Only a few lines further on, he argues that the kind of affection (*mawadda* and *taḥābb*) which can be said to exist between the sexually immoral will be transformed into hatred, certainly by the next life, but in most cases during this earthly existence. (For the particular opinion that all wanton loves will turn to enmity in the hereafter, on which he is consistent, he had the authority of Koran 43:67, "Intimate friends will be foes to one another on that day, save the God-fearing.")[67] Comparison with other passages of the *Ighātha* shows that the terminological distinction between *ʿishq* and *mawadda* does not suffice to resolve the contradiction apparent here.[68] It must be concluded that in each case Ibn al-Qayyim's stance is tailored, perhaps inadvertently, to his immediate purpose. This is a rare carry-over in the doctrinal sphere from his method in polemics. Evidently, not all points of theory were sacrosanct to the writer. Certain of his ideas, it seems, like the mode of his expression and the structure of his works, could be altered to suit the needs of his argument.

Issues such as the authenticity of the *ḥadīth "Man ʿashiqa . . . ,"* the motivation of chastity, and the question of whether love ceases with union, which arise in Ibn al-Qayyim's treatment of profane *naẓar*, are major problems in the scholar's teaching on love. These are not the only aspects of his doctrine which come up in the same context. Others we have seen are the principle of the lesser evil, the conception of *ʿishq* as idolatry, and a negative approach to most music and poetry.

The fact that a wide range of topics emerges in Ibn al-Qayyim's discussion is not without significance; it demonstrates that he thought of *naẓar* as a key issue in the theory and practice of love. The sheer volume of his attack against "looking," extending over a tenth of *Rawḍat al-muḥibbīn* alone and involving the repudiation or reinterpretation of material purported to be from recognized authorities, the countering of rational proofs, and the discrediting of the theory of chaste love, inevitably led to the inclusion of a variety of questions. But the essential thing to notice is that all these questions are undeniably pertinent to the author's treatment of the practice. *Naẓar* thus appears as a unifying theme around which many of the other aspects of Ibn al-Qayyim's theory of love may conveniently be grouped. Perhaps this reflects the fact that the Ḥanbalites were concerned primarily with behavior and only secondarily with ideas.

The object of Ibn al-Qayyim's discussion of *naẓar* as related thus far is the preservation of conventional standards of morality. The basic argument is simply that looking causes *ʿishq*, while *ʿishq* in turn leads to fornication or pederasty. Intentions as well as acts are stressed. A man will not be punished if he earnestly strives to overcome an illicit passion. But deliberate persistence in the *ʿishq*-love brought on and sustained by looking is to be condemned even when the limits of chastity are respected. As an excessive degree of attachment, albeit unsullied by carnality, *ʿishq* entails the devotion of obedience and worship, which are properly religious attitudes, to a human object. It therefore constitutes a violation of the canon that all earthly affections must be subordinated to love for God. The equation of *ʿishq* with idolatry which is implicit in this view, it should be remarked, underlies Ibn al-Qayyim's polemic against *naẓar* as practiced by the Sufis.

Sufi naẓar

In the context of profane relationships what is most often, although not exclusively, referred to by *naẓar* is the furtive and perhaps repeated glance (*naẓra*) towards a potential or actual beloved. In the domain of mysticism the word more frequently denotes the prolonged gaze towards an object of great beauty, by ancient convention usually a comely and still beardless youth.[69] Among the Arab Sufis at least two notable exceptions to this general rule, Ibn al-Fāriḍ in his *Tā'īya* and Ibn al-ʿArabī in *Tarjumān al-ashwāq*, sought their inspiration from feminine objects. Ibn al-ʿArabī specifically condemned keeping company with youths, while, not without reservations, allowing it with women.[70] The beautiful person, or object, was variously held to be an indication of the divine beauty, a vehicle of theophany, a locus of temporary incarnation, or, in the monist or premonist view, an object in which the divine beauty, although inherent in all creatures, is most clearly perceived. As a reflection of these opinions he was commonly termed *shāhid*, or witness.

In his *Kitāb ʿaṭf al-alif al-maʾlūf* Abū 'l-Ḥasan al-Daylamī remarks that the word *shāhid* has two meanings. In one sense it signifies a *shāhid ʿadl* (in Islamic law a witness beyond reproach) who informs one of the uniqueness of the artisan who created him. This usage, in which the term can apply, according to al-Daylamī's explanation, to any exceptional work of God, was acceptable to orthodox Muslims and to the Ḥanbalites in particular. But the mystic points out that in another higher sense the word *shāhid* applies to a witness who informs one of his having recently been in the presence (*mashhad*) of the universal beauty (*al-ḥusn al-kullī*) and of his having been set apart by his maker from the rest of his works. Elucidating this second meaning, al-Daylamī argues that every beauty is derived from the universal beauty. But beauty reveals itself only in proportion to its proximity to this original source and in the degree allowed by the nature of its earthly locus. If, therefore, one perceives a manifest beauty, he can infer two things: that it is close to its source and that its locus is free from corrupting accidents. Al-Daylamī concludes from this that all *shāhid*s are in a sense alike, although some are more manifest than others.[71] It was to doctrines of this sort, based in one way or another on the Platonic ladder of being, that Muslim orthodoxy objected.

An opinion similar to that of al-Daylamī but more fully expressed is found in the *Mashāriq* of al-Dabbāgh. This later writer, whose clear commitment to the progressive apprehension of beauty's stages presupposes at least the initial presence of a *shāhid*, goes so far as to justify the use of a human being to this end. He does not specify the sex, but in the context of Muslim society the severe limitations on the availability of young girls for such purposes should be obvious. Allowing an imaginary opponent to ask, as might a Ḥanbalite, why he directs his attention primarily to human forms with their many temptations when all creatures in existence are tokens of their creator, al-Dabbāgh replies that the perfection and beauty of the "Artisan" are to be inferred more completely as the objects contemplated themselves contain more perfections and greater beauty. Plants, for example, possess more perfections than inanimate objects, while animals possess still more perfections than plants. Man possesses all of the perfections of the three lower stages of being and, moreover, through his possession of a rational soul, resembles the angels. The most sublime indications of the creator's perfection are to be found therefore in the contemplation of man's highest aspect, his rational soul; and the gateway to this for the majority of mystics is the contemplation of external human beauty.[72]

Replying specifically to the objection that to deduce the perfection and beauty of God from human figures exposes one to greater dangers than to draw one's inferences from inanimate objects, plants, and animals, al-Dabbāgh stipulates that the path of sacred love is closed to all but the most favorably endowed of souls. Thus the religious devotion of most men is limited to the lower levels of perfection. Many have worshipped lifeless objects. The Magians, for example, deified fire, while the Hindus, Greeks, and pagan Arabs erected idols of stone. Others, like certain of the Arabs, have venerated trees, and others still have risen to the level of animal-worship but no higher. Similarly, some will indeed be deterred by the physical lust which may accompany the contemplation of human beauty, and they will be punished accordingly.[73]

By this recognition of the dangers inherent in gazing at human figures, al-Dabbāgh admits that the orthodox objection is to a certain extent valid. But as a good Neoplatonist he points out that these dangers are not essentially different from those encountered in the consideration of lower forms of being. All such hazards are but varieties of the fetters of material existence. The sexually immoral are punished therefore for the same reason as animists and idolators—because they stop short of their true goal. This goal, al-Dabbāgh makes it quite clear, is by no means a physical attachment. What the soul in fact loves is a spirit resembling it, not the body, with which it has no affinity. If this were not the case, then men could love corpses, bodies which no longer possess a soul; but it is the contrary which actually occurs. External beauty, he concludes, is merely a shadow of the spiritual beauty which the mystic lover is required to apprehend.[74]

Beyond such general expositions as that presented by al-Dabbāgh, firsthand information on the *shāhid* teaching is hard to come by. For the most part, further details, often considerably distorted, must be gleaned from the works of the heresiographers, since few texts sympathetic to Sufi *naẓar* have survived the thoroughgoing condemnation of the practice by Muslim orthodoxy. From relatively early times the contemplation of beautiful youths was associated with the doctrine of incarnation (*ḥulūl*). It was consequently stigmatized by most of the major mystic writers, who were usually under the influence of the theologians or traditionists. Negative positions were taken, for example, by Ibn Ḥanbal's contemporary al-Muḥāsibī,[75] al-Junayd (d. 297/910),[76] al-Qushayrī (d. 465/1072),[77] al-Hujwīrī (d. 465–69/1072–77),[78] Abū Ḥāmid al-Ghazālī,[79] and even al-Ḥallāj.[80] Al-Dabbāgh's failure to state explicitly that he was writing in defense of gazing at comely males should be understood in the light of the fact that such an imposing array of authorities had come out against the practice. Among earlier mystics who favored or actually adopted it, Abū ʿAbd al-Raḥmān al-Sulamī, Ibn Ṭāhir al-Maqdisī, and Aḥmad al-Ghazālī (the brother of Abū Ḥāmid), all of whom are mentioned by Ibn al-Jawzī, may be recalled.[81]

Ibn al-Qayyim, following closely his master Ibn Taymīya, expresses the typically orthodox view. Sufi *naẓar* is condemned in the harshest terms in both his earlier and later writings.[82] It may be useful to summarize his observations on the custom as stated in a number of sources. Gazing, according to the Neo-Ḥanbalite scholar, is one of the deceits Satan employs to lead the ignorant astray.[83] It produces in the Sufis an amorous inclination towards their *shāhid*s, male or female. But they call this emotion love to God or love for the sake of God (*li-llāh*) and give other men to think that this is the case. Some mystics in their delusion are convinced that their claim is true, while others know it to be false. In plain fact they are merely adopting companions in the hope of obtaining from them the pleasures of kissing and carnal union or those of association and gazing. They may even term their relationship marriage and imitate the acts of husbands and wives, perhaps exceeding them in frequency and variety of methods.[84]

Behind such behavior lies the fact that the Sufis have elevated the passionate love of bodily forms (*ʿishq al-ṣuwar*) to the status of a religion. They maintain that through the experience of love they draw near to God, justifying their opinion on one or more of four untenable premises—that love purifies the soul, that by disciplining the heart through attachment to a single human object love prepares a man to devote himself exclusively to God, that beautiful bodily forms are loci of divine manifestation, or that God is incarnate in or united with the beloved.[85] Ibn Taymīya had remarked a practice which reflected the last of these views, noting that a mystic might kiss his beloved and say to him, "Thou art God."[86] On the issues of incarnation and union in particular, both Ibn al-Qayyim and his teacher point out that the

Sufis were of two opinions—some holding that God indwells or unites with specific beings as the Christians pretended with regard to Jesus or the extreme Shīʿites concerning ʿAlī, others teaching that he indwells or is united with all existent things, even dogs, pigs, and other ritually unclean objects, in accordance with the views of certain "Jahmites" and the teachings of Ibn al-ʿArabī, Ibn al-Fāriḍ, and their followers.[87] For this latter group, who are ordinarily the worst offenders in the Ḥanbalite view, there is no distinction between the lawful and the unlawful, just as there is no difference between the essence of one thing and that of another.[88]

Despite the evident diversity which he remarks in their doctrines, Ibn al-Qayyim seems to put all Sufis who cross over the bounds of traditional sexual morality in one unredeemable class. Since they set up their beloveds as equals to God, their love constitutes idolatry (*shirk*);[89] and such idolatry in love is an unpardonable sin.[90] Their sin is greater than that of ordinary idolators. The idol worshippers in pre-Islamic Arabia did not go so far as to claim that God actually appeared in the stones they erected. Indeed, the immoral among mystic lovers commit a more serious sin than either idolators or sodomites. They combine the transgressions of the two groups—worshipping their minions and copulating with their idols.[91]

The major points stressed in Ibn al-Qayyim's observations on Sufi *naẓar* are the evil consequences of the practice, its blasphemous nature, and the unforgivable idolatry entailed by the type of love it produces. In their ensemble, these remarks clearly represent a reaction of *nomos* religion to a typical element of the *eros* system. The mystical contemplation of beauty was the first step in the ascent of the Platonic ladder and was considered the most effective means of further spiritual progress. It constituted a denial of the this-worldly conception of salvation and the corresponding legalistic emphasis which characterized orthodox faith. To the traditionist party, the mystics' adoption of *naẓar* was at best a grave error in choice of means; at worst it was merely an attempt to provide a cover for immorality. In either case the practice opened the way to antinomian behavior and threatened the ethical foundations of prophetic Islam. Even if carnality were not involved, the gaze itself violated the injunctions of Koran and Sunna alike. But the orthodox had good reason to believe that the rule of chastity was not always respected. One Sufi, accused by Ibn Taymīya of sexual immorality, boldly retorted, "And what if I have done this!"[92] The dangers of gazing were particularly exacerbated, moreover, in the context of mystical monism, which the Neo-Ḥanbalites knew to be a rapidly spreading philosophy.[93] Thus, although Sufi *naẓar* was rejected on fundamentally the same grounds as, for example, the prior existence of souls, the practice was even less to be tolerated than beliefs of this sort and was censured in stronger words. It affected the all-important realm of action. The mystic's fixing of his gaze on the *shāhid* was for its advocates the first step to salvation. For its opponents it was the first step towards the working out of the dire implications of *eros* doctrine for traditional morality.

The vision

In the theological context, the Ḥanbalite teaching on *naẓar* has as its primary focus the doctrine of the beatific vision. This may appear to be a separate issue; the questions raised often differ considerably from those mentioned in connection with profane and mystical love. But there is none the less a degree of continuity, for the more extreme of the mystical interpretations of *naẓar* conflicted with traditionist theology by supposing the possibility of the vision in this life. The Ḥanbalites were most sensitive to the divergence between the Sufi and the orthodox views, and it was at times with specific reference to this issue that they dealt with the practice of gazing.[94] Both Ibn Taymīya and Ibn al-Qayyim rejected the assertion of the mystics, replying that the vision will occur only in the next life.[95] In some ways, however, the position of the two men with regard to the vision was not unlike that taken by more moderate Sufis. This fact, I will suggest, involved a certain inconsistency in their thought.

The beatific vision, according to the argument Ibn al-Qayyim presents, is clearly affirmed by tradition.[96] But it is likewise known to be possible by reason; for the greater the perfection of a thing, the more worthy it is of being seen.[97] Contrary to the teaching of the *mutakallimūn*, the vision is truly the consummation of sacred love, and man will experience pleasure in it.[98] Indeed, since it is the ultimate fulfillment of man's love to God, the vision is infinitely the greatest of the pleasures of Paradise.[99] To be veiled from god, by implication, is a punishment more grievous than the fire of Hell.[100] The pleasure experienced in the vision is proportional to one's love for God, which, in turn, is proportional to one's knowledge of him.[101] Thus the greatest pleasures of this world are knowing and loving God, since they lead to (and increase) the joy of beholding him. All other earthly pleasures are to be judged according to this same criterion.[102]

It will be observed that Ibn al-Qayyim, following Ibn Taymīya but against the speculative theologians, adopts the ancient Sufi view that the beatific vision is the culmination of religious love. Moreover, he does not simply pay lip-service to the opinion but incorporates it into his system of thought, drawing from it certain inferences for the evaluation of temporal pleasures. Perhaps wrongly, this doctrine was not suspect in the eyes of traditionist Muslims. Massignon was mistaken in asserting that the heretics Ibn ʿAṭāʾ (executed 309/921–22) and al-Ḥallāj (executed 309/922) were "the first to proclaim that the principal joy of Paradise is a recompense for the grace of having loved God: the divine vision."[103] The doctrine dates at the latest from al-Muḥāsibī (d. 243/857), who related from his contemporary Dhū 'l-Nūn (d. 245/860) that the highest hope of the true lover is to behold the face of God.[104] The idea thus grew up in circles which were not entirely foreign to nascent Ḥanbalism,[105] and its acceptance by the school and by other similarly inclined groups, if not a sign of the strictest consistency, is at least historically understandable. That al-Muḥāsibī had in mind the very idea referred to by Massignon seems to be confirmed by the fact that he also recorded the related and equally ancient opinion that the true lover must renounce the pleasures of Paradise (in favor of contemplating the divine beauty). The mystic transmitted this opinion, apparently with approval, from Abū Sulaymān al-Dārānī (d. 215/830–31) through the moralist Muḥammad b. al-Ḥusayn al-Burjulānī (d. 238/852–53) and also from Ḥasan al-Baṣrī (d. 110/728).[106]

Significantly, this corollary doctrine is denied by Ibn al-Qayyim as it was by his teacher. In their view Paradise comprehends all the favors of the next life, including the vision, and is therefore desirable in itself.[107] It is undoubtedly the mark of those ignorant of God, according to Ibn al-Qayyim, to desire, after the manner of the majority of the speculative theologians, only the created rewards of Heaven—the drink, the lovemaking, and the fine garments. But it is likewise inconceivable that a living being—the author means a "whole man" in the *nomos* sense—should be completely deprived of his natural will (*irāda*) and hence desire only God and not his favors. One may be tempted to believe otherwise in occasional moments of ecstasy, but such states are fortuitous and temporary. Permanent detachment from natural wants, even in Heaven, is neither commanded, nor desirable, nor indeed possible.[108]

The teaching of the Neo-Ḥanbalites on the beatific vision, outlined here and in an earlier chapter,[109] reveals that they were caught in a rather difficult position between the abstractionism of the theologians and the *eros* doctrine of the Sufis. In response to the first group they affirmed the infinite pleasure of the vision, while against the second they taught a physical resurrection and the permanence of natural appetites. They did this, it seems, without regard to the compatibility of the two views they expressed. Hence one searches their works in vain for an adequate explanation of why any man, even a "whole man," would at a given moment in the afterlife exchange what our authors considered the limitless and ever-increasing joy of beholding God's face and hearing his speech for the lowly pleasure of deflowering yet another houri. They simply dismiss uninterrupted contemplation as inconceivable. Their failure to deal with this problem, I believe, may be seen to reflect one or both of two characteristics of their doctrine. First, the omission may be attributed to the fact that their stance was essentially a defensive one—the primary concern being to refute the adversaries to either side of them rather than to clarify difficulties in their own system. Second, and this is perhaps the more fundamental reason, it may be conjectured that they did not explain the problem because they could not; and they could not, I suggest, because their stress on the infinite joy of the beatific vision, inherited from early Sufism, was foreign to their basic religious viewpoint. Fortunately a saying of the Prophet, cited by Ibn al-Qayyim in a related context, spared them the effort. They had it on authority that the vision is not continuous: "The highest of the people of Paradise," the Prophet reportedly stated, "is the one who looks at the face of his Lord twice each day."[110] One is reminded of the use of technical jargon in Western academic disciplines since the eighteenth century. To paraphrase Goethe's Mephistopheles, where an idea is lacking, a *ḥadīth* is always ready to take its place.

A brief recapitulation is perhaps in order. We may begin by recalling that the Neo-Ḥanbalite treatment of love's causes turned on three basic issues—affinity, beneficence and beauty, and looking. Affinity—in earthly affections a bond of essential similarity—became in religious love a relationship of absolute complementarity. Beneficence, despite Ibn al-Qayyim's effort to elevate its rank, remained in the final analysis subordinate to beauty. Looking—in the profane context the efficient cause of love—became in the sacred sphere its final cause. To these three issues are related many of the major questions which, as recurrent objects of the Ḥanbalite school's attention, were involved in the formation of the total view of love adopted by its adherents. Most notable among these are the problem of the origin and nature of the soul (the seat of love), the conception of chaste love as a rule of life, the question whether love ends with union, and the controversy surrounding the doctrine of the beatific vision. Behind the position taken by Ibn al-Qayyim and his teacher on these issues there lay almost invariably a dual concern for orthodox dogma as taught by the *ahl al-ḥadīth* and for the moral purity of the community—in more general terms, a basic commitment to the *nomos* tradition. It is interesting to note in this connection that among the elements incorporated by the Ḥanbalites into their own system, it was those most closely akin to the *eros* motif which they handled with the least dexterity and consistency—the idea of affinity in sacred love, beauty as a cause of love (Ibn al-Qayyim, it will be recalled, refused to give a definition of beauty), and the infinite pleasure of the vision of God in Paradise. For the most part the thrust of Neo-Ḥanbalite thought is remarkably uniform; but, as is perhaps universal with religious systems, history and the demands of contemporary polemic had burdened the school with certain unalterable tenets which it could not satisfactorily assimilate.

9. The Kinds and Stages of Love

In the writings of Ibn Qayyim al-Jawzīya one finds a number of differing approaches to the problem of distinguishing and classifying the kinds of love. These approaches, often reflecting the author's views on the causes of love, range from a loosely organized lexicographical study to various treatments of the types and stages of affection. One of his earlier efforts was to establish definitions for fifty-one words used to describe love and its many aspects, most of them taken from a long list of love terminology which Lois Giffen has traced to the *Riyāḍ* of al-Marzubānī. The list itself, given in *Rawḍat al-muḥibbīn*, had reached Ibn al-Qayyim incomplete, probably through Mughulṭāy's *al-Wāḍiḥ al-mubīn*, Shihāb al-Dīn al-Ḥalabī's *Manāzil al-aḥbāb*, or both of these works.[1] For lexicographical information he relies heavily on the *Ṣiḥāḥ* of al-Jawharī, but much of the commentary on individual terms is his own. Thus the definitions frequently reflect his particular religious bias, as does likewise the addition of a word like *khulla* (exclusive love, friendship with God) to al-Marzubānī's list.[2]

Among the truly classificatory treatments of love attempted by Ibn al-Qayyim in the *Rawḍa*, one is found in the context of his discussion of affinity. Two kinds of love, he advances, can be considered to result from this cause (depending on the kind of affinity involved). The first is accidental, purposive love (*maḥabba ʿaraḍīya gharaḍīya*). Ending with the usefulness of the object, it corresponds roughly to Aristotle's loves of pleasure and utility. The second is spiritual love (*maḥabba rūḥānīya*), based on conformity between two souls. Accidental love is not necessarily reciprocal but may be so when the two parties share a similar aim—for example, the desire of a man and a woman for each other. Spiritual love, if one looks beyond mere appearances, invariably turns out to be mutual.[3]

The application of the philosophical term "accidental" (ʿ*araḍī*) to the love of utility is based on traditional usage. By other authors it was employed in opposition to the term "essential" (*dhātī*) to distinguish the love of utility from the love of beauty for its own sake and the love caused by hidden affinity.[4] Ibn al-Qayyim is not entirely consistent in his use of this adjective. In *al-Ṭibb al-nabawī*, another early work, he divides love into three categories: (1) love "in and for God," that is, love for what God does together with love for God himself and his Prophet; (2) love from accord in association—for example, religion, blood-relationship, or profession—or from accord in some shared aim; and (3) love for the sake of an end to be obtained from the beloved. Only the last of these is called accidental or *ʿaraḍī*, whereas in the *Rawḍa* the second category as well as the third would seem to be covered by the term.[5] Writing years later in a sacred context, Ibn al-Qayyim contrasts the love of utility (*ḥubb al-wasāʾil*, love of means), to which the term *ʿaraḍī* refers, not with love proceeding from affinity but with "pure love" (*al-maḥabba al-khāliṣa*). Pure love is that which is directed to the beloved for his perfection and his worthiness to be the object of the emotion. Man attains this love by "passing away" in the object of the beloved's will from that which is sought by his own will, striving towards that object rather than what he desires from the beloved.[6] Considering these different classifications together, it becomes clear that, despite what seems to be an inconsistency in Ibn al-Qayyim's use of the term "accidental," the scholar distinguished the purposive love which this adjective denoted from love based on spiritual affinity on the profane level and love for the divine perfection in the religious context.

So much for the terminological problem. What is most intriguing here is that in the passage which describes "pure love" Ibn al-Qayyim approaches the distinction between acquisitive and disinterested affection. We may immediately ask whether the Ḥanbalite scholar in fact meant to qualify proper love for God as truly disinterested, and, if so, whether and to what extent this attitude carried over into his treatment of human love. Our question itself, however, needs some preliminary clarification. By disinterested love may be meant an affection which is strictly alterocentric and which, in the final analysis, does not revert to the interests of the lover. One might choose flatly to dismiss the possibility that such a love can exist. Although there have been many voices raised against Aristotle's assertion that "it is for himself most of all that each man wishes what is good,"[7] the burden of proof still seems to lie on the objectors. Nevertheless, this completely selfless love is one of the conceptions an author may have in mind. Disinterested love may also be taken to refer to a love based on a higher or more abstract level of self-interest than is generally understood to underlie acquisitive love, although this is a less exact use of the expression. What I intend to show is that the first conception of a truly disinterested love, rightly it would seem, did not occur to the Ḥanbalites as a rational alternative, while the second corresponds perfectly to their point of view.

In this respect, it should be remarked, they were typical representatives of orthodox Muslim thought. Even al-Ghazālī, who in his discussion of love of the beautiful for its own sake comes as close as anyone among the more or less right-thinking scholars to affirming the possibility of a purely disinterested relationship, does not deny that this love seeks some benefit (*ḥaẓẓ*) for the subject. Although according to the theologian's thesis nothing more than the mere perception of the beloved is desired, this perception is itself pleasurable and thus responds to the interests of the lover.[8] Moreover, the hidden affinity by which al-Ghazālī attempts to explain the love which he says seeks neither beauty nor any other benefit—his remarks on the matter notwithstanding—clearly implies a fundamental need on the part of one or both parties which can be satisfied only through possession or union.[9]

That Ibn al-Qayyim had a primarily egocentric conception of love is apparent from a number of aspects of his thought. First, as it will be recalled, he taught that man has an essential need for God, whether it be the need of all creatures for their creator or that of the believer seeking salvation.[10] It is because he held this essential need to exist in man that, in describing the higher or "pure" love for God, a love statedly no longer concerned with favors bestowed but requiring the strictest subordination of one's own will, the Ḥanbalite scholar terms it not only the true but also the *beneficial* love.[11] Loves which are not for God or for his sake, whatever their temporal advantage, he rejects as harmful.[12] The criterion, therefore, remains the individual's own best interest.

It may be observed that Ibn al-Qayyim's entire system of ranking loves, and pleasures as well, is based finally on human self-love. God is the highest object of love and the beatific vision is the sublime pleasure. Other loves and pleasures are judged on the grounds of whether they lead to these; but ultimately it is still man's own greatest happiness which is in question.[13] The fundamental egocentricity of love is affirmed unequivocally in the *Ighātha*:

> No living being renounces that which he loves and desires, when he is able to obtain it, except for something [else] he loves; nor does he undertake that which he hates or fears except to avoid falling into something [else] he hates or fears. The particular func-

> tion of reason is to renounce the lower and less advantageous of two beloveds for the greater and more beneficial and to decide in favor of the less harmful of two undesirable things in order to avoid the more harmful.[14]

Loves which are harmful, it is stated in the same work, proceed only from corrupt knowledge and intention or, as the author expressed it in an earlier text, from ignorance, false belief, and conquering passion. If this were not the case, then no man would choose them.[15] The argument concludes in words which are most revealing:

> For this reason true faith is that which induces the believer to do what benefits him and to abstain from what harms him. . . . Man is in the greatest need of knowing what harms him so that he may shun it and what benefits him so that he may seek it avidly and undertake it, loving the beneficial and hating the harmful. [In this way] his love and his hatred will be in conformity with the love and hatred of God.[16]

As is evident from these assertions, Ibn al-Qayyim preached an enlightened but none the less self-interested love. For him, as for his teacher, acts which do not revert to the interests of the agent are absurd. Ibn Taymīya, it has been seen, held this principle to be true of God as well as of men.[17]

There seems to be no doubt, as his own words in the *Ighātha* demonstrate, that Ibn al-Qayyim considered it possible to equate enlightened self-interest with conformity to the divine will. But his description of the selfless character of pure love still seems to conflict, on the surface at least, with the egocentric assumptions of his psychology. The precise limits of the kind of selflessness he had in mind become clear in his discussion of altruism or *īthār* (giving preference). Admittedly, when at one point he makes a distinction between two types of *īthār*, the scholar takes a significant step towards the recognition of a truly disinterested sentiment. One type of *īthār* he calls mercenary. It is the altruism of the lover who gives preference to his beloved in order to facilitate obtaining from him some desired end. The second type, called the *īthār* of love and will, consists in giving preference to the beloved despite one's own wants. Ibn al-Qayyim acknowledges that altruism of this latter kind, at the moment of its occurrence, appears to have no other motive than the act of benevolence itself. The altruism of love and will, he teaches, is in its own right an object of desire; indeed it is the highest of the goals sought by the lover.

This opinion would seem to imply that self-seeking love, properly directed, ends in true disinterestedness. But when Ibn al-Qayyim attempts to explain the case of men who give up to others those goods of which they have only enough for themselves, his doctrine of egocentrism reasserts itself. It may be asked, he observes, how such altruism is possible, since the soul is created with a natural selfishness (*majbūla ʿalā 'l-athara*). His reply to this question, although expressed in theistic terms, resembles the argument advanced by Aristotle. The selfless man may be seeking to acquire nobility of character, of which *īthār* or altruism is the supreme manifestation. The personal advantages to be gained from such conduct are obvious, for God has created men with a natural inclination to love the benevolent and hate the selfish. Again, the selfless man may be seeking to respect unfailingly the rights which God has granted Muslims over each other. As a precaution against falling short of his obligation, he goes beyond it. The result is that he obtains a good reputation in this life and a high reward in the next, and thus—Ibn al-Qayyim's remark parallels the passages cited earlier—"there reverts to him from his selflessness something preferable to that which he sacrificed." But even such ego-based altruism as this is limited by a more important consideration, one which again springs from self-interest. With regard to specifically worldly goods a man may indeed give to another things he needs for himself, although this is not an obligation; but he must be niggardly in the matter of sharing with other men the time he should devote to acts of worship and obedience to God.[18]

In human relationships, therefore, while a sensation of unmotivated benevolence may occur, no strictly disinterested altruism can exist. But there is a higher altruism, consisting in giving preference to God by doing what he loves and shunning what he hates, whatever one's own immediate interests may demand. Upon such selflessness as this, according to Ibn al-Qayyim, depends the true realization of love to God and man's salvation and beatitude.[19] At this point we notice once again the original conflict. The greatest of pleasures, the divine vision, is experienced in proportion to man's love for God.[20] But this love in turn, and hence the pleasure desired from the vision, now appear to be dependent upon utter selflessness. The obvious solution is certainly the right one. In order to be acceptable to God, conformity of will and acts of obedience must be sought by the Muslim for their own sake without regard to future reward or punishment. The desire for them must arise spontaneously from within him as though they did not constitute the means to salvation. For Ibn al-Qayyim the illusion of true selflessness—and it is an illusion—is *possible* in interpersonal relationships, but it is *necessary* in the religious life.

A method of classifying the types of love which recurs with great frequency in Ibn al-Qayyim's works is the threefold division: love to God, love for his sake and "in" him, and love "with" God. This classification, already referred to in the discussion of Ibn Taymīya's teaching,[21] is essentially an ancient one, having its roots in prophetic tradition. In an "authentic" (*ṣaḥīḥ*) *ḥadīth* recorded by both al-Bukhārī and Muslim, the Prophet is reported to have said: "He who possesses three things experiences the sweetness of faith: he to whom God and his Prophet are more beloved than all else; he who loves a man, loving him only for the sake of God; and he who hates to return to unbelief after God has rescued him from it, just as he would hate to be thrown into the fire [of Hell]."[22] What is most interesting about the Neo-Ḥanbalite adaptation of the categories suggested in this tradition is the new stress on love "with" God, which, especially in the doctrine of Ibn al-Qayyim, is equated with idolatry or *shirk*.[23]

Ibn al-Qayyim expresses this division variously, either in its basic threefold form or in expanded and more detailed versions. Emphasizing its significance for the life of piety, he calls it in one place the "forking of the ways which separates monotheists from idolaters" and in another the "distinction which all men are required to make."[24] In *Kitāb al-rūḥ* he carefully defines and distinguishes love "in" God and love "with" God. Love "in" God, consisting in loving what he loves, follows directly from love to God and is incumbent upon every true lover.[25] Correspondingly, hatred of all that God hates is demanded. Love "with" God is of two kinds: that which is harmful to the essence of monotheism (*tawḥīd*) and hence constitutes idolatry and that which mars the perfection of sincerity and love to God but does not exclude the lover from the Islamic faith. The first is a love which implies worship of its object —whoever or whatever it may be. The second comprises a variety of natural loves for persons and possessions—women, children, gold, silver, horses, other livestock, and farmland, for example. These persons and possessions, as is the case more commonly with unlawful women and beardless youths, may at times be the objects of idolatrous love. Ibn al-Qayyim specifies that they may be loved in three ways. They may be loved as aids to worship and obedience to God in the same manner that women and perfumes were loved by the Prophet, in which case they belong to the category of things loved for the sake of God (*li-llāh*). Or they may be loved as objects conforming to one's nature and appetites, in which case love for them is permissible and goes unpunished so long as they are not given priority over what God loves. Such affections, however, mar the perfection of religious love. Or again, they may be loved as ends in themselves, taking precedence over what God loves. In this last case the lover does an injustice to his own soul.[26] It is the second kind of love which Ibn al-Qayyim describes as the love "with" God which does not exclude from Islam, while the third, if not clearly the same as the idolatrous variety, is dangerously close to it in the scholar's view.

A later expansion of this division, expressed in Ibn al-Qayyim's *Ighāthat al-lahfān*, details six kinds of love—three beneficial and, corresponding to these, three which are harmful:

BENEFICIAL	HARMFUL
1) love to God	4) love for that which cuts short love to God or diminishes it
2) love "in" God (*fī 'llāh*), love for what God loves (as above)	5) love of that which God hates
3) love for that which aids in obedience	6) love "with" God, the essence of idolatry (*aṣl al-shirk*)

In this scheme there is an obvious polarity between love to God and love "with" God. The other loves fall along a continuum between the two, with the canonically neutral affections mentioned above being included in the first degree of harmful love.[27] The prime example of love "with" God, here as in other contexts, is passionate *ʿishq*. We will return to Ibn al-Qayyim's association of *ʿishq* with idolatry further on in this chapter.[28]

It has already been observed that one of the primary functions of faith for the Neo-Ḥanbalite scholar is to enable man to distinguish between harmful and beneficial loves.[29] The criterion he offers believers for the evaluation of loves is easy to infer from the ranking we have just seen. In his earlier as well as his later works the loves considered to be most beneficial are love directed to God and those attachments which follow from it, for example love for the Prophet and the Koran,[30] while the most harmful loves are those directed to forbidden objects for their own sake, as the scandalous passion for young boys.[31] The opposition between such loves is straightforward. It is with affections lying between them that the problem of discrimination is posed. Here the test is whether and to what extent the affections constitute either aids to obedience or distractions from proper devotion. An application of this principle is found in Ibn al-Qayyim's justification of love for one's wife or lawful concubines. Such love is normally beneficial and is considered part of man's perfection because it protects both the male and the female parties from sin. The stronger the bond of affection, the greater the protection afforded. In this sense even love for a lost wife or slave-girl is counted as praiseworthy. The jurist recognizes, of course, that love for a wife or concubine may at times distract from devotion; but the advantages procured, in his view, usually outweigh the accompanying drawbacks.[32]

It should be remarked that this reasoning, with its particular stress on distraction from the religious life as a criterion for moral judgments, was applied in a wider context by the Ḥanbalites. On the relatively safe assumption that their school was not alone in this, it may be surmised that the principle had significant effects on the contemporary and subsequent history of Muslim thought. Ibn al-Qayyim lists a number of arts, disciplines, and even specific categories of thinking which he censures on the very same grounds he uses to declare certain types of love harmful. The source of all good and evil, he argues, is thought, and the best thoughts are those which dwell on the resurrection. To be condemned as distractions which yield more harm than good are thoughts devoted to such things as: the quality of the essence and attributes of God; chess, music, drawing, and painting; true but spiritually useless disciplines like the details of logic, mathematics, and physics; most of the philosophical sciences; speculation about how to obtain one's desires and pleasures; hypotheses which are impossible or have not occurred, for example, "What if I found a treasure?"; the particulars of other people's situations; means of obtaining goals which are illicit and, moreover, those which are permissible but have not been commanded by God; the genres of poetry; and, finally, mental conjectures (*muqaddarāt dhihnīya*) which have no existence in reality, there being too many of these, Ibn al-Qayyim remarks, in the theory of jurisprudence (*uṣūl al-fiqh*) and medicine.[33] The implications of this attitude for the intellectual life of late-medieval Islam are too many and too complex to be discussed here and merit a study of their own.

The stages of love

An especially interesting aspect of Ibn al-Qayyim's treatment of the kinds of love is found in his arrangement of its stages. His work in this context commands attention because it demonstrates how the Neo-Ḥanbalites reworked in accordance with their own system the established hierarchies of basic love terminology. Lists of the stages of love, usually including between seven and ten items, are not uncommon in medieval Islamic texts. It is worth remarking, that this tradition is still alive and has found a place in the Muslim literature of English expression. A fine example of the use of such ladders of affection appears in a recently published work by an Indian scholar.[34] In these lists, particularly in the case of contrasting secular and mystical rankings, considerable differences of order and terminology may be noticed (cf. tables below); but it is important to realize that the more strictly profane enumerations could always be put to use by mystics.[35]

As varied as the lists are, there does seem to have existed a certain measure of consensus. Most lists have such terms as *istiḥsān* (approval), *irāda* (will), *mayl* (inclination), and *ʿalāqa* (attachment) in the first two places. *Mawadda* (affection) also is usually an early stage. *Maḥabba* (love), where it occurs, follows *mawadda*. *Khulla* (bosom friendship, unique love) is an earlier stage than *ʿishq* (excessive love) in the majority of cases, while *ʿishq* is most often the last term which refers specifically to the affection of love itself. *ʿIshq* is usually followed by *tatayyum*, *walah*, or both—terms which describe the enslavement and the bewilderment of the lover respectively. The source of this general pattern is apparently the hierarchy adopted by Ibn Dāwūd in *Kitāb al-zahra* (table 3, A) or one similar to it.

One of the most typical lists is given by Ibn al-Jawzī, with no attribution, at the beginning of his passage on the degrees of love in *Dhamm al-hawā* (table 1, A). It is quoted in *Munyat al-muḥibbīn* by Marʿī b. Yūsuf, who ascribes it to "a certain gnostic."[36] But since Ibn al-Jawzī often introduces sections of his book with a few words of his own, this list may well represent the ranking he personally preferred. In any case, along with the other lists cited in the *Dhamm* (tables 3, B; 4, A and C), it differs significantly from those proposed by Ibn al-Qayyim (tables 1, C; 2). The new Ḥanbalism could no longer accept the rankings handed down by tradition, and the rearrangement of the stages of love is just one more instance of the school's efforts begun under Ibn Taymīya to establish a rationally consistent doctrine.

Ibn al-Qayyim establishes two kinds of lists, a shorter one referring specifically to profane relationships and a longer composite type including basic terms of sacred as well as profane love. *Maḥabba* is absent from all these lists, presumably because it was considered the generic term for love. *Walah* (derangement or bewilderment), the highest stage for many earlier authorities, is likewise totally excluded, most probably in response to Sufi interpretations which represented by this and similar terms the final stages in the path of self-annihilation (*fanā'*) (table 5 and n. 34). *Tatayyum* (enslavement, thralldom), generally held to be equivalent to *taʿabbud* (servitude, worship), is main-

TABLE 1. *Ḥanbalite Lists of the Stages of Profane Love*[a]

A. Ibn al-Jawzī[b]	B. Ibn Taymīya[c]	C. Ibn al-Qayyim[d]
1. *istiḥsān* (approval, finding beautiful)	1. *ʿalāqa*, attachment of the heart to the beloved	1. *ʿalāqa*, cause is *naẓar*
2. *irādat al-qurb* (the will to be near the beloved)	2. *ṣabāba*, tender and ardent longing	2. *ṣabāba*
3. *mawadda* (affection)	3. *gharām* (infatuation)	3. *gharām*, love that sticks to the heart as a creditor (*gharīm*) sticks to his debtor (*gharīm*)
4. *maḥabba* (love, *caritas*)	4. *ʿishq*	4. *ʿishq*, excessive love
5. *khulla* (bosom friendship, unique love)	5. *tatayyum*, to become the servant of a person who is not worthy to be one's master. (Note the moralizing tone of Ibn Taymīya's comment on *tatayyum* and the absence of *maḥabba* from his list.)	5. *shaghaf*, love which has reached the pericardium (*shaghāf*)
6. *hawā* (passion, desire), causes the lover to fall (*yahwī*) into the desires of the beloved by destroying his power of self-control		6. *tatayyum* = *taʿabbud.* The heart becomes a servant to one who is not worthy to be its master.
7. *ʿishq* (excessive or passionate love, *eros*, *amor*)		
8. *tatayyum* (enslavement, thralldom). The beloved becomes the owner of the lover, who finds no other in his heart; thus *Taym Allāh*, "the Slave of God."		
9. *walah*, derangement, loss of discernment (Ibn al-Jawzī's definition)		

a. In these tables, suggested English equivalents are given in parentheses. Other comments are those of the authors of the various lists.

b. *Dhamm*, p. 293.

c. Marʿī b. Yūsuf, *Munya*, fol. 8a. Cf. Ibn Taymīya, *al-Tuḥfa al-ʿIrāqīya*, p. 76, where the same list is found.

d. *Ighātha*, p. 26; cf. *ibid.*, p. 302, where, as in Ibn Taymīya's list, *shaghaf* is omitted.

TABLE 2. *Composite Lists by Ibn al-Qayyim Comprehending Profane and Sacred Love*

A. Early[a]	B. Late[b]
1. *ʿalāqa*	1. *ʿalāqa*
2. *ṣabāba*	2. *irāda* = inclination
3. *gharām*	3. *ṣabāba*
4. *ʿishq*, not applicable to God because it implies excess	4. *gharām*
5. *shawq* (longing, desire)	5. *widād* = *mawadda*
6. *tatayyum* = *taʿabbud*, the last of the [imperfect] stages of love	6. *shaghaf*
7. *khulla*, the perfection of love, achieved only by Abraham and Muḥammad	7. *ʿishq*
	8. *tatayyum*
	9. *taʿabbud*, higher than *tatayyum*
	10. *khulla*

a. *Dā'*, pp. 266–67.
b. *Madārij*, III, pp. 18–19.

TABLE 3. *Ẓāhirite and Derivative Lists*

A. Ibn Dāwūd[a]	B. Niftawayh[b]	C. Ibn Ḥazm[c]	D. Walī al-Dīn al-ʿIrāqī[d]
1. *istiḥsān*, from *naẓar*	1. *irāda*	1. *istiḥsān*	1. *istiḥsān*, from *naẓar* and *samāʿ*
2. *mawadda*	2. *maḥabba*	2. *iʿjāb* (admiration)	2. *mawadda*, result of prolonged thought about beloved
3. *maḥabba*	3. *hawā*	3. *ulfa* (familiarity, companion-ship)	3. *maḥabba*, spiritual intimacy
4. *khulla*	4. *ʿishq*	4. *kalaf* (obsession), according to Ibn Hazm, has same meaning as the word *ʿishq* used in poetry	4. *khulla*
5. *hawā*	5. *tatayyum*	5. *shaghaf* (deep love)	5. *hawā*
6. *ʿishq*			6. *ʿishq*
7. *tatyīm*, (transitive form of *tatayyum*)			7. *tatayyum*
8. *walah*			8. *walah*

a. Ibn Dāwūd, *Zahra*, pp. 19–21.
b. Ibn al-Jawzī, *Dhamm*, p. 294.
c. Ibn Ḥazm, *Akhlāq*, pp. 51–52; also in A. R. Nykl, *Dove's neck-ring*, pp. xxv–xxvi.
d. Parallels Ibn Dāwūd's list. Marʿī b. Yūsuf, *Munya*, fol. 8b.

TABLE 4. *Other Lists, Profane*

A. One of the *ʿulamāʾ*[a]	B. One of the *ʿulamāʾ*[b]	C. One of the *ḥukamāʾ*[c]	D. al-Ghazālī[d]
1. *mayl* (inclination)	1. *mayl*	1. *ʿalāqa*	1. *muʾānasat al-ṭabīʿa* (communion of nature)
2. *mawadda*	2. *ʿalāqa*	2. *ḥubb*	2. *mayl*
3. *khulla*	3. *ḥubb* (love)	3. *hawā*	3. *mawadda*
4. *ṣabāba*	4. *mawadda*	4. *khulla*	4. *maḥabba*
5. *ʿishq*, highest stage of love proper	5. *khulla*	5. *ʿishq*	5. *ishtiyāq* (longing)
6. *walah*	6. *ṣabāba*	6. *walah*	6. *walah*
7. *tatayyum*	7. *ʿishq*	7. *tatayyum*	7. *ʿishq*
	8. *walah*		
	9. *tatayyum*		

a. Ibn al-Jawzī, *Dhamm*, p. 293.
b. Marʿī b. Yūsuf, *Munya*, fol. 8a-b.
c. Ibn al-Jawzī, *Dhamm*, p. 294.
d. *ʿIshq* is exceptionally placed higher than *walah.* Al-Ghazālī, *Iḥyāʾ*; cited by Valiuddin, *Love*, pp. 4–5.

tained in the lists of both types. The adoption of this term to indicate the highest stage of profane love reflects Ibn al-Qayyim's teaching that *ʿishq* at its worst implies worship of the beloved and thus constitutes idolatry. The penultimate position of *tatayyum* in the composite lists, on the other hand, reflects the scholar's view that the most sublime station the majority of believers may attain is characterized by servitude and conformity of will. The word *khulla*, connoting extreme intimacy, which represents the final stage in the composite arrangements, is very significantly lacking in the profane lists. One of Ibn al-Qayyim's primary objections to the hierarchies established by earlier writers seems to have been that *khulla*, the degree of sacred love bestowed only on Abraham and Muḥammad, was assigned a rank lower even than that of *ʿishq*.[37]

Khulla and two other terms appearing in these lists, *ʿishq* and *shawq* (the latter only once; see table 2, A), are the focus of discussions central to the Neo-Ḥanbalite doctrine of love. Some further remarks on these terms will therefore be appropriate.

Khulla

The Koran, like the Old and New Testaments, calls Abraham the "friend" of God, rendering the Hebrew *ōhēb* (lover, friend) and the

TABLE 5. *Mystic and Emanationist Lists*

A. Al-Daylamī[a]	B. Al-Dabbāgh[b]
1. *ulfa*, stringing together of similars	1. Stages of *maḥabba*
2. *uns* (intimate association), prolonged gazing at the beloved	a. *ulfa*
3. *wudd, mawadda, muwāṣala*	b. *hawā*
4. *maḥabba*, increases from majāzīya (metaphorical) to *ḥaqīqīya* (real)	c. *khulla*
5. *khulla*, increases from *khulla* (friendship) to *khalla* (mystical poverty)	d. *shaghaf*
6. *sha'af*, ardent passion for mentioning the beloved	e. *wajd* (ecstasy)
7. *shaghaf*	2. Stages of *'ishq*
8. *istihtār* (reckless infatuation)	a. *gharām* (infatuation)
9. *walah*	b. *iftitān* (seduction)
10. *hayamān* (bewilderment), loss of solace, patience, and any advantage other than the beloved	c. *walah*
11. *'ishq*, final stage	d. *dahsh* (bafflement)
	e. *fanā'* (annihilation)

a. Al-Daylamī, *'Aṭf*, pp. 21–24. Text is corrupt, reading *'ishq* twice for *sha'af* [p. 22]. For ten rather different stages, ending with inebriation and *fanā'*, see *ibid.*, p. 94.
b. Al-Dabbāgh, *Mashāriq*, p. 31.

Greek *philos* by *khalīl*, an adjectival and substantival form which may have the meaning of either the active or the passive participle.[38] As a result of this Koranic usage the corresponding verbal noun *khulla*, typically defined as the beloved's permeating the most secret depths (*sarā'ir*) of the lover,[39] came to be associated by Muslims with an inherited Jewish tradition which made of Abraham's undertaking to sacrifice his son the supreme act of love.[40] The importance of this association for primitive Islam is reflected in certain early arguments regarding sacred love. Ḥasan al-Baṣrī (d. 110/728), seeking to vindicate the controversial view that only those who rise above the distractions of the pains of this world and the pleasures of Paradise can truly love God, is said to have traced the source of the doctrine to an Abrahamic revelation;[41] while the father of "Jahmism," al-Ja'd b. Dirham (executed 128/745–46), expressed his rejection of love between God and man by denying that the Hebrew patriarch was God's friend.[42] In debates on such questions as these, Abraham's *khulla* became a central symbol of religious love. Inevitably the same degree of intimacy with God was ascribed to the prophet of Islam. In a *ṣaḥīḥ* tradition Muḥammad is reported to have said: "God took me as a friend (*khalīl*) just as he took Abraham as a friend."[43]

For Ibn al-Qayyim, it has been seen, the *khulla* ascribed to the two major Semitic prophets represents the upper limit of ordinate love. This is a key element in his doctrine. In Neo-Ḥanbalite works, references to *khulla* as the perfection of love are quite often found independent of ordered lists of amatory vocabulary.[44] Following tradition, the essential nature of *khulla* as conceived by Ibn al-Qayyim is mirrored in the story of the sacrifice of Ishmael, who as ancestor of the Arabs replaces Isaac in the Muslim version of the biblical story. Abraham's devotion to his son was incompatible with his love for God and thus constituted a kind of idolatry or *shirk.* His submission to the command to offer up his son's life was a sign that his heart had been purged of idolatrous love. This is why the actual sacrifice ceased to be necessary.[45] *Khulla* accordingly means the complete and exclusive devotion of love to God. It is the antithesis of *shirk* and, hence, of inordinate *'ishq*. Realized by Abraham and Muḥammad alone, *khulla* is a station *hors-série.* It crowns Ibn al-Qayyim's ladder of love as a relevant but impossible spiritual imperative.

There was clearly no place for *khulla* in the profane ranking. Even the Ẓāhirite Ibn Dāwūd, when including the term below *'ishq* in his list, had been careful to define it as a relationship between human beings.[46] For Ibn al-Qayyim, the concept to which it referred had acquired such significance that the word had to be dropped altogether, at least in technical usage, from the category of secular terms.

A direct threat to the preeminence of *khulla* emanated from certain Sufi circles in which Muḥammad was commonly called the "beloved" rather than the "friend" of God. Ibn al-'Arabī, arch-foe of the Ḥanbalites, puts forward the argument in question in his commentary on his *Tarjumān al-ashwāq*. Love, he advances, is in a particular way characteristic of Islam, since God took Muḥammad alone as *ḥabīb* or beloved. Such attributes as friends (*khalīl*) are applicable to other figures as well.[47] Without mentioning the Andalusian mystic by name, Ibn al-Qayyim rejects the view that the *ḥabīb* is superior to the *khalīl*. Love (*maḥabba*) is a generic term, while *khulla* is quite specific. God loves (*yuḥibb*) the repentent (Koran 2:222), and thus anyone who repents may be called a *ḥabīb* of God; but only two men have been termed *khalīl*.[48] Despite appearances, there is more to this controversy than a mere quibbling over words. Ibn al-ʿArabī, still in the same work, reveals what he means by the *maḥabba* peculiar to Islam when he states that there is no good in a love ruled by reason.[49] Ibn al-Qayyim, by denying the superiority of the *ḥabīb*, is implicitly repudiating this emotional abandon advocated by the Sufi in favor of the Ḥanbalite ideal requiring the conscious subordination of all secondary loves to love for God[50]—an ideal perfectly realized only in the station of *khulla*.

ʿIshq

The love known as *ʿishq* is subjected to extensive treatment in the works of Ibn al-Qayyim, especially in *Rawḍat al-muḥibbīn*, where the author's views are supplemented with numerous selections from *ḥadīth*, anecdotal literature, and poetry—material which is often drawn directly from Ibn al-Jawzī's *Dhamm al-hawā*. Most of the points arising in Ibn al-Qayyim's various discussions of the topic have been touched on in preceding sections of this study, but it will be useful for the sake of a *vue d'ensemble* to summarize here the main aspects of his teaching on this the most controversial of the terms for love. Also, there are a few additional questions which will require attention.

How then did Ibn al-Qayyim define *ʿishq*? According to the definition most widely held by Muslim intellectuals, which was presumably the legacy of popularized Aristotelianism, the word denotes excessive love. Aristotle himself had described love—as opposed to friendship—as "a sort of excess of feeling," adding that "it is the nature of such only to be felt towards one person."[51] Following the majority of earlier authorities, Ibn al-Qayyim adopts as his definition of *ʿishq* the phrase "excess in love" (*al-ifrāṭ fī 'l-ḥubb*), which clearly parallels the first half of the Stagirite's formula.[52] However with regard to the exclusive nature of *ʿishq*, the second element in Aristotle's definition, his exact view may need some elucidation.

There is no doubt that in Ibn al-Qayyim's opinion all true loves have a tendency to become exclusive.[53] In the sacred context, for instance, God alone is properly speaking the object of love, other things being desirable not in themselves but only for his sake. Yet the Neo-Ḥanbalite's entire moral teaching with respect to love is based on the assumption that there are conflicting attractions present in the individual. These, although they may be mutually exclusive when followed to the extreme, are normally considered to occur together in a situation of tension. The task facing the believer is to determine the object most worthy of his love and then to devote himself wholly to it. But is it possible to say that the acknowledged conflict between moral and immoral desires in the religious sphere has a purely secular counterpart in the domain of *ʿishq*—traditionally the paradigm of love to a single object for its own sake? [54] This in fact seems to have been Ibn al-Qayyim's view. In *Ighāthat al-lahfān* he recognizes that fornicators and homosexuals, who obtain full pleasure from their sinful deeds only when these are accompanied by *ʿishq*, often switch from one partner to another. From this observation he concludes that each of the different partners will receive a portion of the worship which is characteristic of excessive passionate love.[55] Of course this conclusion does not conflict with the view that the fundamental nature of *ʿishq*, like that of sacred love, is to seek only one object. It merely stipulates that in actual occurrence this human attachment need not conform fully to its abstract pattern. We will return to some of these same ideas shortly.

Before going on to discuss at somewhat greater length two final aspects of Ibn al-Qayyim's teaching on *ʿishq*, there are a few other points in his doctrine which should be recalled briefly. Again, several of these reveal the indirect influence of antiquity.[56] *ʿIshq*, more typically than any other variety of love, demonstrates the consequences of similarity. Hence, barring the presence of some major obstacle, it will be reciprocal.[57] Among sinners such mutual love will soon turn to hatred, usually in this world but certainly in the next.[58] It can exist with or without carnal desire but is stronger when accompanied by it.[59] For Ibn al-Qayyim, just as for Ibn al-Jawzī and the ancients, the love referred to as *ʿishq* constitutes a disease, and it is of a kind rarely cured once it has set in.[60] It afflicts only an empty heart.[61] It does particular harm to its victim by rendering him unmindful of his spiritual obligations and corrupting his reason and senses.[62] Nevertheless, the emotion of *ʿishq* in itself is neither to be blamed absolutely nor to be praised without qualification. Directed to what God loves, as to one's wife, *ʿishq* can be a laudable aid to religion, as long as it does not grow into a serious distraction from love to God. Towards a woman who for some reason may not be obtained, if conceived unintentionally as from an accidental glance, it is canonically neutral. Cure is desirable (*mustaḥabb*), but God will reward the lover for chaste endurance. *ʿIshq* for a forbidden woman into which one enters intentionally, however, and *ʿishq* for a beardless youth—the latter being a sign that one has fallen from the eye of God—are blameworthy. Cure from such affections is an obligation (*wājib*) for Muslims.[63]

ʿISHQ AS IDOLATRY

Despite his hesitation to censure it unconditionally, Ibn al-Qayyim certainly considered *ʿishq* as it generally occurred to deserve condemnation in the harshest terms. His many exhortations against this excessive love dwell on its intimate relationship with such taboos as fornication and sodomy, and he treats it as both cause and effect of the greatest of sins—*shirk* or idolatry. At one point the scholar may assert that the type of love denoted by *ʿishq* is ascribed in the Koran only to women (Potiphar's wife and her Egyptian friends) and to the perverted tribe of Lot,[64] while elsewhere—referring to the same two groups—he will use stronger words, stating that God attributes this passion only to idolaters.[65] From the latter claim it may be assumed that a prior commitment to idolatry is understood to be the cause of *ʿishq*—the love of Potiphar's wife for Joseph was inordinate because she was an idolatress. Expanding on this point, Ibn al-Qayyim contends that the nearer a man is to idolatry, the more acute his *ʿishq*, whereas, the further he is from idolatry, the further he will be from such excess in love.[66]

But if *ʿishq* is proportional to idolatry, then it must be inversely proportional to monotheistic spirituality (*tawḥīd*), and it is indeed this latter formula which is most often used to express the author's position. In such contexts the causal relationship is reversed. Ibn al-Qayyim states explicitly that passionate love may diminish a man's devotion to God or even uproot it completely. The affection is thus no longer merely one of the consequences of idolatry: *ʿishq* itself is at war with monotheism.[67] Those who, seeking a manifestation of the divine beauty, adopt *ʿishq* as a religion are deluding themselves. In reality they are following the path of the polytheistic Arabs of the Days of Ignorance. They set up the objects of their amorous contemplation as equals to God, loving them as they love him, whether with religious feeling, carnal desire, or both.[68]

The details of Ibn al-Qayyim's argument must not be allowed to cloud his basic point. What he is saying is that inordinate *ʿishq* and proper love to God both pursue their objects as ends in themselves and therefore, like objective idolatry and monotheism, are in their essence mutually exclusive. But the most important fact is that he does not draw his final analogy between formal religious creeds on the one hand and states of the soul on the other. It is strictly the latter which are involved in the comparison. Contradictory professions of faith totally exclude all intermediate positions. But such verbal commitments have only ritual value; they have little to do with true piety. Spiritual states, the primary concern of religion, are another matter. It is the nature of such affects to occur in varying degrees of intensity. Hence two conflicting attractions, however incompatible in their essence, may be present simultaneously in any given individual. It is the relative balance prevailing between the higher and lower desires, nothing more, which actually determines whether a man will be an idolater or a sincere monotheist. This is why Ibn al-Qayyim specifies that the essence of early Arabian idolatry was the association of other beings with God as equal objects of love.[69] In this sense every man has something of the idolater in him—a matter of the utmost gravity, since the one whose love for a creature equals or exceeds his love to God is guilty of a kind of *shirk* which is unpardonable.[70] Such a man worships and magnifies his beloved to a degree appropriate only in the context of sacred love.[71] Considering the stakes, it is hardly surprising that Ibn al-Qayyim seems to make the curtailment or eradication of idolatrous affections the primary function of true religion.[72]

ʿISHQ AS DIVINE LOVE

A final question regarding *ʿishq* was whether the term itself should be applied to the love-relationship between God and man. Early in the course of Muslim history *ʿishq* had been adopted as the preferred word for sacred love by the theologian ʿAbd al-Wāḥid b. Zayd of Basra (d. 177/793–94). This choice was based on a tradition from Ḥasan al-Baṣrī in which God himself speaks (*ḥadīth qudsī*) which contains the phrases "ʿashiqanī wa-ʿashiqtuhu" or "he loved me with *ʿishq* and I loved him with *ʿishq*." According to the explanation offered by Massignon, ʿAbd al-Wāḥid recurred to terms like *ʿishq* and *shawq*, implying desire, rather than to *maḥabba*, which suggests consummation, in deference to those theologians who rejected the possibility of love between God and man. *Ḥubb* (or *maḥabba*) was to regain its own in the teachings of al-Muḥāsibī and Maʿrūf al-Karkhī.[73] This latter development did not mean, however, that the use of *ʿishq* was eclipsed or that the various competing terms came to be universally accepted as interchangeable. It is known from the *ʿAṭf al-alif* of al-Daylamī that the author's instructor in mysticism, the celebrated Ibn Khafīf (Abu ʿAbd Allāh al-Shīrāzī, d. 371/982), opposed the use of *ʿishq* to denote sacred love until he discovered an opinion from al-Junayd supporting it. He then changed his mind and wrote a tract on the question.[74] Al-Daylamī himself says that *maḥabba* is the better term because consensus supports it, but he goes on to name *ʿishq* as the highest stage of religious love.[75] After the time of al-Daylamī the importance of the issue seems to have declined, at least for some major writers. Al-Hujwīrī (d. 465–69/1072–77) mentions the controversy, noting that *ʿishq* implies desire; but he fails to offer any decision of his own.[76]

Only a few years later al-Ghazālī felt it necessary to reassert emphatically the propriety of *ʿishq* as a term denoting man's love to God. *ʿIshq*, he contends, means simply love which is excessive (*maḥabba mufriṭa*) and firmly implanted (*mu'akkada*). Thus when love for God becomes firmly implanted it is rightly called *ʿishq*. Indeed, a man will come to love one having God's attributes to such a degree that even this word will not suffice to express the excess of his attachment. There are nevertheless some who understand from *ʿishq* only the desire for (physical) union (*ṭalab al-wiṣāl*). With such donkeys, he concludes, words like *ʿishq*, *shawq* (longing), and *wiṣāl* (union) must not be used, just as daffodils and sweet basil are to be guarded from cattle.[77] Al-Ghazālī's jibe was aimed directly at those who held the opinion subscribed to less than a century later by the Ḥanbalite Ibn al-Jawzī.[78] To them his defense of *ʿishq*, objectionable enough as stated, must have seemed all the more insolent in view of the fact that he himself, in the profane context, branded the passion as "the extreme of ignorance concerning the goal of sexual intercourse."[79] Ibn al-Jawzī, in his sharp reaction to the use of *ʿishq* in the sense of man's love for God, may well have had al-Ghazālī's position in mind. This was certainly true of Ibn Taymīya, who mentioned the great mystic-theologian by name in connection with his own more tempered rejection of the word.[80]

Ibn al-Qayyim's observations on the use of *ʿishq* to mean sacred love follow the balanced approach of his teacher. Describing the undivided love owed to God, he remarks that this love, "even if it be called *ʿishq*," constitutes the highest good of man.[81] Thus, however great his reservations, our author admits that the usage is at least conceivable. He does not condemn the word *ʿishq* outright but chooses rather to stress its inappropriateness. First, there is no scriptural authority for the use of the term to indicate love between God and man in either direction. Moreover, since like *mayl*, *ṣabāba*, *gharām*, *shaghaf*, and *hawā*, it is equivocal, having both praiseworthy and blameworthy connotations, it is patently unsuitable as a name for sacred love. In particular—Ibn al-Qayyim reverses al-Ghazālī's reasoning—*ʿishq* implies excess, a quality which can be asserted neither of God's love nor, more especially, of man's love for God, since the latter is never equal to its object. Likewise the word may suggest the characteristics of the vine *ʿashaqa* (lablab), to which some etymologists refer in explaining its semantic relation to its root. This plant entwines itself around a tree and is subject to change (of color). Such, clearly, are not proper attributes of love between God and man.[82]

An interesting development is noticeable here in the Ḥanbalite treatment of *ʿishq* as a term for sacred love. Fundamentally the usage is still rejected, but a certain degree of tolerance is evident. The question which presents itself is whether this more relaxed approach reflects an actual softening of attitude or merely another application of the school's new style in polemics, that is, a purely rhetorical concession offered in the hope of rendering their basic position more palatable to readers with Sufi leanings. One should perhaps opt for the second alternative. It is true that Ibn al-Qayyim seems to have had some understanding of how a mystic in ecstasy might be led to employ the word *ʿishq*.[83] But the new tolerance was first expressed by Ibn Taymīya, who was somewhat less involved in the details of Sufism. Moreover, the statements of both writers indicate that they had real hesitations regarding the connotations of the term. It is unlikely, despite the apparent sense of their remarks, that these hesitations were based solely on the nuances of carnality and excess which accompany *ʿishq* in its secular meaning. Such considerations were undoubtedly relevant, but it was quite probably the very fact that the word was associated with mysticism, the major vehicle of *eros* doctrine in Islam, which constituted the underlying motive for their objections. This was in essence the chief concern voiced by Ibn al-Jawzī, and it is difficult to imagine that it failed to trouble his successors.

Shawq (longing, desire)

The word *shawq* occurs in only one of Ibn al-Qayyim's lists of the stages of love (table 2, A), but the concept of longing or desire to which it refers is a prominent theme in his later writings. Already in *al-Dāʾ wa-l-dawāʾ* and *Rawḍat al-muḥibbīn* the term is discussed, although the relevant passages do not reveal a full awareness of the bearing of the problems involved on other aspects of Ḥanbalite teaching.[84] When Ibn al-Qayyim became preoccupied with formal mysticism, however, he devoted increased attention to the question of religious longing, studying it at some length in his lost work *al-Mawrid al-ṣāfī* as well as in *Ṭarīq al-hijratayn* and *Madārij al-sālikīn*.[85] The most thorough of his extant treatments of *shawq*, found in the relatively late *Ṭarīq*, examines the subject under seven rubrics: (1) the nature of longing; (2) its relation to love (*maḥabba*); (3) whether it may be attributed to God; (4) whether it is a factor in man's love to God; (5) whether it ceases or increases with union; (6) the distinction between the terms *shawq* and *ishtiyāq*; and (7) the degrees of longing.

The first two questions are dealt with quickly. 1) Longing or *shawq* is defined as "the journey of the heart in quest of the beloved." The essential element shared by this and other authoritative definitions of the word, the scholar points out, is the implied absence of the beloved. Longing is therefore by nature an unconsummated passion. 2) Its relation to love is that of an effect to its cause. One says: "I long for a thing because I love it," not the reverse. Accordingly, love is a nobler (*aʿlā*, higher) sentiment than longing, the contrary assertions of the mystic Sarī al-Saqaṭī and others notwithstanding.[86] These few remarks represent the core of what Ibn al-Qayyim has to say on the two initial questions.

3) With regard to the attribution of *shawq* to God, certain apologists had argued that the Creator, since he loves men, must also long to meet them, this being universally the case with lovers. As further support of their view they cited a tradition in which God is reported to have said: "The pious have long yearned to meet me, but my longing to meet them is greater." Ibn al-Qayyim related this same saying uncritically in the early work *al-Dā' wa-l-dawā'*,[87] but in the *Ṭarīq* he quotes it only to deny its substance. *Shawq*, like *ʿishq*, may not be ascribed to God, and for identical reasons. The connotations of the word are unsuitable, and explicit authority for its use is lacking in the Koran and the authentic traditions of the Prophet.[88]

4) It may properly be said of man, however, that he longs for God, since this usage is attested in the sacred texts. The Prophet is reported to have uttered in a prayer: "I ask of you the pleasure of beholding your face and a longing to meet you."[89] Up to this point Sufi and traditionist could agree. But the partisans of annihilation (*fanā'*) went a step farther. The great Ḥanbalite mystic al-Anṣārī, and after him the Anda-

lusian Ibn al-ʿArīf in his *Maḥāsin*, had admitted *shawq* or longing as a station of the commonality, but they held it to be a grave deficiency in the elite on the grounds that it implies the absence of the beloved. The method of Sufism, they claimed, is founded on the immediate contemplation of God (*mushāhada*).[90] Ibn al-Qayyim, sensing that to deny longing is in effect to deny love, could not accept this view.

To open his rebuttal, the Neo-Ḥanbalite stipulates that there are two kinds of contemplation: one through knowledge (*maʿrifa*) and another by direct vision (*ʿiyān*). Only the first is truly possible in this world; and it is by no means complete, since it varies with the extent of one's knowledge of God. But what may be said of contemplation through knowledge applies equally to longing. The more man knows of God, the more he will long to increase his knowledge; and as there is no conceivable end to what may be known about God, there can be no end to longing. Such being the case, longing cannot be considered a deficiency in relation to contemplation through knowledge. A similar reasoning holds for the contemplation of "direct vision." Insofar as it may be taken to refer to an experience in this life, the expression "direct vision" must be construed as a metaphor for the presence of the heart before its Lord. Contemplation of this sort does not require that a man cease to desire God; on the contrary, it can only increase one's longing actually to meet him.[91] "Direct vision" may also refer to beholding God in the next life, but even in this context longing cannot be called a deficiency. There are two considerations which bear out this judgment. First, since even the most privileged of the inhabitants of Paradise experience the beatific vision only twice daily, they must continually long for its recurrence. Second, for reasons to be given below, the very assumption that longing can have as its object only one who is absent, in other words, that it must cease with contemplation or union, is to be rejected as false—or, more precisely, as but partially true and therefore misleading. Longing is in fact heightened through contemplation.[92]

5) The assertion that longing increases with contemplation, superficially at least, is at variance with Ibn al-Qayyim's original definition of the term *shawq*. Under his fifth rubric the scholar summarizes the arguments for and against this controversial opinion. Some authorities held that longing, being the "journey" of the heart towards the beloved, must cease with union, while others, taking it to be a consequence of love, maintained that it continues to exist as long as the affection which is its cause endures. Ibn al-Qayyim's introductory remarks, it has been seen, comprehend the aspects of *shawq* cited by each of the two sides. Obliged therefore to recognize the logic of both positions, he

attempts to distinguish two levels of *shawq*—one before and one after union. The initial longing, which has union as its object and consists in a kind of movement towards the beloved, naturally ceases with the attainment of its goal; but it is replaced by a new longing, described in the *Madārij* as ineffable and knowable only through experience.[93] In *Tarīq al-hijratayn* the author is more explicit: longing on the higher level is directed towards the *intensification* of the relationship (*ta-ʿalluq*, attachment) between lover and beloved.[94] All of this obviously recalls Ibn al-Qayyim's comments on the question of whether marital love and other licit human attachments terminate with intercourse.[95] Here, however, the frame of reference is spiritual, and the implication is not simply that *shawq* persists until death. Since the qualities of the object of spiritual longing are infinite, there is, in the next life at least, no limit to the degree of intensity of this emotion and no end to its duration.

6) Many writers made a lexical distinction between the two levels of longing, terming the first *shawq* and the second *ishtiyāq*. Ibn al-Qayyim comes near to accepting this usage in the early *Rawḍa*, where he treats *shawq* (verbal noun from *shāqa*, to arouse longing) as beginning and cause, while specifying *ishtiyāq* (verbal noun from *ishtāqa*, to long) as its consequence. He does not differentiate these two forms when discussing the levels of longing with which we are concerned, however.[96] Bringing up the terminological issue once again in *Ṭarīq al-hijratayn*, he alters his approach, but not in the direction one might expect. In ordinary usage, he notes, *shawq* has come to be hardly more than a "substantive" (*ism maṣdar*) equivalent to the verbal noun *ishtiyāq*.[97] From this remark it is obvious that the author did not choose to take advantage of the technical distinction between the two words. In his mystical works he had to consider carefully the repercussions of what he wrote. His reluctance to adopt this particular terminology is probably to be explained by the fact that it was associated in the minds of his readers with the profane theories of writers like Ibn Dāwūd and, more important in this instance, with the Sufism of Ibn al-ʿArabī.[98]

7) Turning to a strictly mystical method of ranking the levels of *shawq*, Ibn al-Qayyim sets out to comment the gradation of longing established by al-Anṣārī. As was his constant practice in the *Manāzil*, al-Anṣārī had enumerated three degrees of this station: (1) longing for Paradise; (2) longing for God, "sown by the love which grows on the banks of [God's] kindnesses," in which the believer's heart becomes attached to the divine attributes; and finally (3) "a fire ignited by pure

love, spoiling earthly life, depriving of comfort, and deterred by no consolation short of meeting [the beloved]."[99] Unlike the majority of the shaykh's trilogies, this one is acceptable to Ibn al-Qayyim.[100] The reason is not without significance. As Ibn al-Qayyim knew well, the third degree of almost every station treated in the *Manāzil* was somehow construed as an equivalent of *fanā'*, or the annihilation of self. Longing, however, already in the *Manāzil*, and thus considerably before the composition of the *ʿIlal*, had been characterized by al-Anṣārī as a deficiency among the elite.[101] By definition it was incompatible with union of any sort and thus, even at its highest level, did not lend itself to an equation with *fanā'*. Accordingly, the stages of longing as delineated by the mystic did not go beyond what were to Neo-Ḥanbalism the conceivable bounds of religious experience. Ironically, it is in al-Anṣārī's analysis of a station which was for him among the most deficient that his statements come closest to expressing Ibn al-Qayyim's ideal of spirituality.

Fanā' and the stages of mystical love

The key element in al-Anṣārī's Sufism, as may be inferred from what has just been said, is his doctrine of annihilation or *fanā'*. In his early Persian treatise *Ṣad maydān* (apparently the class notes of a disciple) *fanā'* is the ninety-ninth of one hundred "grounds." Surpassed only by *baqā'*, the "subsistence" of God alone, it marks the end of the role allotted to the mystic himself. Love (*maḥabbat*), although it is given as the one-hundred-and-first ground, is not to be taken as a higher station than *baqā'* but rather as the guiding principle of the mystic's progress. It comprises three stages which subsume the entire spiritual journey: rectitude (*rāstī*), or obedience to the law; drunkenness (*mastī*); and annihilation (*nīstī*). The message implied in the arrangement of these stages is that man's love, properly directed, must rise above the fetters of religious convention in which it is conceived and, in the end, consume itself in the abiding love of God.[102]

In the later *Manāzil al-sā'irīn*—a work in which, according to Father de Beaurecueil, al-Anṣārī had moved from a more moralizing doctrine towards greater stress on things properly mystical[103]—*fanā'* is no longer the penultimate station, being followed by eight others, beginning with *baqā'* and ending with *jam*ʿ (concentration) and *tawḥīd* (profession of the divine unity). It remains, however, the dominant motif. Already in *Ṣad maydān, fanā'* characterizes the highest levels of certain stations, for example "reality" (*ḥaqīqat*) and "instant" (*vaqt*).[104] In the *Manāzil*, as has been mentioned, this is the case with almost every station. Thus the placing of *jam*ʿ and *tawḥīd* at the summit of the spiritual itinerary does not reflect a downgrading of the concepts of *fanā'* and *baqā'* in their essence but merely a precision of vocabulary. In fact, the two pairs of terms parallel each other. The highest phase of "concentration" is "the disappearance (*talāshī*) of all that allusion may bear in the essence of God, truly," while the sublime and only real profession of divine unity is God's own unification of himself.[105] Nothing, it will be observed, is expressed by *jam*ʿ and *tawḥīd*, which is not implied more generally by the words *fanā'* and *baqā'* as used in *Ṣad maydān*. Thus in his late *ʿIlal al-maqāmāt*, where the discussion is limited to a few very basic terms, al-Anṣārī once again concludes with a reference to *fanā'* and *baqā'*.[106]

The *ʿIlal* was probably dictated in response to a question concerning a statement made in the *Manāzil*. At issue was al-Anṣārī's pronouncement that all states and stations other than *tawḥīd* are accompanied by deficiencies (*ʿilal*), or traces of the mystic himself.[107] In the *ʿIlal*, the shaykh substantiates his earlier claim by selecting ten of the most typical stations, among them *maḥabba* and *shawq*, and showing how each, although necessary to the commonality, is a shortcoming in the elite. Love to God, the object of our concern here, is the "pillar of faith" among the commonality, but it is the "particular blight (*ʿilla*) of *fanā'*" among the elite, since it implies the continued existence of the mystic.[108] Al-Anṣārī's treatise, as we know, was adopted by the Andalusian Ibn al-ʿArīf as the basis of his *Maḥāsin al-majālis*, a work which likewise stresses the deficiencies of the mystical stations. The *Maḥāsin*, slavishly rehearsing al-Anṣārī's pronouncements, reveals little originality. Most of the analytical passages of Ibn alʿArīf's work are direct quotes from the *ʿIlal*, often combined with sentences from the *Manāzil*. The author's own contribution, although considerably lengthening the text, consists of little more than a selection from the sayings of the early Sufis with some anecdotal material provided by way of illustration.[109]

It will be recalled that both Ibn al-ʿArīf's *Maḥāsin* and al-Anṣārī's *Manāzil* were the objects of detailed commentaries by Ibn al-Qayyim. Both were dominated by the doctrine of *fanā'*, and the Neo-Ḥanbalite writer's concerns reflect this fact. The question of whether al-Anṣārī's conception of *fanā'* was to be understood in the sense of complete annihilation or simply as loss of consciousness of self had become a moot point for later commentators.[110] Monists, ʿAfīf al-Dīn al-Tilimsānī in particular, interpreted the shaykh's doctrine as referring to the cessation of individual existence or, more exactly, to the end of the illusion that the self has a separate existence. Ibn al-Qayyim repudiates this view, arguing that al-Anṣārī's teaching on the divine attributes makes it clear that he could not have been a proponent of monism. To al-Tilimsānī's claim that the term *jamʿ* as used in the *Manāzil* means the concentration of existence (*jamʿ al-wujūd*), the scholar answers that what is in fact intended is the concentration of contemplation (*jamʿ al-shuhūd*).[111] He contends, moreover, that the word *wujūd* itself, in al-Anṣārī's usage, means "finding," not "being" as it is defined by the theologians, philosophers, and monists.[112]

Ibn al-Qayyim's defense of the great Ḥanbalite mystic stops at this point. He recognized frankly that al-Anṣārī had held the annihilation of consciousness of world and self in the contemplation of God to be the goal of Sufism. This goal, according to his own outlook, had nothing to do with Islam.[113] Nevertheless, constrained by the terminology of the times and the framework of the treatises which he was commenting, Ibn al-Qayyim found himself obliged to integrate *fanā'*, at least the word, into his new scheme of mysticism. Following the manner of Ibn Taymīya, the scholar lists three types of *fanā'*: passing away from the existence of that which is other than God (*al-fanā' ʿan wujūd al-siwā*); passing away from the contemplation of the other (*al-fanā' ʿan shuhūd al-siwā*); and passing away from the worship and love of the other (*al-fanā' ʿan ʿibādat* [or: *maḥabbat*] *al-siwā*.[114]

As Ibn al-Qayyim explains it, the first type of *fanā'* is that subscribed to by the monists, whose aim is to free themselves from what they consider to be the illusion of duality between Lord and servant. The denial of the distinction between obedience and disobedience, for Neo-Ḥanbalism perhaps the most objectionable feature of monist doctrine, is held to follow directly from this understanding of *fanā'*. The idea of obedience can be relevant only in the context of a relationship between two separate beings.[115] The second interpretation, described as that held by al-Anṣārī, is said to have been adopted by a large number of later Sufis—the contemplative or *shuhūdī* school. These mystics acknowledged the reality of the distinction between Lord and servant as well as that between obedience and disobedience; but in the state of *fanā'* they ceased to perceive the duality which they professed. Ibn al-Qayyim remarks that some of them, including al-Anṣārī, made *fanā'*, in the sense of loss of perception, the ultimate goal of Sufism, while others deemed it an experience necessary to the spiritual journey but one to be surpassed by *baqā'*, understood here as the persistence of the mystic in awareness. (The latter opinion may have been shared by Abū 'l-ʿAbbās al-Wāsiṭī, Ibn al-Qayyim's instructor in mysticism.)[116] Neither of the *shuhūdī* views is correct, the reader is told. Loss of perception is on the contrary an obstacle in the mystic's path. It may result when an intense religious experience occurs in one too weak to receive it, or it may come about because, out of ignorance, it is pursued as a goal. The best that can be said for this *fanā'* in contemplation is that it is forgivable when it is occasioned by the weakness of the subject.[117]

In this argument Ibn al-Qayyim rejects al-Anṣārī's doctrine of *fanā'* together with the monist position from which he was so careful to distinguish it. He thus challenges the fundamental assumption on which the shaykh had founded his spirituality. Consequently, at any point where al-Anṣārī's teaching on love is predicated on the annihilation of consciousness a negative reaction may be anticipated on the part of the Neo-Ḥanbalite commentator, in whose scheme only the third kind of *fanā'*, passing away from the worship and love of what is other than God, is legitimate. This last *fanā'* occurs simultaneously with the perception of the other. Ibn al-Qayyim reasons that it therefore serves to increase the believer's love. Beholding the other, impossible in the *shuhūdī* experience, affords an opportunity to compare the various objects which compete for man's devotion.[118]

In his *Manāzil* al-Anṣārī had relegated love (*maḥabba*) to an intermediate role, making it the sixty-first of one hundred stations dealt with in the treatise and describing it as "the first of the valleys of *fanā'* and the slope from which one descends to the stages of effacement, . . . the last stage where the vanguard of the commonality meet the rear guard of the elite."[119] Conforming to the pattern he had set for himself in the work, he established three degrees of love. Here is the division as he expressed it:

> The first degree is a love which cuts short evil insinuations, makes one take pleasure in service, and consoles from afflictions. It is a love which sprouts from the consideration of the [divine] attributes, becomes firmly rooted through following the Sunna, and grows as one responds to [one's spiritual] need.
>
> The second degree is a love which incites to give preference to God over any other than him, infatuates the tongue with mentioning him, and attaches the heart to the contemplation of him. It is

> a love which arises (*taẓhar*) from consideration of the attributes, reflection on the signs [of God], and the exercise of the stations.
>
> The third degree is a ravishing love which cuts short expression, renders allusion too subtle [to attain it] (*tudaqqiqu 'l-ishāra*), and is beyond the realm of epithets.[120]

In this arrangement, as in that given in *Ṣad maydān*, love is shown to end in the ineffable state of *fanā'*. If the text leaves any doubt concerning this point, the author makes it quite clear towards the end of his *ʿIlal:* "The love of the elite is their annihilation in the love which God has for them, for all loves lose themselves in God's love for his beloved."[121] Ibn al-ʿArīf, through whose *Maḥāsin al-majālis* Ibn al-Qayyim approached the teachings of al-Anṣārī's *ʿIlal* in *Ṭarīq al-hijratayn*, repeats this statement.[122] His section on love borrows phrases from both the *Manāzil* and the *ʿIlal*, but since he is following the twofold division of mystics into the commonality and the elite (*ʿawāmm, khawāṣṣ*) employed in the latter work, he cites only the first and third of al-Anṣārī's degrees. Ibn al-ʿArīf's omission of the second degree is pointed out in the *Ṭarīq*, where the *Manāzil* is quoted directly to supplement the Andalusian's text.[123]

The first and second of al-Anṣārī's degrees of love are commented carefully and without objection by Ibn al-Qayyim in both the *Ṭarīq* and *Madārij al-sālikīn*.[124] The fact should come as no surprise, since the distinction in this case corresponds perfectly to that made by the Neo-Ḥanbalite writer himself between love for God as a result of his beneficence and love motivated by his perfection and beauty as they may be deduced from the divine names and attributes.[125] Turning to the third degree, however, Ibn al-Qayyim remarks that there is disagreement as to whether it is higher than the second. Al-Anṣārī and his followers, he explains, made "ravishing love" the third and highest stage in accordance with their principle that *fanā'* is the ultimate goal of Sufism. Stricken with such a love, the mystic will pass away utterly from awareness of self, the beloved remaining as though he alone were loving himself. The first two degrees were held to be inferior because they are accompanied by *baqā'* (the subsistence of the lover in a state of perception, according to the preferred Neo-Ḥanbalite usage).[126]

In reply to the partisans of this view, whom we may call the contemplative monists, Ibn al-Qayyim asserts the preeminence of al-Anṣārī's second degree of love, describing it as "the degree of the perfect among lovers." To substantiate his own opinion, he offers a comparison between the religious experiences of Moses and Muḥammad. The Hebrew prophet, it should be mentioned, was a recurring figure in mystical discussions of *fanā'*, the Koranic account of his swoon at God's manifestation on the mountain being cited to provide a historic example of the station.[127] Ibn al-Qayyim argues that Muḥammad, although he had attained the highest degree of love, continued to be attentive to the train of events and the needs of the community. He did not lose consciousness during his Night Journey but was fully capable of receiving the speech and commands of his Lord, as is evident from his returning to God a number of times over the matter of prayer. (Muḥammad, at the suggestion of Moses, succeeded in having the quota of prescribed daily prayers reduced from fifty to five.)[128] The state of the prophet of Islam, the argument concludes, is undoubtedly superior to that of Moses, who fell senseless to the ground while God revealed himself to the mountain![129]

Despite the fact that Ibn al-Qayyim capitalizes on the Sufi theme, it is unlikely indeed that he considered Moses' swoon an instance of contemplative *fanā'*. More probably he was accepting the mystical interpretation of the event merely for the immediate purpose of his demonstration. This assumption would seem to explain why he advances an apparently contradictory view in one chapter of the *Madārij*, where he objects to al-Anṣārī's inclusion of the station of bewilderment (*hayamān*) in the spiritual itinerary. In the mystic's treatment of this station he again cites Moses' loss of consciousness. Ibn al-Qayyim dismisses the example on the grounds that it was the crumbling of the mountain, not the revelation itself, which struck the Hebrew prophet senseless.[130] There is no reason to doubt that the opinion expressed in this context represents the scholar's true assessment of the Koranic incident; otherwise "bewilderment" could be justifiably pursued as a mystical station. But Neo-Ḥanbalite writers had considerable tactical leeway. The first principle of religious polemics as taught by Ibn Taymīya was to address one's contemporaries in their own language. The jurist's student was skillfully exploiting this principle. It is certain that the comparison of Muḥammad's conscious perception with Moses' swoon, when the latter event was understood in Sufi terms, constituted a compelling argument against those who made *fanā'* the highest stage of love, especially since al-Anṣārī and his followers readily acknowledged elsewhere the superiority of the Muḥammadan heritage to the Mosaic.[131]

Ibn al-Qayyim demonstrates the flexibility of his tactics more than once in his repudiation of *fanā'*. The Egyptian women of Sūrat Yūsuf, who cut their hands at the sight of Joseph's beauty, are often cited in mystical treatises along with Moses to illustrate the station. This example is likewise rejected by the Ḥanbalite. The love of Potiphar's wife for Joseph, which was superior to that of her companions, was so because she did not lose control of her faculties as they did. Their love was indeed comparable to *fanāʾ*; but hers, combining stability with contemplation of the beloved, resembled the higher station of *baqāʾ*.[132] Here, clearly, the scholar admits the Sufi analogy solely for the purpose of enhancing his own argument. Elsewhere in his works, as has been seen, Potiphar's wife and the Egyptial women are named together, along with the inhabitants of Sodom, as archetypes of the association between *ʿishq*-love and idolatry.[133]

An interesting if somewhat problematic aside to Ibn al-Qayyim's refutation of the view that sacred love ends in *fanāʾ* is found in *Ṭarīq al-hijratayn.* At one point in that work the author interrupts his argument with a digression on a hypothetical but crucial objection, namely, that opinions about spiritual states are to be accepted only from those who have tasted (*dhāqa*) or experienced them. His reply, outlined in the following few sentences, merits attention. To begin, he argues, the masters of the mystical path are known to agree that true knowledge (*ʿilm*) is more to be trusted than mere experience (*dhawq*). Moreover, it cannot be said that knowledge of a thing is to be accepted only from those who are acquainted with it at first hand, since this is surely not the case with physical conditions such as disease and pain. Finally, one must consider what is meant by the word *dhawq* itself. If it applies strictly to the experience of those who have known something in its highest degree, then no one is to be trusted, for in spiritual matters there is no degree above which there is not another. If, however, *dhawq* is understood to be what is commonly called mystical experience, it is unreasonable to deny that it occurs among men of learning while admitting its possibility among others.[134]

Undoubtedly the passage summarized here reflects Ibn al-Qayyim's awareness of the image his opponents must have had of him. Sensing that the nature of his spirituality, not to mention his sincerity in adopting Sufi terminology, would be suspect in their eyes, he deemed it essential to substantiate his reliability on issues such as *fanāʾ* and sacred love. Whether the passage in fact alludes to aspects of his personal religious life is another matter. In my own research I have found nothing to suggest that he ever experienced annihilation of consciousness, although it is known that he spent much of his time in devotions. It would appear from the remarks in question that he was deliberately leading his readers to believe that he had encountered all of the spiritual states with which they themselves were familiar, whether or not this was actually the case. The tactical advantages he might anticipate from a move of this kind should be obvious.

What may be stated with certainty is that any private experience resembling those pursued by the contemplative monists would have constituted shortcomings within the framework of Ibn al-Qayyim's own system. It should be clear from all that has preceded that his teachings reflect a *nomos* piety foreign to the approach of his Sufi antagonists. The evidence for this conclusion has by no means been exhausted. The scholar's treatment of the fear of God, the fundamental correlative of love in the *nomos* scheme,[135] reveals the conformity of his doctrine to the traditional pattern of legalistic religion in one of its most typical aspects. When al-Anṣārī and Ibn al-ʿArīf attack fear, qualifying it as a deficiency in the elite, Ibn al-Qayyim responds predictably. Unlike love, he admits, fear will indeed end in Paradise. But in this life love without fear and awe does not suffice to bring about the obedience required of man.[136] The message conveyed here is the usual: the pursuit of ecstatic experience must under no circumstances be allowed to interfere with the observance of the many obligations imposed by divine law.

In concluding his discussion of al-Anṣārī's three degrees of mystical love, Ibn al-Qayyim deplores the fact that the shaykh made love not an end in itself but merely one station in the path towards annihilation.[137] The place of love in the conception of *fanā'* which the Neo-Ḥanbalite doctors had formulated was altogether different. According to their teaching, as we have seen, *fanā'* consists in passing away from the love and worship of all that is other than God. In this scheme, the persistence of the mystic's love to God himself, demonstrated by conformity to the divine will, is essential.

But love will inevitably be construed as a *vis unitiva*, and a kind of union must therefore be shown to crown the spiritual ascent. Neo-Ḥanbalism expressed this goal of oneness as a unification of the "objects" (*murād*) of the human and divine wills. The true monists and their bedfellows the incarnationists saw things in another light. To contrast their views with his own, Ibn al-Qayyim characterizes their conceptions of unity or union with specific reference to their bearing on God's attribute of will. The first group, as he neatly phrases it, taught a real union of the mystic to the Willer (*murīd*) himself (*waḥdat al-wujūd*), while the second went only so far as to maintain a specific assimilation of the human faculty of will to its divine counterpart. The dangers for the moral life of the community which the

Neo-Ḥanbalites sensed in these monist heresies have already been mentioned in some detail.[138] The contemplative mystics, for their part, taught a union of perception—the doctrine known as *waḥdat al-shuhūd.* The moral implications of this position, also touched on earlier, may require closer attention here. Through the obliteration of the individual consciousness in *fanā'*, the *shuhūdī* mystics claimed to see all things as God sees them. Proceeding from this claim, it was no more difficult for them than for the true monists to justify an antinomian ethic. The argument seems to have run as follows. Since nothing occurs or exists apart from an act of God which he has willed, and since, further, all of God's acts from his perspective are good, all occurrences and all beings must therefore be deemed good when observed from the divine perspective. Consequently, for the one who sees things only as God sees them, the distinction between good and evil ceases to exist. He knows that whatever he may do, even if it is contrary to express commandments, will be in full accord with the object of God's will.[139]

Ibn al-Qayyim points out that al-Anṣārī and those who shared his views had neglected in their argument the distinction between the creative and prescriptive aspects of the divine will discussed by Ibn Taymīya. This was in his opinion an oversight of the utmost gravity, since according to Ḥanbalite doctrine it is strictly to the object of the *prescriptive* will that men must endeavor to unite their intentions.[140] In this connection the scholar cites another important distinction which the *shuhūdī*s failed to notice—that between the active and passive aspects of acts (*fiʿl* and *mafʿūl*). It is clear from reason, linguistics, and revelation, he asserts, that the traditionist party is right in distinguishing between the "act of doing" (*fiʿl*, infinitive) and the "thing done" (*mafʿūl*, passive participle). With this distinction in mind, it may be admitted that all of God's *afʿāl* ("doings") are in accord with his prescriptive will; but the case is not necessarily the same with his *mafʿūlāt* ("things done" by him), which are properly speaking the "doings" of his servants. These latter acts have certainly been ordained by the creative will, but they may be either good or evil from God's perspective, that is, they may or may not conform to the object of his prescriptive will.[141]

To pursue Ibn al-Qayyim's last point further would take us into the problems of predestination and free will, which fall outside the scope of this study. But the relevance of his reasoning to the question at hand is evident enough. The *shuhūdī* understanding of how God perceives the world must be recognized as incomplete if not altogether false, and hence its implications in the sphere of morals cannot be accepted. This argument, of course, comes on top of another which reasons in the reverse direction. An assessment of the ethical implications of the doctrine of unity of perception shows the doctrine itself to be unsound. In either case the result is the same. The union which consummates sacred love is not a fusion of being, most certainly, but neither is it an identity of perception. It is a union of aims, no more and no less.

The upshot of the Ḥanbalite scholar's teaching, here as elsewhere, is to stress obedience to the divine law. God's aims, to which men must conform their own, cannot be known through ecstasy—source of the heresies of existential and contemplative monism alike. They may best be discovered in the traditional stores of religious knowledge—the Koran and Sunna. It is obedience to the sacred code revealed in these sources, the verbal expression of God's prescriptive will, which is the culmination of "mystical" experience in this life; and obedience is the goal which the reader is admonished to pursue in nearly every chapter of Ibn al-Qayyim's commentaries. Throughout *Ṭarīq al-hijratayn* and *Madārij al-sālikīn*, works totaling more than fifteen hundred pages in the printed editions, the author has skillfully reproduced model mystical treatises and has manipulated the technical vocabulary of Sufism with the virtuosity of a true master only to expound the conventional message of *nomos* religion.

Other facets of Ibn al-Qayyim's doctrine of love could be dealt with here, but our conclusions would remain the same. If the outline I have given is by no means complete, it is none the less representative. With the exception of points on which the scholar merely rehearses the teachings of Ibn al-Jawzī and Ibn Taymīya, this chapter and the three which precede it have covered most of the significant elements of his treatment of love. Certainly there are found in his works lengthy passages on the signs and effects of love, its remedies, the rules governing the behavior of the enamored, and other topics which have received only passing attention in this portion of our study.[142] But Ibn al-Qayyim's approach to these questions follows directly from the basic positions already described, all of which, it may be said, reflect his abiding concern for the spiritual and moral well-being of the community as conceived by the *ahl al-ḥadīth*. Thus in *Rawḍat al-muḥibbīn* his discussions of two typical signs of profane love, jealousy and the unusually frequent concurrence of lovers in matters such as sentiment and disease, become the occasion respectively for treating the sacred jealousy of God and the faithful and the conformity of will required by religious love.[143] In the same book, the chapter on obedience to a secular beloved turns into a refutation of the Sufi doctrine of unity of existence—the unity of aims being proposed in its stead.[144] These examples are typical. Throughout the *Rawḍa* the *nomos* motif constantly reasserts itself.

Cases of transition from the profane to the sacred like the ones we have just mentioned will be recognized as applications of the technique of flexibility in religious debate advocated by Ibn Taymīya. It was this same technique which determined the style and literary form of the works in which Ibn al-Qayyim dealt with controversial topics like love.[145] With the exception of *al-Dā' wa-l-dawā'*, which is frankly homiletic in character, the books which constitute the major sources for the author's doctrine of love conform to the standards of the disciplines in which the subject was most often discussed in technical fashion—belles-lettres, theology, and mysticism. *Rawḍat al-muḥibbīn* is an anthology. *Miftāḥ Dār al-Saʿāda* and *Shifā' al-ʿalīl*, reflecting for the most part the arguments of Ibn Taymīya, resemble works of speculative theology. The *Ṭarīq* and the *Madārij* are cast as mystical treatises.

As should now be clear, any search for a change in fundamental outlook corresponding to the variations in structure, language, content, or even the date of composition of these ostensibly quite dissimilar works would end in frustration. On the other hand, taking into consideration the many points on which Ibn al-Qayyim's stance was unyielding, one may readily assess from the variety of molds utilized to convey his arguments the extent to which he was willing to compromise in order to resolve the conflicts between the orthodox and their adversaries among the cultivated and libertine elite, the theologians, and the more extreme Sufis. It seems that almost any formal concession was acceptable, but no conscious compromise on matters of basic doctrine could be tolerated. Since Ibn al-Qayyim's teaching was comprehensive, and since he had no prominent successor in the field of systematic dogma, this attitude of no compromise on essentials came to dominate Neo-Ḥanbalite thought. The fact had significant bearing on subsequent developments. With the death of this celebrated student of Ibn Taymīya, the effort towards reconciliation had run its course. But later representatives of the Ḥanbalite school were still tempted to write in the same genres as their predecessors. For those who concerned themselves with love, only three alternatives were open—imitation and direct borrowing, codification, or complete disregard for the rigid limits set by the giants of the fourteenth century.

10. The Lingering Tradition: Mar'ī b. Yūsuf's *Munyat al-muḥibbīn*

THE FUNDAMENTAL PRINCIPLES and most of the details of the orthodox Ḥanbalite teaching on love were established once and for all by Ibn Taymīya and Ibn al-Qayyim. But the school continued to produce writers who dealt with love. These men, if they were not always faithful to their predecessors' ideas, at least managed to keep them alive. Their treatment of love, like that of the earlier authorities, took a variety of forms. The fifteenth-century scholar Yūsuf b. Badr al-Dīn, Ibn al-Mabrad (d. 909/1503), wrote another *Censure of passion.*[1] An eighteenth-century Ḥanbalite Emily Post, Muḥammad b. Aḥmad al-Safārīnī (d. 1188/1774), who tells his readers among other things that it is improper to use a piece of bread to wipe one's knife, quotes extensively from Ibn al-Qayyim, the most usual source for later works, when he touches on love and sexual relationships in his book on etiquette. The late-eighteenth- and early-nineteenth-century Wahhābī writer Sulaymān b. ʿAbd Allāh, Ibn ʿAbd al-Wahhāb (d. 1233/1817), codified the views of Ibn Taymīya and Ibn al-Qayyim on the specifically theological aspects of love in his *Taysīr al ʿAzīz al-Ḥamīd.*[3] In our own century, the Egyptian modernist Muḥammad Rashīd Riḍā, although apparently a *shuhūdī* in mysticism,[4] drew heavily on the Neo-Ḥanbalite teaching on love and strongly recommended Ibn al-Qayyim's *Madārij* to present-day mystics interested in the subject.[5]

The first notable reflection of Ibn al-Qayyim's treatment of love is found in the *Dīwān al-ṣabāba* (*Anthology of tender longing*) of Shihāb al-Dīn Aḥmad b. Yaḥyā b. Abī Ḥajala (725/1325–776/1375). Ibn Abī Ḥajala, born in Tlemcen, was the grandson of a celebrated marabout of that city. He grew up in Damascus, where he was presumably exposed to the influence of Ibn al-Qayyim, and eventually settled in Cairo. He was a Sufi of sorts but does not seem to have adhered rigidly to any particular way of thinking. Nominally a Ḥanafite in law, he reportedly would tell the Ḥanafites he was a follower of their rite and the Shāfi-

ʿites that he preferred theirs. In any event, he is described as a Ḥanbalite in dogma and is remembered for his diatribes against the Sufi monists, among whom he singled out Ibn al-Fāriḍ and Ibn al-ʿArabī for special attack. He is said to have been harassed as a result of the virulence of his polemic and thus appears to have shared to a certain extent the fate of Ibn Taymīya and Ibn al-Qayyim. He died in Cairo at the age of fifty-one lunar years.[6]

The *Dīwān al-ṣabāba*, widely read for centuries among the Arab elite,[7] is a charming book which may be loosely described as a catalogue of the themes and motifs of amatory verse. It has a theoretical introduction of some importance, and this section in particular owes much of its content to Ibn al-Qayyim's *Rawḍa*. Ibn Abī Ḥajala borrows Ibn al-Qayyim's reply to the question whether longing (*shawq*) ceases with union;[8] his view that *khulla*, as an exclusive attachment, is the highest stage of love;[9] his solution to the problem of whether love is voluntary or involuntary;[10] his comments on the definition and the description of beauty, including his rejection of symmetry as the essence of beauty;[11] his division of love into "purposive" or "accidental" and "spiritual" affections, the latter being the consequence of affinity and thus reciprocal;[12] the fictional dispute between the eye and the heart over which is responsible for love;[13] various remarks on the signs of love—pallor and jealousy for example;[14] and a number of other opinions.[15] In addition, *Dīwān al-ṣabāba* contains a considerable amount of unacknowledged material for which the *Rawḍa* would seem to be the most likely source.

None the less, the two treatises differ fundamentally. Ibn Abī Ḥajala was a poet, and his *Dīwān al-ṣabāba* is definitely literary in intent. There is a pronounced concern with poetic criticism in the work. The author cites choice lines by various poets on a given theme and then, something Ibn al-Qayyim would not have done, hazards his own opinion as to which are the best. Moreover, stories about the loves of a number of contemporary figures are related, and many things for which Ibn al-Qayyim would have recommended the *ḥadd* punishment are taken for granted. Ibn Abī Ḥajala was an amateur of delicately phrased indecencies. We may recall the enthusiastic verses in praise of the wind which he relates from Ibn Saʿīd al-Maghribī, verses composed by that poet on seeing a lovely boy sleeping beneath a tree, his private parts uncovered by an impertinent breeze.[16] The moralizing tradition typical of Ḥanbalite literature thus had little to offer Ibn Abī Ḥajala. Within a theoretical framework very similar to that of the *Rawḍa* he created what is undeniably a much lighter work.

Munyat al-muḥibbīn

Perhaps the most curious adaptation of the conventional Ḥanbalite approach to the question of love is that found in the *Munyat al-muḥibbīn* of the early eleventh-/seventeenth-century Ḥanbalite scholar Marʿī b. Yūsuf al-Karmī.[17] In this work the sophisticated and often lengthy arguments of Ibn al-Qayyim are absent, the controversial tradition *"Man ʿashiqa . . ."* regains respectability, and the influence of the *eros* mystic Ibn al-ʿArabī makes itself felt. When the author of the *Munya* tends to disagree with his celebrated predecessors in the school of Aḥmad, he does not challenge them outright. He simply neglects to relate their opinions in full. This practice he exploits to his own credit. For example, after stating that he is the first writer to attempt a reconciliation of the opposing views that *ʿishq* is laudable and that it is blameworthy, he proceeds to offer a solution obviously inspired by a parallel passage in the *Rawḍa.*[18] Marʿī definitely knew Ibn al-Qayyim's book, and, as we shall see, he was heavily indebted both to the *Rawḍa* and to Ibn al-Jawzī's *Dhamm al-hawā* for the content of his small treatise.

The affected *tour de force* in rhymed prose which introduces almost all classical Arabic texts is commonly overlooked by readers impatient to arrive at more substantial things. But these introductions may often reveal an author's particular bias, as is the case with the following lines from the opening of the *Munya*:

> Wa-ashkuru man jaʿala ʾl-maḥabbata sajīyata ʾl-uqūli ʾl-salīma, wa-l-ʿishqa ʾl-mubāḥa shīmata ʾl-ṭibāʿi ʾl-mustaqīma. . . . Wa-ashhadu anna Muḥammadan ʿabduhu wa-rasūluhu, sanadu ʾl-ʿāsiqīn wa-sayyidu ʾl-muḥibbīn, ṣallā ʾllāhu ʿalayhi wa-ʿalā ālihi wa-aṣḥābihi ulī ʾl-gharāmi ʾl-mubāḥ. . . .
>
> (And I thank him who made love the natural disposition of sound minds and licit *eros* the characteristic of upright natures. . . . And I bear witness that Muḥammad is his servant and apostle, the stay of the enamored [*ʿāshiqīn*] and lord of lovers, may God's blessing be upon him, his family, and his Companions, those men of licit infatuation. . . .)[19]

Anyone who realizes how unusual the tenor of this introduction is in the context of the tradition we are studying will immediately perceive something of the *idée directrice* of Marʿī's work. The slant is obviously different from that of the *Rawḍa*, where a similar stress on legitimate

ʿishq would seem quite incongruous. Were there not sufficient internal evidence testifying to Marʿī's authorship,[20] one might guess that the *Munya* was not written by a Ḥanbalite at all.

In the course of explaining why he has composed his treatise, Marʿī betrays his favorable attitude towards *ʿishq* once again. Since *maḥabba*-love, he tells the reader, is the food of the spirit and licit *ʿishq* the sign of salvation, and since, furthermore, most people are confused on the issue, he has decided to write a brief work on the subject, one which deals with the truth about love and the necessity of remaining chaste, concealing passion, and avoiding the glance.[21] What, it may be asked, would Ibn al-Qayyim have thought of this proposal? Clearly he would have concurred in proscribing the glance, but it is highly unlikely that he would have alluded to the *ḥadīth "Man ʿashiqa . . . ,"* as is done here, to justify writing about love, and it is certain that he could never have agreed to call even licit *ʿishq* the sign of salvation. Perhaps inadvertently, Marʿī is classifying his predecessor among the "confused."

Why has the author of the *Munya* relaxed the traditional stand of his school against passionate love and left the door open to the influence of Ibn al-ʿArabī? Can his tolerance be attributed to a continued and growing Sufi penetration of Ḥanbalism itself, or is it merely that Marʿī, leading a relatively uneventful life under stable Ottoman-Mamlūk rule, was never forced into the rigid positions taken by the earlier Ḥanbalite polemicists? The details we possess regarding the scholar's education and career do not suffice to give a satisfactory answer to these questions.

Marʿī b. Yūsuf was born in the village of Ṭūr al-Karm near Nablus.[22] He began his studies in Palestine but later moved to Egypt, where, according to al-Muḥibbī, he was to become one of the leading representatives of Ḥanbalism. In Egypt he studied under Muḥammad Ḥijāzī (d. 1035/1625–26), a prolific Shāfiʿite jurist,[23] and Aḥmad b. Muḥammad al-Ghunaymī (d. 1044/1634–35), a Shāfiʿite who eventually turned to Ḥanafism.[24] There is no evidence to suggest that the influence of either of these teachers in any way weakened Marʿī's attachment to his own school. After receiving authorization to teach, Marʿī gave lessons for an undetermined period at al-Azhar and subsequently became shaykh of the Sulṭān Ḥasan mosque. He had enemies, however, and although there is no reason to believe that he was ever persecuted in the same manner as Ibn Taymīya and Ibn al-Qayyim, he did finally lose his position to a wealthy and influential Shāfiʿite contemporary, Ibrāhīm b. Muḥammad al-Maymūnī (d. 1079/1668–69), who had also been a student of al-Ghunaymī. An exchange of polemics between the two men ensued.[25] Marʿī spent the rest of his life teaching, giving *fatwās*, and writing. His literary production was considerable, and his enemies, though numerous, al-Muḥibbī reports, were unable to find fault with his works. He died in 1033/1624.

The list of Marʿī's works given by al-Muḥibbī includes at least ten on jurisprudence and related topics, almost as many on Koranic exegesis, although some of these are devoted to a single verse and may have been quite short, and three or four books each on theology, general history (including a history of the Ottoman sultans), and Sufism. One of his works on Sufism deals with the visiting of tombs, a traditional target of Ḥanbalite attacks. Among his essays on individual subjects, there is a biography of Ibn Taymīya, a work on spirits, tracts on the Mahdī, Jesus, al-Khaḍir, and the Prophet, and a book each on the plague and tobacco-smoking. Marʿī also wrote a number of treatises in the domain of ethics, one of which, *Rafʿ al-talbīs ʿam-man tawaqqaf fī-mā kaffar bi-hi Iblīs*, may have been inspired by Ibn al-Jawzī's *Talbīs Iblīs*, as the title would suggest. Another work, *Riyāḍ al-azhār fī ḥukm al-samāʿ wa-l-awtār wa-l-ghinā' wa-l-ashʿār*, on singing, music, and poetry, might have proved useful as a source for this study, but it is not listed by Brockelmann. Marʿī also compiled a *dīwān* of his own poetry.

On the subject of love, in addition to the *Munya*, the scholar composed a no longer extant work entitled *Taskīn al-ashwāq bi-akhbār al-ʿushshāq*—perhaps another in the series of reworkings of al-Sarraj's book on tragic loves.[26] The *Taskīn* is mentioned in *Munyat al-muḥibbīn* and may therefore be presumed to represent an earlier effort on the part of the author.[27] It is interesting to notice at this point the minor place which Marʿī's works on love occupy beside his numerous volumes consecrated to the disciplines of jurisprudence and Koranic commentary. Indeed, love seems to have received only slightly more attention than such isolated topics as spirits, al-Khaḍir, the plague, and tobacco. This observation does not explain why the scholar demonstrates an attitude of tolerance towards passionate love and the influences of mystical monism, but it suggests the possibility that to deal with love was for him a recreation, a *délassement*, not a task of crucial importance to the defense of sound doctrine and practice as it was for Ibn al-Qayyim. Perhaps this is what accounts for the generally light tone of the *Munya*. On the other hand, without knowing both the context and the relative importance of passages on love in Marʿī's theological and exegetical works, it would be inappropriate to consider this suggestion as anything more than a provisional hypothesis.

In its organization, Marʿī's treatise departs somewhat from the pattern one might have anticipated. Both Ibn al-Jawzī's *Dhamm al-hawā* and Ibn al-Qayyim's *Rawḍa* begin with a discussion of the conflict between reason and passion. The regard (*naẓar*) is dealt with next, and then *ʿishq* and various types of debauchery are treated. Both works conclude with a censure of passion and a list of suggested means to cure it. In contrast, the outline of *Munyat al-muḥibbīn*, by chapters, is as follows:

Introduction.

I. On the demonstration of the true essence of love (*maḥabba*) and its dignity.

II. Various opinions concerning the true essence of love.

III. On the true essence of *eros* (*ʿishq*); its causes and stages; the difference between it and *maḥabba* and *khulla*; its names.

IV. Opinions in praise of *ʿishq*.

V. The censure of passion (*hawā*); a discussion of the heart; the praise of reason (*ʿaql*).

VI. On the signs of *maḥabba* and *ʿishq*; the inebriation, etc., to which they lead when emotion prevails; their consequences.

VII. On longing (*shawq*) and whether it ceases or increases with union; whether it is proper to conceal love; whether in the case of true love (*tamām al-maḥabba*) abandonment on the part of the beloved is conceivable; and whether the beloved shuns the lover out of enmity.

VIII. On directing the ailing lover (*ʿāshiq*) to the Straight Path; on those who were inclined to reprehensible acts.

IX. Admonition against giving free rein to the glance (*naẓar*); the dispute between the eye and the heart; warning against the temptations of young boys and adolescents; poetry on them.

X. On the excellence of poetry; selections of amorous verse.

The discussion of reason and passion, which often opens Islamic works on ethics, has here been placed near the middle of the treatise (chapter five). Although, like Ibn al-Qayyim, Marʿī treats *maḥabba* early in his work, he then turns immediately to *ʿishq*, which in the *Rawḍa* comes only after a lengthy study of *naẓar*. The section in praise of *ʿishq* (chapter four) logically follows the treatment of *ʿishq*, as do the parallel sections in *Dhamm al-hawā* and the *Rawḍa. Naẓar* is removed to the next to the last chapter (chapter nine). Finally, whereas *Dhamm al-hawā* and *Rawḍat al-muḥibbīn* both end with an attack on *ʿishq* and the sins of passion, in the *Munya* this matter is taken up in the eighth chapter, with the tenth chapter, which will leave the final impression on the reader, reserved to a praise of poetry and numerous samples of amatory verse, many of them by the author himself. Undeniably, a good number of the usual topics still find their place in the *Munya.* But those chapters which treat the disadvantages of *ʿishq*, sandwiched as they are between less severe sections, fail to strike the reader with the force of the *remedia amoris* passages which conclude the treatises of Ibn al-Jawzī and Ibn al-Qayyim.

To perceive more fully the way in which the *Munya* differs from the works of earlier Ḥanbalite writers, as well as the extent to which it depends on them, it will be useful, however briefly, to examine Marʿī's comments on reason and passion, the definitions of love, the stages of love, longing, *ʿishq*, glancing and gazing, the signs of love, the remedies of love, and love between God and man.

REASON AND PASSION

Concerning Marʿī's notions on the internal equipment with which men face moral problems, we have in the *Munya* only short depictions of reason and passion, in which the author generally follows the traditional view. He opens his discussion of reason by quoting, almost word for word, Ibn al-Jawzī's introduction to his chapter on the same subject in *Dhamm al-hawā*.[28] Remarking that reason is universally praised, he goes on to cite a number of sayings from recognized authorities to support this view. Of particular interest is this one attributed to the Prophet:

> When God created the intellect, he said to it, "Come forward," and it came forward. Then he said, "Return," and it returned. Then he said to it, "By my glory and majesty, I have created nothing dearer to me than you. In proportion to you I give, I take away, and I punish."

Noting that this *ḥadīth* was rejected by Ibn Taymīya, Marʿī is bold enough to record al-Suyūṭī's favorable opinion of it but makes no pronouncement of his own regarding its authenticity.[29] This seems to be one example of his roundabout way of disagreeing with his Ḥanbalite predecessors. We shall see him employing a similarly oblique technique with respect to the tradition *"Man ʿashiqa. . . ."*

The section of passion in the *Munya* is likewise prefaced with a quotation from Ibn al-Jawzī. The earlier writer's definition of *hawā*, translated above,[30] is given with only slight changes and is followed by Ibn ʿAbbās's remark that *hawā* is never mentioned in the Koran without censure. Marʿī thus subscribes to the accepted view that passion, or the concupiscible appetite, is necessary to survival but is none the less generally blameworthy because few people restrict it to its proper role. Following this secondhand introduction, various sayings condemning passion, many of them borrowed from *Dhamm al-hawā*, are related.[31]

THE DEFINITIONS OF LOVE

After the manner of most other Muslim scholars who dealt with love, Marʿī holds that the many different views advanced concerning *maḥabba* represent the subjective states of those who express them. They are based on the fruits of love, not its essence. Those who truly understand love, the scholar adds, know it to be ineffable, escaping definition. This said, he proceeds to record definitions and descriptions of the emotion from a variety of sources. According to a definition attributed to Abū ʿAbd Allāh al-Qurashī (Ibn Abī 'l-Dunyā), found also in the *Rawḍa*,[32] the essence of *maḥabba* is stated to be an inclination towards a thing with one's whole self and giving preference to the object of that inclination over one's self, one's spirit, and one's wealth. In another, from the mystic Dhū 'l-Nūn al-Miṣrī, *maḥabba* is called "the disappearance of all love from the heart save that of the beloved."[33]

Although he has just acknowledged that love is indefinable, Marʿī expresses unhappiness with the definitions he has collected and attempts one himself. Prefacing his own suggestion with the remark that the definitions offered by the Sufis do not touch the essence of love but only its qualities, he leads the reader to expect more than he can produce. With little originality he writes:

> I hold that the essence of *maḥabba* is a *spiritual* attachment (*taʿalluq nafsānī*) and a *corporal* inclination to an object which suits the nature of the lover, resulting from his apprehending it with his sight—or his insight. Love, then, is the very attachment and inclination to the beloved.[34]

Here the author of the *Munya* has done no more than to improve somewhat on the definition ascribed to Ibn Abī 'l-Dunyā by clearly stressing both the spiritual and the physical aspects of love in a single sentence. He has said nothing new, but he must be given credit for a neat formulation. Since the context appears to be that of sacred love, it is possible that Marʿī's wording reflects Ibn al-ʿArabī's similar stress on the physical as well as the spiritual side of the emotion. This would be a decided innovation in the Ḥanbalite tradition. Most likely, however, the scholar has simply failed to make it clear that he is no longer referring to mystical love alone but to human love in general.

THE STAGES OF LOVE

Earlier it was shown that Ibn al-Qayyim's hierarchies of love terminology were the product of theological considerations.[35] This religious element is lacking in Marʿī's passage on the stages of love, which recalls rather the treatment of the subject by Ibn al-Jawzī. The *Munya* gives five lists of love's stages. Three are apparently borrowed from *Dhamm al-hawā*, one of them being somewhat enlarged. Another, which resembles the profane rankings proposed by Ibn al-Qayyim, is taken from Ibn Taymīya. The last, attributed to a certain Walī al-Dīn al-ʿIrāqī, matches Ibn Dāwūd's list.[36] Marʿī is not entirely free from the influence of Neo-Ḥanbalite doctrine, however. Like Ibn al-Qayyim, he reveals a special concern with *khulla* (exclusive love). He even quotes from *al-Dā' wa-l-dawā'* the scholar's demonstration that *khulla*, with a restricted object, is a higher degree of love than *maḥabba*. But the reasons which prompted this argument do not interest him. For Marʿī, *khulla* is merely that affection which penetrates (*yatakhallal*) the interstices of the heart, not the culmination of sacred love as it is for Ibn al-Qayyim.[37] In none of his three lists which include the term is *khulla* placed above *ʿishq*.

LONGING (*shawq*)

Marʿī opens his treatment of *shawq* with an abridgement of the passage in the *Rawḍa* which deals with the question of whether longing ceases or increases with union. With the exception of a few sayings describing longing, the scholar's remarks are taken almost verbatim from Ibn al-Qayyim's work. The corroborating verses of poetry are also from the *Rawḍa*. Marʿī interrupts his excerpt from the earlier text with the phrase "qāla baʿḍu 'l-muḥaqqiqīn" (one of those who know the matter has said). Strangely, he uses these words to introduce Ibn al-Qayyim's verdict on the question at hand: "The longing which occurs at the time of meeting is different from that which exists during the absence of the beloved."[38] After a long, conscious quote from the *Rawḍa*, Marʿī, deliberately it would seem, neglects to identify his source. The omission may have been innocent. But the scholar goes on to offer what he considers an improvement on Ibn al-Qayyim's solution, and it may have been for this reason that he preferred to leave its illustrious proponent unnamed. "The opinion of those who truly understand love," he writes, "is that there are [three things]—*shawq*, *ishtiyāq*, and *qalaq* (anxiety). *Shawq* subsides upon meeting and union, but *ishtiyāq* is aroused and increases. . . ." Ibn al-Qayyim, we know, mentioned this terminological distinction but refused to accept it. Marʿī's real source for this innovation is probably Ibn al-ʿArabī, whom he cites among other Sufis on the issue and who, of course, did use these very same terms.[39]

ʿIshq

ʿIshq, for Marʿī as well as for Ibn al-Jawzī and Ibn al-Qayyim, is a specific term while *maḥabba* is generic. In support of this view Marʿī gives his version of an argument cited by Ibn al-Qayyim. *ʿIshq*, he notes, is said to occur between human beings but not between men and God, whereas *maḥabba* may be applied to both cases.[40] The use of this particular example, surprising in view of his statements in the introduction to the *Munya*, shows that Marʿī was at least willing to pay lip service to the earlier Ḥanbalite position on *ʿishq*. Summing up a list of sayings on *ʿishq*, the author again reveals his dependence on the prior tradition of his school. Using the formula "*qultu*" ("in my opinion"), he introduces a definition taken directly from Ibn al-Jawzī:

> *ʿIshq* is the acute inclination of the soul towards a form which conforms to its nature. If the soul thinks intensely on this form, it imagines the possibility of obtaining it and begins to hope that it may. From this intense thought is born the malady of the body and the injury of the heart.

This definition, with the exception of the last few words, which may have been in Ibn al-Jawzī's original text, will be recognized from an earlier chapter of this study.[41] Thus, although in his general attitude towards ʿ*ishq*-love Marʿī seems to differ considerably from Ibn al-Jawzī and Ibn al-Qayyim, in his treatment of the definitions of this type of love he shows himself heavily indebted to them. His preferred definition he presents in the very words of Ibn al-Jawzī, and almost all of the other opinions on ʿ*ishq* he records appear to have been borrowed either from *Dhamm al-hawā* or from the *Rawḍa*.[42]

On the question whether ʿ*ishq* is to be praised or blamed, Marʿī is particularly indebted to Ibn al-Qayyim. The observation with which he prefaces his discussion, therefore, will come as something of a surprise to those who are familiar with *Rawḍat al-muḥibbīn*. "People are of two opinions on the subject of ʿ*ishq*," he remarks, "there are those who praise it without reserve and those who blame it absolutely. I have seen no one who has reconciled the views of these two groups." The problem, according to Marʿī's understanding, lay in the fact that both sides had spoken in absolute terms. Sympathizers had not in fact endorsed ʿ*ishq* absolutely but had intended to praise only the licit variety, while detractors had in reality desired to censure only the illicit type. How is it conceivable, he asks, that a rational man should praise the illicit or that a man of perception should revile the characteristic traits of the high-minded? One may mean by licit ʿ*ishq*, the reader learns, an attachment devoid of physical lust or a love which is free of the properties commonly ascribed to ʿ*ishq* and is called by the name only metaphorically. Since it is thus possible to conceive of ʿ*ishq* as a legitimate affection, it cannot be blamed categorically. Nevertheless, Marʿī adds that ʿ*ishq* as known in his day is unquestionably worthy of blame: "It is preferable to censure it absolutely," he writes, "in order to block the door [of sin], as I have held in my book called *Taskīn al-ashwāq bi-akhbār al-ʿushshāq*." The substance of this argument, if not the enthusiasm expressed for licit ʿ*ishq*, seems undoubtedly to have been inspired by the *Rawḍa*, the author's claim to originality notwithstanding.[43]

Marʿī's typical Ḥanbalite approach in this context contrasts with his introduction to the *Munya*. As might be expected, the rigor of his stance here is tempered by another of his statements. The passage on whether ʿ*ishq* is to be praised or blamed is followed by a selection of sayings, anecdotes, and verse extolling the affection, together with others censuring it. Marʿī specifies that the praise is not to be taken as absolute, since it would be improper to condone the illicit side of ʿ*ishq*. He adds—and it is this point which is significant—that ʿ*ishq* should not be praised without reservation because it is not suited to everyone. It is for the "virtuous" (*dhū murū'a*), not for the fanciful.[44] Here the tension between the Ḥanbalite tradition and outside influences reappears. After acknowledging that the *ʿishq* of his day is to be censured unconditionally, Marʿī proceeds to suggest, in characteristically Sufi fashion, that there exists none the less an elite who possess the proper qualifications for this excessive love.

GLANCING AND GAZING (*naẓar*)

Among the causes of love, the author of the *Munya* has little to say about affinity, except indirectly in the definitions of *maḥabba* and *ʿishq* which he cites. Beauty he does not discuss. He devotes considerable attention, on the other hand, to *naẓar.* In general, Marʿī's treatment follows that presented by Ibn al-Jawzī. The author begins with a quotation from *Dhamm al-hawā*[45] and goes on to relate a number of the Koranic verses and *ḥadīth*s against "looking" furnished in that work. Among other sayings, the Prophet's admonition to ʿAlī concerning the repeated glance is given. Ibn al-Jawzī's point that Satan has recourse to youths in order to seduce ascetics who refuse to look at unlawful (*ajānib*) women is likewise mentioned, as is his observation that a budding beard only makes a youth more seductive. Ibn Taymīya too is quoted. Of the selection of poetry offered on *naẓar* the major portion is taken from the *Dhamm* or the *Rawḍa.* Interestingly, however, Marʿī closes his argument with a quotation from Ibn al-ʿArabī, who increasingly appears to have been among his favorite authorities.[46]

THE SIGNS OF LOVE

In dealing with the signs of love, a subject not discussed analytically by Ibn al-Jawzī, Marʿī relies largely on the work of Ibn al-Qayyim. Many of the signs he lists are taken directly from *Rawḍat al-muḥibbīn*. There is a noticeable difference, however, in the way certain signs are treated by the two authors. The religious aspect, which is clearly the ultimate concern in Ibn al-Qayyim's treatise, is neglected in the *Munya.* Whereas the earlier writer took his discussion of the sign of obedience as an occasion to oppose the Sufi doctrine of the unity of existence with the Ḥanbalite concept of the unity of aims, Marʿī has nothing of a religious nature to say under this rubric. Indeed, he relates a celebrated couplet, often cited to stress obedience in love to God, in a form which would suggest that he has consciously avoided all allusion to the sacred sphere. The first line, as cited by Ibn al-Qayyim, reads as follows:

> Taʿṣī 'l-ilāha wa-anta tazʿumu ḥubbahū;
> hādhā muḥālun fī 'l-qiyāsi badīʿū.
>
> (You disobey the *divinity* while claiming to love him;
> this is an impossible and strange logic.)

As given in the *Munya*, the line makes a different point:

> Taʿṣī 'l-ḥabība wa-anta tuẓhiru ḥubbahū;
> hādhā la-ʿamrī fī 'l-qiyāsi badīʿū.
>
> (You disobey the *beloved* while pretending to love him;
> this, by my life, is a strange logic.)[47]

The sign of self-sacrifice for the sake of the beloved, which affords an obvious opportunity for pious remarks, Marʿī likewise deals with in a secular manner, although the corresponding passage in the *Rawḍa* is religious in character.[48] Jealousy, which Ibn al-Qayyim treats extensively in both its sacred and profane aspects, is allotted a single line in the *Munya*.[49]

Marʿī closes his basic list of love's signs with three quotations of a mystical nature. These touch particularly on remembrance or mention (*dhikr*) of the beloved, obedience to him, and desire to meet him.[50] The last point serves as a transition to the drunkenness of love, a subject to which Ibn al-Qayyim devoted an entire chapter of his *Rawḍa*.[51] The following is the purport of Marʿī's remarks and the sayings he relates with regard to this state of the lover. Drunkenness far greater than that experienced by the wine drinker ensues when the lover is overcome by desire and passion. As a result of his perceiving the beloved, the lover experiences a pleasure which is proportional to the strength of his emotion and the fullness of his perception. This pleasure is the cause of inebriation. The latter state, in turn, affects the lover's acts and may even lead to his death.[52]

The state of drunkenness is not approved by Marʿī. How wonderful love can be when it is divine, he exclaims, but when it is satanic the resulting inebriation cannot be excused. Like the stupor produced by wine, it proceeds from a forbidden cause. As drinking is a voluntary act, so is the lover's allowing *ʿishq* to gain control over him.[53] This same argument, we know, was used by Ibn al-Qayyim.[54] Thus once again Marʿī appears as a follower of the Ḥanbalite tradition. Other works were at his disposal, but throughout his treatise he draws mainly on the *Rawḍa*, as in this instance, or on *Dhamm al-hawā*. Aside from his rather frequent dependence on Ibn al-ʿArabī, it is most often not his sources as such but the way he selects from the earlier Ḥanbalite texts which sets him apart from the other writers we have studied. Striking here is the fact that Ibn al-Qayyim's observations of a religious nature on the signs of love have been dropped only to be replaced by the Sufi-like remarks with which Marʿī concludes his treatment of the subject.

THE REMEDIES OF LOVE

The development of *ʿishq*, according to the author of the *Munya*, may be summed up in three stages—initial, medial, and final. In the initial stage the lover should conceal his affection and avoid revealing the name of his beloved to possible slanderers. If he reaches the second stage, there is no harm in confessing his love to the beloved and complaining to him in order to alleviate the suffering he is experiencing. But he must be extremely careful that no one else discover his secret, "lest this be the cause of his perishing." This view has its complement in another passage concerned directly with the concealment of love, where Marʿī maintains that whether or not the lover will reveal his love depends simply on the control he has over his emotions.[55] In no case, however, is the revealing of the beloved's name advocated. If the lover exceeds the limits of reason and reaches the final stage of *ʿishq*, he forfeits his sanity. But he is none the less held responsible for his actions while in this state. Indeed, no one should involve himself in any matter unless he can perceive a way out. Consequently, it behooves the lover to remove himself far from the presence of his beloved before *ʿishq* can afflict him irremediably. Did not Hippocrates claim to have cured every malady save love after it had set in?

So far nothing astonishing. Suddenly, however, Marʿī offers advice which seems unusual coming from a Ḥanbalite after the time of Ibn al-Qayyim: the lover should follow the counsel of the *ḥadīth* "*Man ʿashiqa*. . . ." This tradition, the reader is told, although it may be a fabrication (*mawḍūʿ*) as some have maintained, is none the less too well documented to be rejected outright. Here Marʿī takes issue, in spirit if not literally, with Ibn al-Qayyim. Admittedly the earlier scholar did not categorically repudiate this tradition, allowing that it could well be from Ibn ʿAbbās.[56] But Marʿī's expansion on the point which is made in the saying shows that he was not citing it for the reasons Ibn al-Qayyim had in mind. He records that a certain authority, when asked about lovers (*ʿushshāq*), replied: "He who has the greatest *ʿishq* shall have the greatest reward." *ʿIshq*, Marʿī infers, is a glorious stage for the one who respects its canons. Although, typically, he adds the reservation that it is still better to avoid this amorous attachment, he cannot resist the temptation to relate the following verses, which understandably are not to be found in *Rawḍat al-muḥibbīn*:

Ta-allāhi aḥlifu aymānan mu'akkadatan:
  lā ʿadhdhaba 'llāhu arwāḥa 'l-muḥibbīnā
al-qā'imīna bi-sharṭi 'l-ʿishqi dahrahumū
  ʿalā ʿafāfin, wa-in aḍḥaw mulāmīnā.
Wa-kayfa taṣlīhimū nārun, wa-qad sakanat
  nāru 'l-maḥabbati fī aḥshā'ihim ḥīnā?

(By Allah, I swear a most certain oath:
  God will not chastise the souls of lovers
who obey throughout their lives the law of love (*ʿishq*)
  in chastity, though men may blame them.
And how shall fire consume them, when
  the fire of love has dwelt within them for a time?)

Marʿī proceeds to cite a number of sayings, poems, and anecdotes on chastity, some of them perhaps borrowed from the *Rawḍa*. One of the anecdotes is the one which depicts Ibn Dāwūd relating the tradition "*Man ʿashiqa*. . . ." Among the verse is a poem by Ibn al-ʿArabī on a chaste meeting with the beloved.[57]

The argument then continues in a familiar vein. If the lover's fear of God is not sufficient to restrain him, he should try to marry the object of his affection—if the person in question is a woman. If his beloved is a youth, the lover should strive to marry any woman. Aḥmad b. Ḥanbal said that celibacy is not part of Islam, and the Prophet is known to have married fourteen women. Should marriage with the beloved or another person prove impossible, involvement in one's work or trade and/or removing oneself far from the beloved is prescribed. Thinking on the beloved's shortcomings, as Ibn al-Jawzī suggested, is also proposed as a possible remedy. Finally, if all of the preceding alternatives are impossible or to no avail, then the lover should attempt to meet his beloved in a fashion which cannot lead to illicit acts. In this connection, Marʿī quotes once again Walī al-Dīn al-ʿIrāqī, this time to the effect that a man, if he fears that he will die of love, is permitted to kiss his beloved on the forehead, a kiss being not so grave a matter as death. The beloved must grant the kiss if he knows that refusal will result in the death of the lover.

None of the *ʿulamāʾ*, Marʿī states in concluding, have allowed the lover to obtain anything from his beloved, except the kiss permitted by al-Walī al-ʿIrāqī, and that with the reservation that it must only be done in order to prevent the death of the lover. But the common people, he adds, should not be allowed even this, for they might make of it a pretext for falling into sin.[58] Both of these last remarks are significant. The first signals Marʿī's conditional agreement with the reasoning of the spurious *fatwā* ascribed to Ibn Taymīya, at least insofar as the permissibility of the kiss is concerned.[59] The author of the *Munya* is thus subscribing to a view which Ibn al-Qayyim went to great lengths to counter. The second remark provides one more example of how Marʿī applies the characteristically mystical distinction between the commonality of believers and the priviliged elite.

LOVE BETWEEN GOD AND MAN

Marʿī devotes the first chapter of his *Munya* to a vindication of *maḥabba.* Certain *mutakallimūn*, he informs the reader, hold that God does not love and that what is called his love is, in reality, his will to do good to his servants.[60] This statement refers to the Ashʿarite equation of the divine attributes of love and will which was discussed above.[61] It was a chief element in the argument which denied the possibility of a love relationship between God and man. For the earlier Ḥanbalites, it will be recalled, the question of whether such a relationship existed was a major issue in their polemic against the theologians. Marʿī, dealing with the question in cavalier fashion, seems primarily interested in it as a convenient way to introduce his subject and, perhaps, as a strategem for presenting his reliance on Ibn al-ʿArabī in the most favorable light. The author's defense of love, happily for those unsympathetic to the subtleties of scholastic theology, is short and sweet, if unsophisticated.

The reality of sacred love, Marʿī argues, is supported by Koran, prophetic tradition, and the consensus of the Islamic community (*ijmāʿ*). In the Koran, God and his servants are described as loving each other. An exegesis of the pertinent verse is given in the form of a quotation from the *Futūḥāt* of Ibn al-ʿArabī, to whose authority Marʿī has recourse in this context:

> Since there exists an affinity between God and the world, it is proper for him to say that "he loves them and they love him." Thus God loves and is loved. As lover he acts to influence the universe, while as beloved he afflicts to test the pretention [of love], so that the false pretender may be exposed and the true pretender appear. Also as beloved he rules over his lover. . . .[62]

In the *ḥadīth*, Marʿī finds evidence for the reality of sacred love (*maḥabba*) in the many sayings on the rewards of those who love "in God" (*al-mutaḥābbīn fī 'llāh*). A number of such traditions are cited in his text. Finally, his demonstration concludes, consensus supports the existence of this love because no reasonable man can be found who denies it.[63]

This sketchy apology for the existence of a love relationship between God and man constitutes the bulk of what Marʿī has to say in the *Munya* about love as a properly religious attitude. There are, however, other passages from which something of his views on sacred love may be gleaned. Especially noteworthy in this regard are his remarks on the conventional poetic theme of abandonment by the beloved. Marʿī relates in connection with this theme the contention of certain Sufis that abandonment is unimaginable in the case of complete love because the "spiritual forms" to which, in witnessing the beloved, the lover gives power over his soul are permanent. He also cites al-Shiblī quoting al-Ḥallāj's assertion that separation is impossible between true lovers since it is inconceivable that a thing can endure the privation of its own self.[64] For his own part, Marʿī accepts abandonment as at least an apparent reality and turns his attention to resolving the contradiction between the states of abandonment and union. The lover, he points out, strives for contact and union (*ittiṣāl* and *ittiḥād*), but at the same time he seeks to act in accordance with the will of his beloved. Now the beloved may desire separation. If this is the case, the lover must not seek union, lest his desire be other than that of his beloved.

But how, it may be asked, is it possible for the lover, in attempting to conform his will to that of the beloved, actually to love or to desire the separation. For the solution to this dilemma Marʿī again turns to Ibn al-ʿArabī. The mystic taught that the lover should not love the separation itself but rather the beloved's love for separation. This he held to be analogous to the believer's accepting with satisfaction God's ordaining unbelief: he is content not with the thing ordained but only with God's ordaining it.[65] The lover should also realize, Marʿī adds, that the beloved does not shun him out of enmity or hatred, since love renders this impossible. On the contrary, the beloved's aim is to attract the lover and even to create a certain pleasure. If it were not for the sweet and the bitter in love, the reader is asked, what would be the pleasure of messages and correspondence, for example? Accordingly the lover should see union and abandonment as one, realizing that the intention of the beloved in turning from him is only to strengthen his love.[66]

Taking into consideration Marʿī's defense of *maḥabba* and this discussion of abandonment, it is difficult to escape the conclusion that the scholar's reliance on Ibn al-ʿArabī is somewhat greater than usual when he touches on aspects of sacred love. Ibn al-Jawzī and Ibn al-Qayyim are generally sufficient as authorities for matters pertaining to secular relationships, but they do not appear to have influenced Marʿī's position on love in the religious context to the same extent. Indeed Marʿī comes close to acknowledging some misgivings with regard to the views of his Ḥanbalite predecessors. Commenting a point which arises in his treatment of abandonment, he notes that Ibn Taymīya, among others, expressed opposition to the Sufi opinion that such evils as unbelief and sickness are to be accepted with satisfaction. He adds in explanation that those who opposed the Sufi doctrine did so either because they did not understand it as it had been elaborated by Ibn al-ʿArabī or because they had in mind not the doctrine itself but a misinterpretation of it put forth by the ignorant among the Sufis. Still a Ḥanbalite of sorts, Marʿī is compelled to observe that there is in reality no difference between the point of view of the jurists and that of the mystics.[67] But this remark only serves to place in relief the fact that he is attempting to reconcile two incompatible religious attitudes. The text of the *Munya* clearly reflects an encroachment of *eros* on the *nomos* teaching of orthodox Ḥanbalism. It would be interesting to know to what degree the tension evident in Marʿī's work was typical of other Ḥanbalite thinkers during the century before the great Wahhābī purge.

11. Epilogue: Nomos, Eros, and Thelema

It has not been our objective in this study to impose the *nomos* and *eros* motifs, or for that matter any other preestablished conceptual apparatus, on the material provided by the sources. A rather more flexible approach has been followed in the hope of minimizing any distortion of the Ḥanbalite doctrine of love as it is presented in the texts themselves. It should be recognized, none the less, that the *nomos* and *eros* motifs isolated by Nygren, if they have not been applicable in every case, have proved particularly useful in the analysis and classification of what may be termed properly religious attitudes or theories. Most of the speculation concerning love we have met in the preceding pages, moreover, in its profane as well as its sacred aspects, falls somehow into this category, as does indeed by far the greater part of the recorded thought of medieval Muslim scholars on the subject. Perhaps, then, there is something to be gained by taking another look at Nygren's motifs as they apply in the Islamic context.

Ibn Taymīya and Ibn Qayyim al-Jawzīya held the major opponents of the orthodox position on sacred love to be divided into two groups—the mystics and the speculative theologians. Thus far we have made use of the *nomos* and *eros* motifs respectively to distinguish the basic attitudes exemplified in the thought of the Ḥanbalites themselves on the one hand and the more extreme partisans of Sufism on the other. The stance of the theologians does not conform to either of these schemes, nor is it in any sense a synthesis of the two. It must be recognized, therefore, that we have in effect been dealing not with two but with at least three cardinal motifs, each having its own "characteristic content" and each somehow in conflict or indeed fundamentally irreconcilable with the other two. For the sake of symmetry we may designate by the Greek word *thelema* or "will"[1] the characteristic position of the later Ashʿarite theologians, who as a corollary of their equation of God's love with his will denied the reality of love between God and man. *Thelema*, as originally conceived, had not, of course, the same importance for everyday religious practice as *eros* and *nomos*. It was in its essence the abstract theological stance of a restricted intellectual elite and, confined to the circles in which it arose, need have had little or no influence on conventional morality.

The nearly total divergence of *thelema* from the orthodox *nomos* pattern is readily apparent when certain of the basic tenets of the two schemes are juxtaposed.

THELEMA	NOMOS
God has no anthropomorphic or anthropopathic attributes. He does not love nor does he experience "pleasure," the product of love satisfied.	All the traditional attributes of God truly apply to him, although they are not to be explained. God loves and experiences "joy."
The Koranic references to God's love for men must be interpreted to mean his "willing good" to them.	God's love for men is real and is to be distinguished from the creative aspect of his will. It is a natural consequence of his self-love.
God wills good to some men and evil to others for no cause or purpose.	God acts for the sake of a "wise purpose" (*ḥikma*) which he loves.
God cannot be the object of love.	Men can truly love God in and for himself.
Man's pleasure in the beatific vision is not the result of love satisfied but an independent pleasure created simultaneously.	The pleasure of the vision is the result of the consummation of man's love to God.

In their approach to these questions as well as to many others the speculative theologians who contrived the *thelema* scheme pursued their devotion to God's transcendence to the extreme. They denied one by one, presenting them as mere imagery, all those teachings of scripture which tended to render the divinity accessible to the mind and heart of the ordinary believer.

The opposition of the Neoplatonic *eros* motif to *nomos* was for the most part of another complexion. It is true that the Ḥanbalite-orthodox stress on the anthropomorphic attributes of God was rather foreign to the *eros* system, and it also seems to have been the case that Islamic mysticism had no real need to assert that God loves man—as the example of al-Ghazālī's teaching on this question demonstrates. But with regard to these particular issues on which *nomos* and *thelema* were at variance mystical theoreticians were by no means consistent. Often, in fact, they were close to the orthodox position. Fundamentally the conflict between *eros* and *nomos* centered on the doctrine of the soul and the scheme of salvation. In the typical expression of the *eros* view, it is the presence of the soul—a divine element in man—which constitutes the affinity underlying religious love and makes it possible for man to long for God. Salvation is simply the reascent of the soul to its former abode or, for the stricter *eros* mystics, its reintegration in its original source. We have seen how the Muslim *nomos* theologians we have studied, like their celebrated Christian counterpart Tertullian, attacked each of the three principal theses of the *eros* scheme. The soul has not had, as the mystics claimed, an earlier and higher existence which it can recall and to which it strives to return; rather it is created with or after the body. Nor is the soul a divine or spiritual substance; it is in fact a kind of subtle body. The resurrection, therefore, and thus the next life, is not spiritual but physical.

In the course of this inquiry we have been able to observe a number of other issues on which opposition between *eros* and *nomos* is fairly consistent. Disagreement on these additional matters is by no means constant, but it is sufficiently regular to reveal some of the typical contrasting features of the two motifs as they occur in the Islamic context. A few of the more important points of contention may be summarized conveniently as follows.

EROS	NOMOS
The affinity between God and man which underlies sacred love is (for many authors) one of similarity rather than of complementarity.	The notion of similarity is to be avoided as an explanation of the affinity between God and man. (Ibn al-Qayyim suggests a relationship of complementarity which amounts to total dissimilarity.)
Love is only a *means* to salvation; it is a deficiency among the elite.	Love expressed in service is the perfection of religious experience.

The goal of love is loss of awareness of all but God.	The goal of love is obedience to God with awareness of the world.
Secondary loves (to wife, children, etc.) are distractions.	Secondary loves can be aids in love and obedience to God.
The beatific vision is the only pleasure of Paradise to be desired; the others are distractions.	The lesser pleasures of Paradise are not distractions; they respond to the natural desires of the resurrected "whole man." The vision occurs at most twice daily.
Fear of God is a deficiency in the elite.	Without fear, love is not sufficient to produce piety in this life.
The distinction between good and evil is an illusion and does not exist for the mystic who sees the world from God's perspective.	The distinction between good and evil is objective and should never be neglected, even in the highest stages of the spiritual itinerary.

Of all these issues it is undoubtedly the last which most nearly epitomizes the conflict the Ḥanbalite jurists perceived between *eros* mysticism and orthodoxy. Orthodox Islam, to recall the already familiar, is a legalistic religion which aims at regulating the affairs of the community of believers in this world. Sufism as it appeared to the Ḥanbalites, however it may have been practiced by its adherents, was essentially an antinomian movement. In its theory it was prone to neglect the concerns of this life and the needs of the natural man. The traditional sanctions against immorality tended to be eroded. The mystic who claimed to see all things in the moment of ecstatic union only as God sees them—as divine acts and therefore good—could justify any unlawful deed on this basis.

The *thelema* motif, it will be recalled, could by a slight inversion be exploited to the same end. If God's love is identical with his will, then, if it is granted that he wills all that occurs, it must likewise be admitted that he loves all that occurs. The issue was not entirely academic. The Ḥanbalites knew that some of the more extreme mystics carried such reasoning to its logical conclusion in practice. Their response, as we have seen, was to attempt to demonstrate that, contrary to the assertions of their opponents, God is not oblivious to the distinction between good and evil. In this connection they argued at length to establish that the divine will has a prescriptive as well as a purely creative aspect and that God loathes evil even if, in his wisdom, he is ultimately responsible for its existence. The stress and general tenor of the arguments adduced by the Ḥanbalite scholars against the *thelema* scheme suggest that their primary concern, however blasphemous individual points of dogma may have appeared to them, was with the antinomian ethical implications of the system. *Nomos* thus seems to have clashed with *eros* and *thelema* alike for essentially the same reason—the incompatibility of each with the insistence of prophetic religion on conformity to the divine law.

What, at last, may be said of the relation between *eros* and *thelema*? This matter has not been an object of our study, but it will be useful to consider it here briefly in order to round out our understanding of the three motifs. *Eros* and *thelema* were in fundamental conflict on the crucial issue of the reality of man's love to God, and in their most characteristic Islamic manifestations they likewise tended to diverge on the question of God's love for his creatures. These motifs are, of course, only ideal patterns isolated for the purpose of assessing the conflicts and inconsistencies within the work of any given author. In practice it is somewhat rare to find a writer who is as uniform in his devotion to a particular motif as is al-Juwaynī, say, to *thelema*. We have seen how the Neo-Ḥanbalites, despite the generally remarkable cohesion of their system, integrated into their thought, though not without difficulty, the notion of an affinity between God and man and the conception of the beatific vision as the consummation of sacred love—both of which were fundamentally tenets of the *eros* scheme. We have also seen how the Neoplatonist al-Dabbāgh, yielding to the weight of orthodox tradition, denied the preexistence of the soul and adopted the *nomos* doctrine that the soul comes into being with or after the body. There existed in late medieval Islam a marked and fairly generalized tendency towards eclecticism, and this fact is not without bearing on the relation between *eros* and *thelema.* One of the greatest Muslim thinkers appears indeed to have elaborated a synthesis of these two motifs—a synthesis which, to be sure, was not entirely free of traces of *nomos.*

The eminent eleventh-century (A.D.) exponent of mystical theory al-Qushayrī had taken over the *thelema* scheme virtually intact. God and man, he recognized, are indeed described in the Koran as loving each other. But God's love to men in al-Qushayrī's view is merely one of the many aspects of his will—in this case his will to bestow on a man a certain favor or to specify him with nearness to himself or elevated state. The divine will itself is one attribute, not many, although the names by which it is called vary with its object. Thus, for example, when its object is the infliction of punishment, it is called wrath. Nothing more than this is meant by God's love for men. It is in no way analogous to the inclination or intimacy found in earthly love. Man's love to God, on the other hand, al-Qushayrī describes as a state too subtle to be expressed in words. It can impel an individual to strive to please God and to praise him. But like God's love it comprises nothing which may be called inclination.[2] Sacred love in either direction, by this reckoning, since it lacks the essential element of inclination, falls outside the range of meaning of the word love as it was customarily defined by medieval Muslim scholars. Interestingly, al-Qushayrī goes on in his treatise to relate a number of sayings underscoring the ecstatic character of mystical love, many of which contrast sharply with his own severe representation of human love to God. He concludes by calling love conformity (*muwāfaqa*) in the heart,[3] availing himself of the same noncommittal term which Ibn Taymīya was to use later to characterize the elusive nature of the affinity held to underlie love between God and believers.

The existence of a fundamental conflict between the *thelema* position on man's love to God advanced by al-Qushayrī and the assumptions of the *eros* scheme he was claiming to expound is readily discernible. Abū Ḥāmid al-Ghazālī perceived the contradiction and attempted to resolve it. A student of the Ash'arite theologians, he continued to hold the view that God cannot be said to love men in the precise meaning of the term. Love, he observed, is the inclination (*mayl*) of the soul to that which conforms (to its nature), and such an inclination can exist only in that which is imperfect or deficient. Nothing of the sort can be present in God. God's love is to be understood simply as his enabling certain men (by an act of his *will*) to approach him and his purifying them of animal attributes.[4] Still a mystic, on the other hand, al-Ghazālī was unable to accept the corresponding thesis of the theologians that man cannot truly love God. He taught that man could love God not only for the favors he bestowed but indeed also for himself.[5] Love is a religious obligation. How is it possible, he queried, for something which cannot exist to be imposed as an obligation? How, moreover, can one construe love merely as obedience, after the fashion of some scholars, when the affection of love is clearly prior to obedience and is its cause?[6] Al-Ghazālī's celebrated proof of the reality of human love to God has already been considered. He examines at great length the reasons for which a person might be the object of love and then argues that each of these reasons in actual fact applies only to God himself. It is, however, when he distinguishes the ways in which God and man are said to love each other that he makes the point which is of most immediate concern to us here. God's love to man is metaphorical because it does not satisfy the definition of love, that is, it is not an inclination. Man's love to God is real, because it *is* an inclination.[7]

Al-Ghazālī stands apart from al-Qushayrī by his contention that man can be said to love God in a sense which fully satisfies the accepted definition of the word. Yet he held fast to the Ashʿarite view that God does not truly love man. What he attempted to do, with more or less success, was to combine these two positions into one fairly coherent doctrine of sacred love. It would seem justifiable to say therefore—within the framework of our motifs—that he established a synthesis of *eros* and *thelema.* (Ibn Taymīya described the teaching on love of mystic-theologians like al-Ghazālī as a "mixture.")[8] It should not be said, I believe, that al-Ghazālī simply unburdened mystical theory of a useless and untenable belief in the reality of God's love. It may well be the case that it is unnecessary in the *eros* scheme to affirm that God loves his creatures, but al-Ghazālī's denial of God's love to men was not properly speaking the product of a development within the scheme: it was taken from outside—directly from Ashʿarite theology.

The synthesis al-Ghazālī effected was not entirely free of elements of the *nomos* system. On the question of secondary loves, to cite a familiar issue, he departed from the characteristic teaching of the mystics to take a position similar to that later adopted by the Neo-Ḥanbalites. It is possible for a man to love both God and this world. Secondary loves are to be judged by the ultimate object sought. Approved by the theologian as varieties of "love in God" are, among others, such affections as love for one's teacher as a means to attain a spiritual benefit or love for a wife as a means to escape the snares of passion. A person may in fact be loved for the sake of temporal as well as spiritual goods. This is permissible when the worldly good in question is not harmful to the religious life. Harmful worldly goods are, of course, to be despised, although only by the reason or intellect, as the scholar observed with insight, not by human nature.[9]

Fully aware of and no doubt sincerely sharing the fundamental concern of prophetic Islam for the social order, al-Ghazālī espoused the opinion regarding secondary loves which was most consistent with this concern. His synthesis was scrupulously constructed so as to confer not only intellectual but also moral respectability on the *eros* scheme. He hoped to appeal to the traditionist party as well as to the speculative theologians. But the painstakingly balanced system he elaborated still contained in germ the mystic denial of the distinction between good and evil which the Neo-Ḥanbalites saw as the gateway to antinomianism. It is true that in some contexts al-Ghazālī distinguishes between things loved and hated by God.[10] But the reader of his chapter on love will find him writing that God considers exclusively his own essence and acts (which must be good). God does not consider other things as though they were other than himself, for only his essence and his acts truly exist. In the same connection the author quotes Abū Saʿīd al-Mīhanī to the effect that God loves only himself—a phrase interpreted to mean that he loves the *all*, that is to say once again, his essence and his acts.[11]

The thesis advanced in this passage of the *Iḥyā'* could easily be exploited by the contemplative or existential monist to justify an antinomian philosophy. The reasoning we have seen before. Granted the single additional proposition that the spiritually advanced see existence only from God's perspective, it would follow necessarily that the distinction between good and evil is an illusion of the commonality having no meaning for the elite. By no means to be overlooked in this connection is the fact that al-Ghazālī was himself a contemplative if not a pre-existential monist in his mystical teaching. He held the supreme stage of the mystic's advancement to consist in passing away from world and self to behold all things as one.[12] The notion of beholding all things as one is, of course, tantamount in this context to seeing the world from God's perspective. Thus we discover that not only the first but also the second essential premise of the antinomian argument is in fact advanced in the text of the *Iḥyā'*. Al-Ghazālī seems to have demurred at carrying this argument through to its conclusion, presumably in view of its ethical implications. But, whether unwittingly or by design, he left the door ajar for others.

The fact that al-Ghazālī aspired to harmonize theology and mysticism is, of course, well known. What has been said here regarding his synthesis of *eros* and *thelema*, consequently, is in no sense offered as a novel observation on the general character of his theological system. Nothing more has been intended than to demonstrate the applicability of Nygren's motifs, as we have expanded them to suit the Islamic context, to one aspect of al-Ghazālī's thought. On first view, then, it might be surmised that we have merely reformulated with regard to the specifiic what was already known about the general. But this is not precisely the case. The matter with which we are dealing lies very close to the heart of the theologian's teaching—as near as the concepts of love and desire have traditionally been to the core of theistic mysticism. We have adopted for the study of this central issue a method of analysis which obliges us to attach each element in his teaching to a particular internally coherent pattern of religious thinking, rather than, say, to its genetic source in a given author or series of authors—whose work might reveal a similar eclecticism. In this way we have been able to detect and place in perspective certain quite basic problems in al-Ghazālī's system. These problems, in turn, can be seen to reflect points on which the conflicting outlooks he was attempting to reconcile were in fact irreconcilable. Thus his assertion that man's love to God is made possible by a hidden affinity—a relation difficult to conceive except as involving both parties—makes his corresponding denial of the reality of God's love to man seem somewhat out of place. The latter view represented what was originally the conclusion of theologians who rejected altogether the existence of an affinity between God and man. The discrepancy could hardly have escaped the notice of the more rigorous Ashʿarite scholars.

In so far as al-Ghazālī's synthesis represented an attempt to placate the orthodox traditionist party it was seriously weakened by the presence of similar inconsistencies. Foremost among these was the mystic's unwillingness to repudiate—at least with uniformity in all contexts—those tenets of the *eros* system which gave it its antinomian character. The enormous success which his works enjoyed among the scholars of subsequent generations, therefore, must have been a matter of great concern for such strict constructionists as Ibn Taymīya and Ibn Qayyim al-Jawzīya. However moderate al-Ghazālī's own views on ethical matters, his synthesis of *eros* and *thelema* gave an aura of legitimacy to an eclectic trend in mystical thought which they saw as a kind of unholy alliance of theology and mysticism against the primitive religion of the Koran and the moral order it had established.

To be sure, this fusion of Ashʿarism and mystical theory constituted but one of the threats, albeit a major one, to which the Neo-Ḥanbalite doctors addressed themselves. But it is typical of the syncretizing philosophies with which they were confronted and provides an excellent illustration of how the nature of the challenge conditioned the nature of the response. Al-Ghazālī sought to make his mystical doctrine intellectually palatable by giving it the garb and some of the substance of speculative theology. Ibn Taymīya and Ibn al-Qayyim, as we have seen, although with more unswerving devotion to their original principles, were following an analogous course of action. It is to a very great extent against the background of their opponents' growing eclecticism that we must understand their own decision, counter to the precepts and prior practice of their school, to exploit the vocabulary and methods of theology and philosophy in a reasoned defense of the *nomos* doctrine of scriptural Islam.

For the historian of the idea of love the teaching of Ibn Taymīya and Ibn Qayyim al-Jawzīya is particularly interesting, since it is among the most complete and thoroughly worked out medieval statements of the *nomos* scheme. Love was a or perhaps the central doctrinal issue in the theology of these Ḥanbalite writers. Ibn al-Qayyim calls it the foundation of religion and asserts that all the revealed books turn on the question of love to God.[13] As we know, a substantial part of the two men's work was devoted to the subject. Admittedly their thinking on the many and varied facets of love is nowhere set down—in their published works at least—as a fully elaborated theory in the fashion we have met it in the course of this study. I have been obliged to reconstruct a good number of their arguments piece by piece using short passages and at times even isolated sentences from books and tracts on a multitude of topics. The book which comes closest to presenting a comprehensive theory of love is Ibn al-Qayyim's *Rawḍat al-muḥibbīn*, but this work apparently does not represent the author's most mature thought and leaves aside or skims over many of the major theological problems. Although the same author's *al-Mawrid al-ṣāfī* very probably contained a more complete presentation, we can do little more than conjecture about the contents of this lost text. Nevertheless, whether or not the Neo-Ḥanbalite scholars ever put forward their teaching on love in all its details in a single treatise, their arguments and opinions gathered from a variety of works coalesce, for the most part, into what has the appearance of a systematic and coherent doctrine. In all but a few respects their teaching is faithful to the *nomos* pattern.

Marʿī b. Yūsuf's *Munyat al-muḥibbīn* offers an example of one way in which the doctrine of these earlier authorities was preserved or distorted by later writers. Marʿī attempted to balance his heavy reliance on his predecessors in the Ḥanbalite school by introducing into his work opinions taken over from the *eros* tradition. Other writers, as we have noted, borrowed, imitated, or codified in accordance with their particular purpose. To be sure, our understanding of how Ibn Taymīya and Ibn Qayyim al-Jawzīya influenced the men who came after them remains sketchy at best. Of the subsequent evolution of the Ḥanbalite *nomos* doctrine—a long and complex process which extended over more than five centuries, reaching virtually to the present—we know only too little. But with some degree of confidence we may assume that the fundamental outlooks or "motifs" in conflict continued to be very much the same.

Appendix: On Links with Romance Poetry

THE ARGUMENT AGAINST the theory of Arabic influence on Provençal poetry and the conception of love in late medieval European literature seemed sound enough when it was first advanced. The mere cataloguing of common motifs is clearly no substitute for conclusive evidence of imitation or borrowing, which must be sought in the verse of the troubadours themselves.[1] Subsequently, however, some evidence, albeit tenuous, has been presented to support the Arabic theory. E. Lévi-Provençal, pursuing a suggestion made earlier by Nykl,[2] attempted to show that William IX, or another early troubadour who chose to retouch his work, possibly knew colloquial Arabic or was at least familiar with refrains in the language. That William IX should have been acquainted with Arabic is not surprising in view of his Syrian and Spanish expeditions. In his Chanson V, which according to Nykl dates from after the Syrian crusade and shows affinities with the *zajal* form,[3] Lévi-Provençal thought he might have deciphered several lines of Arabic which the poet speaks to two women he meets. Only the Paris manuscript 856 (ed. Jeanroy, p. 35) gives the lines in question. Here is the text with Lévi-Provençal's interpretation of it:

(Aujatz ieu que lur respozi,
Anc fer ni fust no y mentaugui,
Mais que lur dis:) aital lati
Tarrababart
Martababelio riben
Saramahart.

In Arabic:

. . . . antĕ llatī
marra b-Ab Ḥār ˘ṯ [Abū Ḥārith]

marra b-Ab Nūr ibĕn
Ṣāram ʿāhart!

Translation:

You are the one who,
first with Abū Ḥārith
and then with Abū Nūr ibn
Ṣāram, prostituted yourself![4]

There are problems of detail in Lévi-Provençal's solution, but it provides a plausible illustration of how these lines may be read as Arabic.[5] Despite the fact that the text does not seem to be a courtly one, the use of what is apparently the Arabic language none the less strengthens the hypothesis of direct filiation in the work of at least one poet. It would not be unreasonable to suppose that borrowings of this nature—if indeed it is one—occurred more than once.

Lévi-Provençal's proposal for the unraveling of these puzzling lines was an encouragement to the proponents of an Arabic influence on Provençal poetry. More recently, however, Emilio García Gómez has gathered evidence for a more exciting thesis, the implication of which may be a two-way exchange. S. M. Stern's publication in 1948 of the Romance *kharjas* (roughly, last or final "refrains") in certain Hispano-Hebraic poems of the *muwashshaḥ* genre was soon complemented by the uncovering of many others in Arabic *muwashshaḥāt*.[6] With the existence of now more than sixty Romance *kharjas* attested, the bilingual *zajal*s of Ibn Quzmān must pass for the moment into the background. García Gómez concludes from the new discoveries that two poetries flourished in Spain side by side and independently of each other after the Muslim invasion, the Arabic and the preexisting Romance. Towards the end of the ninth century, he suggests, with a movement of social integration, the *muwashshaḥ* was invented, a genre which consisted of verses in classical Arabic leading up to a vulgar refrain usually borrowed, in his opinion, from the common stock of Romance lyric.[7] To substantiate his view, García Gómez has assembled considerable evidence implying that the metric system of the *muwashshaḥāt* is syllabic as in Romance languages rather than quantitative as traditional Arabic prosody would require.[8]

The spread of this Andalusian genre to the Arab East through the Egyptian poet Ibn Sanā' al-Mulk (d. 608/1211) is well known. Theoretician as well as imitator of the *muwashshaḥ*, the Ayyubid writer was careful in many of his pieces to replace the "Berber" refrains he found in Maghribi compositions with *kharja*s of his own expressed in vulgar

Arabic and, later, in Persian.[9] The link between the Romance *kharja*s and the subsequent development of European lyric, if less easily documented, seems undeniable in the matter of content. García Gómez describes this link as a bilingual Hispanic cultural core, whose main traits continued to persist for a millenium, the *muwashshaḥ* being represented in Castilian literature by the *villancico*, which clearly resembles it.[10] A similar if not so enthusiastic assessment is given by the Romanist P. Le Gentil. "Among the *khardja*s," he remarks, "were first noted those which discretely but in an evident manner evoke themes which Romanists know well from having encountered them in the Galician *cantigas de amigo*, in the Castilian *villancicos*, and also in the French *refrains* which belong to the rich and varied tradition of the *chanson de femme*."[11]

It may be added that Le Gentil, apparently unaware of the richness and variety of Arabic poetry, exploits this observation to muster yet another proof against the theory of Arabic influence on Romance literature. Both the *muwashshaḥ* and the *kharja* may treat of love, but it is only the latter, he argues, which makes use of the themes of the *chanson de femme*, "unknown to the Islamic tradition and excluded from the Hebrew or Arabic context—thus producing a vigorous effect of contrast. . . ." Le Gentil finds it difficult to imagine how the Arab authors could have invented these themes on their own, for they would otherwise occur more often in the main body of the *muwashshaḥ*. The writers of *muwashshaḥāt*, like the troubadours, he concludes, would seem to have been amateurs of folklore.[12]

It is difficult to know, of course, precisely which of the Romance *kharja*s that have been found predate the poems in which they are included and which may have been composed by the Arab or Jewish writers themselves. But I would like to suggest that the themes of the *chanson de femme* were not unknown in Arabic poetry. The following line comes to mind:

> Taṭāwala hādhā 'l-laylu wa-khḍalla jānibuh
> wa-arraqanī an lā khalīla ulāʿibuh
>
> (This night is long and its flank dark,
> and I am sleepless because I have no
> sweetheart to play with.)

This line and two which follow it are said to have been heard by the Caliph ʿUmar from a woman whose husband was away at war. They represent a characteristic theme of the *chanson de femme*.[13]

Returning to the issue at hand, we may draw this conclusion. Lévi-

Provençal's argument for reading as Arabic the enigmatic lines found in one manuscript of the poems of William IX and the observations of García Gómez and Le Gentil which connect the *kharja*s with the later stream of European poetry indicate that further studies with a comparative orientation, whether concerned primarily with the Arabic or the Romance side, may prove to be extremely fruitful. The question of filiation, in either direction, has gained a certain respectability. Even studies which aim at no more than enlarging the catalogue of parallels between the two literatures can continue, so to speak, with a clear conscience.

Certainly research in Arabic texts can no longer be considered irrelevant to problems in the history of Romance literatures. In particular, various misconceptions on which theories are still being based need to be corrected—for example, the view shared by both García Gómez and Le Gentil,[14] that a feminine lyric is foreign to the Arab context. Even studies of works which appear to have been unavailable in Spain may be useful for comparative purposes. Many Arabic manuscripts are known to have been destroyed on the peninsula, first by al-Manṣūr (d. 595/1199) and later by Cardinal Jiménez. Not only may texts preserved solely in the East have been available in Spain, but also, since Arab authors used to lengthen their works with many borrowings and quotations, it is certain that most stories, poems, or controversies found in Eastern writings were familiar to Western Arabs from their own sources.[15]

Glossary of Arabic Terms

adab. Belles-lettres.
adhān. Call to prayer.
ahl al-ḥadīth. The orthodox traditionist party, literally "the people of the sayings of the Prophet."
ajnabīya. Woman not allowed to a man, belonging to another.
akhbār. Reports, stories about persons or accounts of events. Plural of *khabar.*
akhbārī. Collector and/or narrator of *akhbār.*
ʿalāqa. Attachment, relationship.
ʿaql. Reason, intellect.
baqā'. Subsistence, remaining, permanence in the future.
dhawq. Taste, tasting, experience.
dīwān. Collection of poetry.
fanā'. Annihilation, passing away from self.
faraḥ. Joy.
fatwā. Opinion rendered by a jurist on a legal problem.
fiqh. Jurisprudence.
gharaḍ. Purpose, motive, aim.
gharām. Infatuation, persistent love.
ghazal. Love lyric.
ḥabīb. Beloved.
ḥadd. Technical term for the severe "fixed" penalties—including stoning, crucifixion, cutting off of hand and/or foot, and flogging—prescribed for certain acts forbidden by the Koran. The infliction of these punishments tended to be restricted, both in theory and in practice.
ḥadīth. A saying of the Prophet; the corpus of the sayings of the Prophet as a whole.
hawā. Passion, concupiscible appetite, lust, love.
hawā muttabaʿ. Passion or lust to which one abandons oneself.
hawān. Disgrace, degradation.
ḥikma. Wisdom, "wise purpose."
ḥiyal. Legal stratagems employed for extralegal ends. Plural of *ḥīla.*
ḥubb. Love (generic term).

ḥulūl. Indwelling of the divine in human flesh, incarnation.
imām. Prayer leader; politico-religious leader; founder of a Muslim legal rite.
Irāda. Will, desire.
ʿishq. Passionate love, excessive love.
ishrāqī. Illuminist; Illuminationist; adept of Illuminative Wisdom, the emanationist philosophy of Shihāb al-Dīn Suhrawardī (d. 587/1191).
ishtiyāq. Longing.
isnād. Chain of narrators cited before the text of a prophetic tradition or other report to guarantee its authenticity.
Isrā'īlīyāt. Reports concerning characters or events of pre-Islamic Jewish history.
istiḥsān. Approval, finding beautiful.
īthār. Altruism, giving preference to someone other than oneself.
ittiḥādī. Monist, partisan of the mystical doctrine of existential union with God.
ittiḥādīya. Plural of *ittiḥādī.*
jamʿ. Concentration (Sufi technical term).
kalām. Dialectical theology.
kātib. Scribe or secretary, especially one performing this function in the departments of government.
khalīl. Intimate friend.
kharja. A kind of envoy or final line in a poem of the *muwashshaḥ* genre. In the early examples of these poems the *kharja* is considered to have been typically in the colloquial language (Romance or Arabic) and to have represented the speech of a woman.
khulla. Bosom friendship; unique or exclusive love.
kuttāb. Plural of *kātib.*
ladhdha. Pleasure.
lūṭī. Sodomite.
madhhab. Rite or school of Muslim law.
madrasa. School for the study of the Muslim religious sciences, especially jurisprudence.
maḥabba. Love (generic term).
malāmī. Mystic who adopts a pattern of outward behavior which belies his inward piety, intending thereby to deny himself the praise of men.
"*Man ʿashiqa. . . .*" First words of the alleged saying of the Prophet "He who falls in love, conceals [his passion], is chaste, and dies, is a martyr." (Other versions than that translated here exist, but they begin similarly and convey roughly the same message.)
maṣdar. Verbal noun, infinitive.
mawadda. Affection, love.
mayl. Inclination.
mubtahij. One who experiences delight.
muḥtasib. Market inspector and keeper of public morals.
mulā'ama. Suitability, appropriateness, affinity.
munāsaba. Affinity, relationship, similarity.

murīd. Disciple of a Sufi teacher.
mustalidhdh. One who experiences pleasure.
mutakallimūn. Dialectical theologians.
muwāfaqa. Accord, agreement.
muwashshaḥ. A postclassical, strophic form of Arabic poetry invented in Muslim Spain in the late ninth or early tenth century. Each stanza has rhymes peculiar to itself, but it is followed by a line with rhymes (internal and final) common to the whole poem. The poem may also begin with such a line. That following the last stanza is the *kharja*. (See James T. Monroe, *Hispano-Arabic poetry* [Berkeley, Los Angeles, London: University of California Press, 1974] for numerous examples of the *muwashshaḥ* in Arabic and English translation, along with a good technical definition of the form [p. 392]).
muwashshaḥāt. Poems of the *muwashshaḥ* form.
naql. Tradition, the handing down of knowledge.
naẓar. Looking, gazing, glancing; the amorous regard.
nisba. Relative adjective; a name designating generally a geographical, tribal, or sectarian relationship; a relation, affinity, or "comparison."
'odhrite. See ʿUdhrī.
qāḍī. Judge in Muslim law.
rāwī. Narrator.
rāwiya. Narrator of poetry and tradition.
ṣabāba. Tender and ardent longing.
ṣaḥīḥ. Sound, authentic (of a *ḥadīth*); having a sound chain of transmitters and not in disagreement with an authoritative text.
sakīna. Peace of soul, tranquility.
samāʿ. Listening to song and music; the spiritual concert of the mystics.
shaghaf. Deep love, love which has reached the pericardium, infatuation.
shahāda. The Muslim profession of faith: "There is no god but Allah and Muḥammad is the prophet of Allah."
shāhid. Witness; one who by his beauty bears witness to the uniqueness of his creator.
shawq. Desire.
shaykh. Religious teacher; old man.
shirk. Polytheistic idolatry; setting up rivals or equals to God.
shuhūdī. "Contemplative," pertaining to the mystical doctrine of the loss of awareness of self or the unity of perception; partisan of this doctrine.
Sunna. The sayings and practice of the Prophet.
taʿabbud. Servitude, enslavement, worship.
ṭabaqa. "Generation" of personalities, generally scholars, a division for arranging biographical works.
ṭabaqāt literature. Biographical literature arranged according to "generations."
tafsīr. Koranic commentary.
tatayyum. Enslavement, thralldom.

tawḥīd. Monotheism, profession of the divine unity.
ta'wīl. Metaphorical or allegorical interpretation of Koranic texts.
ʿUdhrī. Of the tribe of the Banū ʿUdhra; platonic, chaste and often fatal (of love).
ʿulamā'. Muslim religious and legal scholars.
uns. Intimacy.
wafayāt. Literally "deaths." Biographical notices arranged by date of death.
walah. Derangement, loss of discernment, distraction, passionate love.
widād. Affection, love.
ya's. Resignation, despair.
zajal. A strophic form of colloquial Arabic poetry related to the *muwashshaḥ* in structure.
zandaqa. A term for heresy, often but not always denoting a heresy of dualist, Manichaean character.
zindīq. Heretic; dualist, Manichaean.
zuhd. Asceticism.
zuhdīyāt. Ascetic *akhbār.*

Notes

CHAPTER ONE

1. Ḥanbalism is one of four rites or schools of sacred law found within the majority Sunnite or "orthodox" branch of the Muslim community. Today the influence of these schools, to the extent that it persists, is restricted in most Muslim countries to matters of ritual and personal status—marriage, divorce, and inheritance.
2. See Fazlur Rahman, *Islam* (London: Weidenfeld and Nicolson, 1966), pp. 198–99.
3. With the exception of Ibn Taymīya these writers have been treated briefly (Ibn al-Jawzīya in somewhat more detail) by Lois Anita Giffen in *Theory of profane love among the Arabs: the development of the genre* (New York and London: New York University Press and London University Press, 1971). Marʿī b. Yūsuf's *Munyat al-muḥibbīn*, the only significant extant work on love by any of these men which is as yet unpublished, has also been discussed in an article by Emilio García Gómez, "Un precedente y una consecuencia del 'Collar de la paloma,' " *Al-Andalus* 16 (1951): 309–330, especially 324–29.
4. For example, Jean-Claude Vadet's *L'esprit courtois en orient dans les cinq premiers siècles de l'Hégire* (Paris: G.-P. Maisonneuve et Larose, 1968).
5. See in favor of the Arabic hypothesis A. R. Nykl, *Hispano-Arabic poetry and its relations with the Old Provençal troubadours* (Baltimore, 1946) and Lawrence Ecker, *Arabischer, provenzalischer, und deutscher Minnesang* (Berne, 1934); and, opposing it, A. Jeanroy, *La poésie lyrique des troubadours*, 2 vols. (Toulouse and Paris, 1934) and D. Scheludko, "Beiträge zur Entstehungsgeschichte der altprovenzalischen Lyrik, II, Die arabische Theorie," *Archivum Romanicum* 12 (1928): 30–127. Jeanroy does not exclude altogether the possibility of an Arabic influence (*Poésie lyrique*, I, pp. 68ff.). Scheludko shows that the parallels established by J. Pizzi in his *Storia della poesia persiana* (Milan, 1887) may be ascribed to sources other than the Arabic or are common motifs to be found in the love poetry of various cultures which had no contact with medieval Europe. R. Bezzola, in *Les origines et la formation de la littérature courtoise en occident*, 2 vols. (Paris: Champion, 1944–60), gives a list of Pizzi's parallels (II, p. 185, n. 6) and Scheludko's arguments against them (II, p. 190, n. 3).
6. Cf. R. Bezzola, *Origines*, II, pp. 153–203. Bezzola's chapter on the question of Arabic influence appears to have been completed long before the date of its publication (1960). On the hypothesis of Arabic influence through Sicily there is Silvestro Fiore's *Über die Beziehungen zwischen der arabischen und der frühitalienischen Lyrik* (Köln, 1956). Fiore treats what he considers to be the influence of the *zajal* form in Italy, but in my hasty perusal of the work I have found no conclusive example of filiation. On further examples of influence, including some in both directions, see the appendix to this study.

7. Cf. Alexander Joseph Denomy, *The heresy of courtly love* (New York, 1947) and "Concerning the accessibility of Arabic influences to the earliest Provençal troubadours," *Medieval Studies* 15 (1953): 147–58.
8. Gustave E. von Grunebaum, "Avicenna's *Risâla fī 'l-ʿišq* and courtly love," *Journal of Near Eastern Studies* (hereafter cited as *JNES*) 11 (1952): 233, 237–38. Von Grunebaum mentioned specifically Apuleius *De Platone* ii, on love as a source of good, and the Latin Asclepius.
9. *Ibid.*, p. 238.
10. Notable exceptions are Hellmut Ritter's analysis of the works of the Persian poet Farīd ul-Dīn ʿAṭṭār and their background in *Das Meer der Seele* (Leiden: E. J. Brill, 1955) and the studies by J. C. Vadet and Lois Giffen.
11. Anders Nygren, *Agape and Eros*, trans. Philip S. Watson (London: S.P.C.K., 1953), p. 35. In the course of my research I have been obliged to use several editions of Nygren's work, including a separate translation of Part I. References not otherwise noted are to the edition here cited. The first part of the original Swedish version was published in 1930, and the second followed in 1936. As a result of the considerable excitement aroused by the work, an English translation of Part I was made available as early as 1932, while the first and second volumes of Part II appeared in English in 1938 and 1939 respectively.
12. See, e.g., M. C. D'Arcy, *The mind and heart of love* (New York: Meridian Books, 1956) and Irving Singer, *The nature of love, Plato to Luther* (New York: Random House, 1966), a partisan work, at least in places, despite the author's express denial. Compare Singer's disclaimer (p. 323) with his statements elsewhere in the text (e.g., pp. 246 and 366).
13. Robert G. Hazo, *The idea of love*, "Concepts in Western Thought Series," Institute for Philosophical Research (New York, Washington, London: Praeger, 1967). Hazo distinguishes seven "critical notions" occurring in discussions of love. These are denoted by: "in the tendential order, five basic terms: tendency in general, acquisitive desire, benevolent desire, sexual desire, and the desire for union; and, in the order of judgment, two basic terms: esteem and valuation." (*The idea of love*, p. 36. For a detailed explanation of the use of these terms see *ibid.*, pp. 11–36.)
14. The *Qiyān* of al-Jāḥiẓ may be read in a French translation by Charles Pellat published in *Arabica* 10 (1963): 121–47. Perhaps the best Arabic text is that found in *Rasā'il al-Jāḥiz*, ed. ʿAbd al-Salām Muḥammad Hārūn (Cairo: Maktabat al-Khānjī, 1384/1964–65), II, pp. 143–82. The *Risāla fī 'l-ʿishq wa-l-nisā'* is printed in *Rasā'il al-Jāḥiẓ*, ed. Ḥasan al-Sandūbī (Cairo: al-Maṭbaʿa al-Tijārīya al-Kubrā, 1352/1933), pp. 266–75; partial translation in Charles Pellat, *The Life and works of Jāḥiẓ*, trans. from the French by D. M. Hawke (Berkeley and Los Angeles: University of California Press, 1969), pp. 257–59.
15. Al-Ḥārith b. Asad al-Muḥāsibī, "*Faṣl fī 'l-maḥabba.*" Quoted in Abū Nuʿaym Aḥmad b. ʿAbd Allāh al-Iṣfahānī, *Ḥilyat al-awliyā'* (Cairo: Maktabat al-Khānjī and Maṭbaʿat al-Saʿāda, 1351–57/1932–38), X, p. 76ff.
16. See Jean-Claude Vadet, *L'esprit courtois*, pp. 379–430, for a lengthy treatment of al-Sarrāj. There is also a long chapter on al-Sarrāj's *Maṣāriʿ* in Muṣṭafā ʿAbd al-Wāḥid, *Dirāsat al-ḥubb fī 'l-adab al-ʿarabī* (Cairo: Dār al-Maʿārif, 1972), II, pp. 311–408. Cf. my remarks on the *Manāzil al-aḥbāb* of Maḥmūd b. Sulaymān al-Ḥalabī (d. 725/1325) below, pp. 100–101 and n. 55.
17. On this important but now lost work, see Giffen, *Theory*, pp. 18–20, 72–74.
18. The first half of Ibn Dāwūd's *Kitāb al-zahra*, the section on love, has been edited by A. Nykl (Chicago: University of Chicago Press, 1932).
19. Al-Kharā'iṭī's *Iʿtilāl al-qulūb* has not been published. I have consulted the MS of the Egyptian National Library (*Adab*, 445). For discussions of the work, see J. C. Vadet, "Littérature courtoise et transmission du *ḥadīṯ*, un exemple: Muḥammad b. Ǧaʿfar al-Ḫarā'iṭī (m. en 327/938)," *Arabica* 7 (1960): 140–66; and Giffen, *Theory*,

especially pp. 15–16, 74–78. For the chapter headings of the Bursa MS of the *I'tilāl* (Ulu Cami, 1535), see Vadet's article, pp. 157–59, and the additions and emendations given by Giffen, *Theory*, p. 75, n. 14.

20. Giffen, *Theory*, pp. 74–79.

21. Ibrāhīm b. 'Umar al-Biqā'ī (d. 885/1480) compiled, for example, an expanded version of al-Sarrāj's *Maṣāri'* entitled *Aswāq al-ashwāq* (MSS Beşir Ağa, 552, and Reisülküttab, 745). In turn, the sophisticated and carefully arranged *Tazyīn al-aswāq* (Cairo, 1291/1874) by the late-tenth-/sixteenth-century medical authority Dāwūd b. 'Umar al-Anṭākī is a reworking and abridgement of al-Biqā'ī's book. On the anonymous and as yet unpublished *Kitāb as'ār al-aswāq*, apparently also based largely on al-Biqā'ī, see Giffen, *Theory*, pp. 45–46.

22. A detailed presentation of my reasons for considering that al-Sarrāj's book lies largely outside the Ḥanbalite tradition will be found in my forthcoming article "Al-Sarrāj's *Maṣāri' al-'ushshāq*: a Ḥanbalite work?" to appear in the *Journal of the American Oriental Society*.

CHAPTER TWO

1. Ibn al-Jawzī was born ca. 511 A.H. in Baghdad, where he spent most of his life. After some early flirtations with asceticism and mysticism, which never entirely ceased to influence him, he turned to scholarship (Ibn Rajab, *Kitāb al-dhayl 'alā Ṭabaqāt al-Ḥanābila*, ed. Muḥammad Ḥāmid al-Fiqī [Cairo: Maṭba'at al-Sunna al-Muḥammadīya, 1372/1952–53], I, pp. 403, 414, Sibṭ Ibn al-Jawzī, *Mir'āt al-zamān*, Vol. VIII [Ḥaydarābād: Dā'irat al-Ma'ārif al-'Uthmānīya, 1370/1951], Part II, p. 482). He was to have a brilliant career not only as a writer but also as a preacher. According to his personal estimate his sermons were always attended by at least ten or fifteen thousand people (Ibn Rajab, *Dhayl*, I, p. 403). Ibn al-Jawzī is also reported to have claimed that as many as 100,000 attended his sermons. (Al-Dhahabī, remarking that in the case of such an attendance most of those present would not have heard what was said, opts for the lower figure. *Tadhkirat al-ḥuffāẓ* [3d ed.; Ḥaydarādāb: Dā'irat al-Ma'ārif al-'Uthmānīya, 1375/1955–1376/1957], IV, p. 1344. Perhaps the sermon was relayed by mosque officials similar to the *muballighūn* mentioned by E. W. Lane, whose duty it was to repeat the *adhān* so that the entire congregation might hear. *The manners and customs of the modern Egyptians* [Everyman's Library], p. 87, n. 2.) Ibn al-Jawzī eventually became recognized as a preacher of the palace and acquired considerable influence. He relentlessly pursued the enemies of Sunnism. On one occasion he was given caliphal authority to persecute the Rāfiḍites. Again, "in 583/1187 he obtained from the vizier Ibn Yūnus [another Ḥanbalite] the condemnation of the shaykh Rukn al-Dīn (d. 611 A.H.), a grandson of 'Abd al-Qādir al-Jīlī, who was accused of holding in his *madrasa*, the Jīlīya, some questionable books on logic and philosophy, in particular, the Ismā'īlī encyclopedia of the Ikhwān al-Ṣafā'" (Henri Laoust, *Les schismes dans l'Islam* [Paris: Payot, 1965], pp. 213, 240–41). The books were burnt and the *madrasa* taken away from al-Rukn and given to Ibn al-Jawzī (Ibn Rajab, *Dhayl*, I, p. 426). Rukn al-Dīn had his revenge three years later. In 590, at his instigation, the Rāfiḍite vizier Ibn al-Qaṣṣāb had Ibn al-Jawzī confined to a house in Wāsiṭ, where, although nearly eighty, he was obliged to wash and cook for himself. He was not released until five years later, when his son was able to obtain his deliverance through the intercession of the Caliph al-Nāṣir's mother (Ibn Rajab, *Dhayl*, I, pp. 426–27; al-Dhahabī, *Tadhkira*, IV, p. 1346). He died soon thereafter in 597/1200.

2. The text of the *Nihāya* in the section on love is replete with acknowledged borrowings from Ibn al-Jawzī. See, e.g., Vol. II (offset of Dār al-Kutub edition; Cairo, n.d.), pp.

136, 139, 141, 145, 146, and 152. Lois Giffen has shown, however, that the unacknowledged passages are also taken from *Dhamm al-hawā* (*Theory*, pp. 146–47).

Brockelmann mentions a *Dhamm al-hawā* by the fifteenth-century Damascene Ḥanbalite scholar Ibn al-Mabrad and another by a certain Yūsuf b. ʿAbd al-Hādī, apparently also of Damascus, neither of which I have seen (*S*, II, pp. 131, 947).

3. Ibn Rajab, *Dhayl*, I, pp. 416–21; ʿAbd al-Ḥamīd al-ʿAlwajī, *Mu'allafāt Ibn al-Jawzī* (Baghdad: Dār al-Jumhūrīya li-l-Nashr wa-l-Ṭabʿ, 1385/1965); *GAL*, I, p. 501 (660). His productivity was legendary. Ibn Khallikān remarks: "We shall close this list of the writings of Ibn al-Jawzī by merely stating that his works are too numerous to be counted. The quantity of sheets which he wrote with his own hand was very great, but people exaggerate when they say that on summing up the number of *kurrāsas* ["The *kurrāsa* generally contains twenty pages."] written by him and taking into account the length of his life, if the former be divided by the latter, it will give nine *kurrāsas* a-day; but this is a result so extraordinary, that it can hardly be admitted by any reasonable man. It is related also that the parings of the reed-pens with which he wrote the Traditions were gathered up and formed a large heap; these, in pursuance to his last orders, were employed to heat the water for washing his corpse, and there was even more than enough for the purpose" (*Wafayāt al-aʿyān*, trans. De Slane [Paris: Oriental Translation Fund of Great Britain and Ireland, 1843–71], II, p. 97). Ibn Taghrībirdī, in his biographical notice on Ibn al-Jawzī, chooses to quote this same passage from Ibn Khallikān (*al-Nujūm al-zāhira* [Cairo: Dār al-Kutub al-Miṣrīya, 1929–49], VI, p. 175). Besides Ibn al-Jawzī's *Talbīs Iblīs* and *Ṣayd al-khāṭir*, cited later, one can mention in addition to *Dhamm al-hawā* at least two more of his printed works which bear on the subject of love: *al-Ṭibb al-rūḥānī* (Damascus: Maktabat al-Qudsī wa-l-Budayr, 1348 A.H.), chap. viii, "On repelling *ʿishq* from the soul," pp. 8 ff.; and *Akhbār al-nisā'* (Dār al-Fikr, n.d.). The latter work, which in this edition is erroneously attributed to Ibn Qayyim al-Jawzīya, contains a considerable number of love stories.

4. Ibn Rajab, *Dhayl*, I, pp. 414–16. Al-Suyūṭī quotes the Ḥanbalite al-Dhahabī on Ibn al-Jawzī's weakness in tradition (Jamāl al-Dīn al-Suyūṭī, *Ṭabaqāt al-mufassirīn*, ed. A. Meursinge (Leiden: S. and J. Luchtmans, 1839), p. 17.

5. Once when Ibn al-Jawzī was told that his only fault was that he was a Ḥanbalite, he indignantly replied:

Wa-ʿayyaranī 'l-wāshūna annī uḥibbuhā
wa-tilka shakātun ẓāhirun ʿan-ka ʿāruhā.

(The slanderers upbraid me because I love her,
clearly a complaint which does not touch you.)
Abū Dhu'ayb of Hudhayl

Then, employing a current mode of argumentation, he added, "Is this a fault of mine, when there is no fault in a cheek flecked with a beauty spot?" He continued, reciting:

Wa-lā ʿayba fī-him ghayra anna suyūfahum
bi-hinna fulūlun min qirāʿi 'l-katā'ibī.

(There is no fault in them but that their swords
are notched from clashing with mounted squadrons.)
Al-Nābigha al-Dhubyānī

Ibn Rajab, *Dhayl*, I, p. 404. For another example of his use of *ghazal* in argumentation, see Sibṭ Ibn al-Jawzī, *Mir'āt al-zamān*, VIII, Part II, p. 493.

6. Ibn Rajab, *Dhayl*, I, p. 413, citing Ibn al-Buzūrī: "He left no discipline or subject without writing a work on it."

7. *Dhamm al-hawā* contains numerous traditions which the author heard from his teacher Muḥammad b. Nāṣir (on whom see Ibn Rajab, *Dhayl*, I, pp. 225–29). Ibn al-Jawzī gave Ibn Nāṣir most of the credit for his knowledge of *ḥadīth* (*ibid.*, p. 226).
8. Shuhda bint Abī Naṣr Aḥmad b. al-Faraj al-Dīnawārī al-Baghdādī (d. 574/1178), a pious woman held to be among the reliable traditionists of Iraq in her time (al-Dhahabī, *ʿIbar*, IV, ed. Ṣalāḥ al-Dīn al-Munajjid [Kuwait, 1963], p. 221; and Ibn al-ʿImād, *Shadharāt al-dhahab* [Cairo: Maktabat al-Qudsī wa-l-Budayr, 1351], IV, p. 248). The same notice is found in both works, with the addition of al-Niʿālī as one of Shuhda's authorities in the former. Her husband built a *madrasa* for the Shāfiʿites. See the notice on Shuhda in Ibn Khallikān, *Wafayāt al-aʿyān*, ed. Muḥammad Muḥyī 'l-Dīn ʿAbd al-Ḥamīd (Cairo: Maktabat al-Nahḍa al- Miṣrīya, 1367/1948), II, pp. 172–73.
9. Ibn Rajab, *Dhayl*, I, p. 100.
10. Cf., for example, Abū al-Ḥasan ʿAlī b. Muḥammad al-Māwardī, *Adab al-dunyā wa-l-dīn* (1st ed.; Cairo: al-Maṭbaʿa al-Kubrā al-Amīrīya, 1316/1898), chap. one, "The excellence of reason and the censure of passion," pp. 4–16.
11. Trans. Richard Bell (*The Qur'ān* [Edinburgh, 1937–39], I, p. 322, v. 45).
12. Ibn al-Jawzī, *Dhamm al-hawā*, ed. Muṣṭafā ʿAbd al-Wāḥid (Cairo: Dār al-Kutub al-Hadītha, 1381/1962), pp. 5–6.
13. *Ibid.*, p. 10.
14. *Ibid.*, p. 7.
15. Ibn al-Jawzī, *Ṣayd al-khāṭir* (Cairo: Idārat al-Ṭibāʿa al-Munīrīya, 1345/1926–27), *faṣl* 75, p. 98.
16. *Dhamm*, pp. 12–13. Ibn Qayyim al-Jawzīya gives practically the same definition of *hawā* (*Rawḍat al-muḥibbīn*, ed. Aḥmad ʿUbayd [Cairo: Maṭbaʿat al-Saʿāda, 1375/1956], p. 463); but the wording of his argument is more sophisticated than that of Ibn al-Jawzī.
17. *Dhamm*, p. 16. See Giffen, *Theory*, pp. 118–20, on *hawā* in the pagan sense of "love" and the Islamic sense of "evil desire" and the attempt of the Ḥanbalites to equate the two.
18. *Dhamm*, pp. 12–15. Ibn al-Qayyim takes these considerations up again (*Rawḍa*, pp. 465 ff.) and extends the list to fifty, the ninth consideration in his list being the first in that of Ibn al-Jawzī.
19. Trans. Maulānā Muḥammad ʿAlī (4th ed.; Lahore: Aḥmadiyyah Anjuman Ishāʿat Islām, 1951).
20. *Dhamm*, p. 16; Ibn al-Qayyim, *Rawḍa*, pp. 25–26, 138.
21. *Dhamm*, pp. 27, 19, 17 respectively; Ibn al-Qayyim, *Rawḍa*, p. 398. Koran 45:28, trans. E. H. Palmer.
22. *Dhamm*, pp. 20–22.
23. *Ibid.*, p. 33.
24. *Ibid.*, pp. 36, 40.
25. *Ibid.*, pp. 58–59, 62.
26. E.g., Ibn Qayyim al-Jawzīya, *ʿUddat al-ṣābirīn* (Cairo: Dār al-ʿUṣūr li-l-Ṭabʿ wa-l-Nashr, n.d.); and Abū ʿAbd Allāh Muḥammad b. Muḥammad al-Manbijī al-Ḥanbalī (d. 777 A.H.), *Tasliyat ahl al-maṣā'ib* (Cairo: Maktabat al-Khānjī, 1347/1929), esp. pp. 116–48.
27. *Dhamm*, p. 63.
28. Jean-Claude Vadet, "Littérature courtoise," p. 149, n. 1.
29. *Dhamm*, p. 70.
30. *Ibid.*, p. 69; Ibn al-Qayyim, *Rawḍa*, p. 168.
31. Cf. *Dhamm*, pp. 77–78, 81, and Ibn al-Qayyim, *Rawḍa*, pp. 435, 442.
32. *Dhamm*, p. 82.
33. *Ibid.*, p. 85.
34. *Ibid.*, p. 86.

35. *Ibid.*, p. 91.
36. *Ibid.*, pp. 93–94.
37. *Ibid.*, pp. 94–95. Cf. al-Ghazālī, *Mīzān al-ʿamal*, ed. Sulaymān Dunyā (Cairo: Dār al-Maʿārif, 1964), p. 318.
38. *Dhamm*, pp. 103–104.
39. Ibn al-Qayyim, *Rawḍa*, pp. 91–92.
40. *Dhamm*, pp. 105, 107.
41. *Ibid.*, pp. 111, 114, 116.
42. Ibn al-Jawzī, *Talbīs Iblīs*, ed. Muḥammad Munīr al-Dimashqī (Cairo: Idārat al-Ṭibāʿa al-Munīrīya, 1928), pp. 170, 173.
43. Unless otherwise indicated, the information relating to Ibn al-Jawzī's classification of the Sufis with regard to *naẓar* is taken from *Talbīs Iblīs*, pp. 265–73.
44. *Ibid.*, p. 169. This is an example of a tendency of Muslim heresiographers to attribute the doctrine of *ḥulūl* to a Manichaean origin. Cf. Ritter, *Das Meer der Seele*, p. 455; "Abū Ḥamza war sicherlich weder ḥulūlī noch zindīq. Der ṣūfī fühlt sich in bestimmten seelenstimmungen durch jedes ding von Gott angesprochen, bezieht alles, was er erlebt, auch banale vorgänge, auf sein verhältnis zu Gott. . . . Aber es ist natürlich doch interessant, dass man ihn als Manichäer bezeichnete."
45. *Talbīs*, p. 171.
46. *Le Dîwân d'ál-Ḥallâj*, ed. and trans. Louis Massignon (new ed. with additions and corrections; Paris: Librairie Orientaliste Paul Geuthner, 1955), p. 41; *Talbīs*, p. 171.
47. According to Ibn al-Jawzī, Abū ʿUbayd Allāh b. Khafīf suspected that these verses might be falsely attributed to al-Ḥallāj (*Talbīs*, p. 171). Massignon, on the other hand, expresses no doubts about their authenticity.
48. Ibn al-Jawzī makes it clear at this point that it is the insistent gaze which is objectionable, not the occasionally necessary brief glance.
49. On Aḥmad al-Ghazālī (d. 520/1126), see Henri Corbin, *Histoire de la philosophie islamique* (Gallimard, 1964), pp. 278–83. Corbin contrasts the Platonic concept of love as found in Ibn Dāwūd, who was the first jurist to render a sentence against al-Ḥallāj, with the esoteric interpretation of Platonic love taught by mystics like Rūzbahān Baqlī (d. 606/1209) and Aḥmad al-Ghazālī. Here, too, the discussion touches on *naẓar*: "Pour Rûzbehân, le sens caché de la Forme humaine, c'est la théophanie primordiale: Dieu se révélant à soi-même dans la Forme adamique. . . . C'est pourquoi Rûzbehân goûtait particulièrement les célèbres vers de Hallâj: 'Gloire à Celui qui manifesta son humanité comme mystère de gloire de sa divinité radieuse'. . . ." Ibn Dāwūd, being a Ẓāhirite (exoterist) could not admit such an interpretation: "Ce que redoutaient le platonicien Ibn Dâwûd aussi bien que les théologiens (néo-hanbalites et autres), c'est le *tashbîh*, une assimilation de Dieu à l'homme qui compromette radicalement la transcendance du monothéisme abstrait, c'est-à-dire la conception purement exotérique du *Tawhîd.* Aussi bien, certains soufis ont-ils eux-mêmes refusé toute possibilité de rapporter l'*eros* à Dieu. D'autres ont considéré l'amant *'odhrite* comme un modèle proposé à l'amant mystique dont l'amour s'addresse à Dieu. Dans ce cas, il y a un transfert de l'amour: tout se passe comme si l'on passait d'un *objet* humain à un *objet* divin. Pour le "platonicien" Rûzbehân, ce pieux transfert est lui-même un piège. Il n'est possible de passer entre les deux gouffres du *tashbîh* et du *ta'tîl* (abstractionnisme) que par la voie de l'amour humain. L'amour divin n'est pas le transfert de l'amour à un *objet* divin; mais métamorphose du *sujet* de l'amour humain" (*ibid.*, pp. 279–80).
50. Some, however, he adds, claim that the early Sufis did practice chaste *naẓar*, giving as evidence the following verses attributed to Abū ʿAlī al-Rūdhbārī (as well as to Nifṭawayh):

Unazzihu fī rawḍi 'l-maḥāsini muqlatī
wa-amnaʿu nafsī an tanāla muḥarramā.

Wa-aḥmilu min thiqli 'l-hawā mā law annahū
'alā 'l-jabali 'l-ṣaldi 'l-aṣammi tahaddamā.

(I promenade my eye in the gardens of charms
and forbid my soul to partake of the forbidden.
And the burden of my passion is so heavy that were it
on the firm, hard mountain, it would fall to pieces.)
Talbīs, p. 269.

51. *Ibid.*, p. 274. I have quoted above two of the traditions related by Ibn al-Jawzī which suggest this conclusion (p. 21).
52. *Ibid.*, p. 222. Cf. Ibn al-Qayyim on *samā'* (*Rawḍa*, p. 154): "Wine is the drink of souls (*nufūs*) and melodies are the drink of spirits (*arwāḥ*). . . ."
53. *Talbīs*, p. 222.
54. *Ibid.*, pp. 227–28.
55. *Ibid.*, p. 170.
56. Ibn 'Abd Rabbih, *al-'Iqd al-farīd*, VI, ed. Aḥmad Amīn, Ibrāhīm al-Abyārī, and 'Abd al-Salām Hārūn (Cairo: Lajnat al-Ta'līf wa-l-Tarjama wa-l-Nashr, 1368/1949), pp. 4–5.
57. Many of the Apostolic Fathers and early apologists of Christianity turned to the Old Testament legalistic concept of love (called the *nomos* motif by Nygren) in reaction to the Platonic *eros* or longing, egocentric love, in which Christian gnostics saw the path to salvation. When Marcion condemned this recourse to *nomos*, Tertullian came to its defense. For him it is neither *eros* as taught by the gnostics nor the *agape* motif preached by Marcion which can effectively bind man to God, but only the fear of punishment and the hope of reward. See Anders Nygren, *Agape and eros*, trans. A. G. Herbert and Philip S. Watson (London: Society for Promoting Christian Knowledge; New York: The Macmillan Co., 1932–39), I, p. 133; II, pp. 35–36, 127–30.
58. Ibn al-Jawzī, *Talbīs Iblīs*, pp. 246–47. Earlier in the same work we are told that man's only portion in his knowledge of God is awe (*hayba*) and reverence (*ta'ẓīm*) (p. 228). This view, like Tertullian's belief that the only secure bond between man and God is fear of punishment and hope of reward, denies the role of love for God and is unacceptable to Neoplatonists and gnostics, whether Christian or Islamic. Cf. Abū Ṭālib al-Makkī's rejection of this view: "Those who have not experienced the stage of *uns* have rejected it just as those who have no knowledge of *maḥabba* have done with that stage, because they imagine it to be similar to the love for creatures, . . . maintaining that only the created being knows and understands *maḥabba*, which they hold to be nothing more than fear (*khawf*) and awe (*hayba*). Among those who held this view was Aḥmad b. Ghālib, known as Ghulām Khalīl, who rejected the teaching of al-Junayd, Abū Sa'īd, and al-Thawrī on *mahabba*. But this is not the doctrine of the early fathers (*salaf*) nor the way of the gnostics (*al-'ārifīn*)." *Qūt al-Qulūb* (Cairo, 1310), II, p. 64.
59. See pp. 107–113.
60. Ibn Dāwūd may have received many of the "Platonic" ideas expressed in this book from his father, the Ẓāhirite imam Dāwūd b. 'Alī al-Iṣfahānī (d. 270 A.H.). He heard from him, for example, the tradition promising a heavenly reward to the chaste lover (see text). We know also that his father reviewed most of *Kitāb al-zahra*, and we may assume that he approved of it (Ibn al-Jawzī, *al-Muntaẓam fī ta'rīkh al-mulūk wa-l-umam*, VI [1st ed.; Ḥaydarābād: Dā'irat al-Ma'ārif al-'Uthmānīya, 1357 A.H.], p. 94).
61. *Dhamm*, pp. 119–23. This information on Ibn Dāwūd was available to Ibn al-Jawzī in al-Khaṭīb al-Baghdādī's history. See *Ta'rīkh Baghdād* (Cairo: Maktabat al-Khānjī and Maṭba'at al-Sa'āda; Baghdad: al-Maktaba al-'Arabīya, 1349/1931), V, pp. 260, 262. Al-Khaṭīb is cited in Ibn al-Jawzī's *isnāds*.

62. *Dhamm*, pp. 147–48.
63. *Ibid.*, p. 153.
64. From Koran 2:30.
65. *Dhamm*, p. 158. Hārūt and Mārūt are two angels mentioned in the Koran (2:102) as having taught sorcery in Babel. There is no doubt that the seductress is to be associated with the planet Venus; for in the first version of the story she is "sent down" to the two angels (p. 156), while in the second her punishment is described in these words: "God extinguished the light of this star and cut her wings" (p. 157). The version translated here is found also in the *Kitāb al-tawwābīn* of Muwaffaq al-Dīn b. Qudāma (ed. George Makdisi [Damascus: Institut Français de Damas, 1961], pp. 2–3).
66. *Dhamm*, pp. 163, 165.
67. There is an exception in *Ṣayd al-khāṭir.* See p. 30 and n. 79.
68. *Dhamm*, p. 179. Cf. Ibn al-Qayyim, *Rawḍa*, pp. 303–305.
69. *Dhamm*, p. 181. Ibn Qayyim al-Jawzīya tells us that the believer is given dignity and beauty in proportion to his faith (*Rawḍa*, p. 220).
70. *Dhamm*, p. 181.
71. *Ibid.*, p. 186. How self-love and *caritas* can exist together was a problem for medieval Christian theologians (Nygren, *Agape and eros*, p. 423 ff.). Ibn al-Jawzī is undisturbed by the dilemma.
72. See below, esp. n. 79.
73. See pp. 69–70, 120, 149–52.
74. *Dhamm*, p. 194.
75. *Ibid.*, pp. 188, 190.
76. *Ibid.*, p. 191; Cf. Ibn al-Qayyim, *Rawḍa*, p. 354.
77. *Dhamm*, p. 189.
78. *Ibid.*, p. 190.
79. *Ṣayd al-khāṭir*, *faṣl* 316, p. 346. At another point Ibn al-Jawzī expresses an altruistic attitude towards women when he advises the man who hates his wife while she loves him dearly to be patient with her. To protect the loathed woman's feelings and to feign love for her is in his view among the greatest of virtues (*ibid.*, *faṣl* 297, pp. 336–37).
80. *Dhamm*, pp. 201–203.
81. *Ibid.*, p. 209.
82. *Ibid.*, p. 200.
83. "As for the analogy (*qiyās*) drawn between one man's cohabiting with another and the tribady of women, it is of the most fallacious kind; for there is no penetration [in the latter]. The counterpart of tribady is, rather, direct contact between one man and another without penetration. Thus, although it is said in a certain tradition traceable (*marfū*ʿ) to the Prophet, 'If one woman sleeps with another, then they are both fornicatresses (*zāniyatān*),' yet the *ḥadd* punishment is not required, because there is no penetration. It is 'fornication' in the generic sense which is applied to them, as in the expressions 'fornication of the eye, the hand, the leg, or the mouth.' " Ibn Qayyim al-Jawzīya, *al-Dā' wa-l-dawā'*, ed. Muḥammad Muḥyī 'l-Dīn ʿAbd al-Ḥamīd (Cairo: Maṭbaʿat al-Madanī, 1377/1958), p. 258.
84. *Dhamm*, pp. 221–22.
85. *Ibid.*, pp. 276–77; also in Ibn al-Qayyim, *Rawḍa*, p. 460.
86. *Dhamm*, pp. 254–56. The same story is related of Sulaymān b. Yasār by Abū Nuʿaym (*Ḥilya*, II, pp. 190–91). On giving precedence to a saint over a prophet, see Ibn Taymīya, *Majmūʿat al-rasā'il al-kubrā* (Cairo: al-Maṭbaʿa al-ʿĀmirīya al-Sharafīya, 1323/1905–1906), I, p. 147.
87. *Dhamm*, p. 278.
88. "He was never apart from a beautiful maid." Ibn Rajab, *Dhayl*, I, p. 412; also al-Dhahabī, *Tadhkira*, IV, p. 1347.

89. *Dhamm*, pp. 279–82. The same words of Aḥmad b. Ḥanbal are quoted also in Ibn al-Qayyim, *Rawḍa*, p. 214.
90. *Ṣayd al-khāṭir*, *faṣl* 75, p. 98.
91. *Dhamm*, pp. 283–84.
92. *Ṣayd al-khāṭir*, *faṣl* 120, pp. 141–42.
93. *Ibid.*, *faṣl* 235, p. 264.
94. *Ibid.*, *faṣl* 256, pp. 287–88.
95. *Ibid.*, p. 288. Cf. *Rasā'il Ikhwān al-Ṣafā'*, ed. Khayr al-Dīn al-Ziriklī (Cairo: al-Maṭba'a al-'Arabīya, 1347/1928), III, pp. 264–65.
96. Ibn al-Qayyim, *Rawḍa*, p. 77. Licit union is recommended, however, as the essential remedy for an illicit passion (*ibid.*, pp. 311–19).
97. *Dhamm*, pp. 290–91. Cf. Ibn al-Qayyim, *Rawḍa*, p. 137.
98. *Dhamm*, p. 293.
99. *Ibid.*, p. 295.
100. Cf., e.g., Abū al-Ḥasan 'Alī b. Muḥammad al-Daylamī, *Kitāb 'Aṭf al-alif al-ma'lūf 'alā 'l-lām al-ma'ṭūf*, ed. J.-C. Vadet (Cairo: Imprimerie de l'Institut Français d'Archéologie Orientale, 1962), pp. 47–53; and Ibn al-'Arabī, *Tarjumān al-ashwāq* (Beirut: Dār Ṣādir, Dār Bayrūt, 1381/1961), pp. 13–14.
101. *Dhamm*, pp. 293–94; Ibn al-Qayyim, *Rawḍa*, p. 46.
102. *Dhamm*, pp. 293–94. Cf. 'Īsā b. Ibrāhīm b. Muḥammad al-Raba'ī, *Kitāb niẓām al-gharīb* (Cairo: Maṭba'a Hindīya, n.d.), art. "*ḥubb*," p. 39: "Wa-l-mutayyamu 'lladhī dhallalahu 'l-ḥubbu wa-sta'badahu, wa-l-taymu 'l-'abdu, wa-minhu summiya Taymu 'llāhi wa-Taymu 'llāti."
103. *Dhamm*, p. 295. Cf. Ibn al-Qayyim, *Rawḍa*, p. 138, citing al-Jāḥiẓ.
104. *Dhamm*, p. 296. Cf. *Rasā'il Ikhwān al-Ṣafā'*, III, p. 263, and Beirut edition (Dār Ṣādir, Dār Bayrūt, 1957), III, p. 272. The printed text of the *Dhamm* has "*'aṣabīya*" erroneously for "*ghaḍabīya.*" In the *Rasā'il* the appetitive soul is termed more completely *nabātīya, shahwānīya* (vegetable, appetitive).
105. *Dhamm*, pp. 296, 294, respectively.
106. *Ibid.*, p. 297.
107. Cf. Ibn Qayyim al-Jawzīya, *Kitāb al-rūḥ* (4th ed.; Ḥaydarābād: Dā'irat al-Ma'ārif al-'Uthmānīya, 1383/1963), question xviii, pp. 271–304; *Rawḍa*, p. 75; and below, pp. 113–17.
108. *Dhamm*, p. 306.
109. *Ibid.*, pp. 310–11.
110. *Ibid.*, pp. 311–13.
111. *Ibid.*, p. 313, n. 1. Cf. al-Ghazālī, *Mīzān al-'amal*, p. 317.
112. *Dhamm*, p. 314.
113. *Ṣayd al-khāṭir*, *faṣl* 330, p. 355.
114. For Ibn al-Jawzī as an authority for "*Man 'ashiqa . . .*," see Aḥmad b. Muṣṭafā Ṭāshköprüzāde (d. 967 A.H.), *Munyat al-shubbān fī mu'āsharat al-niswān* (MS, collection of Sa'd Maḥmūd Khiḍr), p. 20, citing *Kitāb al-nisā'* by Ibn al-Jawzī, perhaps not the same as *Akhbār al-nisā'*, for I have not been able to find the tradition in the edition of that work cited above (n. 3). Cf. al-'Alwajī, *Mu'allafāt Ibn al-Jawzī*, p. 142. For another source mentioning Ibn al-Jawzī as relating this tradition, see Dāwūd al-Anṭākī, *Tazyīn al-aswāq* (Cairo, 1291 A.H.), p. 6. Ibn al-Qayyim (*al-Dā' wa-l-dawā'*, p. 353) remarks that Ibn al-Jawzī mentions the *ḥadīth* among the "fabrications" (*mawḍū'āt*). In a quick search I did not find the tradition in the printed edition of Ibn al-Jawzī's *Kitāb al-mawḍū'āt* (ed. 'Abd al-Raḥmān Muḥammad 'Uthmān, 3 vols., Medina: al-Maktaba al-Salafīya, 1386/1966–1388/1968). However the scholar wrote another work on "very weak" (*shadīd al-ḍu'f*) traditions entitled *al-'Ilal al-mutanāhiya fī 'l-aḥādīth al-wāhiya* (*Mawḍū'āt*, I, p. 35; Brockelmann, *S*, I, p. 918) which I have not seen. In the *Dhamm* Ibn al-Jawzī seems to make an implicit criticism of the tradition's authenticity when he relates that Ibn al-Marzubān reproached Abū Bakr al-Azraq for attributing it to the Prophet (p.

329). For a long discussion, drawing heavily on Ibn al-Qayyim, of the reasons for classifying this *ḥadīth* as a fabrication, see Muḥammad Nāṣir al-Dīn al-Albānī, *Silsilat al-aḥādīth al-ḍaʿīfa wa-l-mawḍūʿa*, I, part 5 (Damascus: al-Maktab al-Islāmī, n.d.), pp. 13–19.

115. An example is the story of a woman who had a daughter by her own son and years later, in order not to lose her, had her son, unawares, marry the girl. *Dhamm*, pp. 448–53.

116. *Ibid.*, pp. 582–83.

117. *Ibid.*, pp. 584–92, esp. pp. 586, 591–92.

118. *Ibid.*, pp. 593–97.

119. *Ibid.*, pp. 600–601.

120. *Ibid.*, pp. 602–33.

121. *Ibid.*, p. 633. "Self-restraint": Arabic *ḥimya* (régime, diet).

122. *Ibid.*, p. 634.

123. *Ibid.*, pp. 634–40.

124. *Ibid.*, pp. 640–46. On *ya's* as an element in the treatment of *ʿishq*, see also Ibn Qayyim al-Jawzīya, *al-Ṭibb al-nabawī*, ed. ʿAbd al-Ghanī ʿAbd al-Khāliq (Mecca: Maktabat al-Nahḍa al-Ḥadītha, 1377/1957), p. 211.

125. *Dhamm*, pp. 647–52.

126. *Ibid.*, pp. 652–53.

127. *Ibid.*, p. 657.

128. *Ibid.*, p. 661.

129. *Ibid.*, p. 663. Notice how close Ibn al-Jawzī comes to the Sufi view of *ʿishq*-love. Cf., e.g., ʿAbd al-Raḥmān b. Muḥammad, known as (Ibn) al-Dabbāgh, *Mashāriq anwār al-qulūb*, ed. H. Ritter (Beirut: Dār Ṣādir, Dār Bayrūt, 1379/1959), p. 99, where *ʿishq* is described as distraction from the world of sense with knowledge (text: *ittiṣāl* [contact or union]) of the spiritual world.

130. *Ṣayd al-khāṭir*, *faṣl* 63, pp. 81–83.

131. See p. 25.

132. Ibn al-Jawzī refers to the immoral practices of certain sects in his *Talbīs*. The Bābakīya, a sect which died out long before Ibn al-Jawzī's time, are mentioned as an example. They were said "to meet together, both men and women, one night in the year and put out the lamps. Then they would rise up to meet the women, and every man of them would spring upon one. Their claim was that whoever caught a woman might legitimately possess her on the grounds that the case is analogous to that of hunting, which is permissible" (p. 104). Similarly, the Khurramīya are cited for the unrestrained pursuit of their desires (pp. 105–106). Whether or not these charges were true, it is reasonable to assume that Ibn al-Jawzī believed them to be so.

133. The rivalry mentioned earlier between Ibn al-Jawzī and one of the successors of the great Ḥanbalite mystic ʿAbd al-Qādir al-Jīlī, Rukn al-Dīn, may have had its source in a prior enmity towards ʿAbd al-Qādir himself. Could Ibn al-Jawzī have been jealous of the shaykh's position? During the early period of the scholar's own success in the Abbasid capital, Muwaffaq al-Dīn b. Qudāma was able to relate as follows: "We entered Baghdad in the year 561 and found that the Shaykh ʿAbd al-Qādir had attained the highest rank in knowledge (*ʿilm*), deeds, wealth, and legal consultation. It was sufficient for a student to see him and no one else!" (Ibn Rajab, *Dhayl*, I, pp. 293–94). Such recognition of the Sufi coming from a fellow Ḥanbalite may well have been a hard pill for Ibn al-Jawzī to swallow. There is indeed some evidence that he actually was hostile towards ʿAbd al-Qādir: Ibn Rajab reports that Ibn al-Jawzī was said to have written a book in which he disapproved of many things about the shaykh (*ibid.*, p. 295). It does not seem too farfetched to surmise that his hostility towards ʿAbd al-Qādir and his family may have contributed to his negative attitude with regard to Sufism.

134. *Talbīs*, p. 167.
135. *Ibid.*, pp. 162–67, 169.
136. *Ṣayd al-khāṭir, faṣl* 88, pp. 109–110.
137. *Ibid., faṣl* 317, p. 347.
138. *Ibid.*, pp. 347–48.
139. Ibn al-Jawzī as a rule recommends moderation, not abstinence. He tells his readers that the best policy in sexual matters is to follow the mean (*Ṣayd al-khāṭir, faṣl* 35, p. 45). His emphasis on avoiding attachment to this world is evident from his words cited in the preceding paragraph: "His heart does not find its tranquility in wife or child, nor does it cling to the hem of love for any person. . . ."
140. *Ṣayd al-khāṭir, faṣl* 19, pp. 13–14.
141. *Ibid., faṣl* 37, p. 48.
142. *Ibid., faṣl* 36, p. 47.

CHAPTER THREE

1. Ibn Taymīya did not entirely neglect earthly love of course, and works of his other than those considered here may well contain expanded treatments of the subject. I have not seen, for example, his manuscript treatise entitled *Qāʿida fī 'l-maḥabba* (Brockelmann, *S*, II, p. 122). At any rate one comes across a number of brief discussions of *ʿishq*-love, such as the one contained in the jurist's *Amrāḍ al-qulūb* ([Cairo: al-Maṭbaʿa al-Salafīya, 1386/1966–67], pp. 26–30), although these quickly shift to matters pertaining to sacred love. Treatments of sacred love moreover, like that found in his *al-Tuḥfa al-ʿIrāqīya* ([published in one volume with the just mentioned *Amrāḍ al-qulūb*], esp. pp. 62–86), touch on profane affections and the general nature of love at a number of points. There are also of course passing remarks on earthly love in many of the author's works. Thus Ibn Taymīya comments in one context, following Koran 30:21, that the institution of marriage is based on love or affection (*mawadda*) and sympathy (*raḥma*) between husband and wife. This being the case, he asks, how is a woman to be forced to live with someone she cannot bear? (Ibn Taymīya, *al-Masāʾil al-Mārdīnīya* [Damascus: al-Maktab al-Islāmī li-l-Ṭibāʿa wa-l-Nashr, 1383/1964], p. 116). Ibn Taymīya's view on obliging a woman to marry against her will accordingly differs from that of traditional Ḥanbalism.
2. Many if not most of the views advanced in Ibn Qayyim al-Jawzīya's writings on profane love must however be attributed to the inspiration of Ibn Taymīya. A case in point is Ibn al-Qayyim's approach to the tradition "*Man ʿashiqa* . . . ," which parallels in substance that of his teacher. Neither of the two authors is convinced that the *ḥadīth* is authentic, but both accept that it expresses in hyperbolic terms a certain truth. Cf. Ibn Taymīya, *Amrāḍ al-qulūb*, p. 28, and below, pp. 135–37.
3. Laoust, *Essai sur les doctrines sociales et politiques de Taḳi-d-Dīn Aḥmad b. Taimīya, canoniste ḥanbalite né à Ḥarrān en 661/1262, mort à Damas en 728/1328* (Cairo: Imprimerie de l'Institut Français d'Archéologie Orientale, 1939), pp. 7, 10.
4. *Ibid.*, pp. 12–18; above, chapter 2, n. 133. Al-Muwaffaq's literary production was immense. We may recall here his *Mughnī* and a still unpublished *Kitāb al-mutaḥābbīn fī 'llāh.*
5. Laoust, *Essai*, p. 79.
6. *Ibid.*, pp. 85–94.
7. *Ibid.*, p. 89.
8. See *ibid.*, pp. 115–17.
9. *Ibid.*, pp. 117–23.
10. *Ibid.*, p. 128.
11. *Ibid.*, pp. 139, 143.

12. *Ibid.*, p. 148. Imprisoned at the same time was his student Ibn Qayyim al-Jawzīya.

13. Ibn Taymīya, *al-Iḥtijāj bi-l-qadar* in *Majmū'at al-rasā'il al-kubrā*, cited hereafter as *MRK* (Cairo: al-Maṭba'a al-'Āmirīya al-Sharafīya, 1323/1905–6), II, p. 115. For an Ash'arite argument to the effect that God cannot be the object of love in a real sense, see Imām al-Ḥaramayn al-Juwaynī, *Kitāb al-irshād*, ed. Muḥammad Yūsuf Mūsā and 'Alī 'Abd al-Ḥamīd (Cairo: Maktabat al-Khānjī, 1369/1950), pp. 239–40; French translation in *El-Irchad*, ed. and tr. J.-D. Luciani (Paris: Imprimerie Nationale, 1938), p. 218. See also below, pp. 56–60.

14. Ibn Taymīya, *Iḥtijāj*, *MRK*, II, p. 115.

15. Printed in Cairo (?), 1357/1938–39.

16. Ibn 'Aqīl retracted his opinions under Ḥanbalite pressure in 465/1072 (George Makdisi, *Ibn Qudāma's Censure of speculative theology*, edition and translation of Ibn Qudāma's *Taḥrīm al-naẓar fī kutub ahl al-kalām* [London: Luzac and Company, Ltd., 1962] p. xiv).

17. Ibn Taymīya, *Kitāb al-nubūwāt* (Cairo: Idārat al-Ṭibā'a al-Munīrīya, 1346/1927–28), p. 68.

18. Cf. al-Anṣārī al-Harawī, *Kitāb manāzil al-sā'irīn*, edition and French translation by S. de Laugier de Beaurecueil (Cairo: Imprimerie de l'Institut Français d'Archéologie Orientale, 1962), Arabic text, p. 11; French, p. 55.

19. The doctrine of *ḥikma* was advanced by the Mu'tazilites and refuted by the Ash'arites. See, for example, al-Shahrastānī, *Nihāyat al-iqdām*, edited with an English paraphrase by Alfred Guillaume (London: Oxford University Press, 1934), Arabic text, pp. 397–404; English, pp. 126–30.

20. Laoust, *Essai*, p. 471. For the context of Ibn Taymīya's statement on *munāsaba* and his affirmation that a kind of accord can indeed exist between God and man, see Ibn Taymīya, *Tafṣīl al-ijmāl* in *Majmū'at al-rasā'il wa-l-masā'il*, short edition (both editions hereafter referred to as *MRM*), III (Cairo: [Maṭba'at al-Manār], n.d.), pp. 65–66; *Qā'ida sharīfa fī 'l-mu'jizāt wa-l-karāmāt*, *MRM* (short ed.), III, pp. 32–34; *Nubūwāt*, p. 71; and *Minhāj al-Sunna al-nabawīya* (Cairo: al-Maṭba'a al-Amīrīya, 1321–22/1903–5), III, p. 100.

21. Ibn Taymīya, *Iḥtijāj*, *MRK*, II, p. 130; *Minhāj*, III, pp. 98–99.

22. L. Gardet and G.-C. Anawati, *Mystique musulmane* (Paris: Librarie Philosophique J. Vrin, 1961), pp. 161–62.

23. L. Gardet, *Dieu et la destinée de l'homme* (Paris: Librairie Philosophique J. Vrin, 1967), p. 396.

24. Ibn Taymīya, *Minhāj*, III, p. 99. Cf., however, Ibn Qayyim al-Jawzīya's verses equating love to God with accord (*wifāq*), and accord with obedience to his command, in his early didactic poem *al-Qaṣīda al-nūnīya* (ed. and cmt. Muḥammad Khalīl Harās [Cairo: Maṭba'at al-Imām, n.d.], p. 514). In view of the many statements to the effect that God is to be loved "*li-dhātihi*," both in Ibn Taymīya and in Ibn al-Qayyim, these early verses cannot be taken at face value.

25. Michel Allard, *Le problème des attributs divins* (Beirut: Imprimerie Catholique, 1965), p. 143, citing Laoust, *La profession de foi d'Ibn Baṭṭa* (Damascus: Institut Français de Damas, 1958), p. 160 and n. 1. Note that Laoust cautions against the very position Allard has taken: "Il ne faudrait pas en conclure que le hanbalisme en arrive à proscrire sans appel ces deux notions [*shawq* and *maḥabba*] sans lesquels on conçoit mal l'existence d'une vie religieuse."

26. Cf. Allard, *Attributs divins*, p. 73, quoting H. Ritter on Islamic confessions of faith (*'aqā'id*): "If one wishes to understand them correctly, it must always be realized that they represent line by line a refutation of adversaries" ("Philologika II," in *Der Islam*, XVII [1928], p. 253).

27. Al-Barbahārī's *Kitāb al-Sunna* is preserved in part in Ibn Abī Ya'lā, *Ṭabaqāt al-Ḥanābila*, ed. Muḥammad Ḥāmid al-Fiqī (Cairo: Maṭba'at al-Sunna al-Muḥammadīya, 1371/1952), II, pp. 18–43.

28. Ibn Abī Yaʿlā, *Ṭabaqāt*, II, p. 34.
29. *Ibid.*, p. 36.
30. *Ibid.*, p. 39.
31. Cf. Allard's similar treatment of this particular phrase (*Attributs divins*, p. 131, n. 3).
32. Ibn Taymīya himself places precisely the same interpretation on such counsels as these. Those who follow the path of love alone, he remarks, can be observed to violate the sacred law to an extent unknown among those who follow the path of fear. For this reason, he adds, orthodox religious authorities advised in their writings that those who dwelt on love (*maḥabba*) without mentioning fear should be avoided. One similar statement the jurist cites in this context is attributed in fact to a well-known mystic, Dhū 'l-Nūn al-Miṣrī. Once when a group of people spoke about love in his presence Dhū 'l-Nūn reportedly admonished them to cease mentioning the perilous affection lest their souls be taken in by it. Ibn Taymīya, *al-Tuḥfa al-ʿIrāqīya*, p. 83.
33. Ibn Abī Yaʿlā, *Ṭabaqāt*, II, pp. 19–20; cited by Allard, *Attributs divins*, p. 103.
34. Allard, *Attributs divins*, p. 214.
35. Ibn Abī Yaʿlā, *Ṭabaqāt*, II, p. 18; cited by Allard, *Attributs divins*, p. 52.
36. Laoust, *Ibn Baṭṭa*, pp. 167–71.
37. Allard, *Attributs divins*, p. 294.
38. Ibn Abī Yaʿlā, *Ṭabaqāt*, II, p. 43.
39. Allard, *Attributs divins*, p. 336, citing Ibn Ṭāhir al-Baghdādī, *Kitāb uṣūl al-dīn* (Istanbul, 1346/1928), p. 101. Italics mine.
40. Allard, *Attributs divins*, p. 47; Ibn ʿAsākir, *Tabyīn* (Damascus, 1347/1928–29), p. 413.
41. *A vindication of the science of kalam*, ed. and trans. by R. J. McCarthy, S.J., in *The theology of al-Ashʿarī* (Beirut: Imprimerie Catholique, 1953), Arabic text, pp. 87–97; English text, pp. 119–34.
42. McCarthy, *The theology of al-Ashʿarī*, Arabic, pp. 95–97; English, pp. 131–34. Argument discussed and summarized by Allard, *Attributs divins*, pp. 206–10.
43. George Makdisi, *Ibn ʿAqīl et la résurgence de l'Islam traditionaliste au XIe siècle (Ve siècle de l'Hégire)* (Damascus: Institut Français de Damas, 1963), pp. 235–36.
44. Makdisi, *Ibn ʿAqīl*, p. 236, citing al-Khaṭīb, *Ta-rīkh Baghdād*, II, 256; Laoust, *Essai*, p. 78; and Ibn al-Bannā, *Autograph diary of an eleventh-century historian of Baghdad*, edition and translation by George Makdisi, *Bulletin of the School of Oriental and African Studies* (hereafter cited as *BSOAS*) 18 (1956): 12.
45. Ibn Taymīya, *Nubūwāt*, p. 68. For this view in the *Irshād* of al-Juwaynī, see n. 13.
46. Ibn Abī Yaʿlā, *Ṭabaqāt*, II, 201.
47. *Ibid.*, p. 205. In any of these works, it may be noted, as well as in a *Kitāb al-ṭibb* (on medicine), the *qāḍī* may well have had occasion to deal with the subject of love.
48. *Ibid.*, pp. 208, 210.
49. *Ibid.*, p. 227.
50. George Makdisi, *Ibn ʿAqīl*; and "Nouveaux détails sur l'affaire d'Ibn ʿAqīl," *Mélanges Louis Massignon* (Damascus: Institut Français de Damas, 1956–57), III, pp. 91–126.
51. Makdisi, *Ibn ʿAqīl*, pp. 407–9; Ibn Rajab, *Dhayl*, I, p. 144.
52. Unidentified. See Makdisi, *Ibn ʿAqīl*, p. 409; and Ibn Rajab, *Dhayl*, I, p. 144.
53. For the text of the retraction, see Ibn Rajab, *Dhayl*, I, pp. 144–45; French translation in Makdisi, *Ibn ʿAqīl*, pp. 426–28.
54. Makdisi, *Ibn ʿAqīl*, pp. 412–18.
55. *Ibid.*, p. 423; citing al-Subkī, *Ṭabaqāt al-Shāfiʿīya* (Cairo: al-Maṭbaʿa al-Ḥusaynīya, 1905–6), III, p. 13; and Ibn ʿAsākir, *Tabyīn*, p. 271.
56. "Our Ḥanbalite companions wanted me to abandon certain *ʿulamā'*, which would have deprived me of useful knowledge." Ibn Rajab, *Dhayl*, I, p. 143.
57. Ibn Taymīya, *Nubūwāt*, p. 68; *Minhāj*, III, pp. 97–98; *Iḥtijāj*, *MRK*, II, p. 131; *Fatāwā*

(Cairo: Maṭbaʿat Kurdistān al-ʿIlmīya, 1326/1908–1329/1911), I, pp. 206–207; Makdisi, *Ibn ʿAqīl*, p. 526. For al-Juwaynī's affirmation of the beatific vision, see his *Irshād*, pp. 181–85; trans. Luciani, pp. 169–72; and his *al-ʿAqīda al-Niẓāmīya*, ed. Muḥammad Zāhid al-Kawtharī (Cairo: Maṭbaʿat al-Anwār, 1367/1948), pp. 27–29. For his denial of the believer's pleasure in the vision itself, see *ibid.*, pp. 45–46, and below, p. 59.

58. Ibn Taymīya, *Minhāj*, III, p. 98; al-Juwaynī, *Irshād*, pp. 239–40; trans. Luciani, p. 218; *al-ʿAqīda al-Niẓāmīya*, p. 45.
59. Ibn Rajab, *Dhayl*, I, pp. 146, 150–51.
60. *Ibid.*, p. 146.
61. *Ibid.*, p. 144.
62. Makdisi, *Ibn ʿAqīl*, p. 450.
63. *Ibid.*, pp. 451–52. On Ashʿarism in the *Niẓāmīya*, strictly speaking a school established for the teaching of *fiqh*, see, e.g., Robert Brunschvig, "Muʿtazilisme et ašʿarisme à Baġdād," *Arabica*, Volume spécial publié à l'occasion du mille deux centième anniversaire de la fondation de Baġdād," (Leiden: E. J. Brill, 1962), p. 355.
64. Makdisi, *Ibn ʿAqīl*, p. 434.
65. *Ibid.*, pp. 451, 508.
66. Ibn al-Jawzī, *Muntaẓam*, VI, p. 332; cited by Allard, *Attributs divins*, p. 84.
67. George Makdisi, *Ibn Qudāma's Censure of speculative theology*, pp. 36–37.
68. Ibn Taymīya, *Fatāwā*, I, p. 374.
69. *Ibid.*, p. 379.
70. L. Gardet and M.-M. Anawati, *Introduction à la théologie musulmane* (Paris: Librairie Philosophique J. Vrin, 1948), p. 63.
71. Ibn Taymīya, *Fatāwā*, I, pp. 379–80.
72. Allard, *Attributs divins*, pp. 86–87; citing Ibn Taymīya, *Minhāj*, IV, p. 145.
73. Allard, *Attributs divins*, pp. 87–88; citing the list of Ibn Taymīya's borrowings from the *Maqālāt* of al-Ashʿarī given in Ritter's edition of that work.
74. In *MRK*, I, pp. 318–86. This treatise is identical with that entitled *Aqwam mā qīl fī-l-mashīʾa wa-l-ḥikma wa-l-qaḍāʾ wa-l-qadar wa-l-taʿlīl* in *MRM* (short ed.), III, pp. 113–70.
75. Ibn Taymīya, *al-Furqān bayn al-ḥaqq wa-l-bāṭil*, *MRK*, I, pp. 20–21.
76. See pp. 58–59.
77. Allard, *Attributs divins*, p. 222; A. N. Nader, *Le système philosophique des muʿtazila* (Beirut: Edition Les Lettres Orientales, 1956), pp. 88–95. Ibn Fūrak, however, attributes the equation of love and will to al-Ashʿarī. See Ibn Qayyim al-Jawzīya, *Shifāʾ al-ʿalīl* (Al-Ṭāʾif: Maktabat al-Maʿārif, n.d.), p. 180.
78. Together with willing, the seven most commonly accepted attributes.
79. Abū Bakr Muḥammad b. al-Ṭayyib al-Bāqillānī, *al-Inṣāf fī-mā yajib iʿtiqāduhu wa-lā yajūz al-jahl bi-hi*, ed. Muḥammad Zāhid b. al-Ḥasan al-Kawtharī and ʿIzzat al-ʿAṭṭār al-Ḥusaynī ([Cairo]: Maktab Nashr al-Thaqāfa al-Islāmīya, 1369/1950), pp. 34–36; *Kitāb al-tamhīd*, ed. Richard J. McCarthy, S.J. (Beirut: Librairie Orientale, 1957), pp. 27–28. Al-Hujwīrī, who argues for essentially the Bāqillānian opinion on love, claims it was held by al-Muḥāsibī and al-Junayd (*Kashf al-maḥjūb*, trans. Nicholson, p. 307).
80. Al-Bāqillānī, *Inṣāf*, p. 40. Ibn Taymīya cites this view as that of Ibn Kullāb and his followers (*Nubūwāt*, p. 72).
81. Koran 2:205.
82. Al-Bāqillānī, *Inṣāf*, p. 143.
83. Al-Bāqillānī, *Tamhīd*, p. 284; cf. *Inṣāf*, p. 146.
84. Al-Bāqillānī, *Inṣāf*, p. 144.
85. See p. 56.
86. Al-Juwaynī, *Irshād*, pp. 238–40; trans. Luciani, pp. 217–18.
87. *Ibid.*, p. 250; trans. Luciani, pp. 227–28. The details of al-Juwaynī's doctrine fall be-

yond the scope of this study, but one apparent inconsistency should be remarked. While asserting the complete identity of God's love with his will, al-Juwaynī, after the fashion of al-Bāqillānī, calls God's love his will to do good (*irādat al-iḥsān*) (*al-ʿAqīda al-Niẓāmīya*, p. 45), and he does virtually the same for God's mercy (*raḥma*), which he calls his will to benefit (*irādat al-inʿām*) (*Irshād*, p. 145; trans. Luciani, p. 138).

88. *Ibid.*, pp. 239–40; trans. Luciani, p. 218. Cf. also *al-ʿAqīda al-Niẓāmīya*, p. 45.
89. Al-Juwaynī, *al-ʿAqīda al-Niẓāmīya*, p. 45.
90. See p. 48.
91. Al-Juwaynī, *al-Aqīda al-Niẓāmīya*, pp. 45–46.
92. Allard, *Attributs divins*, p. 253.
93. Ibn Taymīya, *Fatāwā*, I, pp. 207–208. Al-Jaʿd b. Dirham is also held to have been the first to maintain the doctrine of the created Koran.
94. Cf., e.g., Ibn Taymīya, *Iḥtijāj*, *MRK*, II, p. 118; and *Risālat al-iklīl*, *MRK*, II, p. 14.
95. "And they [certain Sufis, including the Ḥanbalite al-Anṣārī] held that God's will, love, and satisfaction are one—in which they were in accord with the Qadarites. . . ." The Jahmites and the Muʿtazilites "claim that there is no difference between will, love, and satisfaction." Ibn Taymīya, *Iḥtijāj*, *MRK*, II, pp. 117–18.

CHAPTER FOUR

1. He attempted to salvage the idea of man's free will, however. The problem of the reconciliation of God's decree and human moral responsibility in Neo-Ḥanbalite theology deserves further study.
2. Ibn Taymīya, *al-ʿAqīda al-Wāsiṭīya*, *MRK*, I, p. 389.
3. See p. 58.
4. See pp. 69–71.
5. *Minhāj*, III, p. 102. The essentials of this doctrine were by no means original with Ibn Taymīya. According to al-Ghazālī, both good and evil proceed from the divine will. But good is willed and approved (*murād marḍī*), while evil is willed and loathed (*murād makrūh*). It is ignorance to say that evil is not from God, but it is forbidden to reveal the secret workings of his decree. Al-Ghazālī, *Iḥyā'*, XIV, p. 140. (Ibn Taymīya, it will be seen, tries to unravel this secret.) The eclectic Fakhr al-Dīn al-Rāzī (d. 606/1209) expresses a similar view. Rejecting the Ashʿarite interpretation of Koran 39:7, "He is not pleased with unbelief in his servants," he writes: "Unbelief and acts of disobedience, even though they occur by the will of God, do not occur by the love of God or his good pleasure (*riḍā*)." Fakhr al-Dīn al-Rāzī, *Kitāb al-arbaʿīn fī uṣūl al-dīn* (Ḥaydarābād: Dā'irat al-Maʿārif al-ʿUthmānīya, 1353/1934–35), p. 246. The potential list of such examples is quite long.
6. *Minhāj*, III, pp. 102–103.
7. See pp. 51–52.
8. In *MRK*, II, pp. 87–145.
9. *Iḥtijāj*, *MRK*, II, p. 118.
10. It is not clear whether this addition, not found in al-Juwaynī, was culled by Ibn Taymīya from an unidentified Ashʿarite source or whether it represents an expansion of the argument provided by the jurist himself for his readers. In either case, as will be seen, he takes exception to the idea expressed in this particular phrase.
11. *Iḥtijāj*, *MRK*, II, pp. 118–19.
12. See p. 63.
13. *Iḥtijāj*, *MRK*, II, p. 119.
14. Al-Bāqillānī, *Inṣāf*, p. 146. Al-Bāqillānī makes this statement in connection with his interpretation of Koran 39:7, "He is not pleased with unbelief in his servants." This

text is treated in virtually the same manner as the passage which asserts that God does not love iniquity (Koran 2:205). Being pleased with a thing or satisfaction (*riḍā*) with it, he maintains, is to praise it, to reward the one who performs it, and to make it a religious way (*dīn*) and a holy law (*shar*ʿ). Accordingly, the statement that God is not pleased with unbelief means that he does not praise or reward it and that he does not consent to its being a religion or holy law. This has nothing to do, however, with his willing its existence.

15. For a statement of the congruence of decree and will, see Ibn Qayyim al-Jawzīya, *Shifā' al-ʿalīl* (Al-Ṭā'if: Maktabat al-Maʿārif, n.d.), p. 69, title and first lines of chapter twelve.
16. Ibn Taymīya could not accept the application of the distinction "as a religion or holy law" to both love and will, since it implied the equivalence of the two. In his own thought, as will be seen (pp. 64–67), he made use of the distinction with respect to God's will alone.
17. Cf. Gardet and Anawati, *Introduction à la théologie musulmane*, pp. 62–64.
18. *Iḥtijāj*, *MRK*, II, pp. 119–20; *Nubūwāt*, p. 46. Elsewhere Ibn Taymīya addresses to the argument of al-Bāqillānī the same criticism which he used against that of al-Juwaynī: according to the proponents of this argument, what does not occur in the way of faith and piety is neither loved nor consented to by God. (*Irāda*, *MRK*, I, p. 333).
19. Al-Bāqillānī, *Inṣāf*, p. 40; see above, p. 57.
20. See pp. 70–71.
21. The text (*Iḥtijāj*, *MRK*, II, p. 126) has *ahl al-ṣafā'* erroneously for *ahl al-ṣuffa*. Ibn Taymīya deals with the theological problems concerning this group in a separate treatise, *Ahl al-ṣuffa wa-abāṭīl baʿḍ al-mutaṣawwifa*, in *MRM*, I, pp. 25–60.
22. *Iḥtijāj*, *MRK*, II, p. 126.
23. *Ibid.*, pp. 127–28.
24. *Tafṣīl al-ijmāl*, *MRM*, III (short edition), p. 74.
25. *Risālat al-iklīl*, *MRK*, II, pp. 22–23.
26. *Ibid.*, pp. 23–24. See also, for example, *Qāʿida sharīfa*, *MRM*, III (short edition), pp. 32–34, where Ibn Taymīya argues that if God's attribute of love is to be denied because it would require that its object be suitable or *mulā'im*, which in turn implies a need on the part of God, then the attribute of will must be denied on the same grounds.
27. *Minhāj*, III, p. 100.
28. Al-Kaʿbī, probably after al-Naẓẓām (d. 231/845–46), had claimed that "God may not be qualified as willing in the strict sense, even though he is thus described by the revealed law with respect to his acts. What is meant by his willing them [his own acts] is that he is their author and creator, and what is meant by his willing acts [of men] is that he commands them. Likewise what is meant by saying that he wills from all eternity is that he knows from all eternity." Quoted by Nader in *Le système philosophique des muʿtazila*, p. 88, citing among other sources al-Shahrastānī, *Nihāya*, p. 238. The opinion of al-Kaʿbī was also known to al-Juwaynī (*Irshād*, p. 63; trans. Luciani, p. 67).
29. *Risālat al-iklīl*, *MRK*, II, p. 24.
30. Cf. Romans 9:18, "Therefore hath he mercy on whom he will have mercy, and whom he will be hardeneth."
31. Cf. Psalm 135:6, "Whatsoever the Lord pleased, that did he"; and Romans 9:19, "For who hath resisted his will?" These verses are cited by St. Thomas Aquinas in *Summa contra gentiles*, I, 72, 10.
32. Other examples referring to the creative will cited by Ibn Taymīya are:

> "Wa-lā yanfaʿukum nuṣḥī in aradtu an anṣaḥakum in kāna 'llāhu yurīdu an yughwiyakum" (Koran 11:34).

(And my advice will not avail you, if I will to give you advice, if God wills to mislead you.)

"Wa-law shā'a 'llāhu mā 'qtatalū wa-lākinna 'llāha yafʿalu mā yurīdu" (Koran 2:253).

(And if God had willed they would not have fought each other, but God does what he wills.)

33. *Minhāj*, III, p. 103; I, pp. 266–67; Ibn Taymīya, *Marātib al-irāda*, *MRK*, II, pp. 69–70.
34. *Minhāj*, III, p. 103.
35. *Ibid.*
36. Cf. Laoust, *Essai*, p. 168.
37. Cf. *Minhāj*, III, p. 102, and *Irāda*, *MRK*, I, p. 333.
38. *Irāda*, *MRK*, I, p. 333. Al-Bāqillānī, in answer to the question whether God created the world for a motive (*dāʿī*), a causative factor (*muḥarrik*), or a purpose (*gharaḍ*, term included in one MS), states that God created for none of the reasons suggested (*lā li-shay'in mim-mā sa'alta*). His justification for this view is that such terms as motive and purpose apply only to one who is deficient or subject to need and of whom it may be said that he attracts the beneficial and repels the harmful. But this may be said only of one who is subject to pain, pleasure, and natural inclinations and aversions (*Tamhīd*, p. 30).
39. Al-Shahrastānī, *Nihāya*, pp. 397–98; see also Nader, *Le système philosophique des muʿtazila*, p. 80.
40. Al-Shahrastānī, *Nihāya*, p. 400.
41. Cf., e.g., Koran 14:4; 16:93; 35:8; and 74:31.
42. *Irāda*, *MRK*, I, p. 328.
43. *Ibid.*, p. 328.
44. Al-Shahrastānī, *Nihāya*, p. 402.
45. *Ibid.*
46. See, for example, n. 38 for the position of al-Bāqillānī.
47. Al-Shahrastānī, *Nihāya*, p. 403.
48. *Ibid.*, pp. 401–402; al-Juwaynī, *Irshād*, p. 152; trans. Luciani, p. 144.
49. *Minhāj*, I, p. 126. *Gharaḍ*, according to Ibn Taymīya, may have the connotation of passion or a blameworthy intention and thus may imply an injustice.
50. *Irāda*, *MRK*, I, p. 325.
51. *Ibid.*; *Iḥtijāj*, *MRK*, II, p. 137.
52. *Irāda*, *MRK*, I, p. 325.
53. *Ibid.*, pp. 325–26. See pp. 67–68.
54. *Ibid.*, pp. 319, 325; *Iḥtijāj*, *MRK*, II, p. 137. Al-Ghazālī uses the term *ḥikma* in a similar fashion. Everything has a *ḥikma*, hidden or evident, beneath which lies an aim (*maqṣūd*) which is the object of love (*Iḥyā'*, XII, p. 82).
55. *Minhāj*, III, pp. 103–104.
56. See p. 69.
57. Ritter, *Das Meer der Seele*, p. 554, citing ʿAṭṭār, *Ilāhī-nāme*, ed. Hellmut Ritter (Leipzig, 1940), p. 4.
58. *Ibid.*
59. For Plotinus God is *eros*: he loves himself and enjoys his own perfection. For the Christian Father Origen, like Plotinus a disciple of Ammonius Saccas, God is lover of himself (*ἀυτοῦ ἐρως*) (Nygren, *Agape and eros*, I, pp. 155–56). In the same tradition, Gregory of Nyssa (d. ca. 395) argued that, since God is beautiful and since beauty is necessarily loved by those who know it, God, knowing himself, must love himself (*ibid.*, II, p. 224). Dionysius the Areopagite makes God's ecstatic self-love the source of the "dynamic nature of the universe" (*ibid.*, II, p. 363). Carrying the idea into medieval Latin Christianity, Scotus Erigena, translator of the Pseudo-

Dionysius, maintained that it is not truly men who love God, but God who loves himself through men: "Non vos estis, qui amatis. . . . Ipse amat . . . seipsum in vobis" (*ibid.*, II, p. 390 and n. 2). See also n. 66 below.

60. Ritter, *Meer*, p. 559.

61. Al-Daylamī, *Kitāb ʿaṭf al-alif al-maʾlūf ʿalā ʾl-lām al-maʿṭūf*, ed. J. C. Vadet (Cairo: Imprimerie de l'Institut Français d'Archéologie Orientale, 1962), pp. 24–28. For a French translation of this text, see Louis Massignon, "Interférences philosophiques et percées métaphysiques dans la mystique hallagienne: notion de 'l'essentiel désir' " in his *Opera minora*, II (Beirut: Dar al-Maaref, 1963), pp. 231–34.

62. Al-Daylamī, *ʿAṭf al-alif*, pp. 36–37; Massignon, "Notion de 'l'essentiel désir' " p. 235. Cf. Aristotle *Metaphysics* xii. 7. 1072b; 9. 1074b35.

63. Al-Ghazālī, *Iḥyāʾ*, XIV, pp. 97–98.

64. Miguel Asín Palacios, *El Islam cristianizado* (Madrid: Editorial Plutarco, 1931), pp. 243–44.

65. *Minhāj*, III, p. 102; *Irāda*, *MRK*, I, p. 374.

66. Cf. the argument of Aquinas: "Furthermore, every perfection and goodness found in creatures is proper to God in an essential way, as was proved above. But to love God is the highest perfection of the rational creature, since thereby it is somehow united to God. Therefore, this love is found in God in an essential way. Therefore, of necessity God loves Himself. And thus He wills Himself to be." *Summa contra gentiles*, I, 80, 6; trans. Anton C. Pegis (New York: Image Books, 1955).

67. *Minhāj*, III, pp. 101–102; *Irāda*, *MRK*, I, p. 374. A corollary drawn by Ibn Taymīya from the subordination of God's love for men to his self-love is that his love for them is proportionate to their doing what he loves (*Irāda*, p. 374).

68. Cf. *Minhāj*, III, p. 102.

69. *Irāda*, *MRK*, I, pp. 375–76.

70. Cf. Ibn Qayyim al-Jawzīya, *Miftāḥ Dār al-Saʿāda* (Cairo: Muḥammad ʿAlī Ṣubayḥ wa-Awlāduhu, n.d.), I, pp. 6, 8.

CHAPTER FIVE

1. Cf. *Irāda*, *MRK*, I, p. 372; *Nubūwāt*, p. 45; *Fatāwā*, I, p. 207.
2. The name *Wadūd* occurs in Koran 11:90 and 85:14.
3. Ibn Taymīya manages this by relating the first (and third) form *maṣdar "widād"* to the third form *"muwādda"* and thus to the reciprocal form *"tawādd."* See *Nubūwāt*, pp. 71–74.
4. Cf. p. 5.
5. See pp. 108–109, 110–111.
6. Ritter, *Meer*, p. 409; al-Jāḥiẓ, *Kitāb al-qiyān* in *Rasāʾil al-Jāḥiẓ*, ed. ʿAbd al-Salām Hārūn, II, pp. 168–70. See G. E. von Grunebaum, "Avicenna's *Risâla fî ʾl-ʿišq* and courtly love," p. 236, for the same idea in al-Masʿūdī's *Murūj al-dhahab* and the *dīwān* of al-ʿAbbās b. al-Aḥnaf.
7. Ibn Dāwūd al-Ẓāhirī, *Kitāb al-zahra*, p. 15. Cf. Plato *Symposium* 189–93.
8. Ibn Ḥazm, *Ṭawq al-ḥamāma*, Arabic text with French translation by Léon Bercher (Algiers: Editions Carbonel, 1949), pp. 14–20; French translation pp. 15–21.
9. Ibn Qayyim al-Jawzīya, *Rawḍa*, pp. 73–75. See below, pp. 113–17.
10. See n. 13.
11. Al-Ghazālī, under the influence of mysticism, is an exception. He allows love from man to God but not the reverse. See pp. 110–11.
12. Ṣadr al-Dīn al-Qunawī, *al-Nafaḥāt al-ilāhīya*, MS Hekimoğlu 513, the first pages; quoted in Arabic with German translation by Ritter (*Meer*, p. 506).
13. *Fatāwā*, I, pp. 206–207.

14. *Nubūwāt*, p. 71; *Tafṣīl al-ijmāl*, *MRM*, III (short edition), p. 65.
15. *Minhāj*, III, p. 99.
16. *Tafṣīl al-ijmāl*, *MRM*, III (short ed.), p. 66.
17. See pp. 117–19.
18. Ibn Sīna, *Risāla fī 'l-ʿishq*, ed. with approximate French translation by M. A. F. Mehren in *Traités mystiques d'Aboû Alî al-Hosain b. Abdallâh b. Sînâ ou d'Avicenne* (Leiden: E. J. Brill, 1894), Arabic, pp. 18, 22–23, and ff.; French, pp. 11–12 and ff. See also Henry Corbin, *Avicenna and the visionary recital*, tr. Willard R. Trask (New York: Pantheon Books, 1960), p. 46.
19. *Nubūwāt*, pp. 83–84.
20. See pp. 58–59.
21. Asín, *El Islam cristianizado*, pp. 242–43.
22. *Nubūwāt*, p. 66. This argument is analogous, on another level, to the question whether desire (*shawq*) ceases with union or continues after it. See below, pp. 167–71.
23. *Nubūwāt*, p. 75. Cf. Abū 'l-Barakāt Hibat Allāh b. ʿAbī Malkā al-Baghdādī, *al-Muʿtabar fī 'l-ḥikma* (Ḥaydarābād: Dā'irat al-Maʿārif al-ʿUthmānīya, 1357/1938–39–1358/1939), III, p. 45.
24. Al-Shahrastānī, *Nihāya*, Arabic text, pp. 8–9; English paraphrase, pp. 2–3; and Arabic, p. 31; English, p. 13.
25. Abū 'l-Barakāt al-Baghdādī, *Muʿtabar*, III, p. 33.
26. *Ibid.*, p. 43; see also p. 44, where the theologians are represented as arguing that the question "why" (*li-ma*) is inappropriate with respect to the divine will.
27. *Ibid.*, p. 34; *Irāda*, *MRK*, I, p. 377; see, also, above, pp. 64, 65–67.
28. Abū 'l-Barakāt, *Muʿtabar*, III, pp. 35–41. See also Solomon Pinès, *Nouvelles études sur Awḥad al-zamān Abu-l-Barakāt al-Baghdādī* (Paris: Librairie Durlacher, 1955), pp. 28–32, for a French translation of the end of the philosopher's chapter on time (*Muʿtabar*, pp. 39–41).
29. Abū 'l-Barakāt al-Baghdādī, *Muʿtabar*, III, p. 45. In the passage quoted, Abū 'l-Barakāt does not actually commit himself to the view that God wills phenomena, but this seems to be the view consistent with his theistic philosophy, and it is the one Ibn Taymīya ascribes to him.
30. Cf. *Nubūwāt*, p. 76, where the concept of a first necessitator without a will (*mūjib bi-lā mashī'a*) is rejected.
31. Ibn Taymīya, *Sharḥ ḥadīth ʿImrān b. Ḥuṣayn al-marfūʿ "Kāna 'llāhu wa-lam yakun shay'un qablahu," MRM*, III (short ed.), pp. 179–83.
32. *Irāda*, *MRK*, I, p. 385.
33. *Nubūwāt*, p. 75. The Ashʿarites would, of course, interpret a man's hatred for the destruction of his house as an aspect of his will for its continued existence, this continued existence, at the time it is willed, being still a nonexistent.
34. See pp. 71–73.
35. *Nubūwāt*, p. 76.
36. *Ibid.*, pp. 90–92; see above, pp. 64–65.
37. *Nubūwāt*, pp. 90–92.
38. *Ibid.*, p. 76.
39. *Ibid.*, p. 93.
40. *Ibid.*, pp. 94–95. To a last-resort Ashʿarite objection according to which, if God's joy is considered an attribute of perfection, then he would be lacking that perfection prior to obtaining his beloved, Ibn Taymīya answers that the absence of the beloved and the joy his presence would yield is itself an aspect of perfection as long as God's wise purpose (*ḥikma*) does not require the existence of these things (*ibid.*, p. 95). This argument reflects the jurist's general principle that any denial of God's attributes on the grounds that they imply a deficiency or that he seeks perfection through another than himself is invalid, because God is the ultimate source of all

things. Thus one can say only that he seeks perfection through his own acts, which is in the view of Ibn Taymīya, as has been seen, no more than saying that he is perfected through his attributes and essence. *Irāda, MRK*, I, pp. 375–76; also, p. 377.

41. Cf. the opinion of al-Ghazālī summarized below (p. 166) to the effect that man may love God with ʿ*ishq*. Ibn Taymīya remarks in his *Fatāwā* that he has dealt with al-Ghazālī's view elsewhere (I, p. 208).
42. *Nubūwāt*, p. 94.
43. See p. 25.
44. *Minhāj*, III, p. 98.
45. *Irāda, MRK*, I, p. 371; *Iḥtijāj, MRK*, II, p. 128.
46. *Minhāj*, III, p. 98.
47. *Iḥtijāj, MRK*, II, p. 130.
48. See p. 48.
49. *Nubūwāt*, p. 66.
50. Cf. the summary of Ashʿarite arguments, p. 59.
51. *Iḥtijāj, MRK*, II, p. 130; *Irāda, MRK*, I, pp. 372–73.
52. *Iḥtijāj, MRK*, II, p. 130; *Minhāj*, III, p. 98; *Irāda, MRK*, I, p. 373.
53. *Iḥtijāj, MRK*, II, p. 130.
54. *Minhāj*, III, p. 101.
55. See p. 48.
56. *Minhāj*, III, p. 99.
57. *Ibid.* The tradition begins, "Aḥibbū 'llāha li-mā yaghdhūkum bi-hi min niʿmatin. . . ." Ibn Taymīya is at times less critical of this tradition just as he can also be more positive about the kind of love it prescribes. He states in one text, for example, that love to God for his beneficence, although the believer in this case loves in fact only himself, is none the less laudable and not to be blamed. Using a Sufi distinction, he calls this the love of the commonality, the love of the elite being that which is directed to God solely because he is worthy to be loved. The elite, the jurist remarks, are those who seek the pleasure of beholding the face of God. *Al-Tuḥfa al-ʿIrāqīya*, pp. 84–85.
58. See p. 59.
59. *Nubūwāt*, p. 68.
60. Cf. al-Juwaynī, *al-ʿAqīda al-Niẓāmīya*, pp. 45–46, and above, p. 59.
61. *Nubūwāt*, pp. 77–78.
62. Ibn Taymīya accuses Abu Ḥāmid al-Ghazālī of stressing asceticism (*zuhd*) more than the true monotheism (*tawḥid*) taught by the prophets, that is, the worship of God alone, "which includes," he writes, "love for God alone and absolute renunciation of love for the created unless it is loved by God, in which case [this love] is subsumed under love for God. This is in contrast to the one who loves it *with* God, which constitutes *shirk*." *Nubūwāt*, p. 79. See above, p. 76.
63. See preceding note and p. 82.
64. *Minhāj*, III, p. 98.
65. Cf. pp. 70–71.
66. Margeret Smith, *An early mystic of Baghdād* (London: The Sheldon Press, 1935), p. 40. The report is also mentioned by Ritter in connection with the Persian poetry of Farīd al-Dīn ʿAṭṭār (*Meer*, p. 508).
67. Massignon, *Essai*, pp. 218, 215 and n. 5.
68. Abū Ṭālib al-Makkī, *Qūt*, II, p. 69.
69. Asín, *El Islam cristianizado*, pp. 244–45.
70. Those Sufis, Ibn Taymīya argues, who in accordance with this view claim to have subdued their will so that they no longer pursue its objects, are deluded and have in fact gone to extremes in their obedience to their own wills and loves (*Fatāwā*, I, p. 209).
71. *Ibid.* Ibn Taymīya mentions also a remark attributed to al-Shiblī. On hearing some-

one exhort the populace with these words, "Some of you desire this world and some the next," al-Shiblī observed: "And what of the one who desires God?"

72. *Ibid.*, pp. 208–209. See also *Nubūwāt*, p. 68.
73. *Irāda*, *MRK*, I, p. 372. See also *Marātib al-irāda*, *MRK*, II, p. 72.
74. *Iḥtijāj*, *MRK*, II, pp. 135–36 and 141.
75. Koran 2:165, adapted from Pickthall's translation. Brackets are mine; parentheses, Pickthall's. The Arabic *"ka-ḥubbi 'llāh,"* which corresponds to the English beginning with "just as . . ." is ambiguous. Pickthall reads here: "loving them with a love like (that which is due) of Allah (only)." Ibn Taymīya considers this verse and suggests an interpretation which is that of the English translation given in the text (*Iḥtijāj*, *MRK*, II, pp. 133–34). The "rivals" or *andād* represent a rather frequently recurring theme in the Koran. Cf. Koran 2:22; 14:30; 34:33; 39:8; 41:9.
76. *Iḥtijāj*, *MRK*, II, pp. 115–16. Koran 3:31; trans. Pickthall.
77. See on this last point *Iḥtijāj*, *MRK*, II, pp. 133–36.
78. *Irāda*, *MRK*, I, p. 371.
79. See n. 74.
80. Cf. Koran 45:23 and above, pp. 16–17.
81. See, e.g., Muḥammad b. Muḥammad b. Muḥammad al-Manbijī, *Kitāb al-samāʿ wa-l-raqṣ* (a collection of Ibn Taymīya's opinions), *MRK*, II, pp. 277–315, and Ibn Taymīya, *Risāla fī ahl al-ṣuffa*, *MRM*, I, p. 38, on *samāʿ*, and *al-Waṣīya al-kubra*, *MRK*, I, pp. 285–86, on *naẓar*.
82. Al-Juwaynī, *Irshād*, p. 258; trans. Luciani, pp. 233–34.
83. *Iḥtijāj*, *MRK*, II, p. 120.
84. *Ibid.*, p. 121.
85. Al-Anṣārī, *Manāzil al-sā'irīn*, Arabic text, p. 11; French, p. 55.
86. God's "love" for a given event, of course, meant one thing for Ibn Taymīya and quite another for the stricter Ashʿarites. For examples of Ibn Taymīya's statements concerning al-Anṣārī, see *Iḥtijāj*, *MRK*, II, pp. 116, 122–23, 143, and his *al-Ḥujaj al-naqlīya*, *MRM*, II, pp. 11–12.
87. On this question Ibn Taymīya prefers the views of another great Ḥanbalite mystic, ʿAbd al-Qādir al-Jīlānī, who stressed God's commandments and prohibitions in his teaching. He also mentions al-Junayd in the same context (*Iḥtijāj*, *MRK*, II, p. 143; Ibn Taymīya, *Risāla fī 'l-hajr al-jamīl*, *MRM*, I, p. 3).
88. *Iḥtijāj*, *MRK*, II, pp. 90–91; *Irāda*, *MRK*, I, pp. 335–36.
89. On MSS of al-Tilimasānī's commentary, see Brockelmann, *S*, I, p. 774. See also below, p. 98.
90. Ibn Taymīya, *Ḥaqīqat madhhab al-ittiḥādiyīn*, *MRM*, II (short ed.), p. 79.
91. *Ibid.*, p. 131. See also Ibn Taymīya, *Kitāb Shaykh al-Islām*, *MRM*, I (long ed.), pp. 177–78, and *al-Furqān bayn al-ḥaqq wa-l-bāṭil*, *MRK*, I, p. 145.
92. *Iḥtijāj*, *MRK*, II, pp. 137–38.
93. *Ibid.*, pp. 91–92; *Irāda*, *MRK*, I, p. 326.
94. *Iḥtijāj*, *MRK*, II, pp. 122–23.

CHAPTER SIX

1. In his *Madārij al-sālikīn* (ed. Muḥammad Rashīd Riḍā, 3 vols.; Cairo: Maṭbaʿat al-Manār, 1331–33/1912–15), Ibn al-Qayyim remarks that it would have been better to treat the mystical stations after the manner of the earlier authorities (e.g., Abū Ṭālib al-Makkī and al-Junayd) but that it is necessary to address one's contemporaries in their own technical language (I, pp. 74–75). Cf. Ibn Taymīya's similar observation (above, pp. 54–55).
2. The Jawzīya served as a Ḥanbalite court of law (H. Laoust, EI^2, III, p. 821).

3. *Al-Qaṣīda al-nūnīya*, pp. 326–27; 608, 1.6; 609, 1.3.
4. Ibn Kathīr, *al-Bidāya wa-l-nihāya*, XIV (Cairo: Maṭbaʿat al-Saʿāda, 1358/1939), p. 234. Cf. also the report of al-Dhahabī, cited by Ibn Ḥajar (*al-Durar al-kāmina* [Ḥaydarābād: Dā'irat al-Maʿārif al-ʿUthmānīya, 1349–50/1930–31], IV, p. 401) and Ibn Taghrībirdī (*al-Nujūm al-zāhira*, X, p. 249). The meeting occurred in 713 according to Laoust (*EI*², III, p. 821).
5. Ibn al-Qayyim expressly names al-Wāsiṭī as his teacher (*Shifā' al-ʿalīl*, p. 32).
6. Ibn Rajab, *Dhayl*, II, p. 393; Ibn Ḥajar, *Durar*, I, p. 90. Al-Wāsiṭī was born on the eleventh or twelfth of Dhū 'l-Ḥijja 657/1259, or a little more than three years before Ibn Taymīya, if one accepts Ibn Rajab's dates, or as early as the 640s according to Ibn Taghrībirdī (*al-Manhal al-ṣāfī*, I, ed. Aḥmad Yūsuf Najātī [Cairo: Dār al-Kutub al-Miṣrīya, 1375/1956], p. 196).
7. Ibn Rajab, *Dhayl*, II, p. 359. Al-Wāsiṭī's *Mukhtaṣar al-sīra al-nabawīya*, abridged from Ibn Hishām's life of the Prophet, and a mystical work, *Miftāḥ ṭarīq al-muḥibbīn wa-bāb al-uns bi-Rabb al-ʿĀlamīn al-mu'addī ilā aḥwāl al-muqarrabīn*, are still extant in manuscript (Brockelmann, *GAS*, II, p. 162; new ed., p. 208).
8. Ibn Rajab, *Dhayl*, II, p. 360.
9. *Ibid.*, p. 393. Part of al-Wāsiṭī's letter is preserved in al-Safārīnī's *Ghidhā' al-albāb* ([Cairo: Maṭbaʿat al-Nīl, 1325/1907–1908], p. 47), but the passage quoted offers no evidence concerning the circumstances in which the letter was composed.
10. Ibn Rajab, *Dhayl*, II, p. 394. See also the statements of al-Wāsiṭī concerning Ibn Taymīya recorded by Ibn Shākir (*Fawāt al-Wafayāt*, ed. Muḥammad Muḥyī 'l-Dīn ʿAbd al-Ḥamīd [Cairo: Maktabat al-Nahḍa al-Miṣrīya, 1951], I, pp. 66–67).
11. See Ibn Rajab, *Dhayl*, II, p. 360.
12. For bibliographical data, see, n. 1. The editor, Rashīd Riḍā, erroneously called the *Madārij* Ibn al-Qayyim's only book on Sufism (*Madārij*, I, editor's intro., p. 8).
13. Laoust, *Essai*, p. 147.
14. Ibn Ḥajar, *Durar*, III, p. 401.
15. *Ibid.*, p. 403; Laoust, *EI*², III, p. 822, citing Ibn Kathīr, *Bidāya*, XIV, pp. 216, 235.
16. See pp. 46, 82–83.
17. Ibn al-Qayyim's quotations from Ibn Taymīya are cited by Ibn Rajab (*Dhayl*, II, p. 402). Cf. also remarks by Ibn al-Qayyim concerning his teacher (*ibid.*, pp. 402–403).
18. *Ibid.*, p. 448.
19. Even many of Ibn al-Qayyim's earliest works give the impression that his teacher was already dead at the time they were written. This is implied by the occurrence of such expressions as "our shaykh used to say . . ." and the use of the formula "*raḥimahu 'llāh*," equivalent to "the late," after Ibn Taymīya's name. Cf. Ibn al-Qayyim, *Ijtimāʿ al-juyūsh al-Islāmīya*, ed. Zakarīyā ʿAlī Yūsuf (Cairo: Maṭbaʿat al-Imām, n.d.), p. 157; *Kitāb al-rūḥ*, 4th ed. (Ḥaydarābād: Dā'irat al-Maʿārif al-ʿUthmānīya, 1383/1963), p. 54; *Rawḍa*, pp. 216, 292.

The partial chronology to be established in this chapter, representing the first such endeavor to my knowledge, is largely the byproduct of research relating specifically to Ibn al-Qayyim's doctrine of love and is consequently based on readings more limited in scope than might be desired. Although some supplementary research has been undertaken for the purpose, the periodization suggested is by no means definitive. Most often, a direct reference in a given book to an earlier composition constitutes the grounds for the order decided upon; but there are a few uncertain links, and in several cases a work has been assigned to a period on the basis of style or subject. It is, of course, conceivable that the author, after completing a later text, on occasion saw fit to insert a reference to it in an earlier one. If this in fact happened, some of our findings may be invalid. The danger of error resulting from such inserted citations would seem to be obviated, however, by the fact that no case of two works referring to each other has been observed. Moreover, the fact that the order of composition suggested here appears to reflect a relatively consistent evolution of Ibn al-Qayyim's style and interests tends to confirm its validity.

20. Ibn al-Qayyim's *Kitāb al-maʿālim* is cited in another of his early works, *al-Tibyān fī aqsām al-Qur'ān* (ed. Muḥammad Ḥāmid al-Fiqī [Cairo: al-Maktaba al-Tijārīya al-Kubrā, 1352/1933], p. 234; see also n. 1). See n. 22 on the *Tibyān*. The *Maʿālim* dealt with such topics as *ḥiyal* and Koranic analogies as does the extant work known as *Iʿlām al-muwaqqiʿīn* (transliteration followed by Brockelmann and generally by the Library of Congress; also transliterated *Aʿlām al-muwaqqiʿīn*). See Ibn al-Qayyim, *al-Fawā'id* (Cairo: Idārat al-Ṭibāʿa al-Munīrīya, 1344/1925–26), p. 8.
21. Cited in Ibn al-Qayyim's *Miftāḥ*, II, p. 97. On the *Miftāḥ*, see n. 31.
22. Cited in Ibn al-Qayyim's *al-Dā' wa-l-dawā'*, ed. Muḥammad Muḥyī 'l-Dīn ʿAbd al-Ḥamīd (Cairo: Maṭbaʿat al-Madanī, 1377/1958), p. 294. Another *tafsīr* monograph by Ibn al-Qayyim is cited in *al-Dā' wa-l-dawā'*, the *Kitāb īmān al-Qur'ān*, which is no longer extant (*Dā'*, p. 48). Cf. Ibn Rajab, *Dhayl*, II, p. 450. On *al-Dā' wa-l-dawā'*, see following note.
23. Placed among Ibn al-Qayyim's early works on grounds of (1) style (less sophisticated than that of his later works), (2) content (heavy reliance on *ḥadīth* and other material not his own), (3) lack of any reference to later works, and (4) a possible indirect allusion to the *Dā'*, suggesting familiarity with its subject matter, in the *Miftāḥ* (II, p. 269; cf. *Dā'*, pp. 2–3).
24. Placed among the early works for generally the same reasons as *al-Dā' wa-l-dawā'* (see preceding note) and on the basis of a claim by ʿĪsā Iskandar al-Maʿlūf to have found quotations—I have not identified them—from *Rawḍat al-muḥibbīn* in *Miftāḥ Dār al-Saʿāda* (cited in Aḥmad ʿUbayd's introduction to the first edition of the *Rawḍa*, p. *dāl*). Other evidence consists of lines of poetry found in later works which apparently have been culled from the *Rawḍa* (cf. *Miftāḥ*, I, p. 139, and *Rawḍa*, pp. 19, 263; *Miftāḥ*, I, p. 151, *Rawḍa*, p. 18; Ibn al-Qayyim, *Ṭarīq al-hijratayn wa-bāb al-saʿādatayn* [Cairo: Idārat al-Ṭibāʿa al-Munīrīya, 1358/1939], p. 266, *Rawḍa*, p. 265; *Ṭarīq*, p. 380, *Rawḍa*, pp. 183, 282; and *Ṭarīq*, pp. 432–33, *Rawḍa*, pp. 29, 81); a possible abridged quote from the *Rawḍa* (p. 264) in the *Ṭarīq* (p. 398); and a clear development in a commentary on four verses by Abū 'l-Shīṣ from *Rawḍa* (pp. 69–70, 278) to *Ṭarīq* (pp. 393–94). There is also an abridged quote from the *Rawḍa* in the latest of Ibn al-Qayyim's works discussed here, *Ighāthat al-lahfān min maṣāyid al-Shayṭān* (ed. Muḥammad Ḥāmid al-Fiqī [Cairo: Muṣṭafā al-Bābī al-Ḥalabī wa-Awlāduhu, 1357/1939], II, pp. 125ff. Cf. *Rawḍa*, pp. 55ff.). See also *Ighātha* (ed. Fiqī), I, p. 135.
25. *Kitāb al-rūḥ*, p. 62. The work is also mentioned in *Miftāḥ* (II, p. 156) under the title *Kitāb al-rūḥ wa-l-nafs*.
26. See chapter three, n. 24, for bibliographical data. The *Qaṣīda* was written prior to *Rawḍat al-muḥibbīn*, which quotes extensively from it (*Rawḍa*, pp. 252–57).
27. *Ijtimāʿ al-juyūsh al-Islāmīya* was written prior to *al-Dā' wa-l-dawā'*. In the latter work (p. 209) Ibn al-Qayyim states that he has quoted a certain opinion of al-Ashʿarī in another book, alluding, it would seem, to his *Ijtimāʿ* (p. 206).
28. Cited by Ibn al-Qayyim in the *Miftāḥ* (I, p. 285) and listed by Ibn Rajab as *al-Fatḥ al-Qudsī* (*Dhayl*, II, p. 450). The work dealt with God's *ḥikma* and man's responsibility for sin. The "wise purpose" underlying the divine decree that man should sin, according to Ibn al-Qayyim, was the creation of an opportunity for repentance, which is loved by God (*Miftāḥ*, I, pp. 286–87).
29. Two of Ibn al-Qayyim's major extant works, *Ḥādī al-arwāḥ* and *Zād al-maʿād* with these characteristics as criteria, would appear to belong to the earlier period.
30. See p. 94.
31. The fact that Ibn al-Qayyim mentions *Miftāḥ Dār al-Saʿāda* in most of his later works shows it to be a relatively early composition and likewise indicates the importance the author assigned to it. Cf. *Shifā' al-ʿalīl*, p. 181; *Ṭarīq*, p. 483 and

n. 1 (mentioning his discussion of the comparative benefits of the date palm and the grape in another place, presumably referring to *Miftāḥ*, I, pp. 230–33); *Madārij*, I, p. 49; III, p. 317; *Ighāthat al-lahfān min maṣāyid al-Shayṭān* (Cairo: al-Maṭba'a al-Maymanīya, 1320/1902), p. 291. (Unless otherwise noted, all references to the *Ighātha*, especially in subsequent chapters, are to this older edition.)

32. Cf. Ibn al-Qayyim's own description of the work in *Miftāḥ*, II, p. 273.

33. References to the *Ṣawā'iq* throughout are to the published abridgment of the work by Shaykh Muḥammad b. al-Mawṣilī entitled *Mukhtaṣar al-Ṣawā'iq al-mursala* (Cairo: Maṭba'at al-Imām, 1380/1960–61).

34. In *Shifā' al-'alīl* Ibn al-Qayyim mentions his *Miftāḥ* by name (p. 187) and promises a work against *ta'wīl* (p. 122), to be identified with the *Ṣawā'iq*. Thus *Shifā' al-'alīl* was written after the *Miftāḥ* and before *al-Ṣawā'iq al-mursala.* Another work mentioned in the *Shifā'*, and presumably, therefore, written at an earlier date, is a treatise on the "*aḥkām ahl al-milal*" (the status of the followers of the protected religions). The author is apparently alluding to the work known as *Aḥkām ahl al-dhimma* edited by Dr. Subḥī al-Ṣāliḥ (Damascus: Maṭba'at Jāmi'at Dimashq, 1961 [i.e. 1963?]). An extract from this work, *Sharḥ al-shurūṭ al-'Umarīya* (Damascus: Maṭba'at Jāmi'at Dimashq, 1961), has also been made available by the same editor.

35. *Miftāḥ*, I, p. 47; II, pp. 89, 119.

36. *Ṭarīq*, p. 72. *Al-Mawrid al-ṣāfī*, which Ibn al-Qayyim calls in the *Ṭarīq* his "big book on love," is to be identified with the "big book on love" mentioned in the *Madārij* (II, p. 29; III, p. 13), where it is also claimed that some hundred proofs are furnished in the work.

37. See *Ṭarīq*, pp. 248, 265, and Ibn al-Qayyim, *Badā'i' al-fawā'id* (Cairo: Idārat al-Ṭibā'a al-Munīrīya, n.d.), II, p. 87. The *Tuḥfa* is apparently earlier than *al-Mawrid al-ṣāfī*, since the section just cited in *Badā'i' al-fawā'id*, dealing with the etymology of *ḥubb*, refers the reader to the *Tuḥfa* for further treatment of the topic rather than to the *Mawrid.* Had the *Mawrid* already been completed at the time of the writing of the passage in *Badā'i' al-fawā'id*, Ibn al-Qayyim would presumably have directed his readers to that work instead. This is admittedly a very weak argument; but it is certain, at least, that the *Tuḥfa* cannot postdate *al-Mawrid al-ṣāfī* by long, since both works are mentioned in the *Ṭarīq* (pp. 72, 248, 265). It is not possible on the basis of my evidence to set an early limit for the composition of the *Tuḥfa*, but its subject matter and the fact that it is not, to my knowledge, mentioned in the author's earlier works, suggest that it belongs to the period following the completion of *Miftāḥ Dār al-Sa'āda.* Although almost always cited simply as *al-Tuḥfa al-Makkīya*, the book is probably to be identified with the work referred to under the similar title *Tuḥfat al-nāzilīn bi-jiwār Rabb al-'Ālamīn* in the *Madārij* (I, p. 126). Ibn Rajab's listing of only the first title among the works of Ibn al-Qayyim (*Dhayl*, II, p. 450) tends to confirm this identification. If the two titles do in fact refer to the same book, it is possible to add that the *Tuḥfa* dealt with the reality of the distinction between good and evil as well as with the subjects I have already mentioned in the text.

38. Cf. Ibn Rajab, *Dhayl*, II, p. 450. *Qurrat 'uyūn al-muḥibbīn* must be earlier than the *Madārij*, in which it is mentioned (I, p. 50), but I have no evidence other than the nature of its subject-matter for placing it in this particular period.

39. Published in Spanish translation with an introduction by Miguel Asín Palacios under the title *El místico Abulabás Benalarif de Almería y su "Mahasin al-Machalis"* (Madrid: Imp. Sáez Hermanos, 1931). A French version of Asín's study and translation, with the Arabic text included, appeared later ("Collection de textes inédits relatifs à la mystique musulmane," Vol. II: Paris: Librairie Orientale Paul Geuthner, 1933).

40. Al-Anṣārī's "*'Ilal al-maqāmāt,*" published by Serge de Laugier de Beaurecueil, O.P., in "Un petit traité de 'Abdallah Ansari sur les déficiences inhérentes à certaines

demeures spirituelles," *Mélanges Louis Massignon*, I (Damascus: Institut Français de Damas, 1956), pp. 153–71. Father de Beaurecueil's edition having appeared only in 1956, Asín was unaware of the source of Ibn al-ʿArīf's *Maḥāsin* and was consequently led to overestimate its originality (Asín, *El Místico Abulabás*, intro., pp. 9–11; Fr. trans., pp. 13–16). In fact the stations treated by Ibn al-ʿArīf had all been dealt with in much the same words by al-Anṣārī in his *ʿIlal*. The theoretical expressions of Ibn al-ʿArīf, if indeed he was the author of the *Maḥāsin*, are little more than direct quotes from the *ʿIlal*, or, at times, the *Manāzil*. (Cf. Asín's introduction [Sp., p. 13; Fr., p. 18], citing Ibn al-ʿArabī's *Futūḥāt* [(Būlāq, 1293 A.H.) I, p. 119, l. 19], where the *Maḥāsin* is termed a book "attributed to' Ibn al-ʿArīf; and Asín's remark [Sp., pp. 6–7; Fr., pp. 8–9] that among Ibn al-ʿArīf's biographers only Ibn Khallikān, under the title *Majālis*, mentions the *Maḥāsin*.) The coda which summarizes the argument of the *Maḥāsin* is likewise taken straight from the *ʿIlal*. Moreover, the fact that Asín found the *Maḥāsin* mentioned only by Ibn al-ʿArabī and Ibn Khallikān led him to conclude that the work enjoyed little popularity among either oriental or Maghribī mystics. The fact that Ibn al-Qayyim deemed the treatise important enough to merit a commentary would seem to contradict this view. It would be possible to attribute the Ḥanbalite's interest simply to the importance of the *Maḥāsin* for Ibn al-ʿArabī, but the relatively large number of extant MSS of the work, many of them unknown to Asín at the time of his research, indicates that Ibn al-ʿArīf's manual had a fairly widespread reception. At least one other commentary is also known to have been written—*al-Qawānīn*, by Ibn al-Mar'a b. Dahhāq of Málaga (d. 610/1214), a teacher of the celebrated monist Ibn Sabʿīn (Brockelmann, *GAL*, I, p. 434 [new ed., p. 559]; *S*, I, p. 776).

41. A work by al-Anṣārī on the deficiencies of the mystical stations is mentioned in the *Madārij* (III, p. 310). Ibn Rajab, Ibn al-Qayyim's student, was likewise aware of the existence of the work (*Dhayl*, I, p. 66).

42. In his *Ṭabaqāt al-Ṣūfīya* al-Anṣārī claimed that he spoke stronger words than the mystic martyr al-Ḥallāj but that he was not spurned by the commonality because the meanings of his utterances remained hidden from those who were not suited to receive them (S. de Laugier de Beaurecueil, O.P., *Khwādja ʿAbdullāh Anṣārī* [Beirut: Imprimerie Catholique, 1965], pp. 270–71, quoting and translating al-Anṣārī, *Ṭabaqāt*, ed. ʿAbd al-Ḥayy Ḥabībī [Kabul, 1341/1961], pp. 320–31). See also Beaurecueil, *Anṣārī*, p. 11. The text in question was cited by Massignon in French translation together with the Persian original prior to the edition of the *Ṭabaqāt* (*Passion*, p. 368 and plate opposite). Massignon's translation is misleading, however, and Beaurecueil's improved version is open to question at several points. Part of the problem certainly stems from al-Anṣārī's Persian. I am indebted to Dr. Iraj Dehghan for his help in understanding the difficulties of the passage.

43. See pp. 89–90 and n. 89. I owe the observations expressed in the text concerning the style of the *Manāzil* and the link between Ibn al-Qayyim's *Madārij* and the commentary by al-Tilimsānī to Father de Beaurecueil, who kindly shared with me some of the conclusions of his own research on these works.

44. *Madārij*, I, editor's intro., p. 8. *Madārij al-sālikīn* can be assumed to have been composed later than the following works, each of which it cites: *Ṭarīq al-hijratayn*, cited as *Safar al-hijratayn* (I, pp. 49, 272; II, p. 29), the title given it by Ibn Rajab as well (*Dhayl*, II, p. 449); *al-Mawrid al-ṣāfī*, cited in the *Madārij* as his "big book on love" (II, p. 29; III, p. 13); *Qurrat ʿuyūn al-muḥibbīn* (I, p. 50); *Tuḥfat al-nāzilīn bi-jiwār Rabb al-ʿĀlamīn* (= *al-Tuḥfa al-Makkīya* [?]) (I, p. 126); *al-Ṣawāʿiq al-mursala* (III, p. 226); *Miftāḥ Dār al-Saʿāda* (I, p. 49; III, p. 317); and *Ighāthat al-lahfān fī ṭalāq al-ghaḍbān*, not to be confused with the *Ighāthat al-lahfān* used in this study (III, p. 197).

45. *Madārij*, II, p. 230. Ibn al-Qayyim later mentions and describes briefly a large completed work on *samāʿ* in his *Ighāthat al-lahfān min maṣāyid al-Shayṭān* (ed. Fiqī, I,

pp. 267–68). Perhaps the manuscript mentioned by Brockelmann under the title *al-Kalām fī mas'alat al-samā'* (*S*, II, p. 127) is to be equated with this work. Not having seen the manuscript in question, I can offer this identification only on a conjectural basis.

46. If it is possible to equate the treatise on *samā'* proposed in the *Madārij* with that mentioned as a completed work in *Ighāthat al-lahfān* (see preceding note), then the *Ighātha* may be assumed to be later than the *Madārij*. Brockelmann admittedly refers to two manuscripts by Ibn al-Qayyim on *samā'* (*S*, II, p. 127), but it is reasonable to suppose that only one work could answer to the description of a "big book" given in both the *Madārij* and the *Ighātha*. Moreover, it does not seem likely that Ibn al-Qayyim would have referred in the *Madārij* only to a large work projected for the future, if the important treatise described in the *Ighātha* had already been completed. Internal evidence in one or both of the extant manuscripts on *samā'* may help to establish the dating of the *Ighātha* with more certainty, but the work is, in any case, an undeniably late production. Among the earlier texts it mentions, in addition to the treatise on *samā'*, are *al-Ṣawā'iq al-mursala* (*Ighātha*, ed. Fiqī, I, p. 45); his "big book on predestination," i.e. *Shifā' al-'alīl* (ed. Fiqī, II, p. 114); and *Miftāḥ Dār al-Sa'āda* (ed. Fiqī, II, pp. 125, 138). The *Ighātha* also contains sections which are apparently abridged from the author's *Ḥādī al-arwāḥ*, *I'lām al-muwaqqi'īn*, and *Hidāyat al-ḥayārā*.

Two other works ascribed to Ibn al-Qayyim, both compilations of his thoughts and opinions, seem to contain at least a fair amount of material from a relatively late period of his life. One, *Badā'i' al-fawā'id*, which was known to Ibn Rajab (*Dhayl*, II, p. 450), mentions, as I have remarked in n. 37, *al-Tuḥfa al-Makkīya* (*Badā'i'*, II, p. 87). It was thus compiled after the composition of that work, presumably by the author himself. The second, called simply *al-Fawā'id*, mentions his "big book on predestination," alluding to the late *Shifā' al-'alīl* (p. 25), but also cites such early efforts as *al-Ma'ālim* (p. 8) and *Ijtimā' al-juyūsh al-Islāmīya* (p. 4). However, the occurrence of a rhymed prose differing from Ibn al-Qayyim's typical style (cf. p. 104), together with the use of such expressions as "the most learned Ibn al-Qayyim said . . ." (p. 93), indicate the *Fawā'id* was compiled by someone other than Ibn al-Qayyim himself. The fact that the book, unlike *Badā'i' al-fawā'id*, is not mentioned in Ibn Rajab's long, if admittedly incomplete, list of the scholar's works (*Dhayl*, II, pp. 449–50) tends to confirm this hypothesis.

For the dating of Ibn al-Qayyim's *'Uddat al-ṣābirīn* (on patient endurance) as well as for a number of his other works I have no substantial information. However, I do not claim to have noticed all of the relevant internal evidence, and it may well be possible not only to determine the approximate dating of these remaining works but also to refine further the periodization I have been able to suggest.

47. *Rawḍa*, p. 1.
48. *Ibid.*, pp. 21, 463. Cf. Ibn al-Jawzī, *Dhamm*, p. 12.
49. Cf. *Rawḍa*, pp. 398, 463–78, and Ibn al-Jawzī, *Dhamm*, pp. 12–34.
50. *Rawḍa*, pp. 8, 10.
51. Aḥmad 'Ubayd, in his introduction to the *Rawḍa*, thought that this might explain the author's carelessness with traditions in the work (p. *hā'*). Cf. Ibn al-Qayyim's apology for the faults in his treatise on the grounds that it was composed during his absence from his homeland and his library (p. 12).
52. See Rashīd Riḍā's comments in his introduction to Ibn al-Qayyim's *Madārij* (p. 8).
53. *Rawḍa*, p. 13.
54. Cf. the discussion of the *ḥadīth* "*Man 'ashiqa . . .*" in *Rawḍa*, pp. 180–82.
55. The purpose of al-Ḥalabī's *Manāzil al-aḥbāb* was to demonstrate through citations of anecdotes and verse the chaste character of the early Arab lovers (MS Top Kapı, Ahmet III, 2471, fols. 1b, 147b–48a). On the compiler, see Ibn Rajab, *Dhayl*, II, p.

378. For further remarks on al-Ḥalabī and his work, consult Giffen, *Theory*, pp. 31–33 and *passim.*
56. H. Laoust has previously remarked this similarity between Ibn al-Jawzī and Ibn al-Qayyim (*Essai*, p. 491).
57. Cf. the passage on *ghurba* (estrangement) in *Madārij*, III, pp. 122–30.
58. The MSS on *samā'* mentioned by Brockelmann (*S*, II, p. 127) may very well contain additional late passages on profane love, but I have not yet had the opportunity to examine them.

CHAPTER SEVEN

1. *Madārij*, III, p. 6.
2. See pp. 193–95.
3. C. G. Jung, *Contributions to analytical psychology*, trans. H. G. and Cary F. Baynes (London: Routledge and Kegan Paul, 1928), p. 207; quoted by Robert G. Hazo, *The idea of love*, p. 5, n. 2.
4. Ibn al-'Arīf, *Maḥāsin*, Sp. trans. Asín, pp. 33–34; Arabic, p. 90.
5. *Ṭarīq*, p. 381; cf. *Madārij*, III, p. 235.
6. *Madārij*, III, p. 6.
7. *Ṭarīq*, p. 402; Abū 'l-Qāsim 'Abd al-Karīm b. Hawāzin al-Qushayrī, *al-Risāla al-Qushayrīya* (Cairo: Dār al-Kutub al-'Arabīya al-Kubrā, 1330/1912), p. 144. Al-Jāḥiẓ had made a like comment earlier: "Love (*al-ḥubb*) is [simply] a name which stands for the meaning for which it was prescribed; it has no explanation" (*Qiyān*, in *Rasā'il al-Jāḥiẓ*, ed. 'Abd al-Salām Hārūn, II, p. 167). Approximately the same remark is made by the mystic al-Dabbāgh (d. 696/1296–97) in his *Mashāriq anwār al-qulūb*. One can only allude to love, he declares, it cannot be defined (*Mashāriq*, p. 20). Muḥammad b. Dāwūd considers love subtle, invisible, and inscrutable (*Zahra*, pp. 1–2).
8. *Rawḍa*, pp. 18–20.
9. *Ṭarīq*, pp. 381–407.
10. *Madārij*, III, pp. 6–11.
11. *Ibid.*, p. 11.
12. *Ṭarīq*, pp. 399–400. Cf. Ibn al-Qayyim's rejection of a similar definition in the *Madārij* (III, p. 8). In the *Rawḍa* he uses *mayl* to define the more general term *hawā*, or passion (p. 20).
13. *Ṭarīq*, p. 400.
14. *Ibid.*, pp. 384, 391, 401; *Madārij*, III, pp. 8–9.
15. See pp. 107, 120.
16. Hazo, *The idea of love*, p. 13.
17. *Madārij*, III, p. 10; *Ṭarīq*, p. 425.
18. Cf. Ibn al-'Arīf, *Maḥāsin*, Sp. trans. Asín, p. 34.
19. *Ṭarīq*, pp. 402–403.
20. *Ibid.*, pp. 406–407.
21. *Agape* doctrine makes God, considered as an outside factor separate from both subject and object, the efficient as well as the final cause of disinterested love among men—an affection otherwise impossible. Nygren, *Agape and eros*, p. 216.
22. *Rawḍa*, p. 65. An exception to this rule may occur, according to Ibn al-Qayyim, where the qualities of the beloved, his beauty for instance, are not perfect. The lover may none the less see his qualities as faultless, for love is blind. When the ruthless Omayyad governor of Kufa al-Ḥajjāj b. Yūsuf said to 'Azza, the beloved of the poet Kuthayyir, "You are not as Kuthayyir described you," the woman re-

plied, "O Emir, he did not see me with the eye with which you have seen me" (*ibid.*).

23. See pp. 74–77.
24. Saint Thomas Aquinas expresses this idea repeatedly and quite specifically: "Omne quod appetit aliquid, appetit illud in quantum habet aliquam similitudinem cum ipso. Nec similitudo illa sufficit quae est secundum esse spirituale; . . . sed oportet quod sit similitudo secundum esse naturae" (*De veritate*, Q. 22, Art. 1); again, "Similitudo, proprie loquendo, est causa amoris" (*Summa theologica*, Part I–II, Q. 27, Art. 3, Reply obj. 4). Cited by H. D. Simonin, "Autour de la solution thomiste du problème de l'amour," *Archives d'histoire doctrinale et littéraire du moyen âge* 6 (1931): 248, 258. In the *Summa contra gentiles* Aquinas voices the same idea: "There is a likeness or congeniality between the lover and the one he loves" (I, 91, 6; trans. Anton C. Pegis [New York: Image Books, 1955], pp. 278–79).
25. Plato cites a similar saying. Cf. *Phaedrus* 240.
26. In Greek thought similarity appears most often as a cause of friendship; complementarity, as a cause of erotic love. Plato's thinking on these relationships, however, is not always immediately discernible. In the *Lysis*, Socrates at first accepts as a given the assertion of the poets that God ever leads like to like, but he quickly modifies his view. At the end of the dialogue, in accordance with his didactic method, he leaves the matter undecided. In the *Phaedrus* the philosopher admits similarity, particularly in age, as a basis for friendship but not for love, remarking that the lover, being older, is unlike the beloved (240). The homosexual love implied here, of the older, more experienced man for the green but seductive youth, is clearly a relationship of complementarity. The Athenian in the *Laws*, however, recognizes two types of love—the love of similars and that of contraries. He also mentions the question of reciprocity, an almost universally acknowledged consequence of *munāsaba* in Islamic thought. As he expresses it, the "attachment between opposites is fierce and furious, and we do not often find it reciprocated, whereas that founded on similarity is equable and permanently reciprocal" (*Laws* viii. 837; trans. A.E. Taylor). Interestingly, the Athenian proceeds to state that both factors may be present in a third kind of love.

    Aristotle, primarily concerned with friends rather than with lovers, stresses similarity. It is similarity (in virtue) which is the basis of true and lasting friendship; and, he insists, an affection must be mutual and recognized to be called by that name. Affection based on utility or pleasure ends when the object ceases to be useful or pleasant (*Ethics* viii. 1155b–1156a). Aristotle is not unaware of the love of contraries, which, he remarks, seeks an intermediate state, as the dry desires to become moist, not wet; but he dismisses the subject as foreign to his inquiry (*ibid.* ix. 1159b). The Muslim understanding of *munāsaba* (affinity) as a cause of erotic love, it should be added, seems to be patterned more often on Aristotle's similarity-friendship doctrine than on Plato's love of complementarity.
27. Cf. Hazo, *The idea of love*, p. 32, and Irving Singer, *The nature of love*, p. 54. Singer, taking the myth to mean that love is the search for a state of wholeness, i.e., a union of complementarity, criticizes Freud for having interpreted it as expressing "a need to restore an earlier state of things." Cf. Plato *Symposium* 189–93.
28. See pp. 109–112, esp. pp. 111, 112.
29. See p. 4.
30. Al-Masʿūdī, *Murūj al-dhahab*, Arabic text with Fr. trans. by C. Barbier de Meynard, VI (Paris: Imprimerie Nationale, 1871), pp. 376–77, 381–82.
31. See pp. 110–11, 113.
32. Trans. A. J. Arberry in his English version of Ibn Ḥazm's *Ṭawq al-ḥamāma* (London: Luzac, 1953), p. 27.
33. *Rawḍa*, p. 71.
34. Al-Masʿūdī, *Murūj*, VI, pp. 268–76; al-Daylamī, *ʿAṭf*, pp. 30–31. The attribution of

the definitions is not necessarily reliable. Al-Masʿūdī and al-Daylamī at times ascribe them to different individuals.

35. *Rawḍa*, p. 76.
36. Al-Jāḥiẓ, *Qiyān, Rasā'il al-Jāḥiẓ*, II, pp. 168–70.
37. Al-Daylamī, *ʿAṭf*, pp. 31–32.
38. Ibn Taymīya, *Fatāwā*, I, pp. 206–207.
39. Al-Hujwīrī, *Kashf al-maḥjūb*, trans R. A. Nicholson ("E.J.W. Gibb Memorial," XVII; London: Luzac, 1967), p. 308.
40. Al-Ghazālī, *Iḥyā'*, XIV, p. 51.
41. *Ibid.*, V, pp. 147–48.
42. *Ibid.*, VI, pp. 182–83.
43. *Ibid.*, XIV, pp. 60–61.
44. *Ibid.*, pp. 95–99.
45. Ibn al-ʿArabī, *al-Futūḥāt al-Makkīya* (Cairo: Dār al-Kutub al-ʿArabīya, 1329/1911), II, p. 189.
46. Ibn Dāwūd, *Zahra*, p. 5.
47. *Ibid.*, pp. 14–16.
48. *Ibid.*, pp. 20–21.
49. Ibn Ḥazm, *Ṭawq*, ed. Bercher, pp. 14–16, 20, 28; *Kitāb al-akhlāq wa-l-siyar*, ed. and Fr. trans. Nada Tomiche (Beirut; Commission Internationale pour la Traduction des Chefs-d'Œuvre, 1961), Ar. p. 51; Fr., pp. 61–62.
50. Ibn Ḥazm, *Ṭawq*, p. 18; Ibn Dāwūd, *Zahra*, pp. 20–21.
51. Ibn Ḥazm, *Ṭawq*, p. 14.
52. Al-Masʿūdī, *Murūj*, VI, pp. 379–81. For some further remarks on Ibn Ḥazm's teaching on the prior creation of souls and their peregrinations from their first abode to their ultimate home in Heaven or Hell, see Nada Tomiche's introduction to *Kitāb al-akhlāq wa-l-siyar*, p. xxxiii, citing his *Fiṣal* (Cairo, 1317/1899–1900), I, p. 4; III, pp. 131–34; IV, p. 70; V, p. 87.
53. Al-Dabbāgh, *Mashāriq*, pp. 52, 56.
54. *Ibid.*, p. 65.
55. *Ibid.*, pp. 54–55. Al-Dabbāgh implies elsewhere in the text that *munāsaba* is constituted by an almost exact likeness (*ibid.*, p. 8).
56. *Ibid.*, p. 5.
57. Cf. Seyyed Hossein Nasr, "Shihāb al-Dīn Suhrawardī Maqtūl," *A history of Muslim philosophy*, ed. M. M. Sharif (Wiesbaden: Otto Harrassowitz, 1963–66), I, p. 393 and n. 64.
58. See pp. 113–15.
59. *Ṭibb*, p. 208. Ibn al-Qayyim cites in support of his view the *ḥadīth*s "Souls are regimented battalions, . . ." and "No man loves a tribe but he will be resurrected with them (*Lā yuḥibbu 'l-mar'u . . .*)" (*ibid.*, p. 209).
60. *Rawḍa*, pp. 65–67. A line of poetry which immediately precedes this definition in Ibn al-Qayyim's text is, in any case, ascribed to Ibn Dāwūd (Ibn al-Jawzī, *Dhamm*, p. 302).
61. *Rawḍa*, pp. 66–67. Loves for such varied objects as food, altruism, and knowledge are also attributed to a relationship of similarity (*ibid.*, pp. 67–68).
62. *Ibid.*, pp. 69, 75; *Tibb*, pp. 209–210.
63. *Rawḍa*, pp. 72–73, 285.
64. *Ibid.*, pp. 73–75. The same opinion is expressed by Ibn al-Qayyim in his early monograph *al-Tibyān fī aqsām al-Qur'ān.* The spirit, as confirmed by a saying of the Prophet, is first present in the foetus after three periods of forty days. Any prior movement of the foetus is caused by something other than the spirit. *Tibyān*, p. 339.
65. *Rawḍa*, pp. 140–41. In his *Shifā'*, Ibn Sīnā's precise teaching is that human souls can have no *individual* existence prior to the creation of the body. They are of one genus, he argues, and if it be supposed that they come into being before their

bodies, they cannot be multiple in this earlier existence. It is only with the coming into being of the body that the individuation of souls can occur. *Psychologie d'Ibn Sīnā (Avicenne) d'après son oeuvre aš-Šifā'*, ed. (Vol. I) with Fr. trans. (Vol. II) by Ján Bakoš (Prague: Editions de l'Académie Tchécoslovaque des Sciences, 1959), Arabic text, I, pp. 220, 221; French trans., II, pp. 158, 159.

66. Ibn al-Qayyim mentions and often refutes Ibn Ḥazm's arguments in a number of places in *Kitāb al-rūḥ* (cf. pp. 188, 271, 297–99).
67. Trans. Mawlānā Muḥammad ʿAlī. Cf. Ritter, *Meer*, pp. 339–40.
68. *Rūḥ*, p. 293. See above, pp. 36–37.
69. Cf. especially the argument against Ibn Ḥazm's interpretation of Koran 7:11, "And We indeed created you [pronoun understood by Ibn Ḥazm to mean all living men], then We fashioned you, *then* We said to the angels: Make submission to Adam." According to the Ẓāhirite's exegesis, this verse implies that all men were created before the time when God commanded the angels to bow down to Adam. Since their bodies were not then in existence, the verse must therefore refer to the creation of their souls. Ibn al-Qayyim answers that it is possible to address the now living but in fact to have in mind only their ancestors. He finds support for this assertion in Koran 2:55, "And when *you* [the Jews in general] said: O Moses, we will not believe in thee till we see Allāh manifestly, so the punishment overtook you while you looked on." The point Ibn al-Qayyim wishes to make is clear enough. This verse, although addressed to all Jews, and particularly those alive at the time it was first uttered, refers to a situation which involved only one generation of the early Hebrews. Similarly, the first verse is addressed to mankind in general, but insofar as it expresses a specific sequence of events, it applies strictly to Adam—the only man created before the angels were commanded to make submission to him. See *Rūḥ*, pp. 297–99, esp. p. 298. The Koranic verses here cited are from the translation of Mawlānā Muḥammad ʿAlī. The italics in both cases are mine.
70. *Rūḥ*, pp. 302–303.
71. *Ibid.*, p. 304.
72. See p. 7.
73. Nygren, *Agape and eros*, pp. 298–99.
74. See pp. 112–13.
75. Nygren, *Agape and eros*, pp. 336–40.
76. See esp. *Rūḥ*, pp. 63, 308–318, 332–346, 356, 358, 362–63, 370.
77. Soul and body must both be resurrected for punishment or reward according to Ibn al-Qayyim. If there is no body after death, then there is no soul. The body may admittedly disintegrate in the grave, but God is able to gather its parts together. *Fawā'id*, pp. 5–6.
78. Nygren opposes *nomos* to the primitive Christian *agape* motif, which he describes as "love breaking down the scheme of law" (*Agape and Eros*, p. 251).
79. The Koranic authority for this attitude lay in such verses as these: "Say: if you love God, then follow me and God will love you, . . ." (3:31) and, "Spend in the path of God, and do not be cast by your own hands into perdition. Do good: Surely God loves those who do good" (2:195).
80. Cf. pp. 75–76, 110–11.
81. *Madārij*, III, p. 152.
82. *Ṭarīq*, p. 391. Cf. above, p. 76.
83. In *Rawḍat al-muḥibbīn* Ibn al-Qayyim used the word *muwāfaqa* to denote the affinity between subject and object which is among the causes of love. He specified, moreover, that this *muwāfaqa* is called *munāsaba* or *mulā'ama* in relationships between creatures. There is no mention in the passage of the union of objects of will, however. See *Rawḍa*, p. 65.
84. Al-Anṣārī, *Manāzil*, Ar., p. 71; Fr., p. 105.

85. *Madārij*, III, p. 131.
86. On the two professions of God's unity, the first of his lordship and the second of his divinity, see, e.g., Ibn Taymīya, *Irāda*, *MRK*, I, pp. 335–36; *Iḥtijāj*, *MRK*, II, p. 116; Ibn al-Qayyim, *Shifā' al-ʿalīl*, p. 377; *Ighātha*, pp. 293–94. The distinction parallels that between the existential (*kawnī*) and prescriptive (*dīnī*) aspects of the divine will. As Lord, God is creator and sustainer. As Divinity, he is object of worship and love; but he is also *one who loves* and, therefore, a lawgiver, since his love extends to specific acts as well as to individual creatures. For the same distinction expressed in different terms, see Ibn al-Qayyim's *Ijtimāʿ*, pp. 46–47.
87. *Madārij*, III, p. 131; al-Anṣārī, *Manāzil*, Ar., p. 89; Fr., p. 119.
88. See Ritter, *Meer*, pp. 362–68.
89. See p. 75.
90. *Fawā'id*, p. 52.
91. Al-Ghazālī, *Iḥā'*, XIV, p. 51.
92. See al-Ḥārith b. Asad al-Muḥāsibī, *Risālat al-mustarshidīn*, ed. ʿAbd al-Fattāḥ Abū Ghudda (Aleppo: Maktab al-Maṭbūʿāt al-Islāmīya, n.d.), pp. 94–95, for an early source; al-Daylamī, *ʿAṭf*, pp. 47, 108–110; Ritter, *Meer*, p. 479, on Ibn al-ʿArabī; and al-Dabbāgh, *Mashāriq*, pp. 30, 4, 59–62.
93. Al-Ghazālī, *Iḥyā'*, XIV, pp. 46–47, 50. Al-Ghazālī also distinguishes between love to God proceeding from true hope in his promises and love to God founded on his prior beneficence (*ibid.*, V, p. 154), but these two types may again be grouped together for our purposes.
94. *Dā'*, pp. 333, 336–37, 339; *Miftāḥ*, II, pp. 90–91.
95. In Arabic, "Jubilati 'l-qulūbu ʿalā ḥubbi man aḥsana ilayhā." Cf. al-Muḥāsibī, *Mustarshidīn*, pp. 94–95; al-Ghazālī, *Iḥyā'*, XIV, p. 47; al-Daylamī, *ʿAṭf*, p. 47, where love for a benefactor is called "*maḥabba jiblīya*"; and Ibn al-Qayyim, *Dā'*, p. 333, paraphrasing Ibn Masʿūd's saying.
96. *Ṭarīq*, pp. 410–412.
97. *Miftāḥ*, II, pp. 89, 91.
98. See, e.g., al-Muḥāsibī, *Mustarshidīn*, pp. 94–95; Asín, *El Islam cristianizado*, p. 249, on al-Ghazālī; and, for comparison, *Georges Vajda, L'amour de Dieu dans la théologie juive du moyen âge* (Paris: J. Vrin, 1957), pp. 94–95, on Baḥya Ibn Paqūda (ca. 1100 A.D.). Baḥya taught that love to God may result from his beneficence but that pure love is for his essence. This pure love, which seeks nothing for itself, is not a thing humanly possible. Rather, it is a reward for obedience, but not such a reward as one could anticipate. Christian writers also placed love for God in his essence or "for his sake" on a level above love to him as benefactor, that is, love to him for one's own sake. Consider, for example, the four stages of sacred love distinguished by St. Bernard of Clairvaux (discussed in Nygren, *Agape and Eros*, pp. 645–48).
99. See p. 83.
100. *Ṭarīq*, p. 415, commenting on a statement made by Ibn al-ʿArīf.
101. *Ibid.*, p. 412.
102. *Madārij*, II, pp. 44–45.
103. *Fawā'id*, pp. 182–83. Cf. *Rawḍa*, pp. 414–15.
104. Of course Ibn al-Qayyim might have presented this same view in another fashion, arguing that the sensation of joy which results from receiving a gift or being the object of some kindness is in fact no more a response to self-love than is joy aroused by the perception of beauty.
105. Al-Ghazālī, *Iḥyā'*, XIV, p. 48; Plato *Hippias major* 290–94. Beauty is a cause of love, as al-Ghazālī explains it, for the simple reason that every beautiful thing is pleasurable, while everything pleasurable is loved by the one who enjoys it (*Iḥyā'*, V, p. 147; XIV, p. 44). Despite the fact that his own analysis has reduced the love for beauty to nothing more than another expression of self-interest, al-Ghazālī considers this love

to be an ideal pattern for true love on the human plane because it seeks no advantage other than the perception of the beautiful object. It does not constitute the "love for the sake of God" prescribed by the Prophet, however, since it is possible among unbelievers as well as believers (*ibid.*, XIV, pp. 47–48; V, p. 149).

106. Plotinus *Enneads* i. 6. 1; trans. MacKenna and Page. Cf. Aristotle *Metaphysics* xiii. 3. 1078a-b.

107. *Rawḍa*, p. 231.

108. *Ibid.*, pp. 231–57. The multiple-approaches method Ibn al-Qayyim uses here and, for example, in treating the definition of love is perhaps a fundamental correlate of *nomos* religion, if not its genitor. It is as foreign to Greek discursive thought as *nomos* is to *eros.*

109. *Rawḍa*, p. 222. Cf., e.g., Ibn Ḥazm, *Ṭawq*, Ar., p. 330; Fr., p. 331.

110. *Rawḍa*, p. 220; *Fawā'id*, p. 184.

111. *Rawḍa*, pp. 220–21. The wearing of silken garments is to be praised or blamed on the same grounds (*Fawā'id*, p. 186).

112. Al-Dabbāgh expresses himself in a variety of ways, but this seems to be his meaning. See his *Mashāriq*, pp. 42, 118–19, 100, 123, 125. His distinction between universal and absolute beauty is probably as old as Plato. Diotima appears to separate the universal from the divine beaty —beauty itself (Plato *Symposium* 210–12, esp. 211e–212a).

113. *Dā'*, p. 352; *Rawḍa*, pp. 88–89.

114. *Ighātha*, p. 306.

115. See Ritter, *Meer*, p. 480, quoting Ibn al-ʿArabī's statement of this doctrine in the *Futūḥāt* ([Cairo, 1329], II, p. 542). Cf. al-Dabbāgh, *Mashāriq*, p. 119.

116. *Ṭarīq*, p. 414.

117. *Ibid.*, p. 413; *Miftāḥ*, I, p. 87.

118. *Madārij*, III, p. 225.

119. *Ṭarīq*, pp. 367, 412; *Miftāḥ*, I, p. 184.

CHAPTER EIGHT

1. *Rawḍa*, pp. 88–89.

2. *Ibid.*, p. 88. Ibn Dāwūd seems to have held this view. He notes that, according to the poets, hearing (*samāʿ*) is the partner of *naẓar* (*Zahra*, p. 14). Ibn Ḥazm expressed a more qualified opinion, arguing that the love conceived on hearing a description is not real and that it will either increase or disappear when the person is actually seen (*Ṭawq*, Ar., p. 52; Fr. p. 53). The twelfth-century Provençal poet Jaufre Rudel, whose case may be cited by way of comparison, is reported to have been stricken with love for a certain Countess of Tripoli without having seen her. In his verse he celebrates a faraway love whom he declares never to have seen. Cf. the three poems by Rudel in André Berry, *Anthologie de la poésie occitane*, Provençal texts with French translations (Paris: Stock, 1961), pp. 7–11, esp. the third piece, line 10.

3. *Dā'*, p. 289.

4. *Ibid.*, p. 352; *Rawḍa*, p. 89.

5. In one strictly religious context Ibn al-Qayyim gives a list of ten "causes" involving the subject which lead to love for God, but most of these are actually spiritual exercises intended to *increase* love. Examples are the reading of the Koran with understanding, the performance of canonical obligations and supererogatory works, remembrance of God in every circumstance, having a contrite heart before him, and association with those who truly love him. Contemplation of the divine attributes and beneficence, which may be a true cause of sacred love, is also recommended. See *Madārij*, III, pp. 11–12.

6. Cf. Ibn Dāwūd, *Zahra*, pp. 2, 322–23, holding that only love by choice is to be blamed; al-Masʿūdī, *Murūj*, VI, p. 376; and Hazo, *The idea of love*, pp. 84–86, for a different aspect of the question occurring in Western literature. The Muslim controversy seems inspired ultimately by Aristotle. Cf. *Ethics* iii. 1–5. 1109b–1115a.
7. *Rawḍa*, pp. 144–48.
8. Cf. Aristotle *Ethics* iii. 5. 1114a.
9. *Rawḍa*, p. 149; also, *Shifāʾ al-ʿalīl*, p. 195.
10. *Ṭarīq*, pp. 6–7, 10. A parallel distinction involving patience (*ṣabr*, patient endurance) is made by Ibn al-Qayyim in his *ʿUddat al-ṣābirīn* ([Cairo: Dār al-ʿUṣūr li-l-Ṭibāʿa wa-l-Nashr, Muḥammad ʿAlī Ṣubayḥ, n.d.], pp. 28–29).
11. Ibn al-Qayyim records a fictional dispute between the heart and the eye over which of them is responsible for the conception of love. The liver intervenes to show them that their case is analogous to that of a cripple and a blind man who cooperate to steal fruit from a tree, the blind man carrying the cripple on his shoulders. *Rawḍa*, pp. 104–110. This ancient analogy is attributed to Salmān al-Fārisī. See Merlin S. Swartz, ed. and trans., *Ibn al-Jawzī's Kitāb al-quṣṣāṣ wa'l-mudhakkirīn* ("Recherches publiées sous la direction de l'Institut de Lettres Orientales de Beyrouth," série I: Pensée arabe et musulmane, XLVII; Beirut: Dar el-Machreq Éditeurs, 1971), Ar., p. 48; Engl., p. 130.
12. *Rawḍa*, p. 116.
13. Al-Jāḥiẓ, *Qiyān, Rasāʾil*, II, p. 154. The word *ḥashwīya* seems to have signified those whose scholarship was useless and prolix as well as those who accepted the traditions containing crudely anthropomorphic descriptions of God. The term was applied contemptuously by the Muʿtazilites to the majority of the orthodox traditionist party. See *EI*[1] and *EI*[2], s.v.
14. See, esp., al-Jāḥiẓ, *Qiyān, Rasāʾil*, II, pp. 149, 151, 152–54, 157.
15. *Ibid.*, pp. 160–62.
16. *Ibid.*, pp. 163–64.
17. Ibn Dāwūd, *Zahra*, p. 29.
18. See p. 26.
19. Ibn Ḥazm, *Ṭawq*, p. 92.
20. *Ibid.*, p. 80.
21. *Ibid.*, p. 116.
22. *Ibid.*, p. 322.
23. Cf. Andreas Capellanus's concluding section on "The rejection of love" in his *De arte honeste amandi* (*The art of courtly love*, trans. John Jay Parry [New York: Ungar, 1964], pp. 187–212).
24. See*Rawḍa*, p. 117.
25. Ibn Ḥazm, *al-Akhlāq wa-l-siyar*, Ar., pp. 30–31; Fr., p. 33.
26. Trans. Mawlānā Muḥammad ʿAlī.
27. *Rawḍa*, p. 111.
28. Trans. Mawlānā Muḥammad ʿAlī.
29. *Rawḍa*, pp. 121–22, referring to Koran 24:30–31.
30. *Ibid.*, pp. 111–12.
31. Cf. Ibn al-Qayyim's remarks in *Kitāb al-rūḥ* to the effect that ugly or diseased bodies are generally accompanied by ugly or diseased spirits, while the opposite is the case with beautiful bodies (pp. 65–66).
32. Rawḍa, pp. 123–24. Cf. above, p. 33.
33. *Ibid.*, p. 160.
34. *Ibid.*, pp. 112–16. Some of the same examples as well as a number of others were recorded by al-Daylamī (*ʿAṭf*, pp. 57–63).
35. *Responsa* ascribed to al-Shāfiʿī (*Rawḍa*, pp. 112–14); to Mālik (*ibid.*, p. 114); to Ibn Ḥanbal and Abū Ḥanīfa (*ibid.*, p. 115).
36. *Ibid.*, p. 115.
37. *Ibid.*, pp. 85–86, on two lines attributed to al-Shāfiʿī, and pp. 115–16. 129 on a

fatwā purport to be from the noted Egyptian Ḥanafite Aḥmad b. Muḥammad al-Ṭaḥāwī (d. 321/933).

38. *Ibid.*, pp. 117–19.

39. Sexual relations by night are permitted during fasts (Koran 2:187). Ibn ʿAbbās is reported to have said that intercourse with one's slave-girl (*ama*) is preferable to masturbation, while the latter is preferable to fornication (al-Ghazālī, *Iḥyā'*, IV, pp. 110–11). Al-Ghazālī remarks that both fornication and masturbation, none the less, are forbidden (*ibid.*).

40. *Rawḍa*, pp. 119–20.

41. *Ibid.*, p. 131.

42. *Ibid.*, pp. 132–33. Cf. a similar argument in the *Miftāḥ*, stressing that God's law takes into consideration man's best interests (II, pp. 22–23).

43. *Rawḍa*, p. 134. In another chapter Ibn al-Qayyim recognizes, again without committing himself, that some authorities admit even embracing and kissing an *ajnabīya* as cures for a lover's emaciation, holding these acts to be lesser evils than the use of wine in medical treatment (*ibid.*, pp. 377–78). Perhaps the scholar has allowed himself to be carried away by his subject here (mercy and intercession for lovers), for we have seen that he specifically rejects kissing and embracing together with *naẓar* earlier in the work (p. 133). His position on masturbation cited in the text is roughly that given by Ibn ʿAqīl in his *Fuṣūl*, which is quoted and commented on by Ibn al-Qayyim in *Badā'iʿ al-fawā'id* (IV, pp. 97–98).

44. *Rawḍa*, pp. 91–92; Ibn al-Jawzī, *Dhamm*, p. 104.

45. The version of the *ḥadīth* cited here differs slightly from that related by Ibn Dāwūd (cf. above, p. 89).

46. *Rawḍa*, p. 86.

47. Cf. the distinction between the solaces of the upper and lower parts made by Andreas Capellanus (*The art of courtly love*, pp. 135–36).

48. *Rawḍa*, pp. 83–85. The edition I have used has "*yaʿqid*" for "*yaqʿud*" (he sits) in the text of al-Aṣmaʿī's anecdote and unnecessarily vocalizes "*yajhad*" (presses to the limit) as "*yujhid*" (p. 84). The description of urban love in which these words occur is borrowed from a *ṣaḥīḥ* tradition on ablutions. I have made my translation after correcting the text in accordance with this *ḥadīth* and another version of the anecdote cited by Ibn al-Jawzī. Cf. Ibn Qayyim al-Jawzīya [error for Ibn al-Jawzī], *Akhbār al-nisā'* (n.p.: Dār al-Fikr, n.d.), pp. 39–40. The expression "*shuʿabihā 'l-arbaʿ*" (lit., "her four branches") was understood variously by Muslim scholars to mean: her arms and legs, her thighs and shanks, her labia majora and minora, or her legs and labia majora. See *Ṣaḥīḥ Muslim*, cmt. al-Nawawī, IV (Cairo: al-Maṭbaʿa al-Miṣrīya, 1347/1929), pp. 39–40; *Lisān al-ʿArab* (Būlāq), art. "*SH-ʿ-B*," I, p. 484; art. "*J-H-D*," IV, p. 108.

49. Ibn Dāwūd, *Zahra*, p. 66.

50. *Ibid.*, p. 136. See also the introduction (*ibid.*, p. 1).

51. Ibn Ḥazm, *Ṭawq*, pp. 158–60.

52. *Ibid.*, pp. 172, 178.

53. There is the following consideration, however. The copyist's comment at the end of the extant manuscript of the *Ṭawq* (ed. Bercher, p. 408) clearly indicates that much of the poetry originally included by Ibn Ḥazm has been deleted. Perhaps the text has been abridged or altered in other ways as well. The manuscript, completed in 738 A.H., is presumably later than the one used by Ibn al-Qayyim, if, indeed, the Ḥanbalite scholar knew the entire work firsthand.

54. *Rawḍa*, p. 85.

55. *Ṭibb*, pp. 214–15; *Dā'*, pp. 353–55; *Rawḍa*, pp. 180–82.

56. *Ṭibb*, p. 213.

57. *Ibid.*, p. 213; *Dā'*, p. 355; *Rawḍa*, p. 181.

58. *Ṭibb*, p. 213.

59. *Rawḍa*, p. 182; *Dā'*, pp. 353–55.

60. *Dā'*, p. 355. The translation of the Koranic passage is my own, adapted from Régis Blachère and Mawlānā Muḥammad ʿAlī. The partisans of *naẓar*, it is reasonable to assume, are not among those referred to by the verses. For a more complete discussion of the *ḥadīth* "*Man ʿashiqa* . . . ," see Giffen, *Theory*, pp. 99–115. As Professor Jaroslav Stetkevych has pointed out to me, the *ḥadīth* was already sufficiently familiar by the time of Bashshār b. Burd (d. 167–68/783–85) to be reflected in several verses of that poet's *Dīwān*, as the following:

    Wa-li-l-khayri asbābun, wa-li-l-ʿayni fitnatun;
      wa-man māta min ḥubbi 'l-nisā'i shahīdū.
    Wa-bayḍā'a miksālin ka-anna ḥadīthahā
      idhā ulqiyat minhu 'l-ʿuyūnu barūdū.

    The good has its means, the eye its sedition;
      he who dies from love of womankind is a martyr.
    That [or, many a] idle, white-skinned wench whose conversation,
      when its choicest bits [eyes] were uttered, seemed cooling
        collyrium [or, embroidered cloaks (*burūd*)].

By a skillful play on words, the poet has linked the second verse with the first. Beginning with "whose conversation," the second verse might be translated, "whose prophetic tradition (*ḥadīth*), when its prime utterances (*ʿuyūn*) were revealed (*ulqiyat* [cf. Koran 28:86]). . . ." See *Dīwān Bashshār b. Burd*, ed. Muḥammad al-Ṭāhir Ibn ʿĀshūr, II (Cairo: Lajnat al-Ta'līf wa-l-Tarjama wa-l-Nashr, 1373/1954), p. 162, ll. 7, 8; cf., also, *ibid.*, p. 218, l. 4.

61. *Rawḍa*, pp. 342–43. Three other motives given by Ibn al-Qayyim in this context, although expressed in more general terms, would seem to parallel the first three. These are nobility of character and high aims, desire to procure the pleasure of chastity (which according to the author is greater than that of satisfying one's desires), and knowledge of the evil consequences of illicit pleasures. By the pleasure of chastity Ibn al-Qayyim presumably means the pleasure of obedience to the divine command. Later in the *Rawḍa* the three primary motives are listed again as love for God, love for the houris, and fear (p. 436).

62. *Ibid.*, p. 83.

63. *Ibid.*, pp. 87–88.

64. *Ibid.*, pp. 69, 75.

65. *Ibid.*, pp. 77–78.

66. *Ighātha*, p. 304.

67. *Ibid.*, p. 305.

68. Cf. *ibid.*, pp. 10, 21.

69. Cf. Ritter, *Meer*, pp. 443–47. According to a common *ḥadīth*, dating in Ritter's opinion at the latest from the mid-second century A.H., the Prophet saw God in the form of a beardless youth (*ibid.*, pp. 445–46). It is interesting to find the name of Ibn ʿAbbās in the *isnād* of this tradition. Ibn al-Qayyim, as has been seen above, makes this Companion the source of "*Man ʿashiqa* . . . ," and a saying to the effect that neither blood-money nor retaliation is due when a man is killed by love is also ascribed to him (Ibn Ḥazm, *Ṭawq*, p. 14). According to another *ḥadīth*, those dwelling in Paradise are without beards (Ritter, *Meer*, p. 351). Ritter relates from al-Baghdādī's (d. 1093/1682) *Khizānat al-adab* ([Būlāq, 1291], IV, p. 157) a story which implies that the early Arabs felt the love of youths to be Persian in origin. The Arab poet Ṭulayḥa, on a visit to the Sassanid court, could not understand how the Iranian monarch could become excited over the description of a boy holding a rose (cf. the anecdote about Aḥmad al-Ghazālī, above, p. 23), while the king failed to

comprehend the Arab's weeping over the traces of his beloved's campsite (*Meer*, p. 351). The same homosexual *naẓar* motif, at times with religious overtones, is found in the dialogues of Plato. Phaedrus argues against Aeschylus that Achilles must have been the beloved of Patroclus, not the reverse, since Achilles was the more beautiful of the two and still beardless (*Symposium* 179–80). In the *Laws*, the Athenian advances that there are two types of love for youths—one which seeks a physical fulfillment and another which is satisfied with looking (*Laws* viii. 837). Two remarks by Socrates in the *Phaedrus* are likewise relevant: "But he whose initiation is recent, and who has been the spectator of many glories in the other world, is amazed when he sees any one having a godlike face or form, . . . then looking upon the face of his beloved as of a God he reverences him. . . ." (*Phaedrus* 251; trans. Jowett). Also, "Every one chooses his love from the ranks of beauty according to his character, and this he makes his god, and fashions and adorns as a sort of image which he is to fall down and worship" (*ibid.* 252).

70. Ibn al-ʿArabī, *Futūḥāt*, II, pp. 190–92; Ritter, *Meer*, pp. 352, 480.
71. Al-Daylamī, *ʿAṭf*, pp. 108–110. Cf. Ibn Sīnā's similar view. According to the philosopher, the pleasure experienced in beholding a beautiful form is ennobling as long as both the animal and the rational souls are involved. Beautiful forms are nearer to the First Beloved. Ibn Sīnā, *Risāla fī 'l-ʿishq*, ed. Mehren, in *Traités mystiques d'Aboû Alî al-Hosain b. Abdallâh b. Sînâ*, Ar., p. 15; Fr., p. 8.
72. Al-Dabbāgh, *Mashāriq*, pp. 110–13.
73. *Ibid.*, pp. 113–14.
74. *Ibid.*, pp. 116–17.
75. Al-Muḥāsibī, *Mustarshidīn*, pp. 69–70. The same for song and music: whatever it is forbidden to speak of or to look at, it is likewise forbidden to listen to (*ibid.*, p. 70).
76. Ritter, *Meer*, pp. 461–62.
77. *Ibid.*, p. 471.
78. Al-Hujwīrī, *Kashf*, pp. 416–17. Al-Hujwīrī's approach to song is more qualified: it is lawful or unlawful according to its effect on the mind (*ibid.*, pp. 401–402).
79. Al-Ghazālī, *Iḥyā'*, IX, p. 187. Al-Ghazālī is less stringent regarding song and music: their lawfulness depends on the object towards which they excite love. This is generally an evil object, but the fault does not lie in the essence of music itself (*ibid.*, VI, p. 155).
80. Massignon, *Passion*, p. 796.
81. See p. 23. For a further discussion of the *shāhid* teaching and its development in the Persian language domain, see Ritter, *Meer*, esp. pp. 470–77, where quotations from a variety of sources are collected.
82. See, e.g., *Dā'*, p. 142; *Ighātha*, p. 297. Cf. Ibn Taymīya, *al-Waṣīya al-kubrā*, *MRK*, I, pp. 295–96.
83. *Dā'*, p. 142.
84. *Ighātha*, pp. 297–98.
85. *Ibid.*, p. 306; also *Rawḍa*, p. 122.
86. Ibn Taymīya, *al-Radd ʿalā Ibn ʿArabī wa-l-ṣūfīya*, p. 56; cited by Ritter (*Meer*, pp. 476–77).
87. See Ibn Taymīya's view in al-Manbijī, *Kitāb al-samāʿ wa-l-raqṣ*, *MRK*, I, pp. 285–86, and Ibn al-Qayyim's, stated more briefly, in *Dā'*, p. 142.
88. *Rawḍa*, p. 123.
89. *Ighātha*, pp. 298, 306.
90. *Dā'*, p. 191.
91. Ibn al-Qayyim quoting Ibn Taymīya (*Rawḍa*, pp. 122–23).
92. *Ibid.*, p. 123.
93. Ibn Taymīya's great concern with the ethical implications of this philosophy have already been discussed (pp. 89–91).
94. Cf. al-Manbijī, *Kitāb al-samāʿ wa-l-raqṣ*, *MRK*, I, p. 285.

95. *Madārij*, III, pp. 49, 144, 155–62; Ibn Taymīya, *Risāla fī ibṭāl waḥdat al-wujūd, MRM*, I, p. 99.
96. Cf. the traditions related by Ibn al-Qayyim in the *Rawḍa* (pp. 417ff.).
97. *Ṣawā'iq*, pp. 179–80.
98. *Ṭarīq*, pp. 71–72; *Madārij*, II, pp. 204ff.; III, p. 15.
99. *Dā'*, p. 340; *Miftāḥ*, II, p. 123; *Madārij*, II, p. 43; *Ighātha*, p. 18. Same opinion expressed by al-Ghazālī (*Iḥyā'*, XIV, p. 62).
100. *Miftāḥ*, II, p. 123.
101. *Ighātha*, p. 18. Same opinion again in al-Ghazālī (*Iḥyā'*, XIV, p. 73).
102. *Dā'*, pp. 340–42.
103. Massignon, *Passion*, pp. 38–39.
104. Al-Muḥāsibī, *Faṣl fī 'l-maḥabba*, in Abū Nu'aym al-Iṣfahānī, *Ḥilya*, X, p. 82.
105. Islamic asceticism and mysticism seem to have been nurtured by the same environment that gave birth to Ḥanbalism. Men like al-Junayd and even Abū Ḥamza could be at the same time mystics and companions of Aḥmad b. Ḥanbal.
106. Al-Muḥāsibī, *Faṣl fī 'l-maḥabba* in Abū Nu'aym, *Ḥilya*, X, pp. 84, 81. On al-Burjulānī, see Ibn Abī Ya'lā, *Ṭabaqāt*, I, pp. 290–91. As formulated by Massignon, the opinion of Ibn 'Aṭā' and al-Ḥallāj suggests only that the vision is the *principal* joy of Paradise. It does not necessarily imply that the other joys of the afterlife should be renounced. But Massignon's wording ought not perhaps to be taken at face value. If anything, the Ḥallājian doctrine must have been stronger than that of al-Muḥāsibī.
107. *Madārij*, II, p. 43; above, p. 86.
108. *Ibid.*, p. 45.
109. Chapter five, pp. 83–84.
110. "Inna a'lā ahli 'l-jannati . . . ," cited in *Madārij*, III, p. 35. If it is simply the case that God allows this much and no more to the blessed, then some explanation of why the lesser pleasures of Paradise do not seem painful or at best boring by comparison might be expected. Certainly Ibn al-Qayyim acknowledges in this same context that men will long intensely for the vision between occurrences (cf. p. 169). But to my knowledge, the consideration I have suggested is lacking in Neo-Ḥanbalite writings.

CHAPTER NINE

1. *Rawḍa*, p. 14; Giffen, *Theory*, pp. 87–90. Giffen presents evidence to suggest that Ibn al-Qayyim took the list either from *al-Wāḍiḥ al-mubīn fī dhikr man ustushhida min al-muḥibbīn* (*Mughulṭai's biographical dictionary of the martyrs of love*) (Part I, ed. Otto Spies, Delhi, 1936) by his contemporary 'Alā' al-Dīn Abū 'Abd Allāh Mughulṭāy (d. 762/1360)—seen as the most likely source (cf. *Wāḍiḥ*, pp. 51–52)—or from Maḥmūd b. Sulaymān al-Ḥalabī's *Manāzil al-aḥbāb*. Possibly Ibn al-Qayyim knew both works. In any case he unquestionably became familiar with al-Ḥalabī's *Manāzil* at some point, probably well before he wrote the *Rawḍa*. In *al-Dā' wa-l-dawā'* he mentions the *Manāzil* by name in a section which is clearly indebted to that work (*Dā'*, pp. 323–26, esp. p. 326; cf. *Manāzil al-aḥbāb*, MS Top Kapı, Ahmet III, 2471, fols. 25b–27a, esp. fol. 27a, the marginal addition from another MS). Al-Ḥalabī, but not his work, is also mentioned in the *Rawḍa*, where some lines of his poetry are quoted (pp. 344–45). Ibn al-Qayyim's list has been considerably rearranged but reflects the order of that given in the *Manāzil* sufficiently to suggest the possibility of filiation. The scholar drops items 6, 12, 16, 22, 23, 30, 35–38, 41, 42, 44, 46, 49–51, 56, and 58–62 of al-Ḥalabī's list and adds a number of others, some apparently from Mulghulṭāy's work and some, like *'alāqa*,

hawā, *shawq*, and, particularly, *khulla* (Mulghulṭāy has the form *mukhālala*), which are terms fundamental to his own hierarchies of the stages of love. Cf. *Rawḍa*, p. 14 (where *sha'af*, although defined later like the other terms [p. 23], has been inadvertently omitted) and *Manāzil al-aḥbāb*, fol. 13a.

2. *Rawḍa*, pp. 18–52, esp. pp. 45–47, 51–52.
3. *Ibid.*, p. 75, also, p. 69. Cf. Aristotle *Ethics* viii. 1. 1156a.
4. Cf. al-Dabbāgh, *Mashāriq*, pp. 30–31.
5. *Ṭibb*, pp. 209–210. Perhaps Ibn al-Qayyim originally wrote that love for the sake of an end to be obtained from the beloved is "purposive" (*gharaḍī*) rather than "accidental" (*'araḍī*). The mere disappearance of a dot over the letter *ghayn* would result in the word's being read as "accidental."
6. *Ṭarīq*, pp. 384–85; also, *Miftāḥ*, I, p. 6.
7. Aristotle *Ethics* viii. 7. 1159a; trans. W. D. Ross.
8. Al-Ghazālī, *Iḥyā'*, V, pp. 147, 149, 154; XIV, pp. 47–48, 50, and esp. p. 45.
9. *Ibid.*, XIV, p. 51.
10. *Ṭarīq*, pp. 6–7; cf. above, p. 126.
11. *Miftāḥ*, I, p. 6.
12. *Ṭarīq*, p. 73.
13. *Dā'*, pp. 339–41.
14. *Ighātha*, p. 287. Cf. *Rawḍa*, pp. 55ff.
15. *Ighātha*, p. 295; *Dā'*, pp. 297–98.
16. *Ighātha*, p. 295.
17. See pp. 69–70.
18. *Ṭarīq*, pp. 385–88. In the same vein, Ibn al-Qayyim argues elsewhere that men only do good to each other for the sake of some personal advantage in this life or the next. If a man sees no advantage for himself, he will not do good to others; for in reality he only desires to do good to himself, exploiting his kindness to another as a means (*Ighātha*, p. 22). In an earlier work the scholar contrasted this human egocentrism with divine self-sufficiency: "Whoever among men loves you and is loved by you desires you only for his own sake and for an end which he anticipates from you; but God loves you for yourself" (*Dā'*, p. 336). For Aristotle's justification of self-sacrifice in egocentric terms, see *Ethics* ix. 8. 1169a-b.
19. *Ṭarīq*, pp. 389–90.
20. See p. 144.
21. See pp. 86–87.
22. "Thalāthun man kunna fī-hi wajada bi-hinna ḥalāwata 'l-īmān: . . . ," translated here as cited by Ibn al-Qayyim in *Rawḍa*, pp. 199–200, and *Madārij*, III, p. 55. Cf., however, *Ighātha*, pp. 292–93, and Muslim, *Imān*, 66. This division is also used by al-Ghazālī, at least in part (cf. *Iḥyā'*, V, pp. 151–53; above, chapter seven, n. 105.
23. *Rūḥ*, p. 434; *Rawḍa*, pp. 292–93.
24. *Rawḍa*, p. 293; *Rūḥ*, p. 434.
25. In *al-Dā' wa-l-dawā'* love for what God loves is called one of the "accompaniments" or inseparable attributes (*lawāzim*) of love "in" and "for the sake of" God, a distinction which allows the author to deal with it as a fourth category (*Dā'*, pp. 276–77).
26. *Rūḥ*, pp. 434–36.
27. *Ighātha*, p. 297.
28. See pp. 164–65.
29. See p. 151.
30. *Dā'*, pp. 333, 344.
31. *Ibid.*, p. 351.
32. *Ibid.*, pp. 346–51; *Ighātha*, pp. 296–97; *Rawḍa*, p. 202.
33. *Fawā'id*, pp. 198–99.

34. Mir Valiuddin, *Love of God, the Sufi approach* (Delhi, 1968), pp. 2–6, 11–40. The list dealt with by Dr. Valiuddin at greatest length consists of ten stages, each divided into five phases. For the most part the material represents a recapitulation of an earlier work; but, significantly, the author states that he has made additions of his own which he hopes will prove useful. The ten basic stages with Dr. Valiuddin's English equivalents are as follows: (1) *ulfa* (attachment); (2) *ṣadāqa* (truth); (3) *mawadda* (". . . marked by the excitation of the heart and passionate desire for the Beloved"); (4) *hawā* (passionate desire); (5) *shaghaf* (violent affection); (6) *khulla* (exclusive attachment to the Beloved); (7) *maḥabba* (affection); (8) "Love" [= *ʿishq*] (excessive and intense affection); (9) *taim* [= *tatayyum*] (enslavement); (10) walah (bewilderment). This list, employed by a modern religious scholar, is strikingly similar to some of the medieval arrangements of profane love-terminology given below, notably in the order of the last three items and the low ranking of *khulla* (see tables 1, A; 3, A, D; 4, A, B, C).
35. Cf. preceding note.
36. Marʿī b. Yūsuf, *Munyat al-muḥibbīn*, MS Dār al-Kutub, Adab 6252, fol. 8a.
37. See p. 161.
38. Koran 4:125," And God took Abraham as his friend (wa-ttakhdha 'llāhu Ibrāhīma khalīlan)." Cf. II Chron. 20:7; Isaiah 41:8; James 2:21–23.
39. Cf. Ibn Dāwūd, *Zahra*, p. 19.
40. See Georges Vajda, *L'amour de Dieu dans la théologie juive*, on the remembrance of Abraham's sacrifice as an act of love in Jewish liturgy and in the Midrash (pp. 10, 43) and likewise on the use of the word *ōhēb* in the Dead Sea scrolls as an epithet for Isaac and Jacob as well as for Abraham (p. 28).
41. Al-Muḥāsibī, *Faṣl fī 'l-maḥabba*, in Abū Nuʿaym, *Ḥilya*, X, p. 81.
42. *Madārij*, I, p. 50; Ibn Taymīya, *Irāda*, *MRK*, I, p. 372.
43. "Inna 'llāha 'ttakhadhanī khalīlan ka-mā 'ttakhadha Ibrāhīma khalīlan."
44. Ibn al-Qayyim, *Jalā' al-afhām fī 'l-ṣalāh wa-l-salām ʿalā khayr al-anām* (Cairo: Idārat al-Ṭibāʿa al-Munīrīya, 1357/1938–39), p. 70; *Ṭarīq*, pp. 306, 381, 413. Cf. Ibn Taymīya, *Irāda*, *MRK*, I, p. 372.
45. *Dā'*, pp. 277–78; *Rawḍa*, p. 46; *Miftāḥ*, II, p. 32; *Jalā' al-afhām*, p. 184; *Badā'iʿ al-fawā'id*, III, p. 223; *Madārij*, III, pp. 19–20.
46. Ibn Dāwūd, *Zahra*, p. 19.
47. Ibn al-ʿArabī, *Tarjumān al-ashwāq* (Beirut: Dār Ṣādir, Dār Bayrūt, 1381/1961), p. 44; cf. trans. Nicholson, p. 69.
48. *Dā'*, p. 278; *Rawḍa*, p. 47; *Madārij*, III, p. 19.
49. Ibn al-ʿArabī, *Tarjumān*, p. 59; trans. Nicholson, p. 77.
50. Cf. p. 88.
51. Aristotle *Ethics* viii. 6. 1158a; trans. W. D. Ross.
52. *Dā'*, p. 312; *Rawḍa*, pp. 25, 26; *Madārij*, III, pp. 18–19. Examples of earlier authors who advance this definition or ones similar are al-Jāḥiẓ (cited by Ibn al-Qayyim, *Rawḍa*, p. 138), Ibn Ḥazm (*Ṭawq*, p. 66), al-Ghazālī (*Iḥyā'*, VI, p. 156), and al-Dabbāgh (*Mashāriq*, p. 96).
53. *Rawḍa*, pp. 289–90.
54. Cf. Ibn Ḥazm, *Ṭawq*, pp. 66–68.
55. *Ighātha*, p. 36.
56. See chapter one, pp. 4–5.
57. *Ṭibb*, pp. 208–210.
58. *Ighātha*, p. 305.
59. In fact, Ibn al-Qayyim is somewhat inconsistent on this point. At times he states that the occurrence of *ʿishq* depends equally on finding an object beautiful (*istiḥsān*) and on desiring it (*ṭamaʿ*) (*Ṭibb*, p. 208; *Dā'*, p. 318). Elsewhere he contradicts this view, once only a few pages after having advanced it. There are various types of *ʿishq*-

lovers, he proposes, not all of whom necessarily desire their beloveds (*Dā'*, p. 352; *Rawḍa*, pp. 88–89). Ibn Ḥazm expresses the opinion that all loves are in some way a function of *ṭamaʿ* (*Kitāb al-akhlāq wa-l-siyar*, Ar., pp. 47–48; Fr., p. 57).

60. *Dā'*, p. 259, *Ighātha*, p. 303; *Ṭibb*, pp. 206, 210. Cf. Ovid *Remedia amoris* ll. 81–82, 91–92.
61. *Ṭibb*, p. 208; *Rawḍa*, p. 138; *Dā'*, p. 309.
62. *Dā'*, pp. 310–12.
63. *Ibid.*, pp. 351–52; *Ṭibb*, pp. 213–14; *Rawḍa*, pp. 199–202; *Ighātha*, pp. 292, 296–97.
64. *Dā'*, p. 304.
65. *Ighātha*, p. 302. The word *ʿishq* itself is not used in the Koran, but Ibn al-Qayyim takes it to be implied by the stories in question (Koran 12:21–35; 7:80–81; 11:77–83; 15:61–74).
66. *Ighātha*, p. 297.
67. *Ibid.*, pp. 286–307. *ʿIshq* when it reaches the stage of idolatry is a far greater sin than either fornication or sodomy, and when it accompanies these practices, it renders them more heinous in the sight of God (*ibid.*, pp. 36, 302; *Dā'*, p. 308).
68. *Ighātha*, pp. 306–307. Cf. Koran 2:165.
69. *Shirk* is the greatest of sins according to Ibn al-Qayyim, and the principle of *shirk* is the devotion of love to more than one object: "Wa-aṣlu 'l-shirki bi-llāh, al-ishrāku fī 'l-maḥabba" (*Dā'*, p. 274).
70. *Ighātha*, p. 330.
71. In the context of another scheme of dividing the types of love—into common or "shared" loves (*mushtaraka*) and particular love (*khāṣṣa*), Ibn al-Qayyim says that there are three kinds of shared love which are appropriate in man and do not imply *shirk*: (1) natural shared love for food and drink; (2) the love of mercy and concern (*raḥma* and *ishfāq*), e.g., the love of a father for his child; and (3) the love of sociability (*uns wa-alf*). These three do not necessarily imply magnification (*taʿẓīm*) of the beloved. Particular love, which requires self-abasement and magnification of the beloved, should be devoted to God alone. *Ṭarīq*, p. 382. Cf. *Dā'*, pp. 307–308.
72. See p. 151.
73. Massignon, *Essai sur les origines du lexique technique de la mystique musulmane* (new ed.; Paris: J. Vrin, 1954), pp. 195–96, 214. Cf. Ritter, *Meer*, p. 560. For the Ḥanbalites, ʿAbd al-Wāḥid b. Zayd was unreliable as an authority on prophetic tradition (*matrūk al-ḥadīth*) (al-Dhahabī, *ʿIbar*, I, p. 270).
74. Al-Daylamī, *ʿAṭf*, p. 5. See *ibid.*, p. 18, for the opinion attributed to al-Junayd.
75. *Ibid.*, pp. 5, 20.
76. Al-Hujwīrī, *Kashf*, trans. Nicholson, p. 310.
77. Al-Ghazālī, *Iḥyā'*, VI, pp. 156–58.
78. See pp. 24–25.
79. Al-Ghazālī, *Iḥyā'*, VIII, p. 183; *Mīzān al-ʿamal*, ed. Sulaymān Dunyā (Cairo: Dār al-Maʿārif, 1964), p. 317.
80. See p. 80 and n. 41.
81. *Rawḍa*, p. 199.
82. *Ṭarīq*, pp. 426–29; *Rawḍa*, p. 26; *Madārij*, III, p. 19; *Ighātha*, p. 292.
83. Cf. *Madārij*, III, p. 19.
84. *Dā'*, p. 267; *Rawḍa*, pp. 28–29. Cf. Giffen, *Theory*, p. 93, on the discussion in the *Rawḍa*.
85. Cf. *Madārij*, II, p. 29.
86. *Ṭarīq*, pp. 424–26; *Madārij*, III, p. 33.
87. "Ṭala shawqu 'l-abrāri ilā liqā'ī, wa-anā ilā liqā'ihim ashwaq" (cited in *Dā'*, p. 267).
88. *Ṭarīq*, pp. 426–29.
89. "Allāhumma bi-ʿilmika 'l-ghayb . . ."
90. Al-Anṣārī, *Manāzil*, Ar., p. 73; Fr., p. 106; *ʿIlal*, in Beaurecueil, *Anṣārī*, pp. 282–83; Ibn al-ʿArīf, *Maḥāsin*, Sp. trans. Asín, p. 37.

91. *Ṭarīq*, p. 431; *Madārij*, III, p. 36.
92. *Madārij*, III, p. 35. The general sequence of Ibn al-Qayyim's discussion as presented here being that followed in *Ṭarīq al-hijratayn*, I have been obliged, for the sake of continuity, to alter slightly the order of this particular argument from the *Madārij* and to neglect its immediate function in that text. Hopefully this has been done without distortion of the author's views.
93. *Ibid.*, III, p. 34.
94. *Ṭarīq*, p. 432. Ibn al-Qayyim also dealt with this question in the *Rawḍa* (p. 29).
95. See pp. 137–38.
96. *Rawḍa*, p. 29.
97. *Ṭarīq*, p. 434.
98. See Ibn Dāwūd, *Zahra*, p. 21; and Ibn al-ʿArabī, *Futūḥāt*, II, p. 364; *Tarjumān*, pp. 82, 186 (cf. Nicholson's paraphrase, p. 89).
99. Al-Anṣārī, *Manāzil*, Ar., p. 74; Fr., pp. 106–107.
100. *Ṭarīq*, pp. 434–37; *Madārij*, III, pp. 36–37.
101. See n. 90.
102. Serge de Beaurecueil, "Une ébauche persane des *'Manāzil as-sā'irīn'*: le *'Kitāb-é ṣad maydān'* de ʿAbdallāh Anṣārī," *Mélanges islamologiques*, II (Cairo: Institut Français d'Archéologie Orientale, 1954), pp. 30–31, 5; Beaurecueil, *Anṣārī*, pp. 194–97.
103. Beaurecueil, "Une ébauche persane," p. 13. See also *ibid.*, pp. 19, 20, on the differing treatment of *tawḥīd*, the profession of divine unity, in the two works. It is also worth remarking that the station of *murūwa* ("virtue" in the etymological sense), treated by al-Anṣārī in *Ṣad maydān* but dropped from the *Manāzil*, is reintroduced by Ibn al-Qayyim in his commentary on the later treatise (*Madārij*, II, pp. 197–98).
104. Beaurecueil, *Anṣārī*, pp. 192–95.
105. Al-Anṣārī, *Manāzil*, Ar., pp. 109–113; Fr., pp. 136–39.
106. Beaurecueil, *Anṣārī*, pp. 284–85.
107. *Ibid.*, p. 144; al-Anṣārī, *Manāzil*, Ar., p. 110; Fr., p. 136.
108. Beaurecueil, *Anṣārī*, pp. 280–81.
109. Cf., e.g., Ibn al-ʿArīf, *Maḥāsin*, Arabic text (Paris, 1933), pp. 91–93 (or *Ṭarīq*, pp. 418, 424), and al-Anṣārī, *Manāzil*, Ar., pp. 71–72, 73–74; *ʿIlal*, in Beaurecueil, *Anṣārī*, pp. 280–83. For further remarks on the *Maḥāsin*, see chapter six, n. 40.
110. Cf. al-Anṣārī, *Manāzil*, pp. 130, n. 1, and 131, n. 1.
111. *Madārij*, I, p. 146; also, I, p. 80; III, p. 337. Cf. the long quote from al-Anṣārī's *Dhamm al-kalām* with French translation given by Beaurecueil (*Anṣārī*, pp. 208–221), especially the ascription to the Jahmites of the view that God is in all things, even in the belly of a dog, the belly of a pig, and entrails (pp. 208–209). Ibn al-Qayyim and his teacher Ibn Taymīya describe the position of al-Tilimsānī and his fellow monists in virtually the same derogatory terms (*Madārij*, III, pp. 288–89; Ibn Taymīya, *Ḥaqīqat madhhab al-ittiḥādīyīn*, *MRM*, II [short ed.], p. 79).
112. *Madārij*, III, p. 139. Beaurecueil translates "*wujūd*" in al-Anṣārī's writings by "découverte" (cf. al-Anṣārī, *Manāzil*, Ar., p. 107; Fr., p. 133).
113. *Madārij*, I, pp. 82–83, 145; III, p. 116.
114. *Ṭarīq*, p. 333; *Madārij*, I, pp. 84–90; III, p. 84. Cf. Ibn Taymīya, *Risāla fī ibṭāl waḥdat al-wujūd*, *MRM*, I, pp. 82–83.
115. *Ṭarīq*, p. 333; *Madārij*, I, p. 83.
116. Commenting on al-Anṣārī's pronouncement to the effect that one who contemplates the divine decree no longer deems good to be good or evil to be evil (*Manāzil*, Ar., p. 11; Fr., p. 55), al-Wāsiṭī explained that in *fanā'* the believer's knowledge of the distinction between good and evil does not come to an end but is merely veiled from him. When he awakes, the earlier stations return to him, firmly established in the new one—*baqā'* (quoted by Ibn al-Qayyim in *Shifā' al-ʿalīl*, pp. 32–34; see esp. p. 33). Ibn al-Qayyim felt compelled to elucidate this commentary in his own terms. An act has two aspects, he remarks, one viewed from God's standpoint as an object

of his decree, in which sense it is always good, and another viewed from man's standpoint as a human act, in which sense it may be either good or evil. Perfection consists in seeing acts in both of these aspects. Some people can do this, the reader is told, while others, those who experience *fanā'*, cannot (*ibid.*, p. 34).

117. *Ṭarīq*, pp. 334–35; *Madārij*, I, p. 84.
118. *Ṭarīq*, p. 335; *Madārij*, I, p. 84.
119. Al-Anṣārī, *Manāzil*, Ar., p. 71; Fr., pp. 104–105.
120. *Ibid.*, Ar., pp. 71–72; Fr., p. 105. On the translation of "tudaqqiqu 'l-ishāra," see *Ṭarīq*, p. 419, and ʿAbd al-Muʿṭī al-Lakhmī al-Iskandarī, *Sharḥ Manāzil al-sā'irīn* (cmt. on al-Anṣārī's *Manāzil* composed at the beginning of the seventh/thirteenth century), ed. S. de Beaurecueil (Cairo: Institut Français d'Archéologie Orientale, 1954), p. 154.
121. Al-Anṣārī, *ʿIlal*, in Beaurecueil, *Anṣārī*, pp. 284–85.
122. Ibn al-ʿArīf, *Maḥāsin*, Sp., p. 40; Ar. (1933), p. 96. Asín's translation has "todos los objetos amables [rendering *maḥābb* in his MS (*maḥabbāt* in the *ʿIlal*)] mueren en el amor de [Dios que es] la Verdad." Ibn al-Qayyim quotes the statement in abbreviated form (*Ṭarīq*, p. 450).
123. *Ṭarīq*, p. 419.
124. *Ibid.*, pp. 415–19; *Madārij*, III, pp. 23–25.
125. See p. 120.
126. *Ṭarīq*, pp. 418–19.
127. Koran 7:143. Cf. al-Kalābādhī, *Taʿarruf*, trans. A. J. Arberry, *The doctrine of the Ṣūfī's* (Cambridge: Cambridge University Press, 1935), p. 123; and Anawati and Gardet, *Mystique musulmane*, pp. 261–71, esp., pp. 267–69.
128. See, e.g., Arthur Jeffery, *Islam* (New York: The Liberal Arts Press, 1958), pp. 38–41.
129. *Ṭarīq*, pp. 419–20. Ibn al-Qayyim uses the same argument against al-Anṣārī regarding the degrees of the station *sirr* (secret). The degree of Moses is *fanā'*; that of Muḥammad, *baqā'* (*Madārij*, III, p. 116).
130. *Madārij*, III, p. 50. Cf. al-Anṣārī, *Manāzil*, Ar., p. 78; Fr., p. 110.
131. Cf. al-Anṣārī, *Manāzil*, Ar., pp. 67–68; Fr., pp. 99–101, on *sakīna*. The first degree is that of the Israelites, received with the Ark of the Covenant. The third is that of Muḥammad and "the believers." A late-eighth-/fourteenth-century commentator of the *Manāzil*, Maḥmūd al-Firkāwī, specifies that the first *sakīna* is that of Moses and Aaron (*Sharḥ Manāzil al-sā'irīn*, ed. Beaurecueil [Cairo: Institut Français d'Archéologie Orientale, 1953], p. 90).
132. *Ṭarīq*, p. 420. Cf. Koran 12:30–31; al-Kalābādhī, *Taʿarruf*, trans. Arberry, pp. 124–25.
133. See p. 164.
134. *Ṭarīq*, pp. 421–22.
135. Cf. Vajda, *L'amour de Dieu dans la théologie juive*, throughout.
136. See, e.g., *Ṭarīq*, pp. 349, 367, 379, 446; *Madārij*, I, p. 292. Cf. al-Anṣārī, *Manāzil*, Ar., p. 20; Fr., pp. 62–63; *ʿIlal*, in Beaurecueil, *Anṣārī*, pp. 278–79; Ibn al-ʿArīf, *Maḥāsin*, Sp. trans. Asín, pp. 27–29.
137. *Ṭarīq*, p. 422.
138. See pp. 89–91.
139. *Ṭarīq*, p. 207.
140. *Ibid.*, pp. 35–36, 392–93, 439; *Madārij*, III, p. 74.
141. *Miftāḥ*, II, p. 111; *Madārij*, II, p. 112; and, esp., *Shifā' al-ʿalīl*, p. 365. In the *Shifā'* Ibn al-Qayyim explains that there are two divine wills and, correspondingly, two kinds of objects of will. The first will is God's (creative) will to act, its object being his act (*fiʿl*), which subsists in him. The second is his (prescriptive) will that man act, and its object (if occurring) is the "object of his act" (*mafʿūl*) and is separate from him. "He may will [prescriptively] that a man act and not will from himself

that he aid him in accomplishing the act," Ibn al-Qayyim adds. This, for example, was the case when God willed that Iblīs (Satan) bow down to Adam but did not will to help him.

142. Especially in the *Rawḍa*; cf. chapters 12, 17, 18, 20, 22, 23, 24, 25, 28, 29.
143. *Rawḍa*, pp. 294–315, 285–87.
144. *Ibid.*, p. 266.
145. See pp. 92, 98, 98–99.

CHAPTER TEN

1. *Dhamm al-hawā*, mentioned in Brockelmann, *S*, II, p. 131.
2. Al-Safārīnī, *Ghidhā' al-albāb*, I, pp. 60–63, 66–73 (cf. Ibn al-Qayyim, *Rawḍa*, pp. 92–101; *Dā'*, pp. 221–23), 74–75 (cf. *Rawḍa*, pp. 91ff., 134–35), 76–79 (cf. *Dā'*, pp. 324–26; *Rawḍa*, pp. 442–43), 79ff. (citing Ibn Taymīya, Ibn al-Jawzī, Ibn ʿAqīl, etc.), 82–83 (cf. *Rawḍa*, pp. 112–13); II, pp. 321–400 (citing Ibn al-Jawzī's *Ṣayd al-khāṭir* and Ibn al-Qayyim's *Rawḍa*, *Madārij*, etc.), 437–440 (cf. *Madārij*, II, pp. 95–99).
3. Sulaymān b. ʿAbd Allāh b. Muḥammad b. ʿAbd al-Wahhāb al-Najdī, *Taysīr al-ʿAzīz al-Ḥamīd fī sharḥ Kitāb al-tawḥīd* (Damascus: al-Maktab al-Islāmī, n.d.), pp. 409–425.
4. Cf. Muḥammad Rashīd Riḍā, *Tafsīr al-Qur'ān al-ḥakīm*, X (2d ed.; Cairo: Maṭbaʿat al-Manār, 1349/1931), pp. 239–40.
5. Cf., e.g., *ibid.*, pp. 232–35, 239–42, esp. p. 241. See also J. Jomier, O.P., *Le Commentaire coranique du Manâr* (Paris: G.-P. Maisonneuve, 1954), pp. 148–50.
6. Ibn al-ʿImād, *Shadharāt al-dhahab* (Cairo: Maktabat al-Qudsī, 1350–51/1931–33), VI, pp. 240–41; Ibn Abī Ḥajala, *Dīwān al-ṣabāba* (on margin of Dāwūd al-Anṭākī, *Tazyīn al-aswāq*; Cairo, 1291/1874), biographical notice on title page abridged from the author's *Maghnāṭīs al-durr al-nafīs*.
7. For a listing of the extant MSS of the *Dīwān al-ṣabāba*, see Brockelmann, *GAL*, II, p. 13 (new ed., pp. 13–14); *S*, II, pp. 5–6. Discussions of the work may be found in Giffen, *Theory*, pp. 38–41, and U. Rizzitano, "Il *Dīwān aṣ-ṣabābah* dello scrittore magrebino Ibn Abī Ḥaǵalah," *Rivista degli studi orientali* 28 (1953): 35–70.
8. Ibn Abī Ḥajala, *Dīwān al-ṣabāba*, I, p. 20; cf. above, pp. 167–68, 170.
9. *Ibid.*, p. 21; cf. above, pp. 159–62.
10. *Ibid.*, pp. 29–33; cf. above, pp. 125–26.
11. *Ibid.*, pp. 35–41; cf. above, pp. 121–22.
12. *Ibid.*, p. 53; cf. above, p. 148.
13. *Ibid.*, pp. 61–63; cf. chapter eight above, n. 11.
14. *Ibid.*, pp. 74, 76ff.; cf. Ibn al-Qayyim, *Rawḍa*, pp. 273–74, 274–75, 294–315.
15. See, e.g., Ibn Abī Ḥajala, *Dīwān al-ṣabāba*, I, pp. 187–88, citing Ibn Taymīya and Ibn al-Qayyim on sexual intercourse.
16. *Ibid.*, p. 95.
17. MSS consulted here are Dār al-Kutub, Adab 6252, copied in 1015 A.H., and my own copy transcribed from Dār al-Kutub, Ṭalʿat, Adab 4648.
18. See p. 192.
19. Marʿī b. Yūsuf, *Munyat al-muḥibbīn wa-bughyat al-ʿāshiqīn*, MS Dār al-Kutub, Adab 6252, fols. 1b–2a.
20. See pp. 186, 192 and n. 43.
21. *Munya*, fol. 2a.
22. All information on Marʿī b. Yūsuf, unless otherwise noted, is taken from al-Muḥibbī, *Khulāṣat al-athar fī aʿyān al-qarn al-ḥādī ʿashar* (Beirut: Maktabat Khayyāṭ, 1966), IV, pp. 358–61. The date of Marʿī's birth is not given by al-Muḥibbī, but it must be

some three decades prior to the year 1015, when one of the MSS of the *Munya* in the Egyptian National Library was copied by a scribe with a Maghribī hand (the MS generally cited in this study).

23. On Muḥammad Ḥijāzī, see al-Muḥibbī, *Khulāṣa*, IV, pp. 174–77.
24. On al-Ghunaymī, see *ibid.*, I, pp. 312–15.
25. On al-Maymūnī, see *ibid.*, pp. 45–46.
26. See chapter one, n. 21.
27. See p. 192 and n. 43.
28. *Munya*, fol. 15a-b. Cf. Ibn al-Jawzī, *Dhamm*, pp. 5–6.
29. *Munya*, fol. 15b.
30. See pp. 15–16.
31. *Munya*, fols. 13a–14b. Cf. Ibn al-Jawzī, *Dhamm*, pp. 12 and, e.g., 16, 17, 30, 31.
32. Ibn al-Qayyim, *Rawḍa*, p. 19.
33. *Munya*, fol. 5a-b.
34. *Munya*, fol. 6a. Italics mine. The MS cited has "*taʿlīq*" for "*taʿalluq*" in Marʿī's definition.
35. See pp. 155–59.
36. *Munya*, fols. 8a–9a. Cf. tables 1,B; 3,A,D (pp. 157, 158).
37. *Ibid.*, fol. 9a-b. Cf. Ibn al-Qayyim, *Dā'*, p. 278.
38. *Munya*, fol. 21a-b. Cf. Ibn al-Qayyim, *Rawḍa*, pp. 28–29.
39. *Munya*, fols. 21b–22a. The quotation mentioned in the text from Ibn al-ʿArabī, not found in the MS cited here, is given in my copy.
40. *Munya*, fol. 9b. Cf. Ibn al-Qayyim, *Rawḍa*, p. 26.
41. *Munya*, fol. 8a. Cf. p. 35.
42. *Ibid.*, fols. 6b–7b. Cf. Ibn al-Jawzī, *Dhamm*, pp. 289–92; Ibn al-Qayyim, *Rawḍa*, pp. 137–40.
43. *Munya*, fol. 10b. Cf. Ibn al-Qayyim, *Rawḍa*, p. 199.
44. *Munya*, fol. 12a. The phrase "lā yanbaghī madḥu 'l-ʿishqi ilā umm" in the MS must be read as "lā yanbaghī madḥu 'l-ʿishqi 'l-harām."
45. *Munya*, fols. 30b–31a. Cf. Ibn al-Jawzī, *Dhamm*, p. 82.
46. *Munya*, fols. 31a, 32b–33a, 34a, 35a-b. For Ibn al-Jawzī's opinions see pp. 20–21, 27–28.
47. *Ibid.*, fol. 17a; Ibn al-Qayyim, *Rawḍa*, pp. 265–66. Italics mine.
48. *Munya*, my copy, passage corresponding to a deletion after the words "fī 'l-qiyāmi min ʿindihi" in the MS cited (6252, fol. 17b, 11. 1–2). Cf. Ibn al-Qayyim, *Rawḍa*, pp. 276–77.
49. *Munya*, fol. 17a. Cf. Ibn al-Qayyim, *Rawḍa*, pp. 274–75, 294–315.
50. *Munya*, fols. 18a–19a.
51. Ibn al-Qayyim, *Rawḍa*, chapter twelve, pp. 150–55.
52. *Munya*, fol. 19a-b.
53. *Ibid.*, fols. 20b–21a.
54. See pp. 125–26.
55. *Munya*, fol. 23a.
56. See pp. 135–36.
57. *Munya*, fols. 24b–25b.
58. *Ibid.*, fols. 28a–30a. Cf. Ibn al-Jawzī's suggestions (above, pp. 39–40) and the *fatwa* ascribed to Ibn Taymīya (discussed above, pp. 131–33).
59. See preceding note.
60. *Munya*, fol. 3a.
61. See pp. 56–60.
62. *Munya*, fols. 2b–3a. The Koranic verse usually cited in this connection is 5:54: "Fa-sawfa ya'tī 'llāhu bi-qawmin yuḥibbuhum wa-yuḥibbūnahu. . . ."
63. *Ibid.*, fols. 3a–4a.
64. *Ibid.*, fol. 23a.

65. *Ibid.*, fol. 24a.
66. *Ibid.*, fol. 24a-b.
67. *Ibid.*, fol. 24a.

CHAPTER ELEVEN

1. Morphologically the Greek θελημα most properly denotes the object of an act of will—something willed. But the word was also commonly used in the sense of the act (τὸ θέλειν) or attribute of will itself. Cf. Ephesians 1:5: "κατὰ τὴν ευδοκίαν τοῦ θελήματος αὐτοῦ (according to the good pleasure of his will)." Its use is roughly equivalent to that of the Arabic *irāda*.
2. Al-Qushayrī, *Risāla*, p. 144.
3. *Ibid.*, p. 148.
4. Al-Ghazālī, *Iḥyā'*, XIV, pp. 95–99.
5. *Ibid.*, V, p. 154.
6. *Ibid.*, XIV, p. 41.
7. *Ibid.*, pp. 96, 99.
8. "They [the mystic-theologians] affirmed that he [God] is loved but denied that he loves, because they were adepts of Sufism alongside their adherence to the teaching of the theologians. They took their doctrine of love from the Sufis, although they made a mixture of it (*wa-in kānū yakhliṭūna fī-hi*)." Ibn Taymīya, *al-Tuḥfa al-ʿIrāqīya*, p. 79.
9. Al-Ghazāli, *Iḥyā'*, V, pp. 150–52.
10. *Ibid.*, IV, pp. 103–104.
11. *Ibid.*, XIV, p. 97.
12. *Ibid.*, XIII, pp. 158–59.
13. Ibn Qayyim al-Jawzīya, *Ighātha*, pp. 329, 292.

APPENDIX

1. See chapter one, n. 5.
2. A. R. Nykl, *A book containing the risāla known as the Dove's neck-ring about love and lovers* (translation of Ibn Ḥazm's *Ṭawq al-ḥamāma* with an introductory study) (Paris: Geuthner, 1931), p. cxiii, n. 46.
3. *Ibid.*, pp. lxxix–lxxx.
4. E. Lévi-Provençal, "Arabica occidentalia, II: 2. Les vers arabes de la chanson V de Guillaume IX d'Aquitaine," *Arabica* 1 (1954): 208–11. Lévi-Provençal's transcription has been kept in the text.
5. In his interpretation Lévi-Provençal thought it necessary to change the "t" in "*tarrababart*" to "m" in order to arrive at the Arabic expression *marra . . . marra* . . . (once . . . and again . . .). I suggest that this "t" need not be considered as a copyist's error if we accept the possibility that the poet was using the similar expression *tāra . . . marra. . .* , with the same meaning. The additional "r" in the manuscript is of little consequence, especially since the syllables *tar* and *tā* are of equal length in Arabic. A. Roncaglia objects to another point in Lévi-Provençal's interpretation, remarking that the words "*aital lati*" hardly need be read as Arabic here, since they are quite understandable in their Provençal meaning, "such Latin," i.e., such language as follows (*Cultura Neolatina* 15 [1955]: 164). If this phrase is read as Provençal, the verb may be taken as first person singular, *ʿāhart(u)*—which is nearer to the text—rather than as second person feminine singular, *ʿāharti*.
6. See S. M. Stern, "Les vers finaux en espagnol dans les *muwaššaḥs* hispano-hébraïques,"

Al-Andalus, 13 (1948): 299–346. Stern later published a book on the subject of the *kharja, Les chansons mozarabes* (Palermo: U. Manfredi Editore, 1953; reprinted in 1964, Oxford, Bruno Cassirer). A résumé and bibliography of *kharja* studies in the fifties will be found in Klaus Heger, *Die bisher veröffentlichten Ḫarǧas und ihre Deutungen* ("Beihefte zur *Zeitschrift für romanische Philologie*," Tübingen, 1960). Heger gives fifty-three *kharjas* together with the *muwashshaḥāt* in which they occur and the attempts which have been made to translate them. The most recent summary is contained in José María Solá Solé, *Corpus de poesía mozárabe* (Barcelona: Ediciones Hispam, 1973). Since the publication of this work, two new discoveries have been discussed by James Monroe in "Two new bilingual *ḫarǧas* (Arabic and Romance) in Arabic *muwaššaḥs*," *Hispanic Review* 42 (1974): 243–64.

7. E. García Gómez, "La poésie lyrique hispano-arabe et l'apparition de la lyrique romane," *Arabica* 5 (1958): 120, 125. This article appeared earlier in Spanish under the title "La lírica hispano-árabe y la aparición de la lírica románica" in *Al-Andalus* 21 (1956): 303–338. The reasons given by García Gómez for his conclusion, that the *kharjas* normally existed prior to the composition of the *muwashshaḥāt* in which they are found, are as follows: (a) the "quality" of the *kharjas*; (b) the "feminine lyricism" which they express, a trait foreign to the Arab social climate; (c) the statements of theoreticians to the effect that one poet may borrow a *kharja* from another; (d) the occurrence of such borrowings in practice; (e) the fact that the *kharja* at times does not conform to the "dominant tone" of the poem, implying that it is not the work of the same poet; and (f) the fact that some *kharjas* bear traces of alteration for the sake of rhyme or meter ("La poésie lyrique," pp. 128–30).

8. *Ibid.*, pp. 131–33. Cf. two articles by García Gómez, "La 'ley de Mussafia' se aplica a la poesía estrófica arábigo-andaluza," *Al-Andalus* 27 (1962): 1–20, and "Estudio del *Dār aṭ-ṭirāz*," *ibid.*, pp. 21–104. The headline-like title of the first article is justified. In it the author demonstrates that the so-called "Law of Mussafia"—the possibility in early Portuguese poetry of having both oxytonic and paroxytonic verses in the same piece, the final syllable of paroxytonic lines being counted—applies to the Arabic *muwashshaḥ*. The second article is a translation with commentary of Ibn Sanā' al-Mulk's theoretical discussion of this genre.

9. Jawdat Rikabi, *La poésie profane sous les Ayyûbides et ses principaux représentants* (Paris: G.-P. Maisonneuve, 1949), pp. 84 and n. 3, 86.

10. García Gómez, "La poésie lyrique hispano-arabe," p. 138.

11. P. Le Gentil, "La strophe zadjalesque, les *khardjas* et le problème des origines du lyrisme roman" (deuxième article), *Romania* 54 (1963): 210. On the *chanson de femme*, see A. Jeanroy, *Les origines de la poésie lyrique en France au moyen âge* (Paris, 1925), pp. 91–101. Typical themes of the *chanson de femme* are the *mal mariée* (the wife who loves without being loved) and the woman whose lover has left for the crusades.

12. Le Gentil, "La strophe zadjalesque," pp. 212–14, 223.

13. Ibn Qayyim al-Jawzīya, *Rawḍat al-muḥibbīn*, pp. 209–210.

14. See (b) in n. 7 above.

15. Lois Giffen has pointed out that Ibn Khayr al-Ishbīlī (502/1108–575/1179) reports studying with Spanish Muslim scholars al-Kharā'iṭī's *I'tilāl al-qulūb*, an important early work on love (see above, p. 9 and n. 19), and the *Akhbār Nifṭawayh.* Giffen, *Theory*, p. 72, n. 10.

Bibliography

ʿAbd al-Muʿṭī al-Lakhmī al-Iskandarī. *Sharḥ Manāzil al-sā'irīn*. Ed. S. de Laugier de Beaurecueil, O.P. Cairo: Imprimerie de l'Institut Français d'Archéologie Orientale, 1954.

ʿAbd al-Wāḥid, Muṣṭafā. *Dirāsat al-ḥubb fī 'l-adab al-ʿarabī*. 2 vols. Cairo: Dār al-Maʿārif, 1972.

Abū 'l-Barakāt Hibat Allāh b. ʿAlī b. Malkā al-Baghdādī. *Al-Muʿtabar fī 'l-ḥikma*. Ḥaydarābād: Dā'irat al-Maʿārif al-ʿUthmānīya, 1357/1938–39–1358/1939.

Abū Nuʿaym Aḥmad b. ʿAbd Allāh al-Iṣfahānī. *Ḥilyat al-awliyā'*. Cairo: Maktabat al-Khānjī and Maṭbaʿat al-Saʿāda, 1351/1932–1357/1938.

Abū Ṭālib al-Makkī. See al-Makkī, Abū Ṭālib Muḥammad b. ʿAlī.

Allard, Michel. *Le problème des attributs divins dans la doctrine d'al-Ašʿarī et de ses premiers grands disciples.* Beirut: Imprimerie Catholique, 1965.

al-ʿAlwajī, ʿAbd al-Ḥamīd. *Mu'allafāt Ibn al-Jawzī*. Baghdad: Dār al-Jumhūrīya li-l-Nashr wa-l-Ṭabʿ, 1385/1965.

Anawati, G.-C., and Gardet, Louis. *Mystique musulmane.* Paris: Librairie Philosophique J. Vrin, 1961. (LC lists first author as Anwati, M.-M.)

Andreas Capellanus. *The art of courtly love.* Trans. of his *De arte honeste amandi* by John Jay Parry. New York: Ungar, 1964. (LC lists the author as André *le Chapelain.*)

al-Anṣārī al-Harawī, ʿAbd Allāh. *ʿIlal al-maqāmāt*. Ed. and trans. with intro. by Serge de Laugier de Beaurecueil, O.P., in "Un petit traité de ʿAbdallah Ansari sur les déficiences inhérentes à certaines demeures spirituelles," *Mélanges Louis Massignon*, I (Damascus: Institut Français de Damas, 1956), pp. 153–71. (LC catalogues these *Mélanges* only under Massignon, Louis.)

———. *Kitāb manāzil al-sā'irīn* (*Les étapes des itinérants vers Dieu*). Ed. and French trans. with intro. by S. de Laugier de Beaurecueil. Cairo: Imprimerie de l'Institut Français d'Archéologie Orientale, 1962.

———. *Ṣad maydān.* Ed. with intro. by Serge de Beaurecueil, O.P., in "Une ébauche persane des 'Manāzil as-sā'irīn': le *'Kitāb-é ṣad maydān'* de ʿAbdallāh Anṣārī," *Mélanges islamologiques*, II (Cairo: Imprimerie de l'Institut Français d'Archéologie Orientale, 1954), pp. 1–90.

al-Anṭākī, Dāwūd b. ʿUmar. See Dāwūd b. ʿUmar al-Anṭākī.

Aristotle. *Nicomachean ethics.* Trans. W. D. Ross.

Asín Palacios, Miguel. *El Islam cristianizado.* Madrid: Editorial Plutarco, 1931.

Avicenna (Ibn Sīnā). *Risāla fī 'l-ʿishq.* Ed. with approximate French trans. by M. A. F. Mehren in *Traités mystiques d'Aboû Alî al-Hosain b. Abdallâh b. Sînâ ou d'Avicenne*, Fascicule III (Leiden: E. J. Brill, 1894).

———. *Psychologie d'Ibn Sīnā (Avicenne) d'après son oeuvre aš-Šifā'.* Ed. (vol. I) with French trans. (vol. II) by Ján Bakoš. Prague: Editions de l'Académie Tchécoslovaque des Sciences, 1956.

al-Bāqillānī, Abū Bakr Muḥammad b. al-Ṭayyib. *Al-Inṣāf.* Ed. Muḥammad Zāhid b. al-Ḥasan al-Kawtharī and ʿIzzat al-ʿAṭṭār al-Ḥusaynī. [Cairo]: Maktab Nashr al-Thaqāfa al-Islāmīya, 1369/1950. (LC lists author as al-Bāḳillānī.)

———.*Kitāb al-tamhīd.* Ed. Richard J. McCarthy, S. J. Beirut: Librairie Orientale, 1957.

al-Barbahārī, Abū Muḥammad al-Ḥasan b. ʿAlī. *Kitāb al-Sunna.* Selection or long passage quoted in Ibn Abī Yaʿlā, *Ṭabaqāt al-Ḥanābila,* II, pp. 18–43.

Bashshār b. Burd. *Dīwān.* Vol. II. Ed. Muḥammad al-Ṭāhir Ibn ʿAshūr. Cairo: Lajnat al-Ta'līf wa-l-Tarjama wa-l-Nashr, 1373/1954.

Beaurecueil, Serge de Laugier de, O.P. *Khwādja ʿAbdallāh Anṣārī (396–481 H./1006–1089), mystique hanbalite.* Beirut: Imprimerie Catholique, 1965. (LC lists author as Laugier de Beaurecueil, Serge de.)

Berry, André. *Anthologie de la poésie occitane.* Paris: Stock, 1961.

Bezzola, Reto Roberto. *Les origines et la formation de la littérature courtoise en occident.* 2 vols. Paris: Champion, 1944–60.

Blachère, Régis. *Histoire de la littérature arabe.* Paris: Adrien-Maisonneuve, 1952–66.

Brockelmann, Carl. *GAL = Geschichte der arabischen Litteratur.* 2d ed. Vols. I, II. Leiden: E. J. Brill, 1943, 1949.

———. *S = Geschichte der arabischen Litteratur.* Supplementbände I–III. Leiden: E. J. Brill, 1937–42.

Brunschvig, Robert, "Muʿtazilisme et ašʿarisme à Baġdād," in *Arabica,* volume spécial publié à l'occasion du mille deux centième anniversaire de la fondation de Baġdād (Leiden: E. J. Brill, 1962), pp. 343–56.

BSOAS = London. University. School of Oriental and African Studies. *Bulletin.*

Corbin, Henry. *Avicenna and the visionary recital.* Trans. from the French by Willard R. Trask. ("Bollingen Series," LXVI.) New York: Pantheon Books, 1960.

———. *Histoire de la philosophie islamique.* Vol. I. Paris: Gallimard, 1964.

Cowburn, John, S.J. *Love and the person.* London: Geoffrey Chapman, 1967.

al-Dabbāgh, ʿAbd al-Raḥmān b. Muḥammad al-Anṣārī. *Kitāb mashāriq anwār al-qulūb.* Ed. H. Ritter. Beirut: Dār Ṣādir, Dār Bayrūt, 1379/1959.

D'Arcy, Martin Cyril. *The mind and heart of love.* New York: Meridian Books, 1956.

Dāwūd b. ʿUmar al-Anṭākī. *Tazyīn al-aswāq.* Cairo, 1291/1874. (LC transliterates author's name Dā'ūd.)

al-Daylamī, Abū 'l-Ḥasan ʿAlī b. Muḥammad. *Kitāb ʿaṭf al-alif al-ma'lūf ʿalā 'l-lām al-maʿṭūf.* Ed. J. C. Vadet. Cairo: Imprimerie de l'Institut Français d'Archéologie Orientale, 1962.

Denomy, Alexander Joseph. "Concerning the accessibility of Arabic influences to the earliest Provençal troubadours," in *Mediaeval Studies* 15 (1953): 147–58.

———. *The heresy of courtly love.* New York, 1947.

al-Dhahabī, Muḥammad b. Aḥmad. *Al-ʿIbar fī khabar man ghabar.* Ed. Ṣalāḥ al-Dīn al-Munajjid and Fu'ād Sayyid. Kuwait, 1960–64– .

———. *Tadhkirat al-ḥuffāẓ.* 3d ed. Ḥaydarābād: Dā'irat al-Maʿārif al-ʿUthmānīya, 1375/1955–1376/1957.

*EI*¹ = *The Encyclopaedia of Islām.*

*EI*² = *The Encyclopaedia of Islam.* 2d ed.

Fiore, Silvestro. *Über die Beziehungen zwischen der arabischen und der frühitalienischen Lyrik.* Köln, 1956.

al-Firkāwī, Maḥmūd. *Sharḥ Manāzil al-sā'irīn.* Ed. with intro. by S. de Laugier de Beaurecueil, O.P. Cairo: Imprimerie de l'Institut Français d'Archéologie Orientale, 1953.

García Gómez, Emilio. "Estudio del *Dār aṭ-ṭirāz,*" *Al-Andalus* 27 (1962): 21–104.

———. "La 'ley de Mussafia' se aplica a la poesía estrófica arábigo-andaluza," *Al-Andalus* 27 (1962): 1–20.

———. "La poésie lyrique hispano-arabe et l'apparition de la lyrique romane," *Arabica* 5 (1958): 113–44.

———. "Un precedente y una consecuencia del 'Collar de la paloma,'" *Al-Andalus* 16 (1951): 309–330.

Gardet, Louis. *Dieu et la destinée de l'homme.* Paris: Librairie Philosophique J. Vrin, 1967.

Gardet, Louis, and Anawati, M.-M. *Introduction à la théologie musulmane.* Paris: Librairie Philosophique J. Vrin, 1948.

al-Ghazālī, Abū Ḥāmid. *Iḥyā' 'ulūm al-dīn*. Cairo: Maṭba'at Lajnat Nashr al-Thaqāfa al-Islāmīya, 1356/1937–1357/1938. (LC transliterates author's name al-Ghazzālī.)

———.*Mīzān al-'amal.* Ed. with an intro. by Sulaymān Dunyā. Cairo: Dār al-Ma'ārif, 1964.

Giffen, Lois Anita. *Theory of profane love among the Arabs: the development of the genre.* New York and London: New York University Press and London University Press, 1971.

Goichon, Amélie Marie. *Lexique de la langue philosophique d'Ibn Sînâ (Avicenne).* Paris: Desclée de Brouwer, 1938.

al-Ḥalabī, Shihāb al-Dīn Maḥmūd b. Sulaymān b. Fahd. *Manāzil al-aḥbāb wa-manāzih al-albāb.* MS Top Kapı, Ahmet III, 2471.

al-Ḥallāj, al-Ḥusayn b. Manṣūr. *Le Dîwân d'àl-Hallâj.* Ed. and trans. Louis Massignon. New ed. with additions and corrections. Paris: Librairie Orientaliste Paul Geuthner, 1955.

Hazo, Robert G. *The idea of love.* ("Concepts in Western thought series," Institute for Philosophical Research.) New York, Washington, London: Praeger, 1967.

Heger, Klaus. *Die bisher veröffentlichten Ḫarǧas und ihre Deutungen.* ("Beihefte zur *Zeitschrift für romanische Philologie.*") Tübingen, 1960.

al-Hujwīrī, 'Alī b. 'Uthmān al-Jullābī. *The Kashf al-mahjúb.* Trans. Reynold Nicholson. ("E.J.W. Gibb Memorial," XVII.) London: Luzac, 1936. (Old LC listing under 'Alī ibn 'Uṣmān.

Ibn 'Abd al-Wahhāb. See al-Najdī, Sulaymān b. 'Abd Allāh b. Muḥammad.

Ibn 'Abd Rabbih, Aḥmad b. Muḥammad. *Al-'Iqd al-farīd.* Vol. VI. Ed. Aḥmad Amīn, Ibrāhīm al-Abyārī, and 'Abd al-Salām Hārūn. Cairo: Lajnat al-Ta'līf wa-l-Tarjama wa-l-Nashr, 1368/1949.

Ibn Abī Ḥajala, Aḥmad b. Yaḥyā. *Dīwān al-ṣabāba.* On margin of Dāwūd al-Anṭākī, *Tazyīn al-aswāq*. Cairo, 1291/1874.

Ibn Abī Ya'lā, Abū 'l-Ḥusayn Muḥammad b. Muḥammad. *Ṭabaqāt al-Ḥanābila.* Ed. Muḥammad Ḥāmid al-Fiqī. Cairo: Maṭba'at al-Sunna al-Muḥammadīya, 1371/1952.

Ibn al-'Arabī, Muḥyī 'l-Dīn. *Al-Futūḥāt al-Makkīya.* Cairo: Dār al-Kutub al-'Arabīya, 1329/1911.

———. *Tarjumān al-ashwāq*. Beirut: Dār Ṣādir, Dār Bayrūt, 1381/1961. (LC transliterates *Turjumān al-ashwāq.*)

———. *The Tarjumán al-ashwáq*. Ed. and trans. with an abridged trans. of the author's cmt. by Reynold A. Nicholson. London: Royal Asiatic Society, 1911.

Ibn al-'Arīf (al-'Irrīf), Aḥmad b. Muḥammad. *Maḥāsin al-majālis.* Spanish trans. with intro. by Miguel Asín Palacios under the title *El místico Abulabás Benalarif de Almería y su "Mahasin al-machalis."* Madrid: Imp. Sáez Hermanos, 1931.

———. *Maḥāsin al-majālis.* Ed. with French trans. and cmt. by Miguel Asín Palacios. ("Collection de textes inédits relatifs à la mystique musulmane," II.) Paris: Librairie Orientaliste Paul Geuthner, 1933.

Ibn al-Dabbāgh. See al-Dabbāgh, 'Abd al-Raḥmān b. Muḥammad.

Ibn al-'Imād, 'Abd al-Ḥayy b. Aḥmad. *Shadharāt al-dhahab.* Cairo: Maktabat al-Qudsī, 1350–51/1931–33.

Ibn al-Jawzī, Abū 'l-Faraj 'Abd al-Raḥmān b. 'Alī. *Akhbār al-nisā'*. (Erroneously ascribed to Ibn Qayyim al-Jawzīya.) N.p.: Dār al-Fikr, n.d.

———. *Dhamm al-hawā.* Ed. Muṣṭafā ʿAbd al-Wāḥid. Cairo: Dār al-Kutub al-Ḥadītha, 1381/1962.
———. *Kitāb al-mawḍūʿāt.* Ed. ʿAbd al-Raḥmān Muḥammad ʿUthmān. 3 vols. Medina: al-Maktaba al-Salafīya, 1386/1966–1388/1968.
———. *Kitāb al-quṣṣāṣ wa-l-mudhakkirīn.* See Swartz, Merlin S., *Ibn al-Jawzī's Kitāb al-quṣṣāṣ wa'l-mudhakkirīn.*
———. *Al-Muntaẓam fī ta'rīkh al-mulūk wa-l-umam.* Vol. VI. 1st ed. Ḥaydarābād: Dā'irat al-Maʿārif al-ʿUthmānīya, 1357/1938–39.
———. *Ṣayd al-khāṭir.* Cairo: Idārat al-Ṭibāʿa al-Munīrīya, 1345/1926–27.
———. *Talbīs Iblīs.* Ed. Muḥammad Munīr al-Dimashqī. Cairo: Idārat al-Ṭibāʿa al-Munīrīya, 1928.
———. *Al-Ṭibb al-rūḥānī.* Damascus: Maktabat al-Qudsī wa-l-Budayr, 1348/1929–30.
Ibn al-Qayyim. See Ibn Qayyim al-Jawzīya.
Ibn Baṭṭa, ʿUbayd Allāh b. Muḥammad. *Al-Sharḥ wa-l-ibāna (La profession de foi d'Ibn Baṭṭa).* Ed. and French trans. by Henri Laoust. Damascus: Institut Français de Damas, 1958.
Ibn Dāwūd al-Ẓāhirī. See Muḥammad b. Dāwūd al-Iṣfahānī.
Ibn Ḥajar al-ʿAsqalānī, Aḥmad b. ʿAlī. *Al-Durar al-kāmina fī aʿyān al-mi'a al-thāmina.* Ḥaydarābād: Dā'irat al-Maʿārif al-ʿUthmānīya, 1349/1930–1350/1931.
Ibn Ḥazm, ʿAlī b. Aḥmad. *Kitāb al-akhlāq wa-l-siyar.* Ed. with intro. and annotated French trans. by Nada Tomiche. ("Collection UNESCO d'oeuvres représentatives.") Beirut: Commission pour la Traduction des Chefs-d'Œuvre, 1961.
———. *The ring of the dove: a treatise on the art and practice of Arab love (Ṭawq al-ḥamāma).* Trans. A. J. Arberry. London: Luzac, 1953.
———. *Ṭawq al-ḥamāma fī 'l-ulfa wa-l-ullāf.* Arabic text with French trans., intro., and notes by Léon Bercher. Algiers: Editions Carbonel, 1949.
———. *Ṭawq al-ḥamāma.* Trans. A. J. Arberry. See *The ring of the dove.*
———. *Ṭawq al-ḥamāma.* Trans. A. R. Nykl. See Nykl, *A book containing the risāla known as the Dove's neck-ring.*
Ibn Kathīr, Ismāʿīl b. ʿUmar. *Al-Bidāya wa-l-nihāya.* Vol. XIV. Cairo: Maṭbaʿat al-Saʿāda, 1358/1939.
Ibn Khallikān, Aḥmad b. Muḥammad. *Biographical dictionary (Wafayāt al-aʿyān).* Trans. De Slane. Paris: Oriental Translation Fund of Great Britain and Ireland, 1843–71.
———. *Wafayāt al-aʿyān.* Ed. Muḥammad Muḥyī 'l-Dīn ʿAbd al-Ḥamīd. Cairo: Maktabat al-Nahḍa al-Miṣrīya, 1948 (vols. II-VI), 1964 (vol. I).
Ibn Manẓūr, Muḥammad b. Mukarram. *Līsān al-ʿArab.* Būlāq, 1300/1882–1308/1891.
Ibn Qayyim al-Jawzīya, Muḥammad b. Abī Bakr. *Akhbār al-nisā'.* See Ibn al-Jawzī, *Akhbār al-nisā'.*
———. *Aʿlām al-muwaqqiʿīn.* See *Iʿlām al-muwaqqiʿīn.*
———. *Badā'iʿ al-fawā'id.* Cairo: Idārat al-Ṭibāʿa al-Munīrīya, n.d.
———. *Al-Dā' wa-l-dawā'.* Ed. Muḥammad Muḥyī 'l-Dīn ʿAbd al-Ḥamīd. Cairo: Maṭbaʿat al-Madanī, al-Mu'assasa al-Saʿūdīya bi-Miṣr, 1377/1958.
———. *Al-Fawā'id.* Cairo: Idārat al-Ṭibāʿa al-Munīrīya, 1344/1925–26.
———. *Ighāthat al-lahfān fī maṣāyid al-Shayṭān.* (On the margin is the author's *Ṭarīq* al-hijratayn.) Cairo: al-Maṭbaʿa al-Maymanīya, 1320/1902.
———. *Ighāthat al-lahfān min maṣāyid al-Shayṭān* (same work as above). Ed. Muḥammad Ḥāmid al-Fiqī. Cairo: Muṣṭafā al-Bābī al-Ḥalabī wa-Awlāduhu, 1357/1939.
———. *Ijtimāʿ al-juyūsh al-Islāmīya ʿalā ghazw al-muʿaṭṭila wa-l-Jahmīya.* Ed. Zakarīyā ʿAlī Yūsuf. Cairo: Maṭbaʿat al-Imām, n.d.
———. *Iʿlām al-muwaqqiʿīn ʿan Rabb al-ʿĀlamīn* together with the author's *Ḥādī 'l-arwāḥ ilā bilād al-afrāḥ.* Cairo: Maṭbaʿat al-Nīl, n.d.

———. *Jalā' al-afhām fī 'l-ṣalāh wa-l-salām ʿalā khayr al-anām.* Cairo: Idārat al-Ṭibāʿa al-Munīrīya, 1357/1938–39.
———. *Kitāb al-fawā'id al-mushawwiq ilā ʿulūm al-Qur'ān wa-ʿilm al-bayān.* Ed. Muḥammad Badr al-Dīn al-Naʿsānī. Cairo and Istanbul: Muḥammad Amīn al-Khānjī, Maṭbaʿat al-Saʿāda, 1327/1909–1910.
———. *Kitāb al-rūḥ.* See *al-Rūḥ.*
———. *Madārij al-sālikīn.* Ed. Muḥammad Rashīd Riḍā. Cairo: Maṭbaʿat al-Manār, 1331–33/1912–15.
———. *Miftāḥ Dār al-Saʿāda.* Cairo: Maktabat wa-Maṭbaʿat Muḥammad ʿAlī Ṣubayḥ wa-Awlāduhu, n.d.
———. *Mukhtaṣar al-Ṣawāʿiq al-mursala ʿalā 'l-Jahmīya wa-l-muʿaṭṭila.* Abridgment of *al-Ṣawāʿiq al-mursala* by Shaykh Muḥammad b. al-Mawṣilī. Cairo: Maṭbaʿat al-Imām, 1380/1960–61.
———. *Al-Qaṣīda al-nūnīya.* See *Sharḥ al-Qaṣīda al-nūnīya.*
———. *Rawḍat al-muḥibbīn wa-nuzhat al-mushtāqīn.* Ed. Aḥmad ʿUbayd. Cairo: Maṭbaʿat al-Saʿāda, 1375/1956.
———. *Al-Rūḥ.* 4th ed. Ḥaydarābād: Dā'irat al-Maʿārif al-ʿUthmānīya, 1383/1963.
———. *Sharḥ al-Qaṣīda al-nūnīya.* A cmt. by Muḥammad Khalīl Harās on Ibn al-Qayyim's *al-Qaṣīda al-nūnīya.* Cairo: Maṭbaʿat al-Imām, n.d.
———. *Sharḥ al-shurūṭ al-ʿUmarīya.* Extract from the author's *Aḥkām ahl al-dhimma.* Ed. Ṣubḥī al-Ṣāliḥ. Damascus: Maṭbaʿat Jāmiʿat Dimashq, 1381/1961.
———. *Shifā' al-ʿalīl fī masā'il al-qaḍā' wa-l-qadar wa-l-ḥikma wa-l-taʿlīl.* Al-Ṭā'if: Maktabat al-Maʿārif, n.d.
———. *Ṭarīq al-hijratayn wa-bāb al-saʿādatayn.* Cairo: Idārat al-Ṭibāʿa al-Munīrīya, 1358/1939.
———. *Al-Ṭibb al-nabawī.* Ed. ʿAbd al-Ghanī ʿAbd al-Khāliq with medical annotations by Dr. ʿĀdil al-Azharī. Mecca: Maktabat al-Nahḍa al-Ḥadītha, 1377/1957.
———. *Al-Tibyān fī aqsām al-Qur'ān.* Ed. Muḥammad Ḥāmid al-Fiqī. Cairo: al-Maktaba al-Tijārīya al-Kubrā, Maṭbaʿat Ḥijāzī, 1352/1933.
———. *ʿUddat al-ṣābirīn.* Cairo: Dār al-ʿUṣūr li-l-Ṭibāʿa wa-l-Nashr (Muḥammad ʿAlī Ṣubayḥ), n.d. (LC may list as *Idat al-ṣābirīn.*)
———. *Zād al-maʿād fī hady khayr al-ʿibād.* Cairo: al-Maṭbaʿa al-Miṣrīya, 1347/1928.
Ibn Qudāma, Muwaffaq al-Dīn ʿAbd Allāh b. Aḥmad. *Censure of speculative theology.* Ed. and trans. with intro. and notes of Ibn Qudāma's *Taḥrīm al-naẓar fī kutub ahl al-kalām* by George Makdisi. ("E. J. W. Gibb Memorial," New Series, XXIII.) London: Luzac, 1962.
———. *Kitāb al-Tauwābīn.* Ed. George Makdisi. Damascus: Institut Français de Damas, 1961.
Ibn Rajab, ʿAbd al-Raḥmān b. Aḥmad. *Kitāb al-dhayl ʿalā Ṭabaqāt al-Ḥanābila.* Ed. Muḥammad Ḥāmid al-Fiqī. Cairo: Maṭbaʿat al-Sunna al-Muḥammadīya, 1372/1952–53.
Ibn Sīnā. See Avicenna.
Ibn Taghrībirdī. Abū 'l-Maḥāsin Yūsuf. *Al-Manhal al-ṣāfī.* Vol. I. Ed. Aḥmad Yūsuf Najātī. Cairo: Dār al-Kutub al-Miṣrīya, 1375/1956.
———. *Al-Nujūm al-zāhira.* Cairo: Dār al-Kutub al-Miṣrīya, 1929–49.
Ibn Ṭāhir al-Baghdādī. *Kitāb uṣūl al-dīn.* Istanbul: Maṭbaʿat al-Dawla, 1346/1928.
Ibn Taymīya, Aḥmad b. ʿAbd al-Ḥalīm. *Ahl al-ṣuffa wa-abāṭīl baʿḍ al-mutaṣawwifa fī-him,* in *MRM,* I, pp. 25–60.
———. *Amrāḍ al-qulūb.* Cairo: al-Maṭbaʿa al-Salafīya, 1386/1966–67.
———. *Al-ʿAqīda al-Ḥamawīya al-kubrā,* in *MRK,* I, pp. 414–69.
———. *Al-ʿAqīda al-Wāsiṭīya,* in *MRK,* I, pp. 387–406.
———. *Al-Furqān bayn al-ḥaqq wa-l-bāṭil,* in *MRK,* I, pp. 2–179.
———. *Al-Hajr al-jamīl,* in *MRM,* I, pp. 2–9.

———. *Ḥaqīqat madhhab al-ittiḥādīyīn aw waḥdat al-wujūd*, in *MRM*, II (short ed.), pp. 55–157.
———. *Al-Ḥujaj al-naqlīya wa-l-ʿaqlīya fī-mā yunāfī ʾl-Islām min bidaʿ al-Jahmīya wa-l-ṣūfīya*, in *MRM*, II (short ed.), pp. 1–54.
———. *Ibṭāl waḥdat al-wujūd*, in *MRM*, I, pp. 61–120.
———. *Al-Iḥtijāj bi-l-qadar*, in *MRK*, II, pp. 87–145.
———. *Al-Irāda wa-l-amr*, in *MRK*, I, pp. 318–86.
This treatise is the same as that entitled *Aqwam mā qīl fī ʾl-mashīʾa wa-l-ḥikma wa-l-qaḍāʾ wa-l-qadar wa-l-taʿlīl* in *MRM*, III (short ed.), pp. 113–70.
———. *Kitāb al-nubūwāt*. See *al-Nubūwāt*.
———. *Kitāb majmūʿat fatāwā Shaykh al-Islām Taqī al-Dīn b. Taymīya al-Ḥarrānī*. Cairo: Maṭbaʿat Kurdistān al-ʿIlmīya, 1326/1908–1329/1911.
———. *Kitāb Shaykh al-Islām Ibn Taymīya ilā shaykh al-ṣūfīya Naṣr al-Manbijī*, in *MRM*, I, pp. 161–83.
———. *Maʿārij al-wuṣūl*, in *MRK*, I, pp. 180–217.
———. *Majmūʿat al-rasāʾil al-kubrā*. Cairo: al-Maṭbaʿa al-ʿĀmirīya al-Sharafīya, 1323/1905–1906. Cited as *MRK*.
———. *Majmūʿat al-rasāʾil wa-l-masāʾil*. Ed Muḥammad Rashīd Riḍā. Cairo: Maṭbaʿat al-Manār, 1341/1922–23ff.
This collection was published in a long (5 vols.) and a short (3 vols.) edition, vol. I being the same in each and vols. II and III of the short edition, although containing some additional material, corresponding to vols. IV and V of the long edition. Cited as *MRM*.
———. *Marātib al-irāda*, in *MRK*, II, pp. 64–79.
———. *Al-Masāʾil al-Mārdīnīya*. Damascus: al-Maktab al-Islāmī li-l-Ṭibāʿa wa-l-Nashr, 1383/1964.
———. *Minhāj al-sunna al-nabawīya fī naqḍ kalām al-shīʿa wa-l-qadarīya*. Cairo: al-Maṭbaʿa al-Amīrīya, 1321/1903–1904–1322/1904–1905.
———. *MRK = Majmūʿat al-rasāʾil al-kubrā*.
———. *MRM = Majmūʿat al-rasāʾil wa-l-masāʾil*.
———. *Al-Nubūwāt*. Cairo: Idārat al-Ṭibāʿa al-Munīrīya, 1346/1927.
———. *Qāʿida sharīfa fī ʾl-muʿjizāt wa-l-karāmāt*, in *MRM*, III (short ed.), pp. 2–36.
———. *Risālat al-iklīl fī ʾl-mutashābih wa-l-taʾwīl*, in *MRK*, II, pp. 2–35.
———. *Sharḥ ḥadīth ʿImrān b. Ḥuṣayn al-marfūʿ "Kāna ʾllāhu wa-lam yakun shayʾun qablahu,"* in *MRM*, III (short ed.), pp. 171–95.
———. *Tafṣīl al-ijmāl fī-mā yajib li-llāh min sifāt al-kamāl*, in *MRM*, III (short ed.), pp. 37–80.
———. *Al-Tuḥfa al-ʿIrāqīya*. Published in one volume with the author's *Amrāḍ al-qulūb*. Cairo: al-Maṭbaʿa al-Salafīya, 1386/1966–67.
———. *Al-Waṣīya al-kubrā*, in *MRK*, I, pp. 262–317.
Ikhwān al-Ṣafāʾ. *Rasāʾil*. Ed. Khayr al-Dīn al-Ziriklī. Cairo: al-Maṭbaʿa al-ʿArabīya, 1347/1928.
Imām al-Ḥaramayn al-Juwaynī, ʿAbd al-Malik b. ʿAbd Allāh. *Al-ʿAqīda al-Niẓāmīya*. Ed. Muḥammad Zāhid al-Kawtharī. Cairo: Maṭbaʿat al-Anwār, 1367/1948.
———. *El-Irchad (Kitāb al-irshād)*. Ed. with French trans. by J.-D. Luciani. Paris: Imprimerie Nationale, 1938.
———. *Kitāb al-irshād*. Ed. Muḥammad Yūsuf Mūsā and ʿAlī ʿAbd al-Munʿim ʿAbd al-Ḥamīd. Cairo: Maktabat al-Khānjī, 1369/1950.
al-Jāḥiẓ, ʿAmr b. Baḥr. *Kitāb al-qiyān*, in *Rasāʾil al-Jāḥiẓ*, ed. ʿAbd al-Salām Hārūn (Cairo: Maktabat al-Khānjī, 1384/1964–65), II, pp. 143–82.
———. *Kitāb al-qiyān*. French trans. by Charles Pellat, *Arabica* 10 (1963): 121–47.
———. *Risāla fī ʾl-ʿishq wa-l-nisāʾ*, in *Rasāʾil al-Jāḥiẓ*, ed. Ḥasan al-Sandūbī (Cairo: al-Maṭbaʿa al-Tijārīya al-Kubrā, 1352/1933), pp. 266–75.

Jeanroy, Alfred. *Les origines de la poésie lyrique en France au moyen âge.* Paris, 1925.
Jeffrey, Arthur (ed.). *Islam, Muḥammad and his religion.* New York: The Liberal Arts Press, 1958.
Jomier, Jacques. *Le Commentaire coranique du Manâr.* Paris: G.-P. Maisonneuve, 1954.
JNES = *Journal of Near Eastern Studies.*
Al-Juwaynī. See Imām al-Ḥaramayn al-Juwaynī.
al-Kalābādhī, Muḥammad b. Ibrāhīm. *The doctrine of the Ṣūfīs (al-Taʿarruf li-madhhab ahl al-taṣawwuf).* Trans. A. J. Arberry. Cambridge: Cambridge University Press, 1935.
al-Kharā'iṭī, Muḥammad b. Jaʿfar. *Iʿtilāl al-qulūb.* MS Dār al-Kutub, Adab 445.
al-Khaṭīb al-Baghdādī, Abū Bakr Aḥmad b. ʿAlī. *Ta'rīkh Baghdād.* Cairo: Maktabat al-Khānjī and Maṭbaʿat al-Saʿāda, 1349/1931.
al-Kutubī, Ibn Shākir, *Fawāt al-Wafayāt.* Ed. Muḥammad Muḥyī 'l-Dīn ʿAbd al-Ḥamīd. Cairo: Maktabat al-Nahḍa al-Miṣrīya, 1951.
Lane, Edward William. *The manners and customs of the modern Egyptians.* ("Everyman's Library.") London: J. M. Dent and Sons, Ltd, 1908.
Laoust, Henri. *Essai sur les doctrines sociales et politiques de Taḳī-d-Dīn Aḥmad b. Taimīya, canoniste ḥanbalite né à Ḥarrān en 661/1262, mort à Damas en 728/1328.* Cairo: Imprimerie de l'Institut Français d'Archéologie Orientale, 1939.
———. "Ibn Ḳayyim al-Djawziyya," in *EI*², III, pp. 821–22.
———. *La profession de foi d'Ibn Baṭṭa.* See Ibn Baṭṭa, *al-Sharḥ wa-l-ibāna.*
———. *Les schismes dans l'Islam.* Paris: Payot, 1965.
Le Gentil, P. "La strophe zadjalesque, les *khardjas* et le problème des origines du lyrisme roman" (deuxième article), *Romania* 54 (1963): 209–250.
Lévi-Provençal, E. "Arabica occidentalia, II: 2. Les vers arabes dans la chanson V de Guillaume IX d'Aquitaine," in *Aribica* 1 (1954): 208–211.
McCarthy, R. J., S. J. *The theology of al-Ashʿarī.* Beirut. Imprimerie Catholique, 1953.
Makdisi, George. *Ibn ʿAqīl et la résurgence de l'Islam traditionaliste au XIe siècle (Ve siècle de l'Hégire).* Damascus: Institut Français de Damas, 1963.
———. *Ibn Qudāma's Censure of speculative theology.* See Ibn Qudāma, *Censure of speculative theology.*
———. "Nouveaux détails sur l'affaire d'Ibn ʿAqīl," in *Mélanges Louis Massignon* (Damascus: Institut Français de Damas, 1956–57), III, pp. 91–126. (LC catalogues these *Mélanges* only under Massignon, Louis.)
al-Makkī, Abū Ṭālib Muḥammad b. ʿAlī. *Qūt al-qulūb.* Cairo, 1310/1892–93.
al-Manbijī, Muḥammad b. Muḥammad. *Kitāb al-samāʿ wa-l-raqṣ*, a collection of Ibn Taymīya's opinions on music and dancing, in *MRK*, II, pp. 277–315.
———. *Tasliyat ahl al-maṣā'ib.* Cairo: Maktabat al-Khānjī, 1929.
Marʿī b. Yūsuf al-Karmī. *Munyat al-muḥibbīn wa-bughyat al-ʿāshiqīn.* MSS Dār al-Kutub, Adab 6252, and Ṭalʿat, Adab 4648.
Massignon, Louis. *Essai sur les origines du lexique technique de la mystique musulmane.* New edition. Paris: Librairie Philosophique J. Vrin, 1954.
———. "Interférences philosophiques et percées métaphysiques dans la mystique hallagienne: notion de 'l'essentiel désir,'" in Louis Massignon, *Opera minora*, II (Beirut: Dar al-Maaref, 1963), pp. 226–53.
———. *La passion d'al-Hosayn-ibn-Mansour al-Hallaj.* Paris: Librairie Orientaliste Paul Geuthner, 1922.
al-Masʿūdī. *Les prairies d'or (Murūj al-dhahab).* Arabic text with French trans. by C. Barbier de Meynard. Vol. VI. Paris: Imprimerie Nationale, 1871.
al-Māwardī, ʿAlī b. Muḥammad. *Kitāb adab al-dunyā wa-l-dīn.* 1st ed. Cairo: al-Maṭbaʿa al-Kubrā al-Amīrīya, 1316/1898.
Monroe, James T. *Hispano-Arabic poetry, a student anthology.* Berkeley, Los Angeles, London: University of California Press, 1974.
MRK. See Ibn Taymīya.

MRM. See Ibn Taymīya.

Mughulṭāy, ʿAlā' al-Dīn. *Al-Wāḍiḥ al-mubīn fī dhikr man ustushhida min al-muḥibbīn. Mughulṭai's biographical dictionary of the martyrs of love.* Part I. Ed. Otto Spies. Delhi, 1936.

Muḥammad b. Dāwūd al-Iṣfahānī. *Al-Niṣf al-awwal min "Kitāb al-zahra"* (The first half of *Kitāb al-zahra*). Ed. A. R. Nykl with Ibrāhīm Ṭūqān. Chicago: The University of Chicago Press, 1932.

Muḥammad Rashīd Riḍā. *Tafsīr al-Qur'ān al-ḥakīm.* Vol. X. 2d ed. Cairo: Maṭbaʿat al-Manār, 1349/1931.

al-Muḥāsibī, al-Ḥārith b. Asad. *Faṣl fī 'l-maḥabba.* Quoted in Abū Nuʿaym, *Ḥilyat al-awliyā'*, X, p. 76ff.

———. *Risālat al-mustarshidīn.* Ed. ʿAbd al-Fattāḥ Abū Ghudda. Ḥalab: Maktab al-Maṭbūʿāt al-Islāmīya, n.d.

al-Muḥibbī, Muḥammad Amīn b. Faḍl Allāh. *Khulāṣat al-athar fī aʿyān al-qarn al-ḥādī ʿashar.* Beirut: Maktabat Khayyāṭ, 1966.

Muslim b. al-Ḥajjāj al-Qushayrī. *Ṣaḥīḥ Muslim bi-sharḥ al-Nawawī* (Muslim's *Ṣaḥīḥ* with the cmt. of al-Nawawī). Cairo: al-Maṭbaʿa al-Miṣrīya bi-l-Azhar, 1347/1929–1349/1930.

McCarthy, R. J., S.J. *The theology of al-Ashʿarī.* Beirut: Imprimerie Catholique, 1953.

Nader, Albert N. *Le système philosophique des muʿtazila.* Beirut: Editions Les Lettres Orientales, 1956.

al-Najdī, Sulaymān b. ʿAbd Allāh b. Muḥammad. *Taysīr al-ʿAzīz al-Ḥamīd fī sharḥ Kitāb al-tawḥīd.* Damascus: Manshūrāt al-Maktab al-Islāmī, n.d.

Nasr, Seyyed Hossein. "Shihāb al-Dīn Suhrawardī Maqtūl," in Mian Mohammad Sharif, ed., *A history of Muslim philosophy* (Wiesbaden: Otto Harrassowitz, 1963–66), I, pp. 372–98.

al-Nawawī, *Ṣaḥīḥ Muslim bi-sharḥ al-Nawawī.* See Muslim b. al-Ḥajjāj al-Qushayrī, same title.

al-Nuwayrī, Aḥmad b. ʿAbd al-Wahhāb. *Nihāyat al-arab fī funūn al-adab.* Offset of Dār al-Kutub edition. Cairo, n.d.

Nygren, Anders. *Agape and eros, a study of the Christian idea of love.* Parts I and II. Trans. Philip S. Watson. London: S. P. C. K., 1953.

———. *Agape and eros, a study of the Christian idea of love.* Part I. Trans. A. G. Herbert. London: Society for Promoting Christian Knowledge, 1932 (reprinted 1937).

Nykl, Alois Richard. *A book containing the risāla known as the Dove's neck-ring about love and lovers.* Trans. of Ibn Ḥazm's *Ṭawq al-ḥamāma* with an introductory study. Paris: Geuthner, 1931.

Ovid. *Remedia amoris.*

Pellat, Charles. *The life and works of Jāḥiẓ.* Trans. from the French by D. M. Hawke. Berkeley and Los Angeles: University of California Press, 1969.

Pinès, Salomon. *Nouvelles études sur Awḥad al-zamân Abu-l-Barakât al-Baghdâdî.* ("Mémoires de la Société des Etudes Juives," I.) Paris: Librairie Durlacher, 1955.

Plato. *Collected Dialogues.* Ed. Edith Hamilton and Huntington Cairns. ("Bollingen Series," LXXI.) Princeton: Princeton University Press, 1969.

Plotinus. *Enneads.* Trans. Stephen MacKenna and B. S. Page.

al-Qushayrī, ʿAbd al-Karīm b. Hawāzin. *Al-Risāla al-Qushayrīya.* Text with marginal notes from the cmt. of Zakarīyā al-Anṣārī. Cairo: Dār al-Kutub al-ʿArabīya al-Kubrā, 1330/1912.

al-Rabaʿī, ʿĪsā b. Ibrāhīm b. Muḥammad. *Kitāb niẓām al-gharīb.* Cairo: Maṭbaʿa Hindīya, n.d.

Rahman, Fazlur. *Islam.* London: Weidenfeld and Nicolson, 1966.

Rashīd Riḍā, Muḥammad. See Muḥammad Rashīd Riḍā.

al-Rāzī, Fakhr al-Dīn Muḥammad b. ʿUmar. *Kitāb al-arbaʿīn fī uṣūl al-dīn.* Ḥaydarābād: Dā'irat al-Maʿārif al-ʿUthmānīya, 1353/1934–35.

Rikabi, Jawdat. *La poésie profane sous les Ayyûbides et ses principaux représentants.* Paris: G.-P. Maisonneuve, 1949.
Ritter, Hellmut. *Das Meer der Seele.* Leiden: E. J. Brill, 1955.
———. "Philologika II," *Der Islam* 17 (1929): 249–57.
Rizzitano, U. "Il *Dīwān aṣ-ṣabābah* dello scrittore magrebino Ibn Abī Ḥaǵalah," in *Rivista degli studi orientali* 28 (1953), pp. 35–70.
al-Safārīnī, Muḥammad b. Aḥmad. *Ghidhā' al-albāb li-sharḥ Manẓūmat al-ādāb.* Cairo: Maṭba'at al-Nīl, 1325/1907–1908.
Ṣaḥīḥ Muslim. See Muslim b. al-Ḥajjāj al-Qushayrī, *Ṣaḥīḥ Muslim bi-sharḥ al-Nawawī.*
al-Sarrāj al-Qāri', Ja'far b. Aḥmad. *Maṣāri' al-'ushshāq.* Ed. Muḥammad Badr al-Dīn al-Na'sānī. Cairo: Maṭba'at al-Sa'āda, 1335/1907.
Sezgin, Fuat. *GAS = Geschichte des arabischen Schriftums.* Vol. I. Leiden: E. J. Brill, 1967.
al-Shahrastānī, Muḥammad b. 'Abd al-Karīm. *Kitāb nihāyat al-iqdām fī 'ilm al-kalām.* Ed. with abridged English paraphrase by Alfred Guillaume. London: Oxford University Press, 1934.
Sibṭ Ibn al-Jawzī, Yūsuf b. Qizughlī. *Mir'āt al-zamān.* Vol. VIII. Ḥaydarābād: Dā'irat al-Ma'ārif al-'Uthmānīya, 1370/1951.
Simonin, H. D. "Autour de la solution thomiste du problème de l'amour," *Archives d'histoire doctrinale et littéraire du moyen âge* 6 (1931): 174–276.
Singer, Irving. *The nature of love, Plato to Luther.* New York: Random House, 1966.
Smith, Margaret. *An early mystic of Baghdad, a study of the life and teaching of Ḥārith b. Asad al-Muḥāsibī A.D. 781*–A.D. 857. London: The Sheldon Press, 1935.
Stern, S. M. *Les chansons mozarabes.* Palermo: U. Manfredi Editore, 1953; reprinted in 1964, Oxford, Bruno Cassirer.
———. "Les vers finaux en espagnol dans les *muwaššaḥs* hispano-hébraïques," *Al-Andalus* 13 (1948): 299–346.
al-Suyūṭī, Jamāl al-Dīn. *Ṭabaqāt al-mufassirīn.* Ed. A. Meursinge. Leiden: S. and J. Luchtmans, 1839.
Swartz, Merlin S. *Ibn al-Jawzī's Kitāb al-quṣṣāṣ wa'l-mudhakkirīn.* Edition and translation with introduction. ("Recherches publiées sous la direction de l'Institut de Lettres Orientales de Beyrouth," série 1: Pensée arabe et musulmane, XLVII.) Beirut: Dar el-Machreq Éditeurs, 1971.
Ṭāshköprüzāde, Aḥmad b. Muṣṭafā. *Munyat al-shubbān fī mu'āsharat al-niswān.* MS, collection of Sa'd Maḥmūd Khiḍr.
Thomas Aquinas, Saint. *On the truth of the catholic faith (Summa contra gentiles).* Book One: God. Trans. Anton C. Pegis. New York: Image Books, 1955.
Vadet, Jean-Claude. *L'esprit courtois en orient dans les cinq premiers siècles de l'Hégire.* Paris: G.-P. Maisonneuve et Larose, 1968.
———. "Littérature courtoise et transmission du *ḥadīṯ*, un exemple: Muḥammad b. Ǧa'far al-Ḫarā'iṭī (m. en 327/938)," *Arabica* 7 (1960): 140–66.
Vajda, Georges. *L'amour de Dieu dans la théologie juive du moyen âge.* ("Etudes de philosophie médiévale," XLVI.) Paris: Librairie Philosophique J. Vrin, 1957.
Valiuddin, Mir. *Love of God, the Sufi approach.* Delhi, 1968.
Von Grünebaum, Gustave Edmund. "Avicenna's *Risâla fî 'l-'išq* and courtly love," *JNES* 11 (1952): 233–38.
Yāqūt b. 'Abd Allāh al-Ḥamawī, *Irshād al-arīb = Mu'jam al-udabā'.* Ed. Aḥmad Farīd al-Rifā'ī. Cairo: Maktabat 'Īsā al-Bābī al-Ḥalabī, n.d.

Index